The Working Programmer's Guide to
Serial Protocols

The Working Programmer's Guide to
Serial Protocols

Tim Kientzle

 CORIOLIS GROUP BOOKS

Publisher	Keith Weiskamp
Editorial Director	Jeff Duntemann
Cover Design	Gary Smith and Bradley Grannis
Interior Design/Layout Production	Tim Kientzle
Editor	Diane Cook

Library of Congress Cataloging-in-Publication Data

Kientzle, Tim
    The Working Programmer's Guide to Serial Protocols with disk / Tim Kientzle
       p. cm.
    Includes bibliography and index.
    ISBN 1-883577-20-9: $39.99

Printed in the United States of America

10 9 8 7 6 5 4 3 2 1

Contents

Preface   xv

Part One   Theory

1 What Is a Serial Protocol?   **3**

Properties of a Good Serial Protocol   4
    Reliability   4
    Robustness   5
    Consideration for Channel   5
    Efficiency   5
    Extensibility   5
    Preservation of File Attributes   6
    Ease of Use   7
    Ease of Implementation   8
Going through Channels   8
    Error Rate   9
    Flow Control   9
    Transparency   10
    Duplex   10
    Burst Length   11
    Delays   11
    Examples of Channels   11
    Error-Correcting Modems   13

2 Anatomy of a Serial Protocol   **15**

Encoding Layer 16
Packetization Layer 17
   Packet Header 17
   Start-of-Packet 17
   Packet Format 18
   Packet Types 19
   Sequencing 21
   Header Check 21
   Inside-Out Packets 22
   Error Detection 23
Reliability Layer 23
   Half-Duplex ACK/NAK 23
   Scripted Dialog 24
   Segmented Half-Duplex 25
   Full-Duplex 25
   Multiple Outstanding Packets 26
   Streaming 27
   Window Sizing and Management 28
   Implementing Reliability 29
Transaction Layer 29
   File Transfers 30
   Conditional File Transfers 31
   Non-File Transfers 32
   Application Commands 32
   Host Commands 33
Session Layer 33
   Initiating the Session 34
   Negotiating Capabilities 34
   Completing the Session 35
   Cancelling the Session 36
   Master/Slave Session Model 36

3 Encoding   **39**

Prefix Encoding 40
Radix Encoding 41
Implementing Encoding 42
   Prefix Encoding Hints 42
   Prefix Decoding Hints 43
   Hexify 44

Unhexify 44
ToBase64 45
FromBase64 46
ToBase85 48
FromBase85 48
Compression 50
Encryption 51

4 Error Detection and Correction   53
Error-Correcting Codes 53
Checksums 54
What You Need to Know About Cyclic Redundancy Checks 55
Implementing CRCs 56
Computing CRCs Slowly 56
Table-Driven CRC Calculation 57
Real CRC Calculators 58
12-Bit and 32-Bit CRCs 59
Understanding CRCs 60
Long Division of Polynomials 61
Polynomials Modulo 2 62
Messages as Polynomials 62
CRCs Defined 63
From Mathematics into C 63
Self-Checking CRCs 64
Other Error-Detecting Signatures 64
Cryptographic Signatures 65

5 Understanding Text Files   67
Control Characters in Text 67
End-of-Line Conventions 68
Character Encodings 69
Small Character Sets 69
Seven-Bit Character Sets 70
Eight-Bit Character Sets 71
Non-Roman Languages 73
Multi-Byte Character Sets 73
16-Bit and 32-Bit Character Sets 74
Converting Between Character Encodings 75
References 76

Part Two   *Design*

6   XModem   **83**

The Protocol 83

       Encoding Layer 84

       Packetization Layer 84

       Reliability Layer 85

       Transaction Layer 86

       Session Layer 86

Analysis 86

Derivatives 88

       XModem-CRC 88

       XModem-K 89

       WXModem 90

7   YModem   **91**

The Protocol 91

       Encoding Layer 91

       Packetization Layer 92

       Reliability Layer 92

       Transaction Layer 92

       Session Layer 93

Analysis 93

Derivatives 93

References 94

8   ZModem   **95**

The Protocol 96

       Encoding Layer 96

       Packetization Layer 98

       Reliability Layer 100

             Transferring File Data Reliably 101

       Transaction Layer 102

             File Transfers 102

             Command Transactions 104

             Free Space Transactions 105

       Session Layer 105

             Initiating the Session 106

             Completing the Session 107

Cancelling the Session 107
Sample Sessions 107
Analysis 110
Performance 111
Derivatives 112
References 112

9 Basic Kermit   **113**
The Protocol 114
Encoding Layer 114
Packetization Layer 116
Reliability Layer 117
Transaction Layer 118
File Transfers 118
Session Layer 119
Analysis 121

10 Modern Kermit   **123**
The Protocol 124
Encoding Layer 124
Packetization Layer 126
Reliability Layer 129
Transaction Layer 129
File Transfers 130
Server Command Transactions 135
Session Layer 140
Analysis 142
References 143

11 Designing Your Own   **145**
Defining Your Needs 145
Protocol Considerations 146
Encoding Layer 146
Packetization Layer 146
Reliability Layer 146
Transaction Layer 147
Session Layer 147
Planning Ahead 147

Part Three   Implementation

12 Coding Issues   **151**
  Why C? 151
  General Conventions 152
  Overview of the Source 154
  Error Handling 155
  Multitasking 155
      Polling: Cooperative "From the Top" 156
      Cooperative "From the Bottom" 157
      Preemptive Multitasking 157

13 Debugging Tools   **159**
  Public Interface 159
  Implementation 161
  Private Routines 162
  Handle Management 162
  Message Selection 163
  Logging Specific Data Types 164

14 Serial Interfacing   **167**
  Public Interface 167
  External Dependencies 169
  Managing the Serial Port 170
  Serial I/O 173
  Miscellaneous Serial Operations 175

15 File Interfacing   **177**
  Public Interface 178
  Definitions 181
  Debugging 183
  Utility Routines 184
  Writing Files 187
  Reading Files 194
  File Queries 198

16 Progress Reporting   **201**
  Public Interface 202
  External Dependencies 203
  Progress Internal Data 204

Initialization and Termination 205
Progress Information 206
Progress Display 208

17 Implementing XYModem   **215**
Public Interface 215
External Dependencies 216
Definitions 217
Utility Functions 221
    Error Handling 221
    Debugging Support 222
    CRC Calculation 223
    Time Conversions 224
Interfaces to External Modules 225
    Serial Interface 225
    Reading Files 228
    Writing Files 230
    Progress Reporting 232
Packet Layer 234
    Sending Packets 235
    Receiving Packets 237
Reliability Layer 241
Transaction Layer 244
    Sending Files 244
    Receiving Files 251
Session Layer 256
Public Interface Layer 259

18 Implementing ZModem   **263**
Public Interface 263
External Dependencies 264
System Dependencies 266
Definitions 267
    ZModem State Structure 267
    ZModem Packet Types 271
    Other ZModem Constants 271
    Initialization Flags 273
Utility Functions 273
    Error Handling 274
    Debugging Support 274

CRC Calculation 276
Time Conversions 278
Parsing of Special Packet Types 280
Interfaces to External Modules 281
Serial Interface 281
Reading Files 288
Writing Files 290
Miscellaneous File Functions 293
Progress Reporting 295
Encoding Layer 296
Receiving and Decoding 298
Packet Layer 301
Sending Packets 301
Receiving Data 308
Reliability 311
Receiving Data Reliably 311
Sending Data Reliably 315
Window Management 315
Sending Streamed Data 319
Miscellaneous Send-Side Reliability 328
File/Transaction Layer 331
Sending Files 331
Receiving Files 335
Session Layer 338
Sender Session 338
Receiver Session 339
Receiving a Command 342
Send Command Session 344
Public Interface Layer 347

19 Implementing Kermit   **351**
Public Interface 351
External Dependencies 352
Definitions 353
Kermit State Structure 353
Utility Functions 354
Error Handling 354
Debugging Support 355
CRC Calculation 356
Interfaces to External Modules 357

Serial Interface 357
Reading Files 360
Writing Files 362
Progress Reporting 363
Encoding Layer 364
Encoding 366
Decoding 371
Packet Layer 374
Sending Packets 376
Receiving Packets 379
Reliability Layer 385
Window Management 385
Sending Data Reliably 396
Receiving Data Reliably 400
Transaction Layer 402
Sending One File 402
Sending Multiple Files 404
Receiving One File 404
Receiving Multiple Files 409
Session Layer 409
Session Initiation 410
Negotiating Parameters 412
Maximum Packet Length 413
Timeout 414
Pad Character 415
End-of-Packet Character 416
Control Prefix Character 416
Eighth-Bit Prefix Character 417
Packet Check Type 418
Repeat Prefix Character 419
Extended Capabilities Bitmap . . . . • 420
Window Size 422
Extended Packet Size 423
Cleanup 424
Server Operation 424
Public Interface 426

Bibliography   431

Index   433

Preface

It has been almost 20 years since XModem was first introduced to the computing world. Since then, a variety of serial protocols have been developed to fill almost every niche. Some are easy to implement, others are fast over good quality connections, still others are designed to get the job done regardless of the system or connection quality. Unfortunately, the informal manner in which some of these protocols were developed means that information about them is often limited to "electronic folklore." This book was written to help address this difficulty in finding good documentation. It covers some of the most popular file transfer protocols, using a consistent terminology and viewpoint. Hopefully, it will serve not only as a reference for these specific protocols, but will also provide ideas and insight for developers who need to create their own protocols.

About this Book

The book is divided into three relatively self-contained parts:

Theory   This part discusses general issues applicable to serial file transfers in general and illustrates common techniques with snippets of code. This part should be especially useful to programmers designing their own protocols.

Design   This part presents the popular XModem, YModem, ZModem, and Kermit protocols. I've used a common framework for all of these protocols to help you better understand the similarities and differences between them.

Implementation   This part provides complete, working implementations of these standard protocols, which should clarify the details of each protocol. Having worked on several very different computer platforms myself, I've included a number of ideas to ease the process of adapting the implementations in this book to your specific needs.

What You Can Do with the Source Code

The program code on the accompanying disk is copyrighted by Tim Kientzle.[1] Normally, you must obtain explicit permission from the author to make more than purely personal use of the code accompanying a book such as this. In three specific situations, however, I will allow you to distribute this code or works based on this code without first obtaining such permission:

- If you develop a *complete application program* incorporating my source code and distribute (commercially, free, or otherwise) the compiled binary *without including my source*, then you can do so provided that you acknowledge my contribution, notify me, and abide by the conditions specified at the top of the file.

- If you develop a *complete application program* incorporating my source code and distribute it with *complete source code to the entire program*, then you may do so provided that you acknowledge my contribution, notify me, and abide by and preserve the notices in each of my source files.

- If you do not own this book, and obtain a copy of some or all of my source code as a part of a complete application program, you may distribute my source code only as part of that application program, under whatever restrictions apply to that application. The copyright notices at the top of each source file must be maintained intact.

The phrase "acknowledge my contribution" means that you put the following notice in a prominent place in your program's user interface and documentation.

> This product is partially based on source code appearing in *The Working Programmer's Guide to Serial Protocols*, Copyright © 1995 Tim Kientzle and Coriolis Group, Inc.

---

[1] If you're not familiar with the implications of this sentence, I recommend M. J. Salone's book *How To Copyright Software*, published by Nolo Press, as a good introduction to the principles of copyright as applied to software.

To notify me of your intent to use my code in a program, send me a letter or postcard (please include your name, company, complete return address and telephone number):

Tim Kientzle c/o The Coriolis Group
7339 E. Acoma Drive, Suite 7
Scottsdale, Arizona, 85260

In any case, you must abide by the terms spelled out at the top of each source file.

If you wish to use the source code from this book in any other way (such as in a communications library), you will need to contact me and obtain my permission first. Depending on the exact usage, obtaining such permission may entail a modest fee. If you're unsure whether you can use the source code in your particular project, it's probably best to ask.

Lies, Damned Lies, and Statistics

Most comparisons of file transfer protocols include a detailed table describing their relative performance under "real world conditions;" I've resisted this temptation. My reasons are perhaps best explained by describing the problems I've seen with other attempts.

First, the tester's particular idea of what constitutes the "real world" very rarely reflects the huge variety of situations in which serial protocols are used. Protocols that are blindingly fast in one environment may fail to work at all in another. Second, the choice of implementation can have a large impact on test results. Minor changes in a protocol implementation can result in enormous speed differences. Third, the choice of test files can skew the results. Ridiculously high performance can be obtained by choosing the right test files. Finally, the results are not often very carefully interpreted. One test chose the "fastest" protocol based on the trivial speed difference of 0.2 percent.

Any "real world" comparison of protocols will inevitably reflect the biases of the tester, deliberate or not. Instead, I provide for each protocol a discussion of the impacts of the protocol design and of which circumstances affect the performance of that protocol. Ultimately, you should try different protocols under conditions that are relevant to you, and judge the results for yourself.

Acknowledgments

Many people have generously contributed to the production of this book. I'd like to particularly thank Frank da Cruz, Chuck Forsberg, Laura Keohane, Tom Lippincott, Les Moss, and Gene Stover, who reviewed early versions of the book and made many helpful suggestions. I'd like to also thank the many people at Coriolis who assisted with the editing, layout, and production, especially Keith Weiskamp, Diane Cook, Gary Smith, and Brad Grannis. Finally, I'd like to thank the members of Delphi's OS9 SIG, who enthusiastically helped me to test the early versions of the code that eventually made its way into this book.

TO BETH

Theory

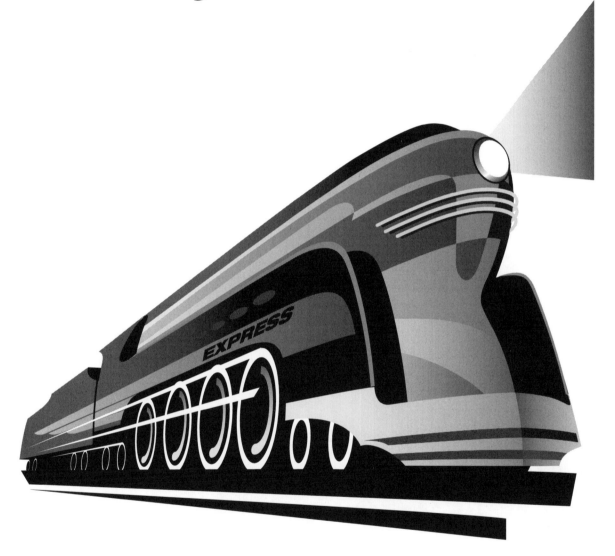

What Is a Serial Protocol? 1

Good serial protocols transfer your data reliably even over rough tracks (or in bad weather). This chapter looks at the fundamentals of serial protocols: what makes a protocol first class and how rough the tracks can be.

Every time you talk to someone, there's the potential for misunderstanding. Usually, this results in nothing more serious than hurt feelings. In some circumstances, however, the stakes are considerably higher. Professional diplomats, whose reputations (and sometimes lives) depend on accurate communication, often start by setting out rules to ensure that all the parties to a negotiation understand each other. These rules are called *protocols*.

In a sense, computers are much like feuding countries: a single misunderstood word can lead to disaster. Like diplomats then, computer programmers have also developed sets of rules to ensure that there are no mistakes when transferring data between different computer systems. These rules are also called *protocols*.

Computer protocols have been developed for many different purposes. I'm primarily interested in the ones originally developed for transferring files over serial connections such as modems. Even though some of these *serial protocols* are now used in other environments, they all have certain elements in common that make it relatively easy to compare them. Protocols designed for other environments have different concerns. For example, protocols used for communicating over radio need to somehow identify both the sender and receiver to avoid confusion when there are more than two parties on the same channel. Because a serial connection only has two ends, such confusion can't occur.

There's one important point here that I want to emphasize. A protocol is *not* a program, nor is it a piece of hardware. A protocol is a specification of how programs can accomplish a certain task, much like an algorithm. Unlike an algorithm, however, a protocol doesn't specify the internal operation of the program, just the external manifestation. A program that "speaks" a particular

3

protocol is called an *implementation* of that protocol. This distinction between a protocol and its implementation is important, and often glossed over. For example, there is a program called "Kermit" which is an implementation of a protocol also called "Kermit."

Properties of a Good Serial Protocol

Before you try to compare different serial protocols, it helps to think about what properties they *should* have. The terms I'm introducing here are fairly standard, so please forgive me if this sounds a little bit like something out of the 1942 Boy Scout manual.

Reliability

A transfer protocol is *reliable* if it knows when something goes wrong. (Whether or not it tells you is, of course, a part of the implementation.) In a poorly-designed protocol, certain combinations of errors can easily sneak past, resulting in damaged data without either the sending or receiving program being aware of the damage.

This is sometimes a subtle issue. For example, many protocols use different packet sizes for transferring data. Small packets turn out to be preferable when the error rate is high, since they are less likely to encounter an error, and less time is required to resend them if they are damaged. On the other hand, when error rates are low, longer packets have relatively less overhead, and so result in faster transfers. So, let's imagine the plight of our brave Boy Scout who decides to switch to shorter packets when the error rate increases:

> After sending packet 48, a glitch in the line causes the sender to believe the packet was incorrectly received, even though the receiver received the packet correctly and stored it in the file. The sender decides to split the old packet 48 into two smaller packets, now numbered 48 and 49. The receiver acknowledges the short 48 but doesn't store it in the file, since it already received a packet numbered 48. It then receives 49 and stores it in the file, oblivious to the fact that it repeats data already received. The transfer then continues, with neither side suspecting that the second half of the original packet 48 was duplicated.

No transfer protocol is perfectly reliable. This hard truth follows from the mathematical fact that no means of detecting errors is perfect; there is always some error or combination of errors that will masquerade as correct data. Nevertheless, well-designed protocols can minimize the chance of undetected errors.

Robustness

Robustness is the property that files are usually transferred correctly; the two sides can recover and continue even when errors do occur. While robustness and reliability usually go hand-in-hand, the two are not the same. For example, YModem-G does check for errors as it transfers data, but has no means of recovering from any errors it might find. This means that YModem-G is reliable but not robust.

Consideration for Channel

The *channel* is the route that data takes from one computer to another; it can involve modems, network interfaces, data routers, and serial ports. A good file transfer protocol can adapt to the limitations of whatever channel is being used. For example, of the protocols in this book, Kermit is the only one that can accurately transfer files even when the channel only allows seven-bit characters. XModem, YModem, and ZModem all require that the channel support eight-bit characters. Channels are discussed in more detail starting on page 8.

Efficiency

An essential part of any transfer protocol is the additional *control information* that is carried along to make sure both ends know what's going on. For example, it's necessary for the sender to notify the receiver where file data begins and ends, even though the begin and end of the file aren't actually part of the file. This control information contributes to *overhead*—non-file data that is transferred as part of the protocol. Protocols with large amounts of overhead will generally be slower than ones with less overhead, since the overhead itself takes time to transfer. For example, one reason the Kermit protocol gained a reputation for being slow, even over fairly nice channels, was that many implementations unnecessarily encoded data to suit the requirements of a more restrictive channel. This additional overhead sometimes increased the amount of data that had to pass through the channel by 50 percent or more, with a consequent reduction in efficiency.

Extensibility

No design is perfect, but good designs account for this fact. Every successful protocol has experienced numerous attempted improvements. For some protocols, these improvements have been relatively painless. For example, the addition of *sliding windows* to the Kermit protocol involved only minor changes, because Kermit had been designed from the beginning to make it easy to add new features.

On the other hand, the addition of windowing to XModem—in the WXModem protocol—required some dramatic changes to the original protocol.

Preservation of File Attributes

Although many people think of a file as simply a stream of bytes, it is actually much more complex. Besides the *contents* of the file, files can also have other attributes:

Name Most systems associate a name with every file. The format of names varies by system. Some systems restrict filenames to as few as six upper case letters. Other systems allow names to use any eight-bit character and be as long as 128 bytes.

Size One of the most popular file transfer protocols, XModem, typically adds junk to the end of each file transferred. For some systems, this causes no problems, but it can wreak havoc with applications that store information at specific offsets from the end of the file.

Creation Date Modern systems often store the time and date on which a file was created.

Modification Date Automated backup software relies on the time at which the file was last altered to determine which files need to be copied.

Permissions Most operating systems attach some information to each file specifying what can be done with that file and by whom.

Record Type In most microcomputer operating systems, a file is simply a sequence of bytes. In contrast, mainframe and minicomputer operating systems often support more complex file types, geared towards efficient handling of large databases. This difference can create extreme problems when transferring data between different systems.

Resources With the advent of Graphical User Interfaces, it has become necessary to attach a variety of additional information to files. To support this information cleanly, some operating systems, most notably Macintosh, associate a small database with each file. This database, called the *resource fork* in Macintosh parlance, contains additional information about the file, such as the preferred font for viewing a text file. In some cases, the corresponding *data fork* is completely empty.

Properties Some operating systems now model files as objects, and allow attachments to any object, including files. These *properties* can be any type of object at all.

Current file transfer protocols use two different mechanisms to transfer these additional file attributes. One approach is to transfer them within the protocol. For example, Kermit has a special packet used to transfer information about the file prior to transferring the file contents. The advantage of this is that if the two systems support comparable information about files, with slight differences, the protocol implementations can translate this information as the file is transferred.

Another approach is to perform *archiving*. Briefly, archiving is a way of encoding one or more files into a single stream of bytes. Usually, this encoding handles filenames and other file information. Some examples of this approach are the `tar` program for Unix, the `zip` programs used on many systems, and the MacBinary standard for transferring Macintosh files using XModem or other protocols. MacBinary encodes certain special information about a file in a header that is attached to the beginning of the file contents, and transferred as part of the file. The major benefit of archiving is that it can preserve information that cannot be represented on the receiving system, because the receiving system can simply store the archived image as an uninterpreted binary file, leaving the data encoded until it arrives on a system where the data can be *dearchived* into a copy of the original file, with all appendages intact.

With the current trend towards byte-stream files with arbitrary attachments, archiving approaches will become increasingly important. Indeed, it may be necessary for designers of new operating systems to consider archiving a fundamental capability, to simplify the transfer of these richly structured files across networks and modems alike. The drawback, of course, is that the proliferation of different archiving methods reduces the chance that a file can be easily transferred between dissimilar systems.

Ease of Use

Ease of use is probably one of the most critical issues in software design in general, and even though it may not seem like a concern at this layer of software design, it does have an impact. One of the major reasons for the development of YModem was that XModem does not transfer multiple files and does not preserve the names of those files. This means that to download a group of files, a user of XModem must repeatedly tell the host which file to send, and then tell the local end to receive a file under the corresponding name. The ability to do this just once to download a group of files was a significant improvement. Similarly, one of ZModem's most popular features stems from a conscious design decision to make the packets used at the beginning of the transfer very easy to recognize. By using ASCII-encoded packets at the beginning of the session and starting them with a single control character that is rarely used by common terminal emulations, ZModem makes it easy for a terminal program to detect when a ZModem transfer is starting, removing the need for the user to manually instruct both ends to start the transfer.

Ease of Implementation

XModem is a good example of a protocol that is both easy to understand and easy to implement. This inherent simplicity was one of the primary reasons for the rapid adoption of XModem, even when arguably better protocols were available. XModem is simple enough that many XModem implementations have been developed without any documentation other than hearsay. This simplicity continues to be a strong argument in favor of XModem.

Going through Channels

Serial protocols exist in part to overcome the gremlins that corrupt data when you try to move it from one computer to another. The path the data takes, whether it's a single bare wire or a series of networks, modems, and data routers, is referred to as a *channel*. Channels are characterized by a number of properties that affect the design and effectiveness of transfer protocols. The most important properties are: error rate, transparency, and delay. This chapter covers these basic channel properties, and closes by looking at the peculiar properties of modern compressing modems.

As an example, for two transfer programs, the channel might include the following steps:

1. The sending program calls a system function.
2. The system function stores the data in a hardware port.
3. The hardware port sends the data through a wire.
4. A modem gets the data from the wire, converts it into a signal suitable for a telephone, and feeds it into a telephone line.
5. The telephone company switching equipment routes it to another modem.
6. This modem converts the telephone signal into a digital signal and feeds it into a wire.
7. A hardware port receives the data and stores it in a special register.
8. A system routine, called by the receiving program, reads the data from that register and returns it to the receiving program.

It is the combination of all of these steps that determines the properties of the channel.

Error Rate

Even the simplest channels experience errors. Electrical signals traveling over a wire can be altered or weakened beyond recognition; serial port buffers can overflow; hardware and software bugs can corrupt or destroy data. Even fiber optics are not immune to errors. The question of interest to a protocol designer is how likely errors are. Generally, the higher the error rate, the more complex the protocol will have to be.

Error rates vary considerably among channels. A direct wire connection has a relatively low error rate. In contrast, a radio signal carrying data from a deep space probe back to Earth has a very high error rate. One of the primary purposes of file transfer protocols is to compensate for the errors that occur in the channel. Chapter 4 (pages 53 to 65) takes a closer look at techniques for detecting and correcting errors in file transfer protocols.

From time to time, someone will propose a file transfer protocol that does not bother to correct errors. While such protocols tend to be both simpler and faster than the protocols I'm interested in here, they've never really caught on. The reason is simply that any such protocol assumes an error-free channel, and such channels are simply not available in practice. Even with error-correcting modems and other guarantees, system bugs and other minor problems still result in occasional errors. Put another way, there is a big difference between a *low* error rate and a *zero* error rate.

Flow Control

One particular way in which bytes can be lost occurs when the receiver is not ready to receive the data that's been sent. This is a common problem with multitasking systems: the receiving computer may be so busy with other tasks that it doesn't have enough time to process incoming data. This isn't just limited to large multi-user systems; modern graphical interfaces can expend considerable amounts of processor time simply updating the mouse cursor. Regardless of the cause, the result is that internal buffers overflow and data is lost. Another contributing factor is that different parts of the channel sometimes operate at different speeds. For example, modems often connect to the computer at a much higher speed than they use over the phone line. In such a situation, it's easy for a faster link to overwhelm a slower one, again resulting in lost data.

Flow control allows the receiver to pause the sender when it's not ready to receive. One common approach is for the receiver to send a control code, usually XOFF, back to the sender to ask it to pause. The problem with this approach, known as *software flow control* is that the character codes used for flow control usually can't be received by a program, since they're preempted by the channel. For this reason, it's preferable to have *transparent* flow control. One way to accomplish this is to use a separate wire, a technique known as *hardware* flow control. Note that transparent flow control doesn't necessarily require a separate wire; for example, error-correcting modems can transparently assert flow control over telephone lines.

Transparency

Flow control characters are a special case of *transparency* problems. The basic idea is that only particular byte values can be put into the channel at one end and reliably appear out the other end. As an extreme example of a channel that's not very transparent, consider a microcomputer communicating with a mainframe through one of the mainframe's terminal ports. Mainframe terminal ports are often designed for humans typing text data one line at a time. As a result, only printable text characters and a few special control codes can be read by a program on the mainframe. There are also limits on line length and the rate at which data can be accepted. Transferring binary files in this situation requires that you somehow compensate for such limitations. Usually, this is done by encoding the data so that the encoded data is acceptable to the channel and the original data can be retrieved by the receiver. Chapter 3 (pages 39 to 51) discusses encoding techniques in more detail.

Duplex

When my young nephews received walkie-talkies for Christmas, it took some effort for their parents to teach them that they had to let go of the "Talk" button before they could hear what the other person was saying. The boys, used to telephones where both people can talk simultaneously, eventually picked up the lesson, and consequently invented a game that involved shoving one walkie-talkie into some nearby adult's hand and running away yelling "talk to me!"

The technical term for the distinction these boys learned is *duplex*. Channels that work like walkie-talkies, where only one person can talk at a time, are said to be *half-duplex*, while channels that mimic telephones are said to be *full-duplex!defined*.

This notion is important because the simplest protocols typically have the property that (under normal conditions) only one side speaks at a time. These protocols are called *half-duplex* by analogy.

Fortunately, commonly available serial channels are all full-duplex (or at least appear to be!), which allows us to consider protocols that exploit this fact.

Burst Length

When flow control is inadequate, there's a very particular pattern that arises. The first data sent through the channel is received with no errors. But, as the data continues to be sent, buffers accumulate data that hasn't been passed along to the next link in the channel. Eventually, a buffer overflows, and data beyond that point is discarded until the buffer empties. The result is a pattern of periodic errors; a certain amount of data is transferred correctly, then errors occur until the two ends stop and resynchronize, and this pattern repeats. The problem with this pattern is that recovering from errors almost always takes longer than merely retransmitting the damaged data, especially in certain full-duplex protocols.

To compensate for this effect, some protocols allow a limit to be sent on how much data they will send before they pause to allow intermediate buffers to empty. By limiting the length of these data bursts, the protocol may be able to successfully transfer data over the channel without having to recover from the periodic errors that occur when buffers overflow.

Delays

For some channels there is a long delay between when the data is sent and when the data is received. Over direct connections or modem connections directly through the telephone network, this delay is minimal. Over public networks and satellite links, however, the delay can be several seconds or more. These delays are a problem for transfer protocols that rely on retransmission for error correction, because the sender must usually keep a copy of data that has been sent until it can get verification that it's been correctly received by the other end. Interestingly, the number of seconds of delay is not as critical to most protocols as the number of bytes *en route* at any given time. At low speeds, even fairly lengthy delays aren't a big problem, because the amount of data in the channel is still low. At higher speeds, even relatively short delays can represent a significant amount of data in transit. Over network connections, especially, there can sometimes be as much as several hundred kilobytes of data in the channel.

Examples of Channels

When designing or evaluating any file transfer protocol, it's important to consider how it will behave over different types of channels. The criteria discussed earlier should all be considered carefully.

To better understand the variety of different effects, here are a few examples of channels with different characteristics:

Computer Serial Ports   Most of the channels I deal with involve data going into or out of a computer through a serial port, making a serial port a part of our channel. As the interface between software and hardware, serial ports can introduce many problems. Two common problems involve transparency—serial ports often use certain characters for special purposes—and flow control.

Wire   A wire between two computers is a relatively nice channel. There's only a short delay, and usually a fairly low error rate.

Modems   Sending data into one modem, through the telephone system, and out another modem is not much worse than a simple wire. Like a wire, there's a small delay, but the rate of errors can be much higher.

Error-Correcting Modems   Error-correcting modems provide a lower error rate, but add a delay while the modems correct any errors they detect. Error-correcting modems also introduce flow-control concerns.

Packet-Switched Networks   Channels often require data to find its way across networks, which vary from single-office local area networks to the globe-spanning Internet. These networks can add considerable delays. In addition, since access to these networks often involves another computer, hence another serial port, there are additional chances for flow control and transparency problems.

Packet Radio   *Packet radio* uses an interface that works much like an error-correcting modem. Communicating data through a packet radio system requires some care, because of the peculiar nature of these interfaces. As a channel, packet radio has a very low error rate, but has long delays, especially when the direction of data reverses. In many ways, it's an extreme form of error-correcting modem, which I'll discuss in more detail in a moment.

Internet   One of the many facilities available on the Internet is the `telnet` program, which allows a user to log in to another computer on the network. This program was designed for interactive text applications; older versions only pass seven-bit data, and even the newer ones reserve certain byte values to coordinate the two ends. Transferring files through a `telnet` connection requires handling not only these transparency problems but also the long and often variable delay caused by the underlying network.

Deep-Space Satellites   Probably the most difficult channel to deal with is one in which delays and error rates are both very high. An extreme example is the radio transfer of data between a computer on Earth and a satellite in deep space. Extremely high error rates and delays as long as several hours require a combination of slow transmission speeds (sometimes as low as ten bits per second), complex mathematical codes to detect and correct certain errors (see page 53), and sophisticated image processing. None of the protocols considered in this book can function over this type of channel.

Error-Correcting Modems

Modern modems containing built-in error correction and compression look quite reasonable at first glance. They have very low error rates, can be configured for complete transparency, provide transparent flow control at each step, and offer a fairly short delay. However, the picture is slightly more complex than this. One of the primary reasons for using such modems is to increase the total throughput, but the throughput of these modems is quite sensitive to subtle changes in the way the modem is used.

A modem with error correction and compression operates in roughly the following fashion: It accumulates data from the computer in a small internal buffer. When the buffer is full, it compresses that buffer, and sends the contents to the receiving modem using a protocol not unlike the ones considered in this book. Once the data is transferred to the receiving modem correctly, the data is uncompressed and sent to the receiving computer.

As long as the sending computer is providing data to the sending modem continuously, this works smoothly. But when the computer stops, the sending modem finds itself with a partially full buffer. After a delay, the modem decides to send the buffer anyway. This delay is usually fairly short, but protocols that operate in short bursts cause this otherwise minor delay to be repeated. The result is a significant reduction in the overall speed at which the modem transfers data. In addition, if data is flowing in both directions, then each modem must alternately handle sending and receiving data. On the other hand, if data is only moving in only one direction, both modems can concentrate on that direction, providing significant increases in throughput.

To obtain the best performance from error-correcting modems, a file transfer protocol should do two things. First, it should send data continuously (without breaks) so that the modem doesn't delay transferring data. Second, it should minimize the *back-channel* data flow, that is, the information that comes from the receiver back to the sender. YModem-G, which has no breaks in the data stream and no back-channel data flow, is possibly the best protocol in this regard, although its total lack of error recovery makes it a poor choice for general use. ZModem and Kermit also provide these two important features.

Anatomy of a Serial Protocol 2

To evaluate or design a protocol, you need to be able to dissect it. This chapter walks you through the components of a serial protocol and shows you different approaches for designing each one.

Good software design proceeds in layers: low layers interface to the operating system (*open file*) or provide simple data manipulation capabilities (*copy string*), while higher layers provide more abstract operations (*find this database entry*). Serial protocols are no different. Lower layers deal with channel issues such as transparency and error detection; intermediate layers guarantee the success of certain operations; higher layers provide user-level transactions.

For networking protocols, there are several standards that define what the layers should be and provide specific guidelines for designing and implementing those layers. However, serial file transfer protocols have not always followed these standard models. Networking protocols have to deal with many issues that simply don't arise in this setting, so many parts of networking models don't apply to serial protocols. After studying and implementing different file transfer protocols over a number of years, I developed my own model to reflect the layers that appear in actual protocols.

If these protocols weren't developed with this type of layering in mind, why am I bothering to develop and explain a layered approach? The biggest reason is to simplify analyzing and comparing these protocols. By stretching each protocol out on a common framework, I hope to be able to easily demonstrate the similarities and differences in these protocols, and hopefully make it easier for those of you who are interested in developing new protocols.

The five layers that I consider when analyzing and implementing a new protocol are:

Application	
Session	Transaction
Reliability	
Packetization	
Encoding	
Operating System	

Figure 2.1   The Five-Layer Model

Encoding   Encoding provides the tools for overcoming such basic channel limitations as lack of transparency.

Packetization   Control information and data must be transferred in a fashion that allows the other end to understand the significance of each piece.

Reliability   By detecting and correcting errors, this layer guarantees the success of basic communications.

Transaction   The reliable communication of data and control information allows you to build the operations that the user is interested in, such as the operation of transferring files.

Session   A framework in which multiple transactions can occur requires some initial negotiation, some way to coordinate which transactions will occur when, and some other general issues.

You may have noticed that these layers aren't necessarily stacked one above the other. For example, the session layer doesn't require the transaction layer in order to start and end a session. Figure 2.1 gives a more realistic view of the dependencies among these different layers.

Encoding Layer

The first issue I consider is how transparent the channel is, and how the protocol encodes all of the things to be sent using only the *alphabet* allowed by the channel. The "things to be sent" include not only the 256 byte values; they also include some *control* information.

For example, basic Kermit reserves a special character to mark the beginning of each packet, and encodes any appearance of that character in the data. That way, if the receiver has some problem, it can re-synchronize by looking for the next occurrence of this reserved character.

There are two basic approaches for this type of encoding. The one used by most current file transfer protocols is *prefix encoding*, which works very well when there are only a few values that must be avoided, and they only occur infrequently in the raw data. Another approach is *radix encoding*, which is better when these assumptions don't hold. These types of encoding are discussed in detail in Chapter 3 (pages 39 to 51).

Packetization Layer

Once you know how to encode data so that it will pass through the channel unmolested, then you can worry about organizing the various required information so that it can be readily interpreted by the receiver. The resulting data structure is variously called a *packet*, *block*, or *frame*. Designing a packet format requires care to ensure that the packet carries all the information that the other layers of the protocol will need.

Packet Header

Typical transfer protocols divide packets into *header* and *data* sections. The header provides some way of easily detecting the start of a packet, tells the receiver how to decode this packet and specifies the purpose of the packet. Table 2.1 summarizes some of the information that commonly appears in the packet header.

This information needn't always be distinct. ZModem, for instance, uses different start-of-packet sequences to indicate different packet formats. Kermit uses the length field to indicate the packet format. YModem uses the sequence number to identify the packet type, and the start-of-packet value to indicate the packet length.

Start-of-Packet

A start-of-packet (SOP) sequence is a special byte or sequence of bytes that lets the receiver find the beginning of a packet easily. This is important because of noise. Inter-packet noise shouldn't affect the protocol's ability to find and correctly decode packets. Besides the fact that damaged packets masquerade as inter-packet noise, the sender of a packet will often deliberately insert additional characters that the receiver should treat as noise. Both Kermit and ZModem add control characters before and after packets to help speed them through line-oriented terminal

Information	Description
Start-of-Packet	Helps the receiver find the packet.
Packet Format	How to decode this packet.
Packet Length	How long the packet is.
Packet Type	The purpose of the packet.
Sequence	Helps the receiver detect lost packets.
Header Check	Checks the header data.

Table 2.1   Typical Packet Header Information

handlers. To the receiver, these extra characters look like inter-packet noise, and should be ignored.

As I mentioned earlier, many protocols use different start-of-packet sequences to indicate the different packet types or lengths. This should be done carefully. If there are too many start-of-packet sequences, it becomes more likely that the receiver will try to decode noise on the line as a valid packet. Even if this does not cause the receiver to receive a spurious packet, it can cause the receiver to lose the next packet and consequently slow the transfer. If there are more than two or three start-of-packet sequences, the header check should include the start-of-packet.

If the protocol is to be used over channels that have lots of noise, then it becomes especially important that the start-of-packet be readily identifiable. This usually means that the encoding should guarantee that the start-of-packet sequence can't occur in encoded data. For example, basic Kermit usually uses a single Control-A as the start-of-packet indicator, and uses an encoding that guarantees no control characters will appear within a packet.

Packet Format

It's not unusual for protocols to have several packet formats. One reason is that there are sometimes different requirements at different stages of the protocol. ZModem, for instance, uses packets encoded in hexadecimal during the startup phase, to avoid problems if packets are accidentally "received" by a command line. Kermit has three different packet formats with different maximum sizes. The original protocol's short packets were inefficient over channels with long delays, so new packet formats were introduced to support longer packet sizes. Similarly, YModem adds a second, longer packet format to XModem.

Both Kermit and YModem occasionally encounter problems because the packet format cannot be determined completely just by examining that packet. These two protocols have a "current error check mode" that affects the type of error check used by the packet. A disagreement about the current error check mode can cause either of these protocols to fail. To avoid these types of problems, it's best if the packet format is completely specified in the packet header.

Packet Types

The packet type indicates the purpose of the packet. In the five-layer model, different packet types are interpreted by different layers. Here are some common packet types that occur in typical protocols:

Acknowledge/Negative Acknowledge   These packets are typically used by the reliability layer to guarantee that packets are transferred correctly. In full-duplex protocols, it is important to make sure that the receiver of such a packet can unambiguously determine which packet is being acknowledged.[1]

Capabilities   At the beginning of a session, the two sides will need to determine which "dialect" of the protocol the other end supports. For simple protocols, an exchange of empty capabilities packets allows for future extensions.

Next Transaction   The capabilities packet can double as a request for the next transaction. In ZModem, the ZRInit packet both communicates the receiver's capabilities, and requests the sender to begin a new transaction.

File Header   Before a file is sent, the receiver needs to know certain facts about the file. This packet transfers the filename and sometimes also carries other file attributes.

File Attributes   As discussed on page 6, files can have many attributes. For simple attributes that are likely to be translatable between systems, such as simple file permissions (whether a file is writable) and the file's creation date, it makes sense to transfer this data explicitly, rather than archiving it (see page 7). In YModem and ZModem, the file header packet carries a number of file attributes. In Kermit, the file header only specifies the filename, and any other attributes are specified in a separate attributes packet.

One attribute that deserves special attention is the file size. There are several good reasons for notifying the receiver of the approximate file size prior to

---

[1]This generally means that the window can't be more than one-half of the number of distinct packet sequence values. For example, Kermit sends packet sequence numbers modulo 64, and is hence limited to a 32-packet window. ZModem uses a 32-bit byte position, and is hence limited to a two-gigabyte window.

transfer: the receiver can check to make sure sufficient disk space is available, the receiver can size buffers to ensure efficient transfer, and the receiver can notify a user of the relative progress of the transfer. The receiver, however, should *not* use the file size to determine how much data to write to the file. This approach, used by YModem, causes problems with files that grow during transmission, and places a burden on the sender to determine the exact size of the data that will be transferred, which is difficult when the file is being converted or created during transmission.

File Data File data is often encoded, either to reduce its size (compression) or to archive other file attributes (see page 7). Over time, many protocols have been extended by adding better encodings; Kermit has recently added locking shifts to reduce the overhead of transferring certain types of files. It's important that the sender know what encoding methods the receiver understands.

Resend Data Instead of using a per-packet acknowledge or negative acknowledge, the receiver of a file may specify which parts of the file should be resent. ZModem uses a simple version of this, and more complex strategies have been proposed to allow data to be initially transferred over a one-way channel (such as broadcast radio), with a later two-way connection allowing the receiver to request data that was not correctly received.

End-of-File Every transaction requires some method for the sender to mark the end of the transaction.

Other Transaction One protocol design decision is whether each transaction has its own packet type, or whether there are a few packet types which are used for many kinds of transactions. An example of the latter is Kermit's "Generic Command" packet, whose data describes the precise transaction being requested.

End-of-Session After all transactions are complete, the sender has to notify the receiver of this fact.

Cancel File transfers can be quite time-consuming, so there should be some way for a user to cancel either a single transaction ("skip this file") or the entire session. Cancel sequences can also be useful for terminating the session if some fatal error occurs, such as when the user pulls out a diskette part way through a file transfer. In case the user needs to type the sequence because the local end has terminated prematurely, the required sequence should be kept simple.

Sequencing

While it's unlikely in well-designed protocols that noise will cause legal packets to be spontaneously generated, it is quite likely that errors can damage a packet so that it is indistinguishable from noise. In this case, the packet is lost. Care must be taken that the loss of a packet is detectable, especially in full-duplex protocols where the sender may not require an explicit acknowledgment of each packet. This is usually accomplished by attaching sequencing information to each packet. XModem, YModem, and Kermit do this in a direct fashion, by attaching a sequence number to each packet. ZModem relies on the packet error check to detect lost packets.[2]

Detecting lost packets is primarily the responsibility of the reliability layer. As you'll see when I discuss reliability issues (starting on page 23), a packet sequence number is only one tool that can be used to help make sure lost packets are detected.

Header Check

In many protocols, a single error check is used both for the header information and the data that follows. In other protocols, there is a separate error check just for the header data. Besides protecting such critical information as packet format, which must often be known before the data part of the packet can be correctly received, the header check also helps to address a subtle protocol problem.

When the receiver sees a damaged packet, it should immediately notify the sender so the packet can be repeated. However, if it sees inter-packet noise, it should probably continue to wait for a possible incoming packet. The problem is how to distinguish between these two cases, especially since a damaged packet often looks like inter-packet noise. The header check helps address this. Because the header is fairly small compared to the data that follows it, it is likely that a header will be received correctly even if the data is damaged. A correct header followed by damaged data can be immediately handled as a damaged packet, without a long delay. Thus, a header check allows the receiver to detect many damaged packets and respond more quickly than it could otherwise.

---

[2]One of the reasons that ZModem uses a very strong 32-bit CRC is because the CRC is responsible for detecting sequencing problems. Other protocols with more explicit sequencing don't need such strong error checks.

Inside-Out Packets

The traditional view looks at data as residing *within* a packet. The idea is that the protocol is primarily an exchange of control information, with data attached as necessary. This is analogous to procedural programming, which focuses on code for manipulating data.

In the last decade, procedural programming has been turned inside-out to obtain object-oriented programming, which might be better called *data-driven programming*. In the same way, we can reverse our view of a serial protocol by focusing on the data first, with the control information being embedded in the data only as necessary.

This view is suggested by the development of *streaming*, which I'll discuss later in more detail. What I want to discuss now is what happens to packets in this view.

Turning the traditional packet inside out results in a flow of data with control nuggets embedded within it. Even in the normal approach, it's possible to think of the start-of-packet sequence as a *control escape*, which indicates that control information follows. This approach requires some re-thinking of the information traditionally associated with packets. For example, if there are no packets, packet sequence numbers are no longer relevant. Control information has to be relevant in the new context.

So, what information can reasonably be embedded within the data flow to help manage that data flow effectively?

Data Position If a transfer is a long stream of bytes, the packet sequence number evolves into a byte position within the data stream.

Error Check Information Each control nugget requires an error check on the nugget itself to safeguard the overall operation of the protocol. You'll also need control nuggets with error check information for the data stream. Probably the best form is to have a CRC (cyclic redundancy checks are explained in Chapter 4) accumulate over the data (but not control information), and whenever a CRC nugget is received, the CRC accumulator is checked and then cleared.

Data Separator Transfer of multiple files will require some form of delimiting to mark the boundaries between files.

Transaction Information Other transactions can be handled either by exchanging packets (control nuggets are just very simple packets), or by encoding data into a continuous stream that is transferred, decoded, and processed on-the-fly. One example of this approach is the transfer of PostScript programs over a network; the PostScript program is transferred over the network as a stream of text data and interpreted as it is received, sometimes generating a stream of data to be transferred back over the network.

Error Detection

There are subtle issues involved in selecting and computing good error checks. Chapter 4 (pages 53 to 65) gives a thorough discussion of the most common error checks and how to compute them.

Reliability Layer

The packet layer provides the necessary functions to create, send, and receive packets. The reliability layer is responsible for interpreting those packets to make sure that data is transferred correctly. If there is only one packet, the sender of a packet can simply wait for a response, and interpret that response to determine if the other side received and understood the packet. If not, the packet is repeated.

This simple approach is known as *half-duplex*, because it only requires the channel to be active in one direction at a time. After a packet is sent, the sender of that packet waits for a response. This method is appropriate when there is only one packet to be sent, such as when the sender notifies the receiver of the name of the next file to be sent. However, it can be very inefficient when you're sending a lot of packets, especially if there are delays while packets traverse from one side to the other.

To address this inefficiency, many protocols switch to *full-duplex* methods to transfer larger amounts of data. These methods take advantage of the fact that both sides can send simultaneously. Rather than waiting for acknowledgment of each individual packet, the sender sends a continuous stream of packets, and the receiver acknowledges them as they are received. As long as the sender doesn't get too far ahead of the receiver, this provides much faster throughput. However, it does complicate recovery from errors.

Half-Duplex ACK/NAK

The simplest way to handle reliability is for each packet to require the receiver of that packet to send an explicit acknowledge (ACK) or negative acknowledge (NAK) packet. XModem and basic Kermit both use this idea fairly directly.

When packet 48 was damaged, the receiver sent a NAK and the sender resent the packet. This picture becomes a bit more complex when you consider the

Sender	Receiver
Packet 47	
	ACK
Packet 48	
	error: NAK
Packet 48	
	ACK

Figure 2.2   Half-Duplex Error Recovery

possibility of lost or corrupted ACKs or NAKs. Either the sender can time out and resend the packet, or the receiver can time out and send a NAK. Either approach works in practice, but problems arise if both sides time out at about the same time. XModem, YModem, and ZModem all time out on the receiver's side, with no time out or a very long time out on the sender's side. Kermit allows the time out to be handled on either side, but is careful to ensure that if both sides time out, the timeouts are sufficiently different to avoid confusion.

Scripted Dialog

One problem with simple ACK/NAK reliability is that the acknowledge or negative acknowledge can be redundant. Consider the following exchange, for example:

A. What's your name?

B. ACK

B. My name is B.

A. ACK

Notice that B's ACK is redundant because the response to A's question implies that B received the question correctly. It's faster to eliminate the redundant ACK. When carried through carefully, this approach leads to what I call a *scripted dialog*, in which ACKs are usually implied by the correct response. There will almost always be some situations in which an explicit ACK is necessary, but this technique can reduce the total number of packets that must be exchanged with a corresponding increase in speed.

Developing a scripted dialog approach requires careful attention, however. In particular, you must make sure that the response does in fact always specify whether or not the previous packet was received. Kermit accomplishes this quite neatly by calling the response packet ACK, and including the response data as part of the ACK packet.

Segmented Half-Duplex

As I mentioned earlier, longer packets are more efficient when there is a long delay on the channel. When there are errors, however, shorter packets are less likely to be damaged, and require less time to retransmit if they are damaged. To be efficient in a variety of situations, you really want both long packets and short packets. One solution to this dilemma is to use a modified half-duplex method in which the sender sends several packets at a time. By sending a large number of packets at one time, you gain the benefits of long packets when there are delays, but since the receiver can request which packets should be resent, error recovery requires less time. One protocol that uses this strategy [10] has the sender send eight packets at a time. After receiving all eight packets or timing out, the receiver responds with a list of the packets that should be resent. Once all eight packets in that group have been successfully transferred, the sender proceeds to the next group. A few protocols use this technique exclusively, and some others, including ZModem (which calls it *segmented streaming*), allow it under certain circumstances.

Although similar to the full-duplex techniques I'll describe in a moment, this is still a half-duplex approach. As such, it works in some situations where full-duplex is impossible, but offers some of the speed advantages of full-duplex approaches. It's not a panacea, however. Good throughput requires a great deal of buffering on both sides, more than is usually required with full-duplex methods, since the receiver's acknowledgment is delayed until the entire group of packets has been sent. In addition, channels that only allow half-duplex often have other restrictions that make this approach unfeasible. Segmented half-duplex does, however, offer a tempting middle ground between the packet size trade-off of basic half-duplex and the inherent complexity of true full-duplex approaches.

Full-Duplex

The scripted dialog approach can result in a significant speedup, but only if there are natural responses. However, when transferring a large amount of data in one direction, as in a file transfer, there are no natural responses during the transfer, so something else is needed.

To speed up file transfers, you could simply have the sender send a continuous stream of data packets and have the receiver notify the sender only when something goes wrong. This method not only eliminates seemingly-redundant ACK packets, it also accelerates the transfer by not requiring the sender to wait for responses.

When it receives bad data, the receiver just sends NAK packets specifying which data to resend.

Unfortunately, this "no news is good news" approach can't provide good protection against certain common errors. For example, if the connection fails, the sender could find itself spending a considerable amount of time dumping data into oblivion. A similar problem occurs if a NAK packet is lost. After the receiver sends a NAK requesting data be repeated, it must wait for some period of time before it can assume the request is lost and repeat it. Otherwise, multiple such requests can prompt the sender to needlessly repeat data. If the sender requires periodic ACKs of good data, it can notice when the receiver has not responded, and can notify the receiver of the problem.

There are two natural questions to ask at this point: How long should the sender continue sending before it requires a response from the receiver? How long should the receiver wait before it assumes a NAK was lost?

The first question is usually abbreviated as: How big should the *window* be? The window is the amount of data the sender will send without expecting a response from the receiver. After it has sent that much data, the window has *blocked* and the sender will wait until it receives some sort of response. The optimal window size depends on the channel delay.[3]

The second question is actually tougher. For example, if the receiver doesn't wait long enough before repeating a NAK, the sender will receive *duplicate NAKs*, prompting it to needlessly resend the same data.[4] If the receiver waits too long, the end-of-file will appear and there can be a long delay while the sender and receiver transfer the remaining shards of data.

This duplicate NAK problem is one of the toughest problems to handle when implementing full-duplex protocols. Many implementations of Kermit and ZModem can get into situations where their throughput degrades considerably from this problem.

Multiple Outstanding Packets

The obvious full-duplex approach is for the sender to continue sending packets, while the receiver returns ACK or NAK packets for each one as it receives it. This approach is called *multiple outstanding packets* to contrast it with half-duplex

---

[3]Some ZModem documentation discusses ZModem operation "without a window." It's more correct to say that some ZModem implementations allow the window to be as large as the file. Every protocol has a window. For half-duplex protocols, for example, the window is exactly one packet.

[4]If the sender sees a duplicate NAK, it *must* respond to the second one; it does not know if the data it resent in response to the first NAK was correctly received or not.

approaches, where only a single packet is outstanding at any given time.[5] This method places a considerable burden on the sender to keep track of which packets have been acknowledged and which haven't. A viewpoint that often helps in understanding and implementing this approach is to look at a NAK from the receiver as being a request for a particular packet. This shows the receiver sending ACKs for correctly received packets, and NAKs for packets that should have been received. In particular, it's possible and even reasonable for the receiver to send a NAK for a packet the sender has not yet sent. Such a NAK simply tells the sender the packet the receiver expects to see next.

This approach has a subtle problem, though. As discussed on page 13, some high-speed modems operate more efficiently when data is moving in only one direction. For optimal throughput with such modems, you want to minimize the number of ACK/NAK packets sent by the receiver. On the other hand, error handling is improved by having frequent responses from the receiver. This means that the optimal frequency for ACK/NAK packets varies depending on the channel. Two approaches that allow some control over the frequency of ACK/NAK packets are to vary the length of data packets, or to have the receiver only acknowledge some of the packets. Kermit uses the former approach, allowing data packets up to 800k in some implementations, while ZModem uses the latter approach, limiting data packets to a modest 1k but having the sender mark which packets the receiver should acknowledge.

Streaming

On page 22, I introduced the idea of a *control escape*, a special byte or sequence of bytes that mark control data embedded in the file data being transferred. This is the idea behind *streaming*, which views the transfer as a continuous dump of data with control information inserted as necessary. Functionally, streaming works similarly to multiple outstanding packets, except it uses a different method to track which data has or has not been correctly received.

Because streaming does not use explicit packets, the receiver can only work with byte position. Unfortunately, if a given CRC check fails, the receiver may not know the byte position of data following that CRC check. Two options are apparent. One is to embed periodic announcements of the byte position so that the receiver can resynchronize. Another is to simply ignore out-of-sequence data. ZModem, in essence, uses both approaches. ZModem's packet headers can be

---

[5]The term *multiple outstanding packets* could also be applied to segmented half-duplex approaches, but I'll only use it to refer to true full-duplex.

viewed as embedded control nuggets in the sense I described on page 22.[6] Because data packet headers convey the current byte position in the stream, the sender does have a means of publishing this data. But, for simplicity, ZModem ignores out-of-sequence data, forcing the sender to resend the data from the point of the error rather than merely resending the damaged data. This approach simplifies the implementation considerably, but sacrifices throughput when there are both long delays and errors.

Window Sizing and Management

In theory, window sizes should always be infinite. The sender should be able to continue sending data regardless of how long it takes the receiver to respond. One of the many reasons this doesn't work in practice involves buffering. The source of data being sent is not always a seekable disk file, so the sender must buffer data internally until it has been acknowledged. Similar considerations apply to the receiver. Since the total amount of data that must be buffered can potentially be as large as the window, there is an obvious problem with infinite windows.

A too-large window impairs error recovery. ZModem, for example, simplifies its window management by ignoring out-of-sequence data. When the receiver sees an error, it ignores all subsequent data until it sees the data it's expecting. This means that the sender must respond to NAKs as quickly as possible. This quick response is hampered by a large window size, which can leave large amounts of now-extraneous data buffered in the channel, data which the receiver must read and discard before it can see the sender's reply.

A too-small window degrades throughput. When the sender has sent a full window's worth of data, it must stop until it gets an acknowledgment from the receiver. If the window is so small that there's insufficient time for a complete round-trip of the channel, the sender will find itself unnecessarily idling.

Combining these considerations tells us that the ideal size for the window depends on the round-trip time. The sender should finish sending the last data in the window just as it receives acknowledgment for the first data in the window. In practice, this round-trip time is relatively easy to measure (simply count how much data you send before receiving a response), although it is prudent to set the window slightly larger to account for variations in the channel round-trip time. The only problem is when the round-trip delay varies significantly, such as when the file is being processed on-the-fly, on multitasking systems, or over networks.

---

[6]More or less. ZModem doesn't guarantee that start-of-packet codes won't appear in data, which complicates the issue.

Implementing Reliability

Reliability functions provide a certain guarantee to their clients. For half-duplex reliability, that guarantee is pretty obvious.

Sender: I guarantee that I will not return until this packet of data is completely and correctly received by the other end.

Receiver: I guarantee that I will not return until I have correctly and completely received the next packet.

For full-duplex reliability approaches, it's more subtle. Guarantees such as those above don't allow for data to be temporarily unaccounted for, which is necessary in a full-duplex situation in which some data should be *en route* at any given moment. What works best is for the file transaction layer to provide a large data buffer (which I call the *window*), and the reliability functions to provide the following guarantees:

Sender: I guarantee that I will not return until some initial portion of the window is correctly received by the other end.

Receiver: I guarantee that I will not return until I have correctly received some initial portion of the remaining data.

Another way of stating the sender's guarantee is that it promises to *reduce the window*. Once the sender has returned, the buffer of data to be sent is smaller, and can be refilled. At any given time, the window structure contains a contiguous part of the file data. For a protocol such as Kermit, which allows data to be transferred out-of-sequence, the sender may have marked some of the data in the middle of the window as having been correctly received, but it will still not return until it has sent data from the beginning of the window.

The full-duplex receiver's guarantee doesn't look much different, but as with the full-duplex sender, the receiver may have received data in the middle of the window, which remains buffered until all preceding data has been received. Unlike the half-duplex case, the full-duplex sender or receiver does not guarantee how much data will be sent or received. A single call to the full-duplex reliable receiver may return one packet of data or a full window's worth.

Transaction Layer

A means for reliably transferring data is the foundation for building useful services. These services are generally called *transactions*, and the particular transaction I'll concentrate on in this book is the transfer of a single file.

File transactions are interesting simply because they are so demanding in terms of efficiency. However, many protocols support other types of transactions. Both Kermit and ZModem, for example, allow an arbitrary system command to be sent to the other side, opening essentially unlimited transaction variations.

File Transfers

The most common type of transaction is the transfer of a file from one machine to another. There are two basic reasons for transferring a file from one machine to another. One is to use the file on the second machine. The other is to store the file for later transfer to a machine that will use the file. This distinction is more important than it may seem, because the receiving machine may not be able to accurately represent the entire file as it exists on the sending machine. A decision must be made whether to translate the file to make it usable on the receiving machine or to somehow store the extra information so that it can be reconstructed when the file reaches its final destination.

As an example, consider transferring a Macintosh file to an MS-DOS machine. The name of the file on the Macintosh may be too long to use on MS-DOS. If the purpose of the transfer is to use the file under MS-DOS, then the exact name is likely not important, and it should be changed to reflect the limitations of MS-DOS. If the file is being stored for later transfer to another Macintosh, it's probably best to store the original name somehow so that it can be recovered when the file reaches that other computer. Filenames are only one such consideration; Macintosh systems also have file types, icons, and a host of other attributes that are meaningless on MS-DOS. This situation is even worse when you consider exchanging files with mainframe systems, where files can be quite a bit more complex than the stream of bytes common on microcomputers and workstations.

Although some file transfer protocols designed for networks attempt to preserve and translate a host of mainframe file attributes, the protocols I'm considering here view a file as simply a stream of bytes with a name and a handful of other specific attributes. Their primary concession to the distinction discussed in the previous paragraph is to provide special handling for text files. Text files are considered usable on any machine and are usually translated to and from a neutral format during transfer. All other files are considered *binary*, and are transferred strictly as-is. For systems whose files aren't simple streams of bytes, archiving programs encode them as a stream. For example, the Macintosh community has developed a standard called MacBinary, which archives a file together with a handful of Macintosh-specific attributes into a single stream of bytes that can be transferred using common protocols. Kermit implementations for VMS and OS/2 take a similar approach to preserving the file properties used on those systems.

Conditional File Transfers

Normally, we think of "file transfer" as deliberately copying a file from one system to another. But there are a number of subtle issues. For example, what should be done if the file already exists on the target system? The answer to this question depends on the intent of the file transfer. Here's a brief list of some of the reasons a file might be transferred:

Backup Copy   The user might be transferring some files to a remote system to keep safe copies. In this case, if a file is unchanged—it has the same time stamp and size as the copy already on the backup system—you would like to avoid transferring it.

Synchronizing Two File Systems   It is increasingly common for a single person to use two or more computers for similar purposes. For example, a person might use a desktop computer in the office and a portable computer when away from the office. Both systems need up-to-date copies of all files. For this application, files that only exist on one system should be transferred to the other, and newer files should be transferred to replace older copies of the same files. Notice that the previous idea ("backup copy") is a special case of this.

Synchronizing Specific Files   In the previous example, it's reasonable to believe that the person may not want the desktop and portable computers to have the exact same files. In particular, the portable is likely to have less storage than the desktop, which might make it desirable to only synchronize those files that already exist on the laptop.

Updating Files   Log files are kept by some critical applications to monitor system usage, maintain accounting information, or record database transactions. Such files typically change only by having new material added to the end, and they can be extremely large. Maintaining a copy on another system is most efficient if only the new part of the file is transferred.

Recovering After a Failure   When a file transfer fails for any reason, a partially-transferred file may be left. Especially if the file is large, you want to transfer only the remaining part of the file.

These different applications show that the question of what to do when a file already exists on the target system can be fairly complex. It becomes even more complex when you attempt to define what it means for a file to already exist. Just because a file has the same name does not mean that it's the same file. Dedicated terminal programs sometimes address this by always storing transferred files in a special area, to reduce the possibility of accidentally overwriting a file which is important to the user. When comparing two files, such issues as the modification date, length, and other factors can all be considered as a basis for comparison. As discussed on page 103, ZModem can even compare the file contents by requesting a file CRC from the sender.

For any protocol, the receiver has the ultimate control over the disposition of a received file. The receiver can choose to overwrite or extend an existing file, or can choose to store the file under a different name or in a different area to avoid destroying an existing file. Having a mechanism to allow the sender to suggest a disposition to the receiver makes it easy for the user to specify the handling of a file regardless of which end is being directly controlled by the user. Kermit's File Attribute packet is an optional extension that both allows the sender to suggest a disposition and allows the receiver to reject the file transfer. ZModem defines a wide range of file dispositions that the sender can suggest to the receiver. ZModem also includes a provision for the receiver to request a CRC of all or part of the file prior to transmission. This CRC provides the receiver with a means of comparing the actual file contents prior to accepting the file.

Non-File Transfers

Often, a stream of data comes from a program or another data source that's not a file, or is sent to something other than a file. For example, the data might be graphics information that should be decoded and displayed on-the-fly, or it might be an archived directory tree to be dearchived as it is received.[7]

Allowing this type of usage requires a great deal of care, primarily in implementation. For example, the ZModem implementation in this book does not support the "infinite window size" common to many ZModem implementations, because that would require either storing the entire file in memory, or assuming that the source of data was, indeed, a seekable file. Fortunately, infinite window sizes are only necessary in unusual situations where the channel buffers inordinate amounts of data, so I lose very little by not supporting it, while gaining the ability to transfer data that does not come from a file without any special consideration of the source of the data.

Application Commands

Many years ago, interacting with an on-line service meant dialing in with a text-based terminal program and typing commands to the remote host. Now, that is

---

[7]I actually know someone who used to back up his computer at home to a computer at work by piping the output of an archiving program into a file transfer utility to be transferred over a modem!

changing; many information services provide a graphical front end program that runs on the user's computer, and uses a reliable protocol to transfer commands to the host and transfer the results of those commands to the user. Electronic mail messages are composed by the user on the local computer using a convenient full-screen editor and then transferred to the host, while messages addressed to the user are transferred to the local computer where they can be stored and read off-line. These front end programs use the same techniques as the file transfer protocols discussed in this book to transfer data and commands in both directions.

Kermit includes an operational mode in which the local program accepts commands to be relayed to the remote Kermit program and interpreted there, with the results transferred back. These commands include listing a directory, changing directories, logging in to a different account, and so on. Some of these commands involve transferring data—a request for a directory listing transfers the text of the listing—while others simply change the operation of the program on the other end. Defining a collection of specific commands that are handled directly by the Kermit server program encourages compatibility between the services offered by different Kermit server programs.

Host Commands

But it's not always possible to build everything into the host program. For this reason, both Kermit and ZModem allow arbitrary text commands to be transferred and executed directly by the host command processor, for instance, the Unix shell or MS-DOS command.com. For Kermit, the output of such a command is automatically transferred back to the user.

Session Layer

Users often will want to do more than a just a single transaction. They will want to transfer multiple files in each direction and perform other tasks. Before any transactions can occur, the two programs need to determine which protocol dialect is in use, and similarly, after all transactions are complete, they need to cleanly finish. The total of all of these actions is a *session*.

Different protocols handle these steps differently. For XModem, there is no negotiation or termination; a session consists of a single file transaction. For Kermit, negotiation and termination are handled for every transaction. This approach allows Kermit to handle any number of transactions with no special considerations; one Kermit program can even be stopped and restarted in the middle of a series of transactions.

In my model, the session layer is also the right place to discuss such issues as terminating when unrecoverable problems occur, even though in implementation, it often makes sense to handle these issues in other layers.

Initiating the Session

Before any protocol events can happen, both ends must know that a protocol is being started. Early systems required users to manually initiate both ends of the protocol, but interest in simplifying the user interface has led to a variety of techniques for allowing one end to start the other end by providing an easily identifiable code that a terminal program or other application can recognize.

One of the early protocols to provide such a scheme was the B protocol developed by CompuServe. Because CompuServe was marketing terminal programs for use with their system, they were in a position to integrate the transfer protocol's operation with the operation of the terminal program. CompuServe's Vidtex programs could be controlled by CompuServe's host software to initiate file transfers in either direction. The host would interpret the user's request for a file transfer, and then instruct the user's terminal program to commence the transaction.

This popular feature spread to many other protocols. ZModem has an easily recognizable packet sent at the start of any file transfer. This packet begins with a control character (CAN) that is not used in common terminal emulations, which makes it easy for these programs to recognize this special packet without interfering with the primary emulation. ZModem also has a convention that the sender types rz<Return> when it starts, in the hope of starting a ZModem receive program on the other end. This approach works well for uploading to Unix (the common Unix ZModem program is called rz) and many bulletin board systems.

Recently, Kermit has standardized a very flexible mechanism to allow automatic initiation and configuration. Kermit implementations use the ANSI/ISO standard *Application Program Command* function [1, 11], which allows an arbitrary command to be sent to an ANSI-compatible terminal program. This feature allows any command from an extensive script language to be sent, including commands to initiate Kermit file transfers. By using a standard mechanism for encapsulating the command, this approach guarantees compatibility with popular terminal emulations.

Negotiating Capabilities

After both ends are operating the same protocol, they must agree on various parameters. For simple protocols, this stage is often merely a formality, in which the two ends exchange empty packets. This allows future improvements to the protocol. For older protocols with a wealth of submodes and other details, this step can be more complex.

Current protocols seem to agree on two points. The first is that the capabilities exchange should be kept short. The common outline is that each end enumerates its capabilities in a single packet, and from that point both ends use only those capabilities common to both sides. The second point is that the session-layer operations should use only the basic protocol. Any extensions or advanced features negotiated during this stage should be used only where they will do the most good, generally in a file transaction. As the protocol evolves over time, the core session remains the same—changes only affect the operation of specific types of transactions.

Completing the Session

When all transactions are finished, the session should end cleanly. In particular, the user shouldn't see a burst of garbage characters as the remote end has a "last laugh."

One sticky problem requires some explanation. Suppose the final exchange looks like the following:

You Say	I Say
X	
	Y
Z	

Clearly, after you send Z, you should simply terminate, since there is no response. But suppose I send Y and don't see your Z for some reason. What should I do? One possibility is that you got my Y but your Z was lost, in which case you'll have already terminated. By that logic, I should simply terminate after I send Y. But what should you do if you send X and don't get my Y? By the same reasoning (I might have sent my Y but you didn't get it), you should simply terminate after not getting a response to your X. This argument can be continued indefinitely.

Something is clearly not right here. If you examine this argument closely, you'll see the problem: "end-of-session" cannot be reliable. Put another way, you can never be certain the other end has agreed to stop. However, it is possible to be certain that both ends agree that a transaction has ended. Protocol implementations should be fairly forgiving of problems ending the session and shouldn't warn the user of errors that don't affect what the user is trying to accomplish. (ZModem's handling of end-of-session is worth studying, however. See page 330.)

Cancelling the Session

It's not uncommon for users to change their minds. As a result, every good file transfer protocol has some way to prematurely terminate a transaction or an entire protocol session. Situations in which this might occur include the following:

- The local end may have to cancel because of a failure of the communications link.

- A single transaction may need to be skipped. The user might decide not to wait for a particularly long file to be transferred, or there might be some error that affects only this transaction.

- The entire session may be cancelled.

- The user may need to terminate the remote because the local end has terminated prematurely, leaving the remote end spitting nonsense at the user's terminal.

The first of these is purely an implementation issue. Any protocol implementation should notice and terminate cleanly if the communications link fails. The last one is more nearly a pure protocol design issue. The keyboard sequence that the user can use to terminate the other end in an emergency should be standard across all implementations of a protocol and should be easy for the user to discover in an emergency. XModem, YModem, and ZModem all use a repeated CAN (Control-X) character. Although the Kermit protocol *per se* does not specify a keyboard sequence, a repeated interrupt character (often, Control-C) will terminate many implementations.

Master/Slave Session Model

Throughout this book, you'll see references to 'sender' and 'receiver.' In practice, of course, users will transfer files in both directions, and many protocols allow the roles of 'sender' and 'receiver' to flip-flop during the session. Often, it's more relevant to ask which end initiates transactions. Typically, a user at one end is transferring files to and from a host machine. When there is only one user, it makes sense for all transactions to initiate from a single end. This end is often called the *master* and the end that simply obeys commands is correspondingly called the *slave*.

In CompuServe's B protocol, all transactions are initiated from the host end. The user commands the host, and the host in turn commands the user's local terminal program to begin a file upload or download. Kermit is exactly the opposite; the local program is the master and the host program is the slave. In other protocols, the roles flip-flop. In ZModem, the sender is always the master; to start a receive, the sender sends a command and the two ends swap roles. When the command is complete, the roles revert. UUCP allows the master to initiate both sends and receives, but it still swaps master and slave to handle transfer requests that have been queued at either end.

Encoding

3

Raw binary data is poisonous to many channels, as anyone who has ever accidentally listed a binary file to the screen can attest. This chapter looks at the fundamental techniques required for developing non-toxic protocols.

When designing a new protocol, the first task is to understand the channel that will be used. Many protocols blithely assume fully transparent channels with a short delay and low error rate. If you know that your protocol will only be used in such environments, you can greatly simplify your protocol design. If not, you have to develop ways to overcome the limitations of your channel.

Encoding is used primarily for dealing with a lack of channel transparency. A certain number of control characters can be usurped by the channel for flow control or other purposes. For example, a common bug among serial routines written in C is for the NULL character to be dropped. The result is that there are more symbols you want to send (usually you'll want to allow all 256 possible byte values) than there are symbols that you can send through the channel.

A mathematical terminology is useful here. Think of the symbols that can be sent through the channel as an *alphabet*. Encoding is the process of building *words* from this alphabet that convey the symbols to be sent. The encoding method to use depends in part on how big the alphabet is compared to the number of words you need to be able to build.

In the ideal case, the alphabet would be large enough to use just one-letter words. In practice, this isn't possible, even if the channel is perfectly transparent, that is, all 256 byte values can be safely used. You actually need more than 256 words. Besides the data in the file, you also need to encode control information, and you want to guarantee that control information isn't confused with file data. The best example of this is the start-of-packet symbol. To make the start of the each packet readily identifiable—so that the receiver can easily re-synchronize after an error—you need to make sure the start-of-packet won't appear in encoded data.

Although there are many different ways to encode data, there are two that are most commonly used. *Prefix encoding* attempts to encode isolated problem values, while *radix encoding* encodes all of the data in a uniform way.

Prefix Encoding

Prefix encoding works well when the alphabet is relatively large. In this encoding approach, certain letters in the alphabet are reserved as *prefix codes*. For example, Kermit usually uses the # character for prefixing control codes. Each byte is encoded separately as either a multi-letter word starting with a prefix code (#A encodes Control-A), or as a single non-prefix letter (A represents itself). Note that the prefix character must always be encoded—Kermit encodes the # prefix as ##.

Kermit actually allows up to three prefix codes. Two are used for prefixing control codes and bytes with the high bit set. These prefixes allow for arbitrary binary data to be encoded using only the printable ASCII characters. The third prefix code allows some simple compression, to help compensate for the expansion from the other encoding. More details on this encoding are given in Chapters 9 (starting on page 114) and 10 (starting on page 124).

If many byte values must be encoded, prefix encoding can expand the data significantly. In the worst case, every byte requires prefixing, doubling the size of the data. One way to reduce this overhead is to use a combination of two different prefixing approaches. The prefixing approach described above is called a *single shift*. Each prefix alters only the next single value, much like the shift key on a keyboard. Just as most keyboards support a *Shift Lock* to simplify typing long sequences of shifted characters, prefix encoding can add a *locking shift* character, which affects *all* the following characters until it is explicitly undone. Such a mechanism has recently been introduced as a Kermit extension, and it has been quite successful at reducing the encoding overhead, especially for text using such character sets as the EUC Japanese encoding and the ISO Hebrew character set. In both cases, text files can consist almost entirely of bytes with the high bit set. A locking eighth-bit prefix reduces the overhead from one prefix for every character to one prefix for the entire file.

Kermit's prefix encoding is both a great strength and a great weakness. On the one hand, this encoding allows Kermit to transfer binary files over very restrictive channels. In fact, Kermit can function over channels that allow only the 95 printable ASCII characters and a single control code. Kermit is the only protocol in this book that works under these conditions.

However, over less-restrictive channels, some Kermit implementations do more encoding than they need to. This practice unnecessarily expands the data, thus increasing the number of bytes that must be sent and reducing the effective speed of the transfer. Fortunately, newer implementations of Kermit can relax their encoding considerably, reducing the overhead and significantly improving the speed of the protocol. This type of flexibility is important in any protocol that strives to be both efficient and work well over a variety of different channels.

Radix Encoding

Prefix encoding isn't very efficient when the alphabet is small, because a large percentage of the bytes will require prefixing, expanding the data significantly. A more efficient approach when the alphabet is restricted is to use *radix encoding*. Only one of the three dictionaries I have at home defines "radix," and that one claims it is "the root of a tree." In this context, however, radix is the "base" of "base 10 numbering."

If it's okay to double the data size, radix encoding can accomplish that with an alphabet of only 16 symbols, by representing each byte in hexadecimal (base 16). By convention, the 16 symbols are the digits and the first six letters (either upper or lower case), but any sixteen characters can be used.

Usually, of course, there are more than sixteen symbols available. Even the most restrictive channels allow all 52 upper case and lower case letters, the 10 digits, and a handful of punctuation characters, which provides enough symbols for base 64 encoding. Base 64 encoding takes a group of three bytes and encodes it using four symbols, earning this encoding the name "four-for-three" encoding. Base 64 encoding is often associated with the Unix `uuencode` program, which is used to encode binary files into text files suitable for transfer through electronic mail. Originally, `uuencode` used the 64 printable ASCII characters from space (character 32) to underscore (character 95). Unfortunately, mail systems can be particularly ugly channels. The encoding was later changed to use tilde ~ (character 126) instead of space, to avoid problems with mail systems that removed trailing and multiple blanks from the text of electronic mail messages. Continuing problems, especially with old mainframes that converted mail text between ASCII and EBCDIC led to the development of the `xxencode` program, which uses only digits, alphabetic characters, and the two punctuation marks + and -.

The 33 percent overhead of base 64 encoding is comparable to the overhead of Kermit-style prefix encoding when applied to binary files. Larger bases can do even better. If you have all 95 printable ASCII characters, you can achieve 22 percent overhead, but special techniques are required. It's usually sufficient to use base 85 encoding, which encodes four bytes into five symbols, giving 25 percent overhead. This encoding is used by the `atob` and `btoa` programs, which are used like uuencode and xxencode to encode binary files for transfer through electronic mail. It's also used by PostScript Level 2 to allow binary graphics data to be embedded within the text of PostScript programs.

Radix encoding may be thought of as a "worst-case" encoding, in that it guarantees that the data won't be expanded by more than a certain amount. By contrast, prefix encoding is a "best-case" encoding, in the sense that it provides no expansion if the data is very nice. By utilizing different packet formats (page 18), it's possible to combine these properties, using whichever encoding provides less expansion. Compression programs such as arc or zip use similar techniques, picking the most appropriate encoding for each item.

Implementing Encoding

Implementing prefix and radix encoding is not particularly difficult, but there are a few techniques that can make these encodings simpler and faster.

Prefix Encoding Hints

When encoding, it is necessary to rapidly classify bytes into those that require encoding and those that don't. One of the fastest and easiest ways to do this is to implement a set of character classification macros similar to those routinely implemented in the standard C header <ctype.h>. These macros use an array of 256 integers, each one encoding the properties of that particular byte value. This array makes it very simple to test to see if a byte needs to be encoded, and if so, how. The following code snippet shows how this can help simplify Kermit-style control and eighth-bit encoding. If possible, the classification array should be an array of char, since on many processors, such arrays can be indexed much faster than arrays of larger data types. If you need more than eight classification macros, you should consider whether it makes more sense to have one array of int or two arrays of char.

```
    char Classify[256];      /* Initialized elsewhere */
#define NEEDSPREFIX8   (1)
#define NEEDSPREFIXCTRL   (2)
#define Needs8BitPrefix(c)   (Classify[c] & NEEDSPREFIX8)
#define NeedsCtrlPrefix(c)   (Classify[c] & NEEDSPREFIXCTRL)
  char *Encode(char *dest, char c)     /* Encode c into dest */
  {
    if (Needs8BitPrefix(c)) { *(dest ++) = PREFIX8; c &= 0x7f; }
    if (NeedsCtrlPrefix(c)) { *(dest ++) = PREFIXCTRL; c ^= 0x40; }
    *(dest ++) = c;
```

```
      return dest;
   }
```

One of the advantages of prefix encoding is that it is selective; you can select at run-time which bytes will be encoded. Using this approach, such alterations can be handled by modifying the `Classify` array. Even if this degree of flexibility isn't necessary, it can be useful to have more than one constant classification array. In that case, the `Classify` variable becomes a pointer, which is updated depending on which of several alternate classifications is in effect. This technique allows different encoding strategies to be used at different times.

Prefix Decoding Hints

Channels can fail to be transparent in several different ways. Not only do they swallow certain characters, channels can also generate spurious characters. For example, mismatches in software flow control can cause `XON` and `XOFF` characters to be generated. To compensate, many protocols deliberately ignore certain characters in the input. Character classification macros like the ones above can be useful in determining which characters to skip during decoding.

These character classification macros can also be used to recognize prefix codes. Admittedly, for most encodings, this degree of flexibility isn't necessary. It's most useful when there is more than one character that represents the same prefix. An example of this is when parity must be ignored; using a character classification array to recognize the character with or without parity is an alternative to stripping parity from each received byte.

```
#define IGNORE   (4)
#define ISPREFIX8  (8)
#define ISPREFIXCTRL  (16)
#define Ignore(c)  (Classify[c] & IGNORE)
#define IsPrefix8(c)  (Classify[c] & ISPREFIX8)
#define IsPrefixCtrl(c)  (Classify[c] & ISPREFIXCTRL)
  char *Decode(char *dest, char *source, int sourceLength)
  {
    char c;
    char toggle8 = 0;
    char toggleCtrl = 0;
    while (sourceLength > 0) {
      sourceLength --;
      c = *source ++;
      if (IsPrefix8(c)) toggle8 = 0x80;
      else if (IsPrefixCtrl(c)) toggleCtrl = 0x40;
```

```
        else if (!Ignore(c)) {
          *dest ++ = (c | toggle8) ^ toggleCtrl;
          toggle8 = 0;
          toggleCtrl = 0;
        }
      }
    }
```

Hexify

Converting a byte at a time into hexadecimal is pretty simple. The only two optimizations are using an array of characters to convert a digit—an integer from 0 to 15—into an appropriate character, and using shifts rather than division to break the byte into two digits.

```
    void Hexify(char *dest, const char *source, int length)
    {
      const char digits[] = "0123456789abcdef";
      while (length -- > 0) {
        *dest ++ = digits[(*source >> 4) & 0x0f];
        *dest ++ = digits[*source ++ & 0x0f]
      }
      *dest ++ = 0;      /* NULL termination */
    }
```

Unhexify

The Unhexify function decodes a string of hex digits. This particular version ignores parity bits, and accepts either lower case or upper case alphabetic characters. It returns the number of bytes decoded. The evenDigit variable keeps track of when to move to the next byte.

The bulk of this routine is involved with converting characters into their digit values. This conversion is simplified somewhat by the fact that the legal characters fall into only three ranges: digits, upper case alphabetic, and lower case alphabetic.

```
    int Unhexify(char *dest, const char *source, int length)
    {
      int c, digit, firstDigit;
      int count = 0, even = TRUE;
      while (length -- >= 0) {
        c = *source ++ & 0x7F;      /* Remove parity bit */
        digit = -1;
        if ((c >= '0') && (c <= '9')) digit = c - '0';
        else if ((c >= 'a') && (c <= 'f'))
```

```
      digit = c − 'a' + 10;
    else if ((c >= 'A') && (c <= 'F'))
      digit = c − 'A' + 10;
    if (digit < 0) return count;      /* Illegal digit? */
    if (even) { firstDigit = digit; even = FALSE; }
    else {
      *dest ++ = firstDigit << 4 + digit;
      count ++;
      even = TRUE;
    }
  }
}
return count;
}
```

ToBase64

This function is similar to `Hexify` except that it collects bits across several bytes. Three bytes give 24 bits, which can be encoded six bits at a time.

There is a trick used here to deal with the one or two bytes that might be stranded at the end of the data. By encoding one byte using two characters and two bytes as three characters, the exact length of the original data can be recovered. Because the encoded data is text, I simply NULL-terminate it rather than returning a length. For simplicity, this function encodes more data than it has to at the end, and takes advantage of a possibly-negative value of `length` to correctly place the terminator.

The encoding vector used here is the one used by the Unix `xxencode` utility. Another possible vector, used by `uuencode`, consists of ~ followed by the 63 ASCII characters from ! through _. Old versions of `uuencode` used a space for the zero digit, rather than ~.

```
void ToBase64(char *dest, const char *source, int length)
{
  const char digits[] = "+-0123456789ABCDEFGHIJKLMNOPQRSTUVWXYZa\
    bcdefghijklmnopqrstuvwxyz";
  while (length > 0) {
    *dest ++ = digits[(source[0] >> 2) & 0x3f];
    *dest ++ = digits[((source[0] << 4) & 0x30) | ((source[1] >>
        4) & 0x0f)];
    *dest ++ = digits[((source[1] << 2) & 0x3c) | ((source[2] >>
        6) & 0x03)];
    *dest ++ = digits[source[2] & 0x3f];
    source += 3;     /* Encoded 3 bytes */
    length −= 3;
```

```
      }
      dest[length] = 0;      /* NULL termination */
   }
```

FromBase64

This function decodes a string in base 64. It illustrates several techniques useful in dealing with larger bases.

The first technique is the method used to decode a character into a digit value. Rather than a lengthy `switch` or a series of `if` statements, this code builds a lookup table that assigns to each character its digit value; a value of −1 indicates that this is an illegal digit. The static variable `decodeFinished` tracks whether or not the table has already been constructed. Note that this table approach requires the use of `unsigned char`.

Often, when using this type of encoding, it's desirable to ignore certain characters, such as control characters, entirely. One way to mark characters to be ignored is to set the entry in the `decode` array to a flag value such as −2. In this example, I've included values for the digit characters with the high bit set; this effectively ignores parity in the data being decoded.

One advantage of this approach is that it makes it very easy to change the characters used. This routine uses the `xxencode` encoding. Switching to the `uuencode` encoding requires merely changing the `digits` string. (If the code formatting looks a bit unusual to you, see page 151 for an explanation.)

```
⟨ Build base-64 decode table 46 ⟩ ==
   if (!decodeFinished) {
      static const char digits[] = "+-0123456789ABCDEFG\
         HIJKLMNOPQRSTUVWXYZabcdefghijklmnopqrstuvwxyz";
      int i;
      for (i = 0; i < 256; i++) decode[i] = −1;
      for (i = 0; i < 64; i++) decode[digits[i]] = i;
      for (i = 0; i < 64; i++) decode[digits[i] | 0x80] = i;
      decodeFinished = 1;
   }
```
This code is used on page 47.

It's easiest to handle the actual decoding four characters at a time. As each character is decoded into a six-bit value, it is added to `num`. Whenever eight bits are accumulated, they are saved to the `dest` array.

Some care is needed to handle short strings. In base 64, four digits represent a three-byte number, which is a problem when we try to encode something that isn't a multiple of three bytes. The convention here is common: a single final byte is encoded in two characters, two trailing bytes in three characters. By peeling off bytes and storing them early, we make it easy to terminate prematurely.

⟨ Decode four characters, **break** on error 47 ⟩ ≡

```
{
    int  i = 0;
    int  numDigits;
    int  digit = 0;

    num = 0;
    while  ((i < 4) && (digit >= 0) && (i < length)) {
        digit = decode[*source ++];
        num = num * 64 + digit;
        i ++;
    }
    numDigits = i;
    length -= i;
    for ( ;   i < 4;  i ++) num = num * 64;
    for (i = 0;  i < (numDigits − 1);  i ++) {
        *dest ++ = num >> (16 − i * 8);
    }
    count += numDigits − 1;
    if  (digit < 0) break;
}
```

This code is used on page 47.

We don't do length checking inside the loop, which means we may end up decoding garbage past the end of the original string. The final return value compensates for this, however. The value in `length` will be negative if we pass the end of the data; `count + length` is then the correct count of the number of bytes decoded.

```
int FromBase64(char *dest, const unsigned char *source, int
        length)
{
    int digit, count = 0;
    long int num;      /* A 32-bit variable */
    static int decode[256];
    static int decodeFinished = 0;

    ⟨ Build base-64 decode table 46 ⟩
    while (length > 0) {
        ⟨ Decode four characters, break on error 47 ⟩
    }
    return count + length;
}
```

ToBase85

Because 85 isn't a power of two, we can't use the bit-shift tricks used in Hexify and ToBase64. Other than that, this function is pretty much the same as the earlier ones.

I've included one compression trick from atob and PostScript, which is the convention that a 32-bit zero is represented by a single z character rather than !!!!!.

```
void ToBase85(char *dest, const char *source, int length)
{
  const unsigned char *p = (const unsigned char *) source;
  unsigned long num;
  const char digits[] =
      "!\"#$%&'()*+,-./0123456789:;<=>?@""ABCDEFGHIJKLMNOPQRS\
      TUVWXYZ[\\]^_`abcdefghijklmnopqrstu";

  while (length > 0) {
    num = ((p[0] << 8 + p[1]) << 8 + p[2]) << 8 + p[3];
    p += 4; length -= 4;
    if (length < 0) {      /* Round up short group */
      switch (length) {
      case -1 :  num |= 0xff;
      case -2 :  num |= 0xffff;
      case -3 :  num |= 0xffffff;
      }
    }
    if ((num == 0) && (length >= 0)) *dest++ = 'z';
    else {
      dest[4] = num % 85; num /= 85;
      dest[3] = num % 85; num /= 85;
      dest[2] = num % 85; num /= 85;
      dest[1] = num % 85;
      dest[0] = num / 85;
      dest += 5;
    }
  }
  dest[length] = 0;      /* NULL termination */
}
```

FromBase85

Again, this function is the same as FromBase64 except generalized to handle a base that's not a power of two.

As before, the `decode` table simplifies translating characters into digit values. Rather than list all 85 digit characters in a string, we cheat and use the ASCII characters beginning with `!`.

⟨ Build base-85 decode table 49 ⟩ ≡
```
if (! decodeFinished) {
  int i;

  for (i = 0; i < 256; i ++) decode[i] = −1;
  for (i = 0; i < 84; i ++) decode[i + '!'] = i;
  for (i = 0; i < 84; i ++) decode[(i + '!') | 0x80] = i;
  decodeFinished = 1;
}
```
This code is used on page 50.

Because the digit characters only go up to `u`, some of the remaining characters can be used to implement a bit of compression. Both `atob` and PostScript use `z` to represent a 32-bit zero, which provides modest compression.

⟨ Decode `z` as a 32-bit zero 49 ⟩ ≡
```
*dest ++ = 0;  *dest ++ = 0;
*dest ++ = 0;  *dest ++ = 0;
source ++ ;  length -- ;
count += 4;
```
This code is used on page 50.

Performing the actual decoding is a bit tricky, because you can't pick off the bytes along the way. Because the base isn't a power of two, you have to first compute the 32-bit number from the five digits, and then break the number into four bytes.

⟨ Decode 5 characters, `break` on error 49 ⟩ ≡
```
{
  int i = 1;
  int numDigits;

  num = 0;
  while ((i < 5) && (digit >= 0) && (length > 0)) {
    digit = decode[*source ++] ;
    num = num * 85 + digit;
    i ++;
  }
  numDigits = 5 − i;
  length −= numDigits;
  for ( ;  i < 5;  i ++) num = num * 85;
  for (i = 0;  i < (numDigits − 1);  i ++) {
    *dest ++ = num >> (24 − i * 8);
  }
```

```
        count += numDigits - 1;
        if (digit < 0) break;
    }
```
This code is used on page 50.

FromBase85 is identical to FromBase64, except for the special handling of the z character.

```
    int FromBase85(char *dest, const unsigned char *source, int
            length)
{
  int digit, count = 0;
  unsigned long num;
  static int decode[256], decodeFinished = 0;
  ⟨ Build base-85 decode table 49 ⟩
  while (length > 0) {
    if ((*source & 0x7f) == 'z') {
      ⟨ Decode z as a 32-bit zero 49 ⟩
    }
    else {
      ⟨ Decode 5 characters, break on error 49 ⟩
    }
  }
  return count + length;
}
```

Compression

Radix encoding is a special case of a much more general technique known as *arithmetic encoding*. Arithmetic encoding is related to such popular compression algorithms as Huffman coding, which leads to the conclusion that it should be possible to create algorithms that simultaneously compress and encode data. The compression would compensate for the encoding overhead, making it possible, for example, to encode data for compatibility with seven-bit data paths with little or no expansion of the data.

In practice, such combined algorithms probably aren't worth the trouble. Since standard compression algorithms result in fairly random binary data, following them with a radix-encoding step will give results that are just as good as a more complex combined approach, with the advantage of being built from standard software components, such as the encoding routines presented on the previous pages. The only practical advantage to combined algorithms that compress data directly into a restricted set of characters is probably a marginal increase in speed.

Compression is often done manually by users who compress data files before transfer and manually uncompress them afterwards. This procedure is especially popular on BBS systems, where storing all files in a compressed format provides a significant reduction in storage requirements.

Kermit and ZModem both offer some compression. Kermit's simple run-length encoding offers modest compression for certain types of data. Its primary advantage is that it is simple, and hence widely implemented. ZModem offers an optional compression based on the patented LZW algorithm. The fact that this algorithm is patented has discouraged its widespread use (although many programs depending on this algorithm were released prior to the patent). In addition, LZW is significantly more complex to implement than Kermit's encoding, which has also slowed its appearance in ZModem implementations.

For now, the complexity and processing requirements of serious compression algorithms make them generally unsuitable for widespread use as an integral part of file transfer protocols. In addition, the potential gains from such compression in the protocol are reduced when they are combined with other compression engines, such as those becoming common in modems. Despite this, I suspect that the steady increase in processing power will make compression a more popular aspect of future protocols.

Encryption

One other possible use of encoding is to encrypt the data so that it is difficult for an eavesdropper to determine what data is being transferred. Again, the computational requirements of good encryption make this fairly expensive. In addition, currently popular channels—telephone and public packet networks—are reasonably secure against casual eavesdropping.

However, encryption will doubtless be an important part of future protocols. Faster processor speeds and new encryption methods are slowly addressing the speed concerns that have made encryption impractical. The need for encryption is increasing with the increasing use of insecure channels such as cellular telephone. Finally, public awareness of data security is increasing, in part due to the media attention given to the Internet worm and the debate over the Clipper chip.

Error Detection and Correction 4

One of the major raisons d'être for file transfer protocols is to provide error-free transfer of data over channels that are not error-free. This requires the ability to find and correct the errors that are inevitably going to occur.

Most transfer protocols use some form of *error-detecting signature* to detect errors, and *retransmission* to correct them. The idea is that the sender computes some special value and "signs" the packet of data with that value. When the sender receives the data, it computes its own signature and compares it with the one received from the sender. An error in transferring the data will cause these two values to disagree. The receiver can then ask the sender to resend that particular packet.

The two most popular error-detecting signatures are *checksums* and *cyclic redundancy checks* (CRCs). Although simple, checksums lack the robust mathematical properties of CRCs. CRCs can be computed efficiently with the code in this chapter, making it reasonable to use them for error detection in most applications.

Error-Correcting Codes

An alternative to resending bad packets is to use an *error-correcting code*. Error-correcting codes have special properties that allow the receiver to tell not only that an error has occurred, but to identify—within limits—exactly what that error was. In contrast, error-detecting signatures can only identify the existence of an error.

Error-correcting codes are useful in situations where resending data is unreasonable. One example presented earlier is that of sending data from a deep space satellite to Earth. The extremely long delays make it unreasonable to ask the satellite to resend data. Error-correcting codes are also used in audio and video applications, since the delay while data is resent cannot be predicted, which interferes with the strict timing requirements of these applications.[1] Sometimes, as with audio compact disks, resending the data (from the studio!) is simply impossible.

The transfer protocols in this book do not rely on error-correcting codes for a number of reasons. The first is that error-correcting codes are more complicated than error-detecting signatures—NASA employs full-time mathematicians just to design new error-correcting codes that can be efficiently computed by the computers carried on satellites. Error-correcting codes also tend to increase the size of data significantly. Finally, error-correcting codes don't correct all errors. Error-correcting codes can be designed that correct any specific number of errors, but codes that correct more errors are significantly more complex. To correct all errors, you have to resort to retransmission anyway.

These reasons combine to make error-correcting codes generally unsuitable for serial protocols. Instead, these protocols rely on error-detecting signatures and some method for the receiver to request that parts of the data be resent. Essentially, they trade reduced complexity in the error detection (choosing simple signatures rather than more complex error-correcting codes) for increased complexity in the higher layers of the protocol.

Checksums

Checksums are the easiest signatures to understand, and largely for that reason, may well be the most widely used type of signature. A checksum simply adds up the values of each byte of data to obtain a signature value. Unfortunately, they aren't particularly effective.

To detect a large number of errors, the signature values must be *uniformly distributed*; that is, on random data any signature value should be about as likely as any other. Unfortunately, checksums do not have this property.[2] Think about the "checksum" obtained by rolling two dice. A sum of 2 provides a very accurate check, since there's only one way to obtain a 2. On the other hand, a checksum of 7 is less helpful; there are many ways to obtain a 7. So, you can see that checksums are not very evenly distributed; some checksums give you more information than others.

Using only the lower eight bits of a larger checksum gives a value with a better distribution. However, shorter signatures are generally less effective at detecting

---

[1]The delay is not predictable because you don't know in advance how many times a single packet of data will have to be resent before it is transferred correctly.

[2]This is a special case of a statistical property known as *The Law of Large Numbers*, which says that sums tend to have *normal* distributions rather than *uniform* distributions.

errors than longer signatures. A well-distributed eight-bit signature will detect only one of every 256 errors.

These considerations mean that checksums are only acceptable when the packets are fairly short, as they are in the original XModem and Kermit protocols. As packet sizes increase, it becomes more likely that any given packet will have an error, and so it becomes more likely that an error will go undetected. Because checksums do not provide well-distributed large signatures, something else is needed.

What You Need to Know About Cyclic Redundancy Checks

I'm well aware that many people will skip much of this chapter because of the modest amount of mathematics in it. I'll summarize a few simple facts about CRCs in advance, so that you can pick up the basics even if you're one of those people whose eyes glaze over when they hear words like "division." The mathematics don't appear for a few more pages, so you're safe until then.

- There are many different CRCs. They are all computed in essentially the same fashion, but vary in length. The most common ones are 12, 16, and 32 bits. The most popular of these is the 16-bit CRC recommended by the CCITT, which is used by XModem, YModem, ZModem, Kermit, and many other protocols.[3] As you can guess, a 12-bit CRC will miss only one error out of 2^{12}, while a 32-bit CRC will miss only one error in 2^{32}.

- The most important aspect of a CRC is its length. Longer CRCs are more effective than short ones at detecting errors.

- As a rule of thumb, eight-bit checksums are reasonable for packets up to about 128 bytes. Beyond that, you should use a CRC. The 16-bit CRC-CCITT is adequate for all but the most demanding situations.

- CRCs can be computed nearly as quickly as checksums, using table-driven algorithms such as the ones given in this chapter. These implementations are both compact and fast. In addition, some minicomputers and mainframes can compute CRCs in hardware. (The DEC VAX has an instruction that computes the 16-bit CRC-CCITT of a sequence of bytes.)

- Because CRCs are easily implemented in hardware or software, they have received widespread use. They are used to detect errors in floppy and hard

---

[3]Each of these protocols also supports other error checks.

Size	Generating Polynomial	Binary
12	$x^{12} + x^{11} + x^3 + x^2 + x + 1$	0x180f
16	$x^{16} + x^{12} + x^5 + 1$	0x11021
32	$x^{32} + x^{26} + x^{23} + x^{22} + x^{16}$ $+ x^{12} + x^{11} + x^{10} + x^8$ $+ x^7 + x^5 + x^4 + x^2 + x + 1$	0x104c11db7

Table 4.1   Common CRC Generating Polynomials

disk interfaces, network software and hardware, program loaders, backup software, revision control systems, and many other products.

Implementing CRCs

Few good descriptions of the mathematics behind CRCs exist, and partly for this reason, CRCs are frequently dismissed as being too complex for common use. Fortunately, despite the mathematical underpinnings, good CRC implementations are both short and fast. In this section, I'll present some efficient code for computing the most popular CRCs, with a minimum of mathematics. The next section will delve into some high-school mathematics so that those of you who want more insight can better understand them.

CRCs are characterized by a parameter called the *generating polynomial*, which is written either as a sum of powers of x or as a string of bits. Three popular generating polynomials are listed in Table 4.1. It's not important at this point that you know what a generating polynomial is, just that different generating polynomials give different CRCs.

The relationship between the binary and polynomial forms is just that the powers of x indicate which bits in the binary form are set, with the convention that 1 in the polynomial form is thought of as x^0. So, for the generating polynomial $x^{16} + x^{12} + x^5 + 1$, bits 16, 12, 5, and 0 are set.

Computing CRCs Slowly

CRCs are calculated on a stream of bits. I'll start with a simple calculator that computes the 16-bit CRC recommended by the CCITT, which creates international communications standards. This calculator isn't very efficient, but will help explain the better ones that follow.

```
short BitwiseCrc16(int bit, short crc)
{
  long longcrc = crc;
  longcrc = (longcrc << 1) ^ bit;     /* next bit */
  if (longcrc & 0x10000) longcrc ^= 0x11021;     /* reduce */
  return (longcrc & 0xFFFF);
}
```

Without going into the mathematics, I'll briefly explain this code so that you can more easily understand the other CRC code that follows. CRC calculations consist of alternating two operations: collect the next bit(s), and reduce the value so far. In this example, the function is called once for each bit of data. The shift and exclusive-or puts this bit into the longcrc variable, and the if statement handles the reduction. One slight modification (checking the bit before the shift rather than after) eliminates the need for a long temporary variable.

```
short BitwiseCrc16(int bit, short crc)
{
  if (crc & 0x8000) crc = (crc << 1) ^ 0x1021 ^ bit;
  else crc = (crc << 1) ^ bit;
  return (crc);
}
```

Table-Driven CRC Calculation

If you look at this operation over the eight bits in a byte, the eight reductions don't depend on the bits being shifted into the low-order end; they only depend on what was already in the high-order byte. Thus, you can rearrange the calculation to collect eight bits and then do eight reductions (or vice-versa). By precomputing the reductions in a table, you end up with a very efficient algorithm. InitCrc16 precomputes the reductions for all 256 possible byte values, using exactly the algorithm in the previous section. Many programs that use CRCs include the table as a list of constants in the source code, rather than computing it at run-time.

```
static short Crc16Table[256];
void InitCrc16()
{
  short i, j, crc;
  for (i = 0; i < 256; i++) {
    crc = (i << 8);     /* Put i into high-order byte */
    for (j = 0; j < 8; j++)
      crc = (crc << 1) ^ ((crc & 0x8000) ? 0x1021 : 0);
    Crc16Table[i] = crc & 0xFFFF;
```

```
        }
    }
```

By using the pre-computed values in the table, `Crc16` can very rapidly update the CRC value. To make this function even faster, it could be modified to accept a pointer and a count, removing the need for a function call for each byte of data.

```
short Crc16(int ch, short crc)
{
    crc = Crc16Table[((crc >> 8) & 255)] ^ (crc << 8) ^ ch;
    return crc & 0xFFFF;
}
```

Real CRC Calculators

If you compare the previous code with the CCITT-CRC16 computations in the XYModem and ZModem source code, you'll notice that the table is identical, but the CRC calculation itself, which I've shown below, is slightly rearranged. There's an interesting mathematical reason for this, but for now, here's a relevant non-mathematical observation: In the first version, if you initialize the `crc` value to zero, the first two bytes simply get shifted directly into the CRC (the zero entry in the table is always zero). That is, the CRC16 of a two-byte buffer is just those two bytes. The alternative version below doesn't have this property. You can get the exact same result from the version above by adding two zero bytes to the end of your data and including those in the CRC calculation. When I discuss the mathematics, you'll see that this change gives a very nice property.

```
short XYZModemCrc16(int ch, short crc)
{
    crc = Crc16Table[((crc >> 8) ^ ch) & 255] ^ (crc << 8);
    return crc & 0xFFFF;
}
```

The Kermit CRC16 shows yet another variation. Kermit computes its CRC backwards, shifting the CRC to the right rather than the left. This reversed direction means that we test the least significant bit rather than the most significant bit, and the CRC constant is reversed from 0x1021 to 0x8408.

```
static short Crc16Table[256];
void InitCrc16()      /* Kermit version */
{
    int i, j, crc;
    for (i = 0; i < 256; i++) {
        crc = i;      /* Start with i in low-order byte */
```

```
      for (j = 0; j < 8; j++)
        crc = (crc >> 1) ^ ((crc & 1) ? 0x8408 : 0);
      Crc16Table[i] = crc & 0xFFFF;
    }
  }
```

The `KermitCrc16` function also reflects this reversal.

```
  short KermitCrc16(int ch,
        short crc) { crc = Crc16Table[(crc ^ ch) & 255] ^
        (crc >> 8);
      return crc & 0xFFFF; }
```

The Kermit protocol reference [3] gives an interesting algorithm for computing this CRC, which takes advantage of the fact that the CRC16 only has a few terms in it's polynomial and those are widely separated. That algorithm, credited to Andy Lowry of Columbia University, calculates the CRC16 four bits at a time rather than eight bits. It's somewhat slower than the versions I've shown here, but it doesn't require a 512-byte table.

12-Bit and 32-Bit CRCs

Other CRCs can be computed similarly. The following function computes a table for the standard 12-bit CRC.

```
  static short Crc12Table[256];
  void InitCrc12()
  {
    int i, j, crc;
    for (i = 0; i < 256; i++) {
      crc = (i << 4);    /* Put i into top of 12-bit value */
      for (j = 0; j < 8; j++)
        crc = (crc << 1) ^ ((crc & 0x800) ? 0x80F : 0);
      Crc12Table[i] = crc & 0xFFF;
    }
  }
```

Notice that the left shift in `Crc12` shifts by 8, because it's computing the CRC one byte at a time. The right shift aligns the high-order byte, and is therefore a shift by four. With similar minor modifications, this code can be used for any CRC of at least eight bits.

```
  short Crc12(int ch, short crc)
  {
```

```
    crc = Crc16Table[((crc >> 4) ^ ch) & 255] ^ (crc << 8);
    return crc & 0xFFF;
}
```

The 32-bit CRC is computed the same way. The ANSI/ISO C standard guarantees that `long` is at least 32 bits, which allows this implementation to be completely portable among compliant compilers.

```
static long Crc32Table[256];

InitCrc32()
{
  int i, j;
  long crc;

  for (i = 0;  i < 256;  i++) {
    crc = (i << 24);      /* Put i into top of 32-bit value */
    for (j = 0;  j < 8;  j++)
      crc = (crc << 1) ^ ((crc & 0x80000000 L) ? 0x04c11db7 L : 0);
    Crc32Table[i] = crc;
  }
}
```

Note that ZModem computes its 32-bit CRC backwards from the `Crc32` function below, just as the Kermit CRC16 is backwards from the X/Y/ZModem CRC16.

```
long Crc32(int ch, long crc)
{
  crc = Crc32Table[((crc >> 24) ^ ch) & 255] ^ (crc << 8);
  return crc & 0xFFFFFFFF;
}
```

Understanding CRCs

(Some of you will want to skip this section on a first reading. The non-mathematical narrative resumes on page 64.)

CRCs are based on a technique for dividing polynomials that's routinely discussed in high-school algebra classes. The key point is to think of the data being transferred as a single long list of bits. By writing this list as a polynomial, a chunk of data becomes a single mathematical entity that can be manipulated as a whole. Put slightly differently, polynomials give a way of computing that treats an entire file as a single mathematical object.

Long Division of Polynomials

Grade-school math classes teach a technique for division often referred to as *long division*. The method looks at the dividend (the part under the division symbol) a few digits at a time.

$$
\begin{array}{r}
508 \text{ rem } 16 \\
37 \overline{)\ 18812} \\
-185 \\
\hline
31 \\
-0 \\
\hline
312 \\
-296 \\
\hline
16
\end{array}
$$

High-school math classes teach this same method for dividing polynomials. As you may recall, division of polynomials is even simpler than division of integers, because only the first term matters. For example, the first step in dividing $2x^4 - 2x^3 - 12x^2 + 12x - 6$ by $x^2 - 3x + 2$ is to divide $2x^4$ by x^2, yielding $2x^2$.

$$
\begin{array}{r}
2x^2 \\
x^2 - 3x + 2 \overline{)\ 2x^4 - 2x^3 - 12x^2 + 12x - 6} \\
2x^4 - 6x^3 + \ 4x^2
\end{array}
$$

The rest of the process is the same as dividing integers. At each step, you divide the leading terms to obtain a new term in the quotient, then multiply and subtract.

$$
\begin{array}{r}
2x^2 + \ 4x - 4 \text{ rem } -8x + 2 \\
x^2 - 3x + 2 \overline{)\ 2x^4 - 2x^3 - 12x^2 + 12x - 6} \text{ rem } -8x + 2 \\
2x^4 - 6x^3 + \ 4x^2 \\
\hline
4x^3 - 16x^2 + 12x \\
4x^3 - 12x^2 + \ 8x \\
\hline
-4x^2 + \ 4x - 6 \\
-4x^2 + 12x - 8 \\
\hline
-8x + 2
\end{array}
$$

If you look back at the original bit-at-a-time CRC calculator, you'll see these same steps: bring another term (bit) into consideration (shift), divide the leading terms (test the high-order bit), multiply (multiply by zero or one), and subtract (exclusive-or). Repeating this procedure for each term (bit) eventually results in a remainder (CRC).

In the sample division just given, because you're dividing by a second-degree polynomial, you always consider three terms at a time. After subtracting, you're left with two terms, so you "shift" another term into consideration, just as the CRC algorithm shifts the next bit into the CRC variable. Also, the CRC algorithm only tests a single bit at each loop, much as the division algorithm only divides the leading terms.

The reduction is the part that doesn't make sense at first glance. The subtraction in the normal division algorithm somehow has been mutated into an exclusive-or operation. Clearly, these aren't ordinary polynomials...

Polynomials Modulo 2

The number system of *integers modulo 2* has only two numbers, zero and one. This number system allows all four of the basic arithmetic operations according to the following tables. Just as in normal arithmetic, division by zero is undefined.

+	0	1		−	0	1
0	0	1		0	0	1
1	1	0		1	1	0

×	0	1		÷	0	1
0	0	0		0	*	*
1	0	1		1	0	1

Using integers modulo 2 to create polynomials gives you some peculiar properties. For example, since $1 + 1 = 0$ in modulo 2, you know that $(x + 1)^2 = x^2 + x + x + 1 = x^2 + 1$, which is very different from what you get using the standard integers.

Messages as Polynomials

Now, consider the word "dog" in ASCII. As a string of bits, it looks like 0110 0100 0110 1111 0110 0111. By considering these bits as the coefficients, you have a 22nd degree *message polynomial*:

$$x^{22} + x^{21} + x^{18} + x^{14} + x^{13} + x^{11} + x^{10} + x^9 + x^8 + x^6 + x^5 + x^2 + x + 1$$

One warning: many people are tempted to equate these polynomials with binary numbers by "substituting 2." That doesn't work. A moment ago you saw that $(x + 1)^2 = x^2 + 1$ in modulo 2. If you "substitute 2," this would mean that $(2 + 1)^2 = 3^2 = 9$ is the same as $2^2 + 1 = 4 + 1 = 5$. It's more appropriate to think of a term such as x^{22} as meaning that there is a one bit in position 22. The polynomial is then just a list of which bit positions hold ones.

CRCs Defined

Now, I'm ready to define a cyclic redundancy check: a CRC is the remainder obtained by dividing the message polynomial by the generating polynomial. The key to translating this into the code I presented earlier is to realize that adding and subtracting polynomials in modulo 2 is really just the exclusive-or operation, as reflected in the addition and subtraction tables shown earlier. The initial bit-at-a-time CRC calculator is just the realization of the long division algorithm for polynomials modulo 2.

From Mathematics into C

Let's take a closer look at this connection. Because CRCs use polynomials modulo 2, there are only two possibilities at each step of the long division algorithm: either it does divide or it doesn't. For example, a 16th degree polynomial divides *any* other 16th degree polynomial. That's the key to the bit-at-a-time CRC calculator. Checking the high-order bit is simply checking to see if a polynomial is 16th degree. If it is, the exclusive-or does the subtraction.

In symbols, if the message polynomial so far is m, and the generating polynomial is g, then m/g can be written in terms of a quotient q and a remainder r.

$$\frac{m}{g} = q + \frac{r}{g}$$

So, assume that's already been done. In particular, you know r, which is the CRC of the message before this bit. If the next bit is b, the new message is $mx + b$. (Multiplying m by x raises each power by one; that is, it performs a left shift.) The previous remainder then tells you something about the new remainder.

$$\frac{mx + b}{g} = \frac{mx}{g} + \frac{b}{g} = qx + \frac{rx + b}{g}$$

This result tells us that the remainder from $\frac{mx+b}{g}$ is the same as the remainder from $\frac{rx+b}{g}$. So, to find out the new remainder (new CRC), just shift the new bit b into the old remainder, and then take the remainder from dividing *that* by g. Because the old remainder was at most 15th degree, the new remainder cannot be more than 16th degree, so the division is just one bit test and a possible exclusive-or. If you look back at the original bit-at-a-time CRC calculator, you'll see that's exactly what it's doing. The nice part about only needing the old remainder to compute the new one is that it's not necessary to look at the entire file to compute the CRC; you only need to keep track of the CRC thus far as you scan through the bits in the file.

Instead of looking at one bit b at a time, you could consider the next *eight* bits at a time, which reveals the table-driven algorithm. Just let $B = b_0x^7 + b_1x^6 + \cdots + b_6x + b_7$ (B is the next byte of the message). Then, as before, the old remainder r becomes the basis for computing the new remainder.

$$\frac{mx^8 + B}{g} = qx^8 + \frac{rx^8 + B}{g}$$

The table is just a tool to quickly compute $\frac{rx^8+B}{g}$.

Self-Checking CRCs

When you send a packet of data, you usually append the CRC to the end of the packet. Examining this practice closely reveals a widely-used trick.

Assume you're computing a 16-bit CRC. Instead of computing the CRC of some message m, you could instead compute the CRC of mx^{16}; that is, append two zero bytes to the end of the message and include them in the CRC calculation. The CRC is simply some remainder r, and you know that $mx^{16} - r$ is divisible by the generating polynomial (the CRC of $mx^{16} - r$ is zero). But remember that in modulo 2, addition and subtraction are the same, so the CRC of $mx^{16} + r$ is also zero. This suggests that you add two zero bytes (for a 16-bit CRC) to the end of the message and use that when computing the CRC. When you send the message, replace those two zero bytes with the CRC. The receiver can then simply compute the CRC of the message and CRC bytes, and compare the result to zero.

The previous paragraph explains the comment I made earlier about the practical CRC implementations implicitly adding zero bytes to the end of the message.

Other Error-Detecting Signatures

Checksums and CRCs are not the only error-detecting signatures available. Several variations on the basic eight-bit checksum have been proposed to address some of the problems. As an example, the algorithm used by CompuServe's B protocol performs the following two steps for each byte of data:

1. Rotate the checksum value left one bit, with the high bit rotating into the low bit.

2. Add the next byte. If there was a carry, increment the checksum.

Kermit's default checksum does something similar, computing a standard eight-bit checksum, and then folding in the top two bits to create a six bit value. Kermit's reasons for this extra calculation are worth exploring. In the original Kermit protocol, an important goal was to keep the packets as short as possible. It was also important that the protocol be usable over seven-bit connections. Taken together, these concerns meant that the packet check needed to be expressible as a single printable ASCII character, which explains the choice of a six-bit error check. Simply taking the bottom six bits of the checksum would have given an error check that completely ignored the high-order two bits of every byte. Any error that only affected the high-order bits would not be detected by a naive six-bit checksum! This observation points out another important property of good error checks: they should depend on all of the bits in the message (they should detect an error in any one bit). To provide this property, the Kermit designers instead computed an eight-bit checksum, which does depend on every bit, and then added the top two bits to the lower six bits to create a six-bit value.

Cryptographic Signatures

Error-detecting signatures are also used in computer security. In that application, however, the goal is to detect *deliberate* modification of data. These signatures are used, for example, to detect alteration of such electronic messages as those that are used in banking networks to transfer money.

CRCs are very good at detecting *random* modification of data. Unfortunately, their simple mathematical properties make it relatively easy to deliberately alter data in such a way that the CRC is still correct. This weakness makes CRCs poor choices for applications in which security is a major concern.

Understanding Text Files 5

Of course, everyone "knows" what a text file is. Unfortunately, not everyone knows the same things! Because files transferred between dissimilar computers are usually text files, it makes sense to take a careful look at what goes in a text file and what can be done to ease the points of disagreement.

Because text files are composed of *characters*, the first step in understanding text files is to understand clearly what a character is. There are two types of characters, *graphic characters* and *control characters*. Graphic characters have a visual representation called a *glyph*, for example, "A," while control characters indicate "non-text" properties. Some control characters indicate the logical structure of the data, such as the *new line* character, which marks the start of a new line. Others control the display of subsequent characters on a display device, for example, the *line feed* character instructs the display device to move the current position down to the next line.

Control Characters in Text

Various control characters are used to indicate breaks between lines, breaks between paragraphs, overstruck characters, the end of the data, or other properties of the text. Different systems vary in the control characters used and the meaning of those characters. To effectively transfer data between different systems, it's usually best to stick to a least common denominator text format.

The least common denominator text format uses end-of-line markers after each line, restricts lines to less than 80 characters (including the end-of-line marker), and uses no other control characters. If other control characters must be used, the following conventions should be adhered to closely:

- Tabs stops are spaced every eight characters.

- Use backspace for overstriking rather than overprinting lines, as overprinted lines are not usually possible on systems that use CR (Carriage Return) as the end-of-line marker.

- When overstriking, print the most important character last, so that on systems that do not support overstriking (such as most character displays) legibility will be maintained. For example, to underline a character, print the underline first, then backspace and print the character.

Even text files that do obey these guidelines can be problematic. For example, many printers cannot support overstriking of any sort, and some text editors do not support tabs.

End-of-Line Conventions

The most important control characters are the ones used to separate lines in a text file. There are at least three different widely-used conventions for representing the end of a line of text, and as many different conventions for what a "line" means. Various systems use any of the following control characters to separate lines:

CR/LF   – CP/M and MS-DOS use two control characters to mark the end of each line. This mimics the operation of text terminals, which require, after every line, both a CR (Carriage Return) to move the current position to the left margin, and an LF (Line Feed) to move down to the next line.

CR   – The Apple Macintosh uses a single CR to mark the end of each line.

LF   – Unix uses a single LF (actually, it's the New Line character, which happens to have the same code) to mark the end of each line of text.

Other variations occur, but are less common. A few systems use LF followed by CR, some use other control characters. But the three listed above cover the vast majority of current systems. To reduce confusion, most serial protocols insist on a particular end-of-line convention, meaning that many implementations need to convert between the native format for their system and the standard format used by the protocol. The serial protocols discussed in this book all use CR/LF for this purpose.

There's also variation in the *meaning* of the end-of-line. Usually, the end-of-line marker breaks the text into short pieces, so that it can easily be displayed with each line from the file appearing on a single line of the display. However, many text editors now automatically handle the wrapping of paragraphs over several lines, which leads to two common variants. One variant, used by many MS-DOS editors, uses two different end-of-line markers. A *soft break* is often represented as a single CR, and indicates a line break inserted by the editor, which can be moved or removed as the program sees fit. A *hard break* is represented by the CR/LF sequence, and marks the end of a paragraph. A hard break is a paragraph break, and should not be changed by the program.

Another variant is to not store soft breaks at all. This scheme, which is more popular with Macintosh editors, uses the end-of-line marker as a paragraph marker. The result is files in which each paragraph is stored as a single long line.

Both of these end-of-line variations cause problems with systems that don't support them. Some editors don't allow lines longer than 80 characters, either refusing to read them, or truncating any longer lines. Thus, it's often a good idea to break long lines into shorter ones and convert soft breaks into hard breaks. On the other hand, this type of conversion can make it more difficult to use the file if the receiving system does use paragraph breaks.

Character Encodings

The characters described above are defined in terms of what they look like or what they mean, but to be manipulated by a computer, they must be represented by numbers in the computer's memory. A *character encoding* is an assignment of specific numbers to specific characters. Although this encoding is usually represented simply as a table, there are patterns in most character encodings that make them easier to understand. For example, EBCDIC (Extended Binary Coded Decimal Interchange Code) sets the eighth bit on all alphabetic and numeric characters, and clears it on all punctuation and control characters. Similarly, ASCII has a convention that lower case characters use numbers 32 higher than their upper case equivalents.

A character together with the number that represents it is called a *code point*. For example, in EBCDIC, the code point for "a" is 0x81, while in ASCII, the code point for "a" is 0x61. This is in contrast to a *character code*, which is a number without any assumption of what character it represents.

Small Character Sets

The first character encodings were designed by equipment vendors for their specific equipment, and varied widely. The Baudot code used by teletypes consists of two sets of five-bit codes, with special *shift* codes to switch between them. Codes like Baudot with five or six bits per character were quite common well into the 1960s.

One of the reasons early computer languages were in all upper case (FORTRAN) or were case insensitive (Pascal) was that many early computers did not support both upper and lower case letters.

Seven-Bit Character Sets

In the mid-1960s, the American National Standards Institute (ANSI) ratified ANSI x3.4, the American National Standard Code for Information Interchange, which came to be known as ASCII. The structure of this seven-bit character encoding, shown in Table 5.1, has influenced many subsequent national and international standards.

In ASCII, the 128 character codes are divided into four sections: the codes 0-31 are used for control characters, 32 is the space character[1], 33-126 are graphic characters, and 127 is another control character.[2]

Although the precise assignments of the graphic and control characters within these regions has varied, this arrangement of 33 control codes, 94 graphic codes, and space has become standard. In particular, it was later adopted by the International Standards Organization (ISO) as the basis for ISO 646. ISO 646 defined a family of seven-bit character encodings by fixing the control codes and most of the graphic codes identically to ASCII. The remaining 12 graphic codes were allowed to vary so that different countries could have character sets reflecting the needs of their particular language. For example, ASCII's } character (code 125) is changed into ü in the German national version, å in the Finnish, and è in the French. Table 5.2 on page 72 shows the differences between a number of ISO 646 character sets.

For languages with relatively small alphabets, seven-bit character sets are often sufficient. However, the limitations become apparent when you try to transfer text internationally. For example, a German user might sign an electronic mail message `Hans Größman`, only to have an American user wonder who `Hans Gr|~man` is. When computers transfer data, they usually consider the data as a sequence of byte values; when the meanings of those bytes change, chaos can ensue.

---

[1] The space character is a bit ambiguous, being sometimes treated as a graphic character and sometimes as a control character. The best approach seems to be to treat it as a completely separate kind of character.

[2] The significance of having all 1's denote the "delete" character goes back to the days of punched tape, when it was convenient to be able to erase a single character by punching out the remaining holes in that column.

	00	10	20	30	40	50	60	70
00	NUL	DLE		0	@	P	'	p
01	SOH	DC1	!	1	A	Q	a	q
02	STX	DC2	"	2	B	R	b	r
03	ETX	DC3	#	3	C	S	c	s
04	EOT	DC4	$	4	D	T	d	t
05	ENQ	NAK	%	5	E	U	e	u
06	ACK	SYN	&	6	F	V	f	v
07	BEL	ETB	'	7	G	W	g	w
08	BS	CAN	(	8	H	X	h	x
09	HT	EM	)	9	I	Y	i	y
0A	LF	SUB	*	:	J	Z	j	z
0B	VT	ESC	+	;	K	[	k	{
0C	FF	FS	,	<	L	\	l	|
0D	CR	GS	-	=	M	]	m	}
0E	SO	RS	.	>	N	^	n	~
0F	SI	US	/	?	O	_	o	DEL

Table 5.1   US ASCII

Eight-Bit Character Sets

The need to transfer text between computers in different countries encouraged the standardization, in ISO 8859, of a series of eight-bit character sets. Each of the ISO 8859 character sets uses US ASCII for the lower 128 code points, and then extends it. Unlike the ISO 646 national character sets, however, each ISO 8859 character set covers several languages. For example, ISO 8859-1 (ISO Latin Alphabet 1) includes the characters needed for Danish, Dutch, English, Faeroese, Finnish, French, German, Icelandic, Irish, Italian, Norwegian, Portuguese, Spanish, and Swedish. ISO 8859-2 (ISO Latin Alphabet 2) covers Albanian, Czech, English, German, Hungarian, Polish, Romanian, Croatian, Slovak, and Slovene. Tables 5.3 and 5.4 on page 77 show these encodings. For comparison, Tables 5.5 through 5.8 show the default encodings used on some popular computer systems.

All ISO eight-bit character sets have a common structure. The lower 128 values are referred to as the *left half.* This half contains 33 *C0* control codes, space, and 94 *GL* graphics codes in the same arrangement used for seven-bit character sets. The *right half* usually consists of 32 *C1* control characters (0x80–0x9f)

Language	23	40	5B	5C	5D	5E	5F	60	7B	7C	7D	7E
British	£	@	[	\	]	^	_	'	{	|	}	~
Canadian-French	#	à	â	ç	ê	î	_	ô	é	ù	è	û
Chinese Roman	#	@	[	¥	]	^	_	'	{	|	}	~
Danish	#	@	Æ	Ø	Å	^	_	'	æ	ø	å	~
Dutch	£	¾	ÿ	½	|	^	_	'	¨	ƒ	¼	'
Finnish	#	@	Ä	Ö	Å	Ü	_	é	ä	ö	å	ü
French	£	à	°	ç	§	^	_	µ	é	ù	è	¨
German	#	§	Ä	Ö	Ü	^	_	'	ä	ö	ü	ß
Hungarian	#	Á	É	Ö	Ü	^	_	ú	é	ö	ü	"
Icelandic	#	Þ	Ð	\	Æ	Ö	_	þ	ð	|	æ	ö
Italian	£	§	°	ç	é	^	_	ù	à	ò	è	ì
Japanese Roman	#	@	[	¥	]	^	_	'	{	|	}	~
Norwegian	§	@	Æ	Ø	Å	^	_	'	æ	ø	å	|
Portuguese	#	'	Ã	Ç	Õ	^	_	'	ã	ç	õ	~
Spanish	£	§	¡	Ñ	¿	^	_	'	°	ñ	ç	~
Swedish	#	É	Ä	Ö	Å	Ü	_	é	ä	ö	å	ü
Swiss	ù	à	é	ç	ê	î	è	ô	ä	ö	ü	û
US ASCII	#	@	[	\	]	^	_	'	{	|	}	~

All ISO 646 character sets are the same, except in the 12 positions listed above. The remaining positions can be deduced from Table 5.1. (Table copied from *Using C-Kermit*, page 172 [5]. Used by permission.)

Table 5.2   Selected ISO 646 National Character Sets

and 96 *GR* graphics characters.[3] In theory, ISO defines sets of 94 or 96 graphics characters, which can then be used to build eight-bit character sets by taking one set of graphics for GL and another for GR.[4] Notice, however, that the C0 and C1 control codes are fixed. In practice, ISO 8859 defines specific combinations which should be adhered to. All of the ISO 8859 character sets use US ASCII as the GL character set, and use GR to provide accented characters (such as Ü), other special characters (such as Þ or ð), and alternate alphabets (such as Cyrillic, Hebrew, Greek, or Arabic).

One result of this arrangement is that text files will have different distributions of seven-bit and eight-bit characters, depending on the language and character set.

---

[3]Note that GL and GR refer to sets of character *codes*, while C0 and C1 refer to sets of *code points*. This is a subtle distinction, but one which becomes important if you study ISO character standards closely. There are such things as *G0* and *G1* sets of code points, but I won't go into those here.

[4]Because GL only has 94 character codes, it obviously cannot accommodate a set of 96 graphics characters.

For example, Italian text files in ISO Latin 1 will have a preponderance of seven-bit characters, with accented and a few special characters appearing in eight-bit forms. On the other hand, Arabic text files in the ISO Latin/Arabic alphabet will tend to have a preponderance of eight-bit characters, with only a few seven-bit control characters and punctuation marks.

Because eight-bit character sets are a convenient way to provide more characters, many computer vendors have developed their own character encodings. IBM has defined several hundred *code pages* that provide different collections of characters for different purposes. With many vendor-specific character encodings, some or all of the ANSI/ISO control code points are used for graphic characters. While this is fine for use within a single computer, it can present problems transferring text across serial connections, which commonly absorb, interpret, or otherwise alter C0 or C1 character codes.

Non-Roman Languages

For ideographic languages such as Japanese, things become significantly more complex. Japanese actually uses three different writing systems. The most important consists of *Kanji* ideograms. An educated Japanese speaker will recognize over 10,000 different Kanji. Japanese also has two different *Kana* alphabets, of about 30 characters each, called *Katakana* and *Hiragana*. One use for Kana is to spell out uncommon words, whose Kanji may not be recognized by potential readers.

In the past, Japanese computer users have often been forced to use Kana, since few computers could support a large set of Kanji characters. Improvements in printer and screen resolution, storage, and input methods have made Kanji processing reasonable. Of course, Kanji support also requires augmenting the character encoding techniques.

Multi-Byte Character Sets

When transferring files over serial connections, the best way to handle large numbers of characters is with *multi-byte* character sets. These character sets generally take one of two forms. One form is to use escape sequences to change between different character sets. Carefully implemented, this approach can provide users with convenient access to a variety of different languages.

Another approach is to use two or more graphic *codes* to represent a single graphic *character*. The Japanese EUC (Extended Unix Code) character set uses this approach. In EUC, roman characters are represented with seven-bit graphic codes from the Japanese Roman ISO 646 character set. Japanese Kanji or Kana characters each use two eight-bit graphic codes. With 96 possibilities for each byte, there are slightly over 9,000 characters that can be represented with a single eight-bit character set. EUC is not the only multi-byte Japanese character set. Sophisticated Japanese terminals obey escape sequences to select among several multi-byte character sets. See [14] for more information about Japanese character encodings.

While convenient for transferring data, multi-byte character sets are awkward for processing data. Simply reading the "next character" from a string can require parsing one or more escape sequences to select a character set and then reading several bytes to determine the specific character. Parsing strings that use multi-byte characters requires always starting from the beginning of the string, since the position of a character within the string cannot be determined without scanning from the beginning.

16-Bit and 32-Bit Character Sets

Rather than trying to parse a stream of bytes into different characters in different character sets, a simpler approach for many applications is to use 16 or even 32 bits per character. In the language of the ANSI/ISO C standard, these are *wide characters*, in which all characters use the same number of bytes, and there is only one character encoding, unlike multi-byte characters, in which there may be multiple encodings and different numbers of bytes per character, even within a single piece of text.

To date, the most successful wide character set has been the *Unicode* character encoding. Unicode's first 256 code positions agree with ISO Latin 1, and it then goes on to cover the characters used by most modern languages, including approximately 30,000 Chinese, Japanese, and Korean ideograms. It has been used as the basis of the ISO 10646 standard, which refers to the Unicode encoding as the *16-Bit Base Multilingual Plane*.

While Unicode adequately covers most of the languages in current use, it was more difficult than you might anticipate to fit all of those characters into a 16-bit character set. To include the characters used in modern Chinese, Japanese, and Korean, a process called *Han Unification* was used to identify characters in the three languages with identical appearances and assign them to a single character code. Even with this, Unicode had to omit many characters that are not currently in widespread use. ISO 10646 will eventually extend the 16-Bit Base Multilingual Plane into a 32-bit character encoding, which should have room for 50,000 or more historical Chinese ideograms, ancient Egyptian hieroglyphic characters, and many others.

With most communications channels geared for eight-bit communications, it may be some time before wide character sets can be conveniently used for transferring data. The primary obstacle is simply that a 16-bit character value must be transferred as two eight-bit values, and Unicode provides no assurances that neither of those eight-bit values will be control codes. Thus, eight-bit channels that usurp certain control codes cannot transparently pass Unicoded data. In addition, since few operating systems currently use Unicode, it's still necessary to convert to/from the operating system's preferred encoding for compatibility with other applications on that system. Thus, modern software design seems to be encouraging a model in which software uses a wide character set such as Unicode/ISO 10646 for processing data internally, and converts to and from whatever single-byte or multi-byte character set is appropriate for exchanging data with other applications or other systems.

Converting Between Character Encodings

As you might imagine from the preceding, converting between different character encodings is rarely easy. The biggest problem is balancing the two contradictory goals of legibility (can people read the result?) and invertibility (can the conversion be undone?). For example, consider the problem of converting from DEC's Multinational Character Set to the IBM Code Page 850, which contains a roughly similar set of characters in different positions. It's pretty clear that 0xc6 ("Æ" in DEC's MCS) should be mapped to 0x92 ("Æ" in IBM's CP850), but what about 0xd7 ("Œ" in DEC's MCS), for which no equivalent exists? One option is to convert this as the two characters "OE," but that makes it impossible to reliably convert back. Maintaining invertibility may require mapping it to some non-alphabetic symbol, which makes it more difficult to read.

Once you decide whether legibility or invertibility is more important, it's fairly routine to build a table which, for each character in one character set, specifies an appropriate conversion in another character set. If your emphasis is legibility, you may need to do some research to determine a good transliteration, which may depend on the *language*, not just on the character set. For example, if you need to transliterate from ISO Cyrillic into US ASCII, you may need to use different conversions depending on whether the original language is Russian or Serbian. Even with one language, there may be several accepted transliterations. If your emphasis is on invertibility, you need to carefully ensure that no two codes are converted to the same value. Invertibility almost always rules out translating one character into more than one character. A legible translation of German "ö" into

US ASCII is "oe," but that causes problems with German words that have "oe" in them, since translating into US ASCII and then back would alter the spelling.

References

The basic references for the material in this chapter are a series of ANSI and ISO standards. The ANSI standards have largely been superseded by the ISO standards, so I'll only mention the most important ISO standards here:

ISO 646   defines the basic structure of seven-bit character sets.

ISO 2022   extends this to eight-bit character sets and multi-byte character sets. It also describes the mechanisms for switching between multiple character sets. Much of the terminology of C0, C1, GR, and GL is defined in this standard.

ISO 8859   defines ten basic international eight-bit character sets. These cover most of the languages that use Roman, Cyrillic, Arabic, Greek, or Hebrew alphabets.

ISO 10646   has defined a 16-bit character encoding and has established the framework for a future larger character encoding.

Of course, formal standards don't exactly make light reading. One of the best books I've seen on character sets and text processing is Ken Lunde's book *Understanding Japanese Information Processing* [14]. It discusses many of the general issues involved in working with multiple eight-bit and multi-byte character sets, and is worth reading even if you're not specifically interested in Japanese character sets. Other good sources of information on this subject are the electronic document *A Kermit Protocol Extension for International Character Sets* [9], and chapters from the C-Kermit and MS-Kermit user's manuals [5, 8].

	00	10	20	30	40	50	60	70	80	90	A0	B0	C0	D0	E0	F0
00	NUL	DLE		0	@	P	`	p		DCS		°	À	Ð	à	ð
01	SOH	DC1	!	1	A	Q	a	q		PU1	¡	±	Á	Ñ	á	ñ
02	STX	DC2	"	2	B	R	b	r	BPH	PU2	¢	²	Â	Ò	â	ò
03	ETX	DC3	#	3	C	S	c	s	NBH	STS	£	³	Ã	Ó	ã	ó
04	EOT	DC4	$	4	D	T	d	t		CCH	¤	´	Ä	Ô	ä	ô
05	ENQ	NAK	%	5	E	U	e	u	NEL	MW	¥	µ	Å	Õ	å	õ
06	ACK	SYN	&	6	F	V	f	v	SSA	SPA	¦	¶	Æ	Ö	æ	ö
07	BEL	ETB	'	7	G	W	g	w	ESA	EPA	§	·	Ç	×	ç	÷
08	BS	CAN	(	8	H	X	h	x	HTS	SOS	¨	¸	È	Ø	è	ø
09	HT	EM	)	9	I	Y	i	y	HTJ		©	¹	É	Ù	é	ù
0A	LF	SUB	*	:	J	Z	j	z	VTS	SCI	ª	º	Ê	Ú	ê	ú
0B	VT	ESC	+	;	K	[	k	{	PLD	CSI	«	»	Ë	Û	ë	û
0C	FF	FS	,	<	L	\	l	|	PLU	ST	¬	¼	Ì	Ü	ì	ü
0D	CR	GS	-	=	M	]	m	}	RI	OSC	-	½	Í	Ý	í	ý
0E	SO	RS	.	>	N	^	n	‾	SS2	PM	®	¾	Î	Þ	î	þ
0F	SI	US	/	?	O	_	o	DEL	SS3	APC	¯	¿	Ï	ß	ï	ÿ

Table 5.3   ISO Latin 1

	00	10	20	30	40	50	60	70	80	90	A0	B0	C0	D0	E0	F0
00	NUL	DLE		0	@	P	`	p		DCS		°	Ŕ	Ð	ŕ	ð
01	SOH	DC1	!	1	A	Q	a	q		PU1	Ą	ą	Á	Ń	á	ń
02	STX	DC2	"	2	B	R	b	r	BPH	PU2	˘		Â	Ň	â	ň
03	ETX	DC3	#	3	C	S	c	s	NBH	STS	Ł	ł	Ă	Ó	ă	ó
04	EOT	DC4	$	4	D	T	d	t		CCH	¤	´	Ä	Ô	ä	ô
05	ENQ	NAK	%	5	E	U	e	u	NEL	MW	Ľ	ľ	Ĺ	Ő	ĺ	ő
06	ACK	SYN	&	6	F	V	f	v	SSA	SPA	Ś	ś	Ć	Ö	ć	ö
07	BEL	ETB	'	7	G	W	g	w	ESA	EPA	§	ˇ	Ç	×	ç	÷
08	BS	CAN	(	8	H	X	h	x	HTS	SOS	¨	¸	Č	Ř	č	ř
09	HT	EM	)	9	I	Y	i	y	HTJ		Š	š	É	Ů	é	ů
0A	LF	SUB	*	:	J	Z	j	z	VTS	SCI	Ş	ş	Ę	Ú	ę	ú
0B	VT	ESC	+	;	K	[	k	{	PLD	CSI	Ť	ť	Ë	Ű	ë	ű
0C	FF	FS	,	<	L	\	l	|	PLU	ST	Ź	ź	Ě	Ü	ě	ü
0D	CR	GS	-	=	M	]	m	}	RI	OSC	-	˝	Í	Ý	í	ý
0E	SO	RS	.	>	N	^	n	‾	SS2	PM	Ž	ž	Î	Ţ	î	ţ
0F	SI	US	/	?	O	_	o	DEL	SS3	APC	Ż	ż	Ď	ß	ď	˙

Table 5.4   ISO Latin 2

	00	10	20	30	40	50	60	70	80	90	A0	B0	C0	D0	E0	F0
00		▶		0	@	P	`	p	Ç	É	á	▓	└	╨	α	≡
01	☺	◄	!	1	A	Q	a	q	ü	æ	í	▌	┴	╤	β	±
02	☻	↕	"	2	B	R	b	r	é	Æ	ó	█	┬	╥	Γ	≥
03	♡	‼	#	3	C	S	c	s	â	ô	ú	│	├	╙	π	≤
04	♢	¶	$	4	D	T	d	t	ä	ö	ñ	┤	─	╘	Σ	⌠
05	♣	§	%	5	E	U	e	u	à	ò	Ñ	╡	┼	╒	σ	⌡
06	♠	▬	&	6	F	V	f	v	å	û	ª	╢	╞	╓	µ	÷
07	•	↨	'	7	G	W	g	w	ç	ù	º	╖	╟	╫	τ	≈
08	◘	↑	(	8	H	X	h	x	ê	ÿ	¿	╕	╚	╪	Φ	°
09	○	↓	)	9	I	Y	i	y	ë	Ö	⌐	╣	╔	┘	Θ	∙
0A	◙	→	*	:	J	Z	j	z	è	Ü	¬	║	╩	┌	Ω	·
0B		←	+	;	K	[	k	{	ï	¢	½	╗	╦	█	δ	√
0C		∟	,	<	L	\	l	|	î	£	¼	╝	╠	▄	∞	ⁿ
0D		↔	-	=	M	]	m	}	ì	¥	¡	╜	═	▌	φ	²
0E		▲	.	>	N	^	n	~	Ä	Pt	«	╛	╬	▐	ε	■
0F		▼	/	?	O	_	o	△	Å	ƒ	»	┐	╧	▀	∩	

Table 5.5   IBM PC Code Page 437

	00	10	20	30	40	50	60	70	80	90	A0	B0	C0	D0	E0	F0
00		▶		0	@	P	`	p	Ç	É	á	▓	└	ð	Ó	-
01	☺	◄	!	1	A	Q	a	q	ü	æ	í	▌	┴	Ð	ß	±
02	☻	↕	"	2	B	R	b	r	é	Æ	ó	█	┬	Ê	Ô	=
03	♡	‼	#	3	C	S	c	s	â	ô	ú	│	├	Ë	Ò	¾
04	♢	¶	$	4	D	T	d	t	ä	ö	ñ	┤	─	È	õ	¶
05	♣	§	%	5	E	U	e	u	à	ò	Ñ	Á	┼	ı	Õ	§
06	♠	▬	&	6	F	V	f	v	å	û	ª	Â	ã	Í	µ	÷
07	•	↨	'	7	G	W	g	w	ç	ù	º	À	Ã	Î	þ	¸
08	◘	↑	(	8	H	X	h	x	ê	ÿ	¿	©	╚	Ï	Þ	°
09	○	↓	)	9	I	Y	i	y	ë	Ö	®	╣	╔	┘	Ú	¨
0A	◙	→	*	:	J	Z	j	z	è	Ü	¬	║	╩	┌	Û	·
0B		←	+	;	K	[	k	{	ï	ø	½	╗	╦	█	Ù	¹
0C		∟	,	<	L	\	l	|	î	£	¼	╝	╠	▄	ý	³
0D		↔	-	=	M	]	m	}	ì	Ø	¡	¢	═	│	Ý	²
0E		▲	.	>	N	^	n	~	Ä	×	«	¥	╬	Ì	¯	■
0F		▼	/	?	O	_	o	△	Å	ƒ	»	┐	¤	▀	´	

Table 5.6   IBM PC Code Page 850

	00	10	20	30	40	50	60	70	80	90	A0	B0	C0	D0	E0	F0
00	NUL	DLE		0	@	P	`	p	Ä	ê	†	∞	¿	–	‡	
01	SOH	DC1	!	1	A	Q	a	q	Å	ë	°	±	¡	—	·	Ò
02	STX	DC2	"	2	B	R	b	r	Ç	ì	¢	≤	¬	"	,	Ú
03	ETX	DC3	#	3	C	S	c	s	É	í	£	≥	√	"	„	Û
04	EOT	DC4	$	4	D	T	d	t	Ñ	î	§	¥	ƒ	'	‰	Ù
05	ENQ	NAK	%	5	E	U	e	u	Ö	ï	•	µ	≈	'	Â	ı
06	ACK	SYN	&	6	F	V	f	v	Ü	ñ	¶	∂	Δ	÷	Ê	ˆ
07	BEL	ETB	'	7	G	W	g	w	á	ó	ß	Σ	«	◊	Á	˜
08	BS	CAN	(	8	H	X	h	x	à	ò	®	Π	»	ÿ	Ë	¯
09	HT	EM	)	9	I	Y	i	y	â	ô	©	π	…	Ÿ	È	˘
0A	LF	SUB	*	:	J	Z	j	z	ä	ö	™	∫		/	Í	˙
0B	VT	ESC	+	;	K	[	k	{	ã	õ	´	ª	À	□	Î	˚
0C	FF	FS	,	<	L	\	l	|	å	ú	¨	º	Ã	‹	Ï	¸
0D	CR	GS	-	=	M	]	m	}	ç	ù	≠	Ω	Õ	›	Ì	˝
0E	SO	RS	.	>	N	^	n	ˉ	é	û	Æ	æ	Œ	fi	Ó	˛
0F	SI	US	/	?	O	_	o	DEL	è	ü	Ø	ø	œ	fl	Ô	ˇ

Table 5.7   Macintosh Character Encoding

	00	10	20	30	40	50	60	70	80	90	A0	B0	C0	D0	E0	F0
00	NUL	DLE		0	@	P	`	p		Ð	©	®	¹	—	ì	ö
01	SOH	DC1	!	1	A	Q	a	q	À	Ñ	¡	–	`	±	Æ	æ
02	STX	DC2	"	2	B	R	b	r	Á	Ò	¢	†	´	¼	í	ù
03	ETX	DC3	#	3	C	S	c	s	Â	Ó	£	‡	^	½	ª	ú
04	EOT	DC4	$	4	D	T	d	t	Ã	Ô	/	·	¯	¾	î	û
05	ENQ	NAK	%	5	E	U	e	u	Ä	Õ	¥	|	˜	à	ï	ı
06	ACK	SYN	&	6	F	V	f	v	Å	Ö	ƒ	¶	˘	á	ð	ü
07	BEL	ETB	'	7	G	W	g	w	Ç	Ú	§	•	˙	â	ñ	ý
08	BS	CAN	(	8	H	X	h	x	È	Ù	¤	,	¨	ã	Ł	ł
09	HT	EM	)	9	I	Y	i	y	É	Û	'	„	²	ä	Ø	ø
0A	LF	SUB	*	:	J	Z	j	z	Ê	Ü	"	"	°	å	Œ	œ
0B	VT	ESC	+	;	K	[	k	{	Ë	Ý	«	»	¸	ç	º	ß
0C	FF	FS	,	<	L	\	l	|	Ì	Þ	‹	…	³	è	ò	þ
0D	CR	GS	-	=	M	]	m	}	Í	µ	›	‰	˝	é	ó	
0E	SO	RS	.	>	N	^	n	ˉ	Î	×	fi	¬	˛	ê	ô	
0F	SI	US	/	?	O	_	o	DEL	Ï	÷	fl	¿	ˇ	ë	õ	

Table 5.8   NeXT Character Encoding

Design

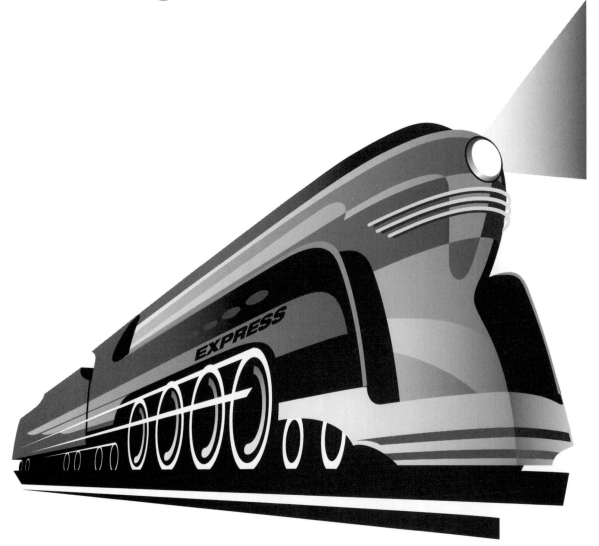

XModem

Primarily because of its simplicity, XModem has spread from its CP/M origins to become one of the most widely implemented file transfer protocols. This simplicity also makes XModem a good place to start examining the design of real-world protocols.

In August 1977, Ward Christensen released an update to his original MODEM communications program for CP/M. Dubbed MODEM2, the program included a facility for transferring files to another copy of the same program with a simple check to verify the integrity of the result.

Christensen's protocol was quickly adopted by other programs. One reason for its popularity was that it filled a need among the computer hobbyists of the time. The fact that the protocol is extremely simple, and thus easy to implement, also contributed. But the most important factor may be that Christensen placed both the protocol and the MODEM2 source code in the public domain. Christensen's generosity allowed many people to add this capability to their programs by adapting his source.

Two of the programs that adopted Christensen's protocol were MODEM7, which added a crude but functional batch capability for transferring multiple files, and XMODEM, a program for RCP/M systems that allowed people to dial into an unattended computer and transfer files. It is this last program that led to the protocol being widely known as "XModem." In the nearly twenty years since XModem's inception, it has become a de facto standard for file transfer.

The Protocol

Christensen made a number of simplifying assumptions in his design of the XModem protocol. Foremost among these was the assumption of a fully transparent, eight-bit channel.

> I ... had an 8-bit UART, so my protocol was an 8-bit protocol, and I would just say "sorry" to people who were held back by 7-bit limitations.
>
> *Ward Christensen* [2]

Christensen also exploited the simple structure of CP/M files. CP/M does not specify the precise length of a file; a file is simply a sequence of 128-byte sectors. It's up to the specific application to determine the precise end of file; text-processing applications conventionally use a Control-Z character. Thus, making each data packet carry precisely one sector made it unnecessary for the XModem protocol to bother with a precise file size or other details.

These two design decisions allowed Christensen to develop a very simple protocol, but at the cost of limiting its use. Although full transparency is common among microcomputer systems and online services, mainframes and many network connections continue to be restricted to seven bit data. Even channels that do support eight-bit data often use special control codes for flow control or other purposes, and are thus incompatible with XModem. XModem's failure to preserve the exact file size causes problems with many application data files that store critical information at fixed offsets from the end of the file.

Encoding Layer

XModem does not encode data. It assumes a fully transparent eight-bit channel.

Packetization Layer

XModem uses single control characters for control packets. Because XModem does not transfer the filename or other information, the only control packets required are ACK/NAK packets to support reliable transfer, and a packet for the sender to specify the end of the transfer.

Data packets are equally simple. The packet sequence numbers begin at one and wrap from 255 to zero. The only interesting point is that the packet sequence

Control Packet	Description
ACK	Receiver acknowledges data packet.
NAK	Receiver requests retransmission of last data packet.
EOT	Sender sends this after last data packet is acknowledged.

Table 6.1   XModem Control Packets

Size	Description
1	SOH (character 0x01)
1	Packet sequence number, modulo 256
1	Complement of sequence number
128	Data
1	Checksum of data, modulo 256

Table 6.2   XModem Data Packet Structure

number has a separate error check to help guard against corruption of this critical value.

Notice that even this simple protocol contains a header check. In this case, since the header contains only a sequence number, the header check only needs to verify that one byte. The choice of a byte complement also helps to detect attempts to use XModem over a seven-bit data path; either the sequence number or its complement will have the high bit set, and will thus be damaged.

Reliability Layer

XModem uses simple half-duplex reliability. For each data packet sent, the receiver responds with an ACK or NAK.

Because XModem performs no encoding, it cannot guarantee that data within a packet will not masquerade as the start of a new packet. This creates a problem when recovering from errors. The receiver must be certain that the last of any old packet is gone before it starts to look for a new packet, lest it be fooled by a coincidental sequence of data within a packet. The usual approach is to program the XModem receiver to wait for an interval of silence before sending a NAK.

A more serious problem is that XModem's single-character ACK and NAK do not specify which packet the receiver expected. This is a problem because these single-character packets can be generated by noise. In particular, if an ACK is generated by noise, the sender will advance to the next packet. To illustrate, imagine the sender sends packet 73, which is damaged en route, but noise alters the receiver's NAK into an ACK. The sender will proceed to send packet 74, and a subsequent NAK from the receiver will prompt the sender to resend packet 74. There is nothing the receiver can do to prompt the sender to go back to packet 73, and the transfer will fail.

Transaction Layer

The only transaction supported by XModem is file transfer. Transfer of a file begins with the receiver sending NAK. The sender responds with the first data packet.

After all the data in a file has been sent, XModem sends a single EOT to mark the end of the file. In some implementations, this EOT was not subject to reliability. Later implementations have changed this, requiring the sender to wait for an ACK before terminating. The reason for this change is to prevent premature termination from an EOT caused by noise. Older receivers will stop immediately when they receive an EOT, which can result in a truncated file if the EOT was spurious. Newer receivers respond with NAK to the first EOT to prompt the sender to repeat it, and only terminate after it is repeated.

Session Layer

An XModem session consists of a single file transfer with no other considerations.

A convention used by some early XModem implementations was to allow a single CAN character to cancel the transfer. Newer implementations have altered this to require at least two consecutive CAN characters to reduce the likelihood of the transfer being spontaneously terminated because a CAN was generated by noise.

Analysis

XModem became popular primarily because it was freely available in Ward Christensen's MODEM2 and was very easy to implement. Unfortunately, XModem has a host of problems that make it significantly less reliable than later protocols. Because later protocols were developed partly in response to the problems in XModem, it makes sense to take a careful look at those problems here.

While not stellar, a single-byte checksum does provide acceptable error detection for XModem's short packets. As mentioned above, XModem's packet format lacks a distinctive start-of-packet, which makes it more difficult to resynchronize after an error. Recovering after an error generally requires waiting for a delay, which severely degrades throughput over moderately noisy channels.

The biggest problem with XModem is its lack of error detection on control packets, which allows spurious packets to be generated by noise. Many later changes to XModem have attempted to address some of the problems caused by this weakness. For example, to prevent premature termination from a spurious CAN character, later XModem implementations require two consecutive CAN characters for a user cancel. To prevent premature termination from a spurious EOT, it has become common to wait for an ACK, which allows the receiver to challenge an

Speed	Seconds Delay	Bytes Delay	Time for 256k	Efficiency
2400 bps	0	0	18:55	96%
2400 bps	1	240	53:03	34%
2400 bps	4	960	2:35:27	12%
9600 bps	0	0	4:44	96%
9600 bps	1	960	38:52	12%
9600 bps	2	1920	1:13:00	6%

Table 6.3   XModem Efficiency with No Errors

EOT by responding with a NAK and looking for a repeat. The one major problem that cannot be easily addressed through such modifications is the synchronization error induced by a spurious ACK.

As a basis for comparison, it's interesting to compute the efficiency of XModem. For every 128 bytes of data, XModem sends a single packet of 132 bytes, and requires a single-byte ACK in response. The total time required for this exchange is the time for 133 bytes plus one complete channel round-trip. It's convenient to express the round-trip delay in terms of the number of bytes that could be sent in that time. For example, the fourth line in Table 6.3 shows a transfer at 9600 bps with a one second round-trip delay. A channel rated at 9600 bits per second carries 960 bytes per second using RS-232 conventions, so the one second delay corresponds to 960 "byte times." This delay raises the total to 1093 byte times to transfer 128 bytes of data, from which you can directly calculate the 12 percent efficiency shown in the table.

If there are errors, the time increases depending on the number of packets that must be resent. For concreteness, assume our channel is 99.9 percent error-free, meaning that one byte out of a thousand is lost or altered.[1] That means that 87.5 percent of our packets will be transferred reliably the first time ($.999^{133}$). The total number of packets sent for the sample 256k file grows from 2048 to 2339 due to the repeated packets. Each retransmission incurs the same costs as a normal packet plus an implementation-dependent delay while the receiver waits for the line to clear. Assuming the receiver waits two seconds after each damaged packet for the line to clear gives the transfer times in Table 6.4.

The marginally higher efficiency for the same delay (measured in byte times) at lower baud rates is due to the impact of the assumed two second error recovery delay.

---

[1] A 0.1 percent error rate is moderately high.

Speed	Seconds Delay	Bytes Delay	Time for 256k	Efficiency
2400 bps	0	0	29:47	61%
2400 bps	1	240	1:08:10	27%
2400 bps	4	960	3:07:14	10%
9600 bps	0	0	13:49	33%
9600 bps	1	960	52:13	9%
9600 bps	2	1920	1:30:36	5%

Table 6.4   XModem Efficiency with Errors

There are two important facts you should understand from these efficiency examples. First, the efficiency of half-duplex protocols is severely reduced when there are delays in the channel. Second, the important measurement for these delays is the delay in byte times.

Derivatives

Due to XModem's popularity, there have been many derivative protocols. The ones discussed below are among the more popular.

XModem-CRC

XModem-CRC replaces XModem's single-byte checksum with the 16-bit CCITT CRC16 (described on page 58) for improved error detection. Only two changes are required to the original XModem protocol. The first change is, of course, replacing the single-byte checksum in the packet format described earlier with a 16-bit CRC. The second is to alter the session initialization so that both ends can agree which of the two possible error checks to use. An XModem-CRC receiver begins by sending a C (character 0x43) rather than a NAK. The sender interprets this C to mean that the receiver expects CRC error checks rather than the default checksum. If the receiver does not get a response to several repeated C characters, it falls back to the standard XModem protocol and sends NAK. This strategy allows XModem-CRC receivers to function with XModem-CRC or plain XModem senders. For an XModem-CRC sender to function with either type of receiver, it must accept either an initial C or NAK and alter its error check accordingly.

Speed	Seconds Delay	Bytes Delay	Time for 256k	Efficiency
2400 bps	0	0	18:18	99%
2400 bps	1	240	22:34	81%
2400 bps	4	960	35:22	51%
9600 bps	0	0	4:34	99%
9600 bps	1	960	8:50	51%
9600 bps	2	1920	13:06	35%

Table 6.5   XModem-K Efficiency with No Errors

It's worth pointing out that XModem-CRC is no more efficient than plain XModem. The only result of replacing the checksum with a CRC is increased reliability; it's less likely that an error will go unnoticed by XModem-CRC than plain XModem.

XModem-K

XModem-K attempts to improve the throughput of XModem over channels with delays by adding a new packet format. This alternate packet starts with an STX (character 0x02) and contains 1024 bytes of data rather than 128 bytes. The sender can use any mix of the two different packet sizes; most senders will use shorter packets at the end of the file when there's not enough data remaining to fill a 1024-byte packet. As an example of the improvement this simple change provides, contrast Table 6.5 with Table 6.3.

The dramatic reduction in transfer time over channels with a delay occurs because XModem-K sends only one-eighth as many packets, and hence spends only one-eighth as long waiting for responses. However, longer packets also bring a penalty. Each time a packet is damaged, it takes longer to resend that packet. In addition, longer packets increase the chance that any given packet will be damaged, which in turn increases the average number of times that a packet will have to be resent.[2] Compare Table 6.6 with Table 6.4. Note that, at this error rate, XModem-K is still marginally faster than plain XModem when there are delays, but when the delays are short, XModem is noticeably faster.

---

[2] In fact, the average packet is resent $\left(\frac{1}{1-e}\right)^p$ times, where e is the error rate and p is the packet size. For $e = .001$, p of 133 gives 1.14 while p of 1029 gives 2.80. With this error rate, a 1024-byte packet is likely to require three attempts before it is correctly transferred, while a short XModem packet will usually make it on the first try.

Speed	Seconds Delay	Bytes Delay	Time for 256k	Efficiency
2400 bps	0	0	1:06:34	27%
2400 bps	1	240	1:18:31	23%
2400 bps	4	960	1:54:26	16%
9600 bps	0	0	28:10	16%
9600 bps	1	960	40:06	11%
9600 bps	2	1920	52:03	9%

Table 6.6   XModem-K Efficiency with Errors

As with any comparison of different protocols under varying conditions, you should treat these values carefully. These calculations make many simplifying assumptions, and will only be generally indicative of the actual behavior of these protocols under specific conditions. The actual efficiencies you'll see will depend on many details of the particular channel and protocol implementation you're using.

WXModem

WXModem attempts to improve XModem's performance when there are both delays and errors by allowing up to four outstanding packets at a time. To support this, WXModem requires some extensive changes to the simple XModem protocol, including the addition of an encoding to allow software flow control to be used in conjunction with WXModem, and modified ACK/NAK packets to identify the packet being acknowledged. Unfortunately, WXModem's decision to allow only four outstanding packets means that it cannot maintain a continuous flow of data over today's faster channels. For this reason, WXModem will still frequently be slower than XModem-K, although a good implementation should be noticeably faster when there are errors.

YModem

YModem is the logical successor to XModem. It retains most of the simplicity of that protocol, but makes a few minor changes to reduce its susceptibility to errors and to allow several files to be transferred at one time.

In the late 1970s, Chuck Forsberg released his YAM (Yet Another Modem) program for CP/M. This program contained a number of innovations. Forsberg developed some simple techniques to improve the reliability and performance of standard XModem, including both the XModem-K protocol and a thorough implementation of "protocol cheating" to improve throughput.[1] YAM also introduced a new protocol based on XModem-K that supported "batch" transfers (the ability to transfer multiple files at one time). This new protocol came to be known as YModem.

The Protocol

YModem is essentially the same as XModem-K, except that it adds a data packet zero to the beginning of each file to carry information about the file, including the filename and exact length. YModem also alters the session layer of the protocol to allow for multiple files to be sent in a single session.

Encoding Layer

Like its predecessor, YModem assumes a fully transparent eight-bit channel, and does no data encoding.

---

[1] Protocol cheating for an XModem receiver involves sending an ACK *before* you receive a packet. This results in the sender seeing the ACK sooner, hence reducing the effective channel delay and improving throughput. The cost is that error recovery is compromised.

Field	Format	Separator	Description
Filename	ASCII	NULL	
File Size	Decimal	Space	
File Date	Octal	Space	Seconds since Jan 1, 1970 UCT
File Mode	Octal	Space	As in Unix
Serial Number	Octal String	none	

Table 7.1   YModem File Information

Packetization Layer

YModem's control packets are the same single bytes used by XModem-CRC, including the C packet used to start a file transfer with CRC error checking rather than checksum. It supports both the short XModem packets (beginning with SOH) and the long packets introduced by XModem-K (beginning with STX).

Reliability Layer

YModem uses the same half-duplex reliability strategy as XModem, with the same potential problems.

Transaction Layer

A YModem file transfer begins with the receiver sending a C or NAK handshake to indicate the transfer should proceed with CRC or checksum error detection, respectively. The sender responds with a special file header packet with sequence number zero. This packet contains two consecutive NULL-terminated strings. The first string contains the filename and the second contains a sequence of file attributes separated by spaces. The fields are outlined in Table 7.1. The packet can be either 128 or 1024 bytes. In either case, the packet is padded to its full length with NULL characters. The filename is mandatory and all other fields are optional. If any file attribute is omitted, all following fields must be omitted. The file size is guaranteed by the sender; the receiver should discard any data beyond the specified file size. In particular, if the sender does not know the size of the data that will be transmitted, such as when a text file needs to be converted to the canonical format, the sender should omit the file size.

The receiver repeats its C or NAK handshake until it successfully receives the file header. Many YModem implementations drop back to XModem after repeating a C handshake and receiving no response. Receivers should repeat the handshake if they receive a bad packet; using a NAK to request retransmission can be misinterpreted by the sender as a request for checksum error detection. After this packet is reliably transferred (acknowledged by the receiver), the receiver repeats the C or NAK handshake.[2] In response, the sender transfers the file data beginning with packet one, as in XModem.

Like XModem, YModem implementations traditionally distinguish 'binary' and 'text' transfers. Binary files are transferred with no alteration. Text files are converted to a canonical format using CR/LF line termination. It is traditional to pad the last packet with Control-Z characters to mark the end of the file for CP/M systems, and to make it easier for other systems to identify and remove this padding.

After the file data is transferred, the sender sends an EOT packet, which must be acknowledged by the sender.

Session Layer

A YModem session consists of repeated file transfers. The session ends when the sender sends a file header packet with an empty filename, and the receiver acknowledges.

Analysis

YModem implements most of the XModem improvements discussed in the previous chapter. As mentioned there, the only major remaining problem is the synchronization problem caused by a spurious ACK. It is possible to sometimes recover synchronization if the sender backs up after a large number of NAKs of the same packet.

YModem's efficiency is essentially the same as XModem-K, except that transfers of multiple files are faster because YModem does not require manual intervention between each file. Tables 6.5 and 6.6 give a more detailed evaluation of XModem-K's efficiency.

Derivatives

As I mentioned at the beginning of this chapter, one of YAM's innovations was the use of protocol cheating to improve throughput. This was doubtless one of

---

[2]Forsberg's documentation of YModem does not specify whether this second handshake must be the same as the first, although there seems to be no reason for it to be different.

the primary ideas behind the development of the YModem-G protocol. YModem-G differs from standard YModem in two respects. The first is the handshake: YModem-G uses an initial G handshake, which implies CRC error checks. The second change is that the YModem-G sender does not expect or wait for acknowledgments to file data packets. It does expect acknowledgments for the final EOT and initial filename packet, but transfer of actual file data proceeds at full speed. By omitting explicit acknowledgments, YModem-G is essentially insensitive to channel delays, at the cost of having no ability to recover from errors. YModem-G is a good choice for benchmarking other protocols, because it will almost always be faster than any alternative when it does work.

To better understand how fast YModem-G is, simply consider that it sends 1029 bytes to transfer 1024 bytes of data, and never waits for a round-trip delay. This means that its efficiency is always 1024/1029 or 99.5 percent, regardless of the channel delay. On the other hand, if there are errors or the channel is not fully transparent, YModem-G's efficiency is zero percent.

References

The most important reference for XModem and YModem is Chuck Forsberg's *XModem/YModem Protocol Reference: A Compendium of Documents Describing the XModem and YModem File Transfer Protocols* [15]. This electronic document, available on several information services and Internet archive sites, collects together a number of different short comments from individuals involved in the evolution of XModem and YModem. It includes the original XModem specification written by Ward Christensen and a description of XModem-CRC written by John Byrns. The bulk of the *Compendium* was written by Forsberg to answer questions about XModem-K, YModem, and YModem-G.

ZModem

8

Despite its name, ZModem has little in common with XModem or YModem. Rather, ZModem is a flexible, full-duplex protocol that was designed to be efficient over common channels, including channels with long delays and software flow control.

The increasing use of YModem in the early 1980s proved problematic for the networks that were expected to carry such transfers. At that time, error-correcting modems providing transparent flow control were uncommon, so most flow control was still handled with XON and XOFF flow control characters. Because YModem requires a completely transparent channel, network nodes had to be able to handle bursts of 1029 bytes without flow control. In addition, YModem, like all half-duplex protocols, is slow when there are channel delays.

In the mid-1980s, windowing Kermit became available, but it was considered complex to implement, and the heavy use of prefix encoding degraded its performance. In 1986, GTE Telenet (now SprintNet) contracted Chuck Forsberg, the inventor of YModem, to design a new protocol to overcome these problems. Under the terms of the contract, the protocol and its implementation were to be public domain, to encourage its widespread adoption.

Forsberg began to modify the existing XModem and YModem protocols to satisfy the new requirements, but ultimately developed a completely new protocol with a number of innovative features. Experience in implementing file transfers for microcomputers and on-line services prompted him to include a variety of small details that helped make ZModem significantly easier to use than its predecessors. Forsberg also aggressively publicized ZModem, distributing implementations of the protocol that could be readily integrated with popular bulletin board software. The public domain source code provided "out-of-the-box" ZModem support for Unix and VAX/VMS and was rapidly incorporated into popular communications software. This widespread adoption, based in part on Forsberg's reputation as the designer of YModem, has made ZModem one of the most popular protocols available today.

The Protocol

ZModem was designed with public access packet-switched networks in mind. These networks have low error rates, but the delays can be fairly long. ZModem accommodates the long delays by allowing unlimited window sizes, and takes advantage of the low error rates with a simple error recovery strategy. The networks are transparent except for a handful of special flow control characters. ZModem's prefix encoding is tailored for low overhead when only a few control characters need be encoded, but makes no provisions for very restricted seven-bit channels.

ZModem works especially well with modems that have built-in error correction and compression. It presents the modem with a continuous stream of data while minimizing the reverse data flow. This strategy allows these modems to attain their maximum throughput. (See page 13 for a discussion of the channel properties of error-correcting modems.)

ZModem is compatible with a variety of different hardware and software restrictions. It provides several ways to limit the flow of data, and provides a half-duplex mode for channels that lack effective flow control.

Encoding Layer

As discussed in Chapter 3, encoding is used to represent a large selection of symbols—usually including 256 byte values for data and several additional control symbols—in a smaller alphabet of bytes that can be transferred through the channel.

For most data, ZModem uses a prefix encoding with ASCII CAN (Control-X, character 0x18) as the prefix code. When the size of the encoded data is not critical (as in most receiver responses) or when transparency is a concern (as with startup packets that may be accidentally received by another program), ZModem uses a hexadecimal encoding, with digits and lower case alphabetic characters, ignoring parity.

ZModem encodes two distinct types of control symbols: three start-of-packet (SOP) codes and four *CRC escapes* used to embed a CRC error check within streamed data. These encodings are indicated in Tables 8.1 and 8.2. The meanings of these codes will be explained in more detail in following sections.

Code	CRC type	Encoding
CAN A	CRC-16	Prefix
CAN B	CRC-16	Hexadecimal
CAN C	CRC-32	Prefix

Table 8.1   ZModem Start-of-Packet Codes

Code	End of packet	Acknowledge Requested
CAN h	No	No
CAN i	Yes	No
CAN j	Yes	Yes
CAN k	No	Yes

Table 8.2   ZModem CRC Escapes

ZModem allows prefix encoding of all 33 seven-bit control characters and their eight-bit counterparts. DEL (0x7f) and its eight-bit counterpart (0xff) are encoded as CAN l and CAN m, respectively. Other control characters are encoded as CAN followed by the control code offset by 64. Some examples are shown in Table 8.3.

ZModem's prefix encoding is selective; the sender can choose which control characters to encode. Five characters must *always* be encoded. The most obvious is the CAN character itself. To avoid conflicts with software flow control, the ZModem receiver ignores XON and XOFF characters and their eight-bit counterparts, and hence those four characters must also be encoded. Traditionally, ZModem senders also always encode DLE (Data Link Escape), a CR that follows @,[1] and their eight-bit counterparts. The escaping of control codes with the high bit set is done to avoid problems due to mismatched parity.

The receiver will always accept encoded control characters. Thus, the sender has two different ways to send most control characters. The startup negotiation allows either side to specify that all unencoded control characters should be ignored, and hence must be encoded; there is no provision for negotiating an intermediate level of control escaping.

---

[1]This protects the SprintNet command-mode escape sequence CR @ CR.

Code	Control Code
CAN @	0x00 (NULL)
CAN A	0x01 (SOH)
CAN B	0x02 (STX)
CAN 1	0x7f (DEL)
CAN 0xc0	0x80
CAN 0xd6	0x86
CAN m	0xff
CAN n	n AND 0xbf
CAN m OR 0x40	m

In the last two examples, n is in one of the ranges 0x40–0x5f or 0xc0–0xdf, and m is in one of the ranges 0x00–0x1f or 0x80–0x9f.

Table 8.3   Examples of ZModem Prefix Encoding

Packetization Layer

A ZModem packet consists of a packet header possibly followed by additional data. Packet headers contain two pieces of information in addition to the SOP sequence and header CRC. Those two pieces of information are a type code from Table 8.4 and a 32-bit argument, stored from least-significant byte to most-significant byte. The type, argument, and CRC are all subject to the encoding specified by the SOP code.

Hexadecimal headers include some additional padding characters that help avoid common problems with flow control or incompletely initialized ports. In

*	SOP	Type	Argument	CRC

The Type, Argument, and CRC are all subject to prefix encoding.

SOP   The start-of-packet codes are CAN A to specify 16-bit CRC or CAN C to specify 32-bit CRC.

Type   Packet types are listed in Table 8.4.

CRC   The CRC is 2 or 4 bytes, depending on the SOP code.

Figure 8.1   ZModem "Binary" Packet Header

*	*	SOP	Type	Argument	CRC	CR	LF	XON

The type, argument, and CRC are all encoded in lower case hexadecimal.

SOP The start-of-packet code is CAN B.

Type Packet types are listed in Table 8.4.

CRC Hexadecimal packet headers always use a 16-bit CRC.

CR/LF These end-of-line markers help speed hexadecimal packets through line-oriented interfaces.

XON This is intended to prevent lock-ups due to spurious XOFF characters or lost XON characters.

The XON is omitted in two situations. The first is after ZAck packets during streaming file transfer. Including the XON in this situation could damage software flow control and cause data to be lost. The second is after the ZFin packets used to terminate the session.

Figure 8.2 ZModem Hexadecimal Packet Header

particular, CR LF helps make sure that the ZRQInit startup packet can be recognized even by line-oriented applications, while the XON helps prevent software flow control lockups. The extra * padding character eases detection of error packets, which are always hexadecimal packets.

These considerations are important for hexadecimal headers because they are used during the initialization, when the other end may not have started—meaning our packets are going to be received by a command line or other program—or may not yet have initialized the connection—meaning that line-oriented input or flow control may be in an unusual state.

The 32-bit argument in the packet header reduces the need for packet data. As a result, only four packet headers—ZSInit, ZFile, ZData, and ZCommand—actually have data following them.

Standard ZModem only allows data to follow prefix encoded headers, so the four packet headers that require data will *always* be sent with prefix encoded headers. Data is prefix encoded, with CRC escapes (see page 97) occasionally inserted. CRC escapes are followed by the CRC accumulated over the decoded data since the last CRC escape. The CRC itself is the same size (16 or 32 bits) as the packet header, and is prefix encoded. Note that a CRC escape is also used to separate

Code	Packet	Layer	Description
0	ZRQInit	Session	Sent to trigger automatic receive
1	ZRInit	Session	Receiver's capabilities
2	ZSInit	Session	Sender's capabilities
3	ZAck	Reliability	Various uses
4	ZFile	Transaction	Filename, etc.
5	ZSkip	Transaction	Asks sender to not send file
6	ZNak	Reliability	Header was garbled
7	ZAbort	Session	Polite termination
8	ZFin	Session	End of session
9	ZRPos	Reliability	Reposition stream
10	ZData	Transaction	File data
11	ZEOF	Transaction	End of file
12	ZFErr	File	File I/O error
13	ZCRC	Transaction	File CRC
14	ZChallenge	Session	Security challenge
15	ZCompl	Transaction	Command completed
16	ZCan	Session	Immediate session cancel
17	ZFreeCnt	Transaction	Request file system status
18	ZCommand	Transaction	Command request

Table 8.4   ZModem Packet Types

streamed data from a following packet header. By convention, only ZData is ever followed by more than one CRC escape.

Reliability Layer

Except when transferring file data, ZModem defaults to a half-duplex scripted dialog approach. There are several good reasons for this. First, during the initialization, some critical parameters are established, which means any further exchange must be delayed. Second, there are still many systems (especially older microcomputers) that cannot overlap serial I/O with disk I/O or cannot overlap serial sending and receiving, and can therefore only use half-duplex protocols. When transferring large amounts of data, efficiency concerns make it reasonable for ZModem to implement multiple strategies, and as you'll see in a moment, it does. However, the efficiency of the initial exchange is not critical, so it makes sense to limit it to a half-duplex approach.

On page 24, I introduced the notion of a *scripted dialog* in which packets are considered acknowledged if a "reasonable" response is received. For example, if the sender sends a ZFile packet to begin a file transfer, there are only three reasonable responses: ZSkip indicates the file should not be sent, ZCRC asks the sender for more information about the file, and ZRPos tells the sender the file position to begin sending from. Any other response indicates the ZFile was lost. Usually, an unrecognized response results in a repeat of the packet.

Transferring File Data Reliably

ZModem's streaming strategy uses very long file data packets with the receiver sending acknowledgments only as requested by the sender. Under good conditions, the sender can request no acknowledgments at all, resulting in no back-channel data flow and providing optimal performance with error-correcting modems.

A ZData header is followed by prefix-encoded data punctuated by CRC escapes. There must be no more than 1024 bytes of data between CRC escapes. These CRC escapes convey two important pieces of information to the receiver:

- Whether an acknowledgment is expected.
- Whether the current packet is ending.

The receiver acknowledges a CRC escape by sending a ZAck packet with the receiver's file position.[2] If any CRC escape is in error, the receiver sends a ZRPos (reposition) request with the receiver's current file position. In response to ZRPos, the sender will send a CRC escape indicating the current packet is ending (but *not* requesting an acknowledgment), and start a new data packet at the requested position.

The sender's ability to control the frequency of acknowledgments allows it to adapt its transmission strategy to deal with various channel or system restrictions. For example, a sender that cannot receive data during disk I/O or while sending can send short data packets with an acknowledgment requested at the end of each one. This approach allows the sender to operate in half-duplex. The sender may also need to use a half-duplex approach—referred to in ZModem literature as "segmented streaming"—because of receiver limitations. Some of the capability bits in the initial exchange indicate whether or not the receiver can support full-duplex transfers, and how much data the receiver or channel can handle at one time.

ZModem also attempts to support senders that cannot "sample" incoming data. Some serial I/O routines do not have any means for testing if there is data available,

---

[2]A CRC escape together with the preceding data is often referred to as a *data subpacket*.

so that data can only be read in a "blocking" fashion, where a program attempting to read data waits for data to become available. Sometimes, such senders can be notified of an "interrupt," usually a break signal or special control character. ZModem allows the sender to specify an Attention string that the receiver will send before any of its packets, thus allowing the sender to be notified when such packets arrive, without having to stop transmitting and wait for a packet.

ZModem uses file position to identify data. The file transfer is receiver-driven; the receiver specifies a file position with ZRPos (reposition) packets and the sender sends data continuously from that position.[3] Whenever there is an error, the receiver sends a new ZRPos and the sender responds by restarting the transfer at the new position. This simplifies the receiver's job; it merely ignores data after an error until the damaged data is received correctly. It also allows the receiver to specify the file position at which the transfer should begin, which provides the basis for ZModem's "crash recovery" feature. If the receiver has a partially-received copy of the file, this transfer can be started at the point where the last transfer stopped.

The sender has a somewhat more difficult task. It tracks the receiver's current file position by observing ZAck packets that arrive in response to its requests. It uses this to limit the amount of outstanding data. If there is a restriction on the burst length or if full-duplex I/O is not possible, it must also periodically end a data packet with a request for acknowledgment and wait for the receiver to synchronize before continuing. A more detailed discussion of the issues faced by the sender begins on page 319.

Transaction Layer

Besides the obvious file transactions, ZModem also supports a generic command transaction that specifies a command to be interpreted by the receiver, and a free space transaction that allows the sender to query the receiver's available disk space prior to sending large files.

File Transfers

ZModem file transactions contain an initial negotiation in which the sender essentially offers a file to the receiver and the receiver decides whether or not to accept it. This negotiation begins with the sender sending a ZFile packet. The argument to this packet specifies which options the sender believes should be used to determine if this file is transferred, as shown in Tables 8.5, 8.6, 8.7, and 8.8.

---

[3]However, good error recovery requires some care. See page 110.

Value	Description
0x01000000	File is binary
0x02000000	File is text
0x03000000	Resume transfer, file is binary

Table 8.5 File Conversion Options

These options deserve some discussion. The "conversion" options indicate how the file should be translated by the receiver. Text files should be converted from the canonical text format (which uses LF or CR/LF to separate lines) to the native format. There are two options to specify a binary file. One of these suggests that the receiver resume an interrupted transfer. Notice that it's impossible for the sender to suggest resuming a text transfer. The "management" options suggest how to handle any file collision. The "transport" options specify any special encoding that will be done to the file as it is transferred. Only one of these is actually supported by standard ZModem. The LZW compressed format is identical to the compressed format used by the Unix `compress` program with 12-bit encoding. Few ZModem implementations currently support this compression, primarily because the compression algorithm is patented. The "extended" options allow for anything that doesn't fit in the other fields. The only one currently defined indicates sparse file transmission, in which the ZData packets may not be contiguous. For the receiver, this merely requires that it not issue reposition requests at the beginning of a new ZData packet; the sender must be careful to synchronize at the end of each packet to avoid lost data.

In deciding whether to accept the file, the receiver can optionally send a ZCRC packet to request a CRC of part or all of the file, so the receiver can check if the file is different from a file the receiver already has. The receiver's ZCRC packet specifies the number of bytes (beginning from the start of the file) to be included in the CRC. The sender responds with its own ZCRC packet containing the 32-bit CRC of the specified data.[4]

Once the receiver has made its decision, it can reject the file with a ZSkip packet, terminating the transaction. If the receiver chooses to accept the file, it sends a ZRPos packet specifying the file position (usually zero) at which the sender should begin. The sender begins sending the file at that point. When the sender has sent all of the file data, it sends ZEOF, which is acknowledged with ZRInit.

---

[4]ZModem does not allow for the possibility that the sender cannot compute a file CRC.

Value	Description
0x00800000	Skip if receiver does not already have file with this name
0x00010000	Receiver should accept if file is newer or longer
0x00020000	Receiver should accept if file has different length or contents
0x00030000	Receiver should append to end of file
0x00040000	Receiver should replace existing file
0x00050000	Receiver should accept if file is newer or nonexistent
0x00060000	Receiver should accept if file has different length or date, or is nonexistent
0x00070000	Receiver should accept only if file is nonexistent

Table 8.6   File Management Options

Value	Description
0x00000100	File is LZW compressed
0x00000200	File is encrypted with the NULL-terminated key attached to the beginning of the file
0x00000300	File is RLE compressed

Table 8.7   File Transport Options

Command Transactions

A command transaction allows the sender to send a command to the receiver to be executed on the host. The transaction begins with a ZCommand packet header followed by a NULL-terminated command string (and CRC escape to verify the string, of course). By convention, the command string is interpreted by the receiving application unless the first character is ! (0x21), in which case the command is passed to the system command interpreter.

Value	Description
0x00000040	Sparse file transmission. ZData packets are not necessarily contiguous.

Table 8.8   File Extended Options

When the command is complete, the receiver responds with a ZCompl packet to finish the transaction. The argument to ZCompl holds the status of the command, with zero indicating normal completion with no errors.

Most ZModem receivers should support the `sz` command, which causes the receiver to recursively begin a new session to send the specified files. In this case, the sender of the command will see a responding ZRQInit to begin the recursive session. When the recursive session is finished (the recursive session must not contain a command transaction!), the ZCompl packet is sent as usual by the original receiver (which is the recursive sender).

Sometimes, commands are intended to be executed asynchronously; that is, the command transfer is intended to begin the specified command without actually waiting for the result. The sender can request this by specifying an argument of 0x01000000 (a 1 in the most-significant byte) in its ZCommand packet rather than the default zero. This value instructs the receiver to immediately return a successful completion rather than waiting on the outcome of the command.

ZModem treats command transactions somewhat specially. In particular, the argument to the ZRQInit packet must contain the code for ZCommand (0x12) in the high-order byte to specify that a command transaction will occur. One use of this special marker is to allow programs that automatically detect ZRQInit to specifically ignore command downloads if they don't support that feature.

Free Space Transactions

The sender can request the amount of free space on the receiver's file system by sending a ZFreeCnt packet. The receiver responds with a ZAck containing the amount of free space. A receiver response of zero means that the information is not available.

Session Layer

The ZRInit packet can be thought of as the receiver's request for a new transaction. After the session initiation, the sender sends its capabilities packet, and the receiver sends its first ZRInit packet. The sender then begins a transaction. Transactions occur back-to-back, with file transfers terminated by ZRInit or ZSkip and free space transactions terminated by ZAck. As described earlier, command transactions are somewhat unique in that a single command transaction occurs in a session all by itself.

Initiating the Session

ZModem's session initiation is designed to remedy many of the problems with XModem and YModem session initiation. In particular, XModem and YModem wait for the receiver to prompt the sender, resulting in a delay if the sender is started after the receiver. ZModem addresses this by having both sides immediately notify the other when they begin, resulting in much quicker startup.

The ZModem sender begins by sending rz followed by CR. This is the command to begin a ZModem receive on many bulletin boards and on-line systems, and allows the user to upload a file without having to give any command to the host. The sender then sends a ZRQInit packet. This easily recognizable packet (CAN B 0 0) can be detected by many applications to provide automatic file transfer. In particular, the CAN character is not used in common terminal emulations, making it easy for terminal emulator programs to support this sequence.

In response to the sender's ZRQInit, the receiver can optionally "challenge" the sender with a ZChallenge packet with a random number, which should be echoed in a ZAck packet. This challenge is intended to guard against the following scenario: On some timesharing systems and networks, it is possible to dump data onto another user's terminal. Because ZModem is designed to support automatic download, it would be possible to download a program to another user's computer without their cooperation. Assuming no errors, the culprit can anticipate every response of the ZModem receiver, and hence affect a download even though such arrangements usually prevent the guilty party from actually observing those responses. This challenge guarantees that the receiver is in fact receiving from a legitimate two-way connection, and thus helps to guard against such abuses. It is traditionally only used when the receiver has been started automatically because the application received ZRQInit.

After the challenge, or in response to the ZRQInit if a challenge is not used, the receiver sends a ZRInit packet with the receiver's capabilities, as listed in Table 8.9. The lower 16 bits of the ZRInit argument specifies the size of the receiver's buffer. The sender will limit the burst size to this value. A value of zero means that full flow control makes the buffer size irrelevant. (Some applications recognize ZRInit (CAN B 0 1) to automatically start a preselected upload.)

If the sender has any limitations that the receiver needs to know about, it has the option of responding to ZRInit with a ZSInit packet. The ZSInit packet can specify control encoding and is followed by data containing the Attention string. The Attention string is NULL-terminated, and can contain characters 0xdd to specify a Break signal or 0xde to specify a 1-second pause. The receiver sends the Attention string prior to any ZRPos or other error packet during file transfer.

Value	Description
0x01000000	Receiver can overlap serial send and receive
0x02000000	Receiver can overlap serial and disk I/O
0x04000000	Receiver can send a break signal
0x08000000	Receiver can decrypt (not used)
0x10000000	Receiver can decompress
0x20000000	Receiver can use 32-bit CRC
0x40000000	Receiver expects control chars to be encoded
0x80000000	Receiver expects eight-bit chars to be encoded (not used)

Table 8.9   ZRInit Flags

Completing the Session

After the last transaction is complete, the sender sends a ZFin packet, the receiver responds with its own ZFin packet, and the sender finishes with the two characters OO (Over and Out). By looking for these final two characters, the receiver can also detect a * character indicating another packet. This would happen if the receiver's ZFin was corrupted, for example. By giving the receiver a chance to verify that its ZFin was received, the session ends more cleanly. If the OO is lost for some reason, or the receiver terminates before it is received, these two characters are unlikely to cause problems with an application or command prompt that receives them.

Cancelling the Session

If the receiver detects an unrecoverable error, it can send a ZFErr packet, indicating a file I/O error, or a ZAbort packet, indicating a user cancel, to request the sender to immediately terminate the session in the usual way.

In more drastic circumstances, a ZCan packet will immediately cancel a ZModem sender or receiver. This special packet consists of 5 CAN (Control-X) characters, and is intended to be easy for users to type. It follows the convention developed by XModem and YModem implementations of allowing two CAN characters to cancel a transfer.

Sample Sessions

To help you understand how ZModem works, here are a few sample sessions. For clarity, I've just identified the packets involved, omitting the lower-level details of the file data transfer.

Sender	Receiver
ZRQInit	
	ZRInit
ZFile *filename*	
	ZRPos
ZData	
File data transferred …	
ZEOF	
	ZRInit
ZFin	
	ZFin

Figure 8.3   Minimal ZModem File Transfer

Sender	Receiver
ZRQInit	
	ZChallenge
ZAck	
	ZRInit
ZSInit	
	ZAck
ZFile *file1*	
	ZSkip
ZFile *file2*	
	ZCRC
ZCRC	
	ZRPos
ZData	
File data transferred …	
ZEOF	
	ZRInit
ZFin	
	ZFin

Figure 8.4   More Complete ZModem File Transfer

Sender	Receiver
ZRQInit	
	ZChallenge
ZAck	
	ZRInit
ZCommand *sz file*	
	ZRQInit
ZRInit	
	ZFile *file*
ZRPos	
	ZData
File data transferred …	
	ZEOF
ZRInit	
	ZFin
ZFin	
	ZCompl
ZFin	
	ZFin

Figure 8.5   ZModem Command Session

The first example (Figure 8.3) is a minimal file transfer session, which is typical of most ZModem file transfer sessions. Note the multiple meanings of the second ZRInit, which both acknowledges the ZEOF and requests the next transaction.

The example in Figure 8.4 is a bit more complete. This example starts with a receiver challenge, which is satisfied by the sender's response. After the initializations, the sender offers *file1*, which the receiver declines. When the sender offers *file2*, the receiver first requests a CRC of the file contents, presumably in order to compare with a preexisting file of the same name. After the sender's reply, the receiver decides to accept the second file. The receiver could use the ZCRC to determine if a preexisting file matched the first part of the file being sent before attempting to resume a transfer. In that case, the ZRPos beginning the transfer would specify the byte offset at which the sender should begin.

Finally, Figure 8.5 shows a command session, in which the sender sends the command *sz file* to the receiver, which responds by initiating a recursive send. Pay careful attention to the termination first of the recursive session, then the command transaction, then the original session.

Sender	Receiver
Send bytes 0–999	
Send bytes 1000–1999	
Send bytes 2000–2999	
Send bytes 3000–3999	Receive 0–999
Send bytes 4000–4999	Error: Request reposition to 1000
Send bytes 5000–5999	Ignore 2000–2999
Send bytes 6000–6999	Ignore 3000–3999
Send bytes 7000–7999	Repeat reposition request
Reposition: send 1000–1999	Ignore 5000–5999
Send bytes 2000–2999	Ignore 6000–6999
Send bytes 3000–3999	Repeat reposition request
Reposition: send 1000–1999	Receive 1000–1999
Send bytes 2000–2999	Receive 2000–2999
Send bytes 3000–3999	Receive 3000–3999
Send bytes 4000–4999	Ignore 1000–1999
Send bytes 5000–5999	Ignore 2000–2999
$\vdots$	$\vdots$

Figure 8.6 ZModem's Response to Duplicate NAKs

Analysis

ZModem was designed to be a relatively simple protocol to implement. One important part of this is ZModem's simple error recovery strategy. Unfortunately, this simple strategy can be quite time-consuming when there are long channel delays.

The basic problem is the *duplicate NAK* problem discussed on page 26. Unlike windowing Kermit, the ZModem receiver will not receive out-of-sequence data. Thus, after any error, the receiver must ignore data after that file position. The problem is that at some point, the receiver must decide that its original error packet was not received and send it again. The sender will receive this duplicate reposition request and must honor it, since the sender has no way of knowing the repeated request is spurious. The effect is outlined in Figure 8.6, which shows how a long delay can result in several requests for the same data. Notice the amount of data ignored by the receiver.

There are several ways in which implementations can address this problem:

- The sender should synchronize after answering a reposition request. Rather than streaming file data from that point, it sends a single short packet ending with an acknowledge request, and waits until the receiver acknowledges. Only after the data is acknowledged does the sender resume streaming transfer.

- The sender should delay answering a reposition request. Rather than responding immediately, the sender should wait several seconds to see if there is another reposition request. If there is, it ignores the first one and only responds to the second one. Even if the sender doesn't wait long enough to actually receive a duplicate reposition request, the pause will reduce the amount of duplicate data, hence speeding recovery from this problem.

- Receivers should avoid sending reposition requests asking the sender to move *forward* in the data stream. Instead, the receiver should simply ignore any duplicate data. If you study Figure 8.6 carefully, you can see that if the receiver requested forward repositions, it would take much longer to recover.

- Receivers should be conservative in repeating reposition requests. Ideally, the receiver will have some way to measure the round-trip delay, and can use this information to wait until there is good reason to believe the original request was lost.

Performance

ZModem is considerably more complex than XModem or YModem, and so I won't give a lengthy analysis of its efficiency. Over good channels, ZModem behaves a lot like YModem-G, simply dumping data with no response required from the receiver. Unlike YModem-G, however, ZModem does do some encoding. Conventional ZModem implementations prefix encode between seven and ten different byte values by default. This results in about three to four percent overhead from encoding, in addition to the injected CRC escapes, which constitute six bytes for every 1024 bytes of data. These numbers suggest that good ZModem implementations should be able to achieve about 96 percent efficiency over good quality connections, depending on the data being transferred and regardless of the delay. Over less transparent connections, ZModem may need to encode all control characters, resulting in about 25 percent overhead from encoding, or about 75 percent efficiency. If it's necessary to fall back to half-duplex reliability, then ZModem performance should approximate that of YModem or other similar protocols.

Analyzing ZModem's behavior when there are errors is quite difficult, and requires making many assumptions about the particular implementations and the channel involved. Generally, as pointed out earlier, ZModem does not behave very well when there are both long delays and errors. In unusually poor conditions,

ZModem's full-duplex streaming can actually become slower than simpler half-duplex approaches, due to the need for the receiver to scan through and ignore data that was already in the channel before the error occurred.

Derivatives

The ZModem specifications provide for a number of extensions. For example, the format of streamed data following a hexadecimal header is left undefined. This is an obvious place to extend the protocol to provide support for seven-bit channels. Similarly, the capabilities exchange and file header define bits to allow for encryption and run-length compression of files, but the details are omitted.

Chuck Forsberg has capitalized on these omissions to develop a proprietary protocol called ZModem-90. ZModem-90 provides these extensions and several others, but, as a proprietary protocol, is only available in programs developed by his company, Omen Technology. In particular, later versions of `rz` and `sz` are *not* public domain, because they incorporate some of these proprietary extensions. (Only versions prior to version 3.0 are public domain.) This restriction has generated some confusion, because the currently distributed version of the ZModem protocol reference still refers to the public domain status of these programs.

References

The original ZModem reference is Chuck Forsberg's *The ZModem Inter-Application File Transfer Protocol* [7]. Unfortunately, Forsberg's documentation omits many details, so it's necessary to also have the source code to the public domain versions of `rz` and `sz` [6] available. Finding the public domain versions of this source code can be difficult, since the newer non-public domain versions have largely displaced the older versions.

More information about ZModem can be obtained by contacting:

Chuck Forsberg
Omen Technology Incorporated
17505-V Northwest Sauvie Island Road
Portland, Oregon 97231, USA
Voice: +1 503 621-3406
Modem: +1 503 621-3746
Email: caf@omen.com

Basic Kermit 9

The design of the original 1981 Kermit protocol was motivated by the desire to transfer files among a wide variety of computer systems. The result was a simple, flexible protocol that works under almost any conditions.

Kermit development began at Columbia University in 1981. While searching for a way to connect a diverse collection of computer systems, the system administrators were dismayed both by the high cost of deploying a commercial solution over the thousands of computers in their care and by the inability of any one product to work with all of the systems they wanted to connect.

Frank da Cruz and Bill Catchings resolved this dilemma by designing and implementing their own protocol, which was named after Kermit the Frog, star of *The Muppet Show*. They drew on ideas from a variety of sources, including the ISO OSI[1] model and a number of experimental protocols that had been developed at other universities. Their original implementations included such diverse platforms as CP/M, DEC-20, and IBM VM/CMS.

The end result is remarkable for several reasons. The first is that it functions in so many different environments. Kermit has been ported to just about every computer system imaginable, from supercomputers to cash registers, and to languages ranging from assembler to Lisp, from Hebrew to Russian. It is one of the very few serial protocols capable of communicating through mainframe protocol converters.

Another remarkable aspect of Kermit is its extensibility. When Chuck Forsberg was contracted to design the ZModem protocol, he initially considered adapting XModem, but was forced essentially to start from scratch. By contrast, the simple half-duplex Kermit protocol from 1981 has been gradually extended to include

---

[1]These palindromic acronyms stand for *International Organization for Standardization* and *Open Systems Interconnection*, respectively.

host commands, full-duplex transfers, automatic download, and a variety of other features, all while maintaining compatibility with the original protocol.

The Protocol

Kermit's original design was guided by the desire to transfer files over very restrictive channels. One type of channel in which the Kermit designers were especially interested was a dial-in connection to a mainframe computer. The front-end port handlers for these systems are line-oriented, collecting a line of text from the user and passing it to the operating system or application program only when a complete line is available. A line of input in this environment is quite limited, with strong restrictions both on the content of the line and its length.

Encoding Layer

In particular, input to a mainframe terminal connection is frequently limited to the 95 printable ASCII characters. It was essential that Kermit be able to represent all of its data using only those characters. The limit on line length means that the packets must be kept small, which in turn requires reasonably compact encoding.

Kermit uses three different encodings. Two are used for encoding small numbers and control characters in packet headers and certain negotiations, while the third is used to encode actual file data. I'll look at each of these in turn.

The packet format that I'll discuss momentarily has a packet sequence number, packet size, and a packet check. To remain compact, each of these integers is encoded as a single ASCII character by adding 32 (space) to the integer value. Thus, sequence number 5 is represented by ASCII character 37 (%). Note that an integer is encoded as a *character*, not a byte value. If the transfer goes through a terminal converter that maps incoming ASCII characters to their EBCDIC equivalents, % will become character number 108, but will still represent the number 5. It is the character that's important. Also note that the largest number that can be encoded this way is 94, which corresponds to ASCII character 126 (~).

While this simple mapping works fine for small numbers, it doesn't allow all control characters to be encoded. In particular, the DEL character (character 127) can't be converted into a printable character by adding 32. Because Kermit needs to encode control characters to negotiate end-of-packet markers, padding, and other protocol features, Kermit defines a correspondence between control characters and printable characters by toggling bit six, that is, by taking the exclusive-or of the character code with 0x40. Control-A (0x01) is conveniently mapped to A (0x41). The troublesome DEL character is mapped to ? (0x3f).

Character	Hex	Decimal	Encoded
NULL	0x00	0	#@
NULL$_8$	0x80	128	&#@
A	0x41	65	A
DEL	0x7f	127	#?
DEL$_8$	0xff	255	&#?
#	0x23	35	##
&	0x26	38	#&

Table 9.1 Kermit Prefix Encoding Examples

These two encodings form the basis of the prefix encoding used for file data. The prefix encoding is performed in three steps, the first two of which are optional:

1. Sequences of the same repeated byte are condensed into a *repeat prefix* (usually ~) followed by the repeat count offset by 32 (this limits the repeat count to a maximum of 94), followed by the encoding of the repeated character. The sequence AAAAA is encoded as ~%A.
2. If the channel does not pass all eight bits, values greater than 127 are encoded with an *eighth-bit prefix* (usually &), and the character is reduced by 128. The sequence of five copies of character 0xc1 is encoded as ~%&A.
3. Any control character is encoded with a *control prefix* (usually #) and then converted into a printable character by toggling bit six. The sequence of five copies of character 0x81 is encoded as ~%&#A.

Table 9.1 shows several examples of this encoding. The actual prefix characters are determined by the startup negotiation. The table shows the recommended values, as indicated above. I've used a subscript 8 in the table to indicate characters that have the high bit set, so that H$_8$ indicates character 200.

Note in particular that the control prefix is also used to prefix literal occurrences of any of the prefix characters; if one of the prefix characters is in the original data, it must be encoded so that the receiver doesn't become confused. For the decoder, if the control prefix is followed by a character that does not represent a valid control code, then the control prefix is dropped and the following character is taken literally. The order of the prefixes is important; #&A is decoded as the two characters &A, while &#A is decoded as a single character 129.

Kermit's repeat-count encoding is not particularly sophisticated, but can effectively compress certain types of files. In particular, executable files sometimes contain large sections consisting entirely of zero bytes.[2] Some text files, especially source code and formatted text files, contain many repeated sequences of spaces or tabs, and are similarly compressible. On other types of files, especially files that have already been through some other compression algorithm, Kermit's repeat-count encoding has essentially no effect.

One important final note about Kermit's prefix encoding. The result of prefix encoding is a sequence of *prefix groups*, each representing a single byte of the original data or a repeated sequence of bytes. The longest prefix group is five characters, and consists of a repeat prefix, a repeat count, an eighth-bit prefix, a control prefix, and a final character. Kermit forbids breaking a prefix group across more than one packet.

Packetization Layer

The full Kermit protocol currently supports three different packet formats, but I'm only going to discuss the original short packet format here. The others are described in Chapter 10 (starting on page 126).

As you can see in Table 9.2, a Kermit packet consists of a four-byte header, up to 91 bytes of encoded data, and a single-byte packet error check. Except for the start-of-packet character, all of the packet header values and the packet error check are represented by seven-bit printable ASCII characters, using the encodings described above. The error check is computed over the entire packet except for the start-of-packet character, and thus serves to protect the packet sequence, length, and type fields as well as the data.

The single-byte error check is computed by taking an eight-bit checksum of the encoded data, and adding the top two bits to the bottom six to form a six-bit result. Symbolically, if s is the eight bit checksum, the error check value is computed as $(((s/64) \bmod 3) + s) \bmod 64$. The six-bit result is offset by 32 to yield the error check character.

Note that the smallest packet has no data, has a length field of 3 (#), and is five bytes long. The longest packet has 91 bytes of encoded data, has a length field of 94 (~), and is 96 bytes long.

The packet type is a single upper case letter. Several of the Kermit extensions add new packet types, but the basic protocol only uses a handful: acknowledge (Y) and negative acknowledge (N) packets respond to sent packets; File (F), Data (D), and End-of-File (Z) are used to transfer files; Send-Init (S), Break (B), and Error

---

[2]As one extreme example, the `uuencode` executable on one Sparc system I checked was 16k long and contained two repeated runs of zero bytes which together were 13k long! Kermit's prefix encoding compressed this file to less than 4k.

Name	Size	Description
Mark	1	Start-of-packet character, usually Control-A.
Length	1	Length of remaining fields after encoding, offset by 32.
Sequence	1	Packet sequence number, modulo 64, offset by 32.
Type	1	Packet type.
Data	variable	Packet data, prefix encoded.
Check	1	Packet error check, offset by 32.

Table 9.2   Kermit Short Packet Format

Name	Code	Description
Acknowledge	Y	Packet received, data field contains response.
Negative Ack	N	Garbled or out-of-sequence packet.
Send-Init	S	Sender's capabilities.
File	F	Filename.
Data	D	File data.
End-of-File	Z	End of file.
Break	B	End of transaction.
Error	E	Terminates file transfer immediately.

Table 9.3   Kermit Packet Types

(E) packets are used to start, end, and cancel the session, respectively. Table 9.3 summarizes these packet types.

Reliability Layer

Basic Kermit uses a simple, half-duplex reliability approach. The sender sends a packet, and the receiver responds with an acknowledgment (Y), which has the same sequence number, and which may carry data responding to the request. If the receiver times out, receives a damaged packet, or receives a packet with the wrong sequence number, it responds with a negative acknowledgment (N) with the sequence number it expected to see.

Thus, Kermit's reliability can be looked at as a request/response exchange. The sender sends a packet, and the receiver responds with an acknowledgment carrying the response to that packet. For example, when the sender sends file data, the receiver may respond with an empty acknowledgment (the usual case), or it may respond with a single 'Y' or 'Z' character, requesting the sender to terminate the file or the session, respectively.

The packet sequence number starts at zero and increments throughout a transaction, and is then reset to zero between transactions.

Transaction Layer

Kermit's notion of "transaction" and "session" differ from the other protocols I've discussed. In particular, most Kermit transactions begin with a capabilities exchange. A Kermit session consists of a single transaction, or, if one end is in "server" mode, any number of transactions back to back. In the latter case, the session ends only when the client invokes a special transaction to terminate the session. I'll discuss server mode in more detail in the next chapter.

File Transfers

A single transaction can transfer any number of files. The transaction begins with the sender's Send-Init (S) packet and the receiver's acknowledgment (Y). For each file, the sender sends a File (F) packet containing the filename, followed by the contents of the file in one or more Data (D) packets, and an End-of-File (Z) packet. After the last file, the sender sends a Break (B) packet, the receiver acknowledges, and the transaction is complete.

Several of these packets have optional arguments. The acknowledgment to the File (F) packet can contain the name the receiver will store the file under (which needn't be the same as the name specified by the sender). As mentioned earlier, the acknowledgment to a Data (D) packet can contain either 'X' to request this file should be cancelled, or 'Z' to request the entire transaction be cancelled. If the transfer of a file is prematurely terminated for some reason, the sender signals this by including 'D' (discard) as the argument for the End-of-File (Z) packet.

Traditionally, Kermit senders have converted the name of the file into a canonical form (only upper case alphanumeric characters and a single period, with eight characters before the period and three after), but this creates problems with like-system transfers. For compatibility with older Kermit receivers, it's wise to include an option to perform this type of translation in the sender, but newer implementations are increasingly placing the burden of filename translation on the receiver, where it belongs.

Session Layer

Many Kermit transactions, including all file transfers, begin with a Send-Init (S) packet and its acknowledgment. The Send-Init packet carries a list of the sender's preferences for how the transaction should take place, while the receiver's acknowledgment carries a similar list. By comparing these two lists, the two Kermit implementations can determine which options will be used. If there are multiple transactions, as in server mode, the parameters are renegotiated for each transaction. Each transaction is completely independent.

Because the configuration exchange determines how prefix encoding will be handled, the data for this packet is encoded explicitly rather than being prefix-encoded.

To allow for new capabilities to be added, the configuration string is extendable. It consists of three parts; the first part holds the basic parameters used by the original protocol, and the other two parts are each extendable to support additional protocol features as they are added. The configuration string may be truncated, and any missing fields will be treated in a default manner. It's even possible (and quite reasonable for simple implementations) to send an empty string. In this case, all of the configurable options are defaulted. Table 9.4 lists the first part of the configuration string. The other two parts are shown in Table 10.12 on page 141.

For the first six fields listed in Table 9.4, the value in the initialization string is non-negotiable. Either I'm telling the other end how I will behave, or I'm telling it how I expect it to behave. In particular, even simple implementations must be able to interpret and obey these first six fields, in case the other end chooses to specify unusual values. The last three fields describe optional features, and hence are only used if both ends agree:

- The packet check must be the same in both the Send-Init (S) packet and the acknowledgment (Y), or the default single-character packet check will be used by both sides. (Alternate packet checks are discussed on page 127.)

- Similarly, the repeat prefixes must agree or repeat prefixing will not be done.

- The eighth-bit prefix is handled slightly differently, because the receiver must be able to initiate eighth-bit prefixing, even if the sender thinks it unnecessary. The special value Y in this field indicates that eighth-bit prefixing is supported, but is not requested. Typically, senders that can support eighth-bit prefixing, but think it unnecessary, will use Y here to allow the receiver to specify this option. If the receiver specifies a valid eighth-bit prefix, both sides will use eighth-bit prefixing. Similarly, if both sides specify the same valid eighth-bit prefix, eighth-bit prefixing will be done. But, if

Field name	Default	Description
Packet Length	80	The largest value that I will accept for the packet length field.
Timeout	5	How many seconds I want you to wait before timing out.
Number Pad	0	Number of padding characters you should send before each packet.
Pad Character	NULL	character you should use for padding, converted to a printable character by toggling bit six.
End-of-Packet	CR	Character you should send after each packet. Contrary to other Kermit conventions, this control character is offset by 32.
Control Prefix	#	Character I will use as a control prefix.
Eighth-bit prefix	none	Character we should both use for eighth-bit prefixing.
Packet check	1	Type of packet check we should both use. The default value is the ASCII character 1 (character 49), representing the standard single-byte packet check.
Repeat prefix	none	Character we should both use for repeat prefixing.

Table 9.4   Kermit Basic Configuration Fields

both sides specify Y, or the two sides specify different prefixes, eighth-bit prefixing will not be done.

Note that for all three prefixes, the valid values include characters from 32 to 62 and from 96 to 126. This restriction is necessary to prevent ambiguities when prefixing control codes; for example, ? can't be used as an eighth-bit prefix, because then it's unclear whether #? is DEL or a literal ?.

A Kermit transaction ends with a Break (B) packet. Typical sessions consist of only a single transaction, so this is also usually the end of the session.

An Error (E) packet will cause any Kermit implementation to immediately terminate. The Error packet contains a text explanation in the data section, which can be displayed to the user.

Basic Kermit does not define a standard way for a user to manually cancel the other end. However, most implementations allow the user to type two or three interrupt characters (commonly Control-C) to terminate the other end.

Analysis

Kermit satisfies its goal of allowing transfer between many different systems quite well. It functions over many channels where protocols such as XModem, YModem, and ZModem cannot function at all. The only systems with which Kermit has problems are a few mainframe protocol converters that are incapable of passing *any* control characters and certain systems that usurp some graphic characters. The former problem can be addressed in implementations by allowing the start-of-packet character to be set to a graphic character, and the latter problem can sometimes be worked around by specific implementations, although fortunately systems with this type of restriction are rare.

One example of these problems is the 'full screen' mode of certain IBM protocol converters. In this mode, the protocol converter performs blank compression, replacing any sequence of spaces with a single space. To use Kermit through such converters requires two changes. First, any sequence of two or more spaces must be sent using a repeat prefix, even though normally a sequence of two spaces would not be encoded. Secondly, the packet error check must be altered so that a space error check cannot occur. The first is purely an implementation detail. The second has been added as a Kermit protocol extension specifically to deal with protocol converters that only support full screen mode. (See the description of the 'B' packet check on page 128.)

This basic Kermit protocol is quite reliable. The six-bit error check is adequate for the small packet size, and all control packets have error checks. The inclusion of a specific sequence number in every packet addresses the synchronization problem that plagues XModem and YModem.

The relative slowness of basic Kermit is often attributed to its encoding, but comparisons to other protocols must be made carefully. While it's true that for random binary data, Kermit incurs about 75 percent overhead when encoding for a seven-bit channel, this figure should not be used when comparing Kermit with protocols that don't function at all over seven-bit channels. It's more appropriate to evaluate Kermit's performance in two situations. The first is transferring seven-bit text over seven-bit channels. In this case, assuming the average line length is 40 characters, Kermit only prefixes the CR and LF occurring between lines, yielding approximately 5 percent encoding overhead, assuming no gains from repeat-count encoding. The second situation is transferring random eight-bit data over eight-bit connections. In this case, the encoding overhead is approximately 25 percent, the same overhead as a ZModem sender that's configured to escape all control characters.

The major problem is that basic Kermit is a half-duplex protocol with short packets. Because the round-trip delay is incurred for every packet, short packets mean that much more time is spent waiting. The result is that when there are non-trivial delays, basic Kermit can be quite slow.

Modern Kermit 10

The features added to Kermit since 1981 have greatly improved upon the original. Today, Kermit is fast and efficient, while remaining completely compatible with the original.

The original Kermit protocol described in the previous chapter satisfies its goals quite well. It transfers files between a wide variety of systems under less than ideal conditions. At the time it was designed, most transfers between dissimilar systems were transfers of text files over direct-dial connections. Because of the preponderance of different computers with different software and capabilities, it was unusual for a non-text file to be usable on more than one type of computer. Public-access networks were still in relative infancy, and the performance issues created by channel delays were not a major concern.

In the years since Kermit's inception, however, usage of file transfer protocols has changed. Binary files are now routinely transferred even between very dissimilar systems. The growth of the Internet and online systems has sparked increasing interest in transferring files over networks. To keep pace with these changes, the Kermit protocol has been extended in a number of ways.

The ongoing improvements to the Kermit protocol are a marked contrast to the situation with XModem, YModem, and ZModem. XModem and YModem have no commonly recognized authority coordinating the efforts of the many people who would improve them. The inventor of ZModem has continued to improve upon ZModem, but has chosen not to make those improvements freely available.

The developers of Kermit, on the other hand, continue to freely distribute the improvements to their protocol and their software. They currently distribute a collection of comprehensive communications packages that provide terminal emulation, file transfer capabilities, and sophisticated connectivity over modems and networks. They also publish and distribute documentation for their software [5, 8] and for the Kermit protocol itself [4]. Unlike most communications software vendors, the software distributed by the Kermit project is aggressively multi-platform and multi-lingual. Kermit software is probably in use in more countries and on more platforms than any other communications software.

The Protocol

The decision to include an explicit capabilities exchange as the first step in a Kermit session has become Kermit's greatest asset. In the years since Kermit's original development, Kermit has come to be used in an increasing variety of environments, and its original designers have responded to the varying demands of those environments by extending the protocol.

- To simplify the use of Kermit by a wide variety of users, Kermit added a *host mode*, in which a menu-driven program running on a microcomputer could provide easy access to files stored on a mainframe.

- To improve its performance over channels with delays, Kermit gained longer packets (up to 900k), and a windowing extension that allowed multiple outstanding packets.

- Reducing the overhead of Kermit's prefix-encoding strategy was the motivation behind the addition of locking-shift prefixing.

- Awareness of the issues involved in international computing led to an extension that provides character set conversion during file transfer.

These sophisticated extensions are not available in every Kermit implementation. However, thanks to Kermit's capabilities exchange, it is possible to transfer files between any two Kermit programs. Any capabilities not shared by both sides will simply not be used. There are a few exceptions to this—some parameters must be known before the capabilities exchange can take place, and a few crude implementations demand certain capabilities before they will work—but in general, the interoperability of different Kermit implementations is remarkably high.

Encoding Layer

The basic Kermit encoding described on page 114 does quite well on text files that contain few control characters. For example, a file containing seven-bit ASCII text with an average line length of 40 characters only needs to prefix the CR and LF that terminate each line, resulting in about 5 percent overhead from encoding. If repeat coding is in effect, and the text file has tabular data aligned with repeated spaces, the compression from repeat coding is likely to compensate for the encoding overhead. Some binary files (especially small executables) have large sections of zero bytes, which compress quite well with repeat-count coding, sometimes resulting in files that are smaller than the originals, even after the overhead of eighth-bit and control prefixing.

However, two particular common types of files do not behave well with the encoding described earlier. The first type are compressed files created by popular compression and archiving programs. Compressed binary data tends to be very random, which means that repeat coding is generally ineffective, and the overhead from prefixing tends to be very high. The second type are text files written in eight-bit character sets, such as ISO Cyrillic or Japanese EUC. In both of these, the lower 128 characters are the common Roman alphabet, so that the majority of the characters in such files have the eighth bit set. Transferring these files over seven-bit connections requires eighth-bit prefixing nearly every character.

Transferring compressed binary files over eight-bit connections has been accelerated by recent additions to popular Kermit implementations allowing the user to specify exactly which control characters should be prefixed. Over reasonably transparent connections, it is sometimes sufficient to prefix as few as three control characters,[1] reducing the overhead due to control prefixing from 25 percent down to less than two percent. There has also been some discussion of adding more sophisticated compression and encoding techniques to provide better performance when transferring binary files over more restrictive channels, but this work is not yet complete.

Transferring files with many eight-bit characters over seven-bit connections is addressed by the addition of an eighth-bit *locking shift*, introduced on page 40. Intuitively, Kermit's locking-shift encoding is done before control, eighth-bit, and repeat encoding is done. A file with eight-bit characters is converted into one with only seven-bit characters by placing SO (Shift Out) before each group of eight-bit characters, SI (Shift In) after the group, and throwing away the eighth bits. After the result is transferred, the receiver sets the eighth bit on each character between SO and SI, and removes the SO and SI characters themselves. On a typical Japanese file using the EUC character code, which may consist entirely of eight-bit characters, this encoding simply places a single SO at the beginning of the file and removes the eighth bit of each character.

---

[1] When using C-Kermit over high-quality connections, only 0, 1, and 129 require prefixing: 0 is used internally by C-Kermit, 1 is the start-of-packet character, and 129 is the start-of-packet character with the high bit set. If software flow control is being used, 17, 19, 145, and 147 will probably require prefixing. The implementation in this book can be modified to function with no prefixing at all over suitably clean channels.

Of course, in practice, there may be SO and SI characters in the original file, which must somehow be marked so the receiver doesn't mistake them for locking shifts. Kermit uses the DLE (Data Link Escape) character for this purpose. DLE is placed before each SO, SI, and DLE that existed in the file before the locking shifts were added. In addition, a DLE must be placed before an SI_8, SO_8, or DLE_8 that has been converted to SI, SO, or DLE as a result of locking-shift encoding.

The encoding described in the previous two paragraphs is sufficient to perform locking-shift encoding that any Kermit receiver supporting this extension will understand. This encoding is done *before* Kermit's normal control and repeat-count encoding. Two additions allow for more compact encoding of certain sequences. Note that these next additions are *optional* for senders, but *not* for receivers.[2]

If your file contains a repeated group of SO or SI characters, prefixing each one separately with DLE results in a sequence that can no longer be compressed. Kermit dodges this by decreeing that a DLE prefix applies to any single compressed group of SO, SI, or DLE characters. Note that a sequence of 100 SO characters requires two prefixed groups, both of which will need to be prefixed with DLE.

There is no need for locking-shift encoding over eight-bit channels, so locking-shift encoding is *always* done in conjunction with eighth-bit prefixing. For example, it's more compact to use the eighth-bit prefix for an isolated eight-bit character than to surround it with SO and SI. If you think of locking shifts and the eighth-bit prefix as *changing* the eighth bit rather than setting it, you see that you can use the eighth-bit prefix within a locking shift section to mark isolated seven-bit characters; between SO and SI, the eighth-bit prefix actually *clears* the eighth bit.

Except for the rule about a DLE applying to the next prefixed group, locking-shift encoding occurs before the normal prefix encoding. In particular, any SO, SI, and DLE characters inserted must be prefix encoded as usual, unless the sender is explicitly configured to not encode those characters.

Packetization Layer

In addition to the basic short packet format discussed on page 116, Kermit supports two extended packet formats and three optional packet checks.

Both extended packet formats are based on the observation that, since the length field in the basic packet format includes the sequence, type, and packet check, it will never be less than three. So, the extended formats use the same

---

[2] It's generally the case that senders can be less robust than receivers. Senders need only guarantee that their output will be correctly decoded. It's desirable, but not necessary, that the output be optimal. Receivers, on the other hand, must be able to correctly decode any legal input.

Name	Size	Description
Mark	1	Start-of-packet character, usually Control-A.
Length	1	Zero or one, offset by 32, to indicate the extended packet format.
Sequence	1	Packet sequence number, modulo 64, offset by 32.
Type	1	Packet type.
Extended Length	2–3	Length of data and packet check, base 95, offset by 32.
Header Check	1	Single-byte error check of previous four fields.
Data	variable	Packet data, prefix encoded.
Check	1-3	Packet error check.

Table 10.1   Kermit Long and Extra-Long Packet Format

four-byte header, but treat a length value less than three as a marker indicating an extended packet format. The extended packet formats follow the basic header with a multi-byte extended length field and a header check computed in the same way as Kermit's default single-byte packet check. The data and packet error check follow this extended header as usual, as indicated in Figure 10.1.

A standard length field of zero is used for *long packets*, which have a two-byte extended length field. A standard length of one indicates an *extra-long packet*, with a three-byte extended length field.

In the long and extra-long packet formats, the extended length field includes only the length of the data and packet error check, unlike the normal packet format. The extended length is represented in base 95, starting with the most significant digit. Thus, a length of 1024 would be stored as *j. Not all Kermit implementations support these extended formats, and they should only be used if the startup negotiation indicates the other end is capable of supporting them.

Kermit's default single-character error check is adequate for normal packets, but something stronger is needed for longer packets. During the initial negotiation, four different packet checks can be negotiated:

1   The type 1 packet check is the standard default six-bit check described on page 116.

Name	**Code**	**Description**
Init	I	Set server parameters.
Text	X	Start of text to be displayed to user, similar to File (F) packet.
Receive-Init	R	Contains filename I want you to send.
Attributes	A	File attributes.
Command	C	Command for host command interpreter to execute, in target system's native command language.
Kermit Command	K	Command for server program to execute, in server's native command language.
Generic Command	G	Command encoded in system-independent manner.
Reserved	T, Q	Used internally by some Kermit implementations.

Table 10.2   Kermit Packet Types, Continued

---

2   The type 2 packet check is a 12-bit checksum of the packet data.

B   This is identical to the type 2 check, except that it is sent as two characters in base 64, with each byte offset by 33 rather than 32. This error check is used when sending files through certain mainframe protocol converters that strip trailing blanks and compress repeated blanks. An implementation that supports this packet check should also slightly modify its encoding when this check is specified, so that any repeated sequence of spaces are repeat-count encoded, even if it enlarges the data.

3   The type 3 packet check is a 16-bit CRC computed as shown on page 58.

Packet checks are sent as one, two, or three characters in base 64, with each byte offset by 32. For example, the 16-bit CRC 0x1a87 is decomposed into 1, 42, 7, yielding the three character error check !I'. For those that prefer to think in binary, the first digit represents the first four bits of the CRC, the second digit holds the next six bits, and the third digit holds the bottom six bits.

Table 9.3 on page 117 listed the basic eight Kermit packet types. Table 10.2 shows the packets that have been added by various extensions. Again, not all Kermit extensions will support all of these packet types.

Reliability Layer

Even in basic Kermit, acknowledgments can be lost. When they are, the receiver can receive a duplicate of a packet it has already correctly received. To resynchronize, the receiver must repeat the same acknowledgment that it used before. Simply generating an empty acknowledgment isn't sufficient, because the data in the acknowledgment can be critical.

For the implementation, the reliability functions in the receiver must store the previous acknowledgment, in case it's needed again. (The alternative is to have special-purpose code for each packet type to recreate the acknowledgment.) In essence, the receiver must cache old packets.

Extending this cache results in both the sender and receiver keeping copies of old packets. If the sender receives a negative acknowledgment (N) for a packet it sent previously, it recalls the packet from the cache and resends it. If the receiver receives a duplicate packet, it repeats the acknowledgment stored in the cache. A packet received out of sequence can be stored in the cache until it's needed.

This simple mechanism allows the sender to send multiple packets before receiving acknowledgments, and allows the receiver to receive packets out of order. When well implemented, the precise size of the cache is not critical (see page 385), but it is simpler and faster if both ends agree on the maximum number of packets that will be outstanding at any time. This number is referred to in Kermit documentation as the *window size*. In the basic protocol, the window size is, of course, one packet, and that is the default value in the negotiation. A window size greater than one allows full-duplex operation, and provides a significant speed improvement over typical channels.

To ease compatibility with older implementations, to avoid having multiple files open at one time, and to avoid some ugly problems during negotiation, Kermit dictates that *only file data is transferred with a window size greater than one*. All other parts of the protocol operate in half-duplex, regardless of the negotiated window size.

Transaction Layer

The file transfers provided in the original Kermit protocol have been extended to provide a host of different transaction types. It's possible, in fact, for Kermit to serve as the primary means of interacting with a host system. A Kermit program running on a mainframe or minicomputer can allow a user to login to the computer, perform a variety of different operations, transfer files to and from the host, and finally disconnect, all from a menu-operated program running on the client. This type of interface is similar in concept to the interfaces being advertised by many online services.

File Transfers

Basic Kermit transfers only the filename and the file data. While adequate for many purposes, it's usually desirable to transfer other information about the file. For instance, in interactive applications, the receiver can provide the user with better progress information if the receiver knows the approximate file size in advance. A discussion of other file attributes and why you might want to transfer them appears on page 6.

Kermit allows a wide variety of file attributes to be transferred using Attribute (A) packets. When both sides support this extension, the file transfer is altered to transfer first the filename, then the file attributes, and then the file data. The data in the attribute packet is a coded string specifying one or more file attributes.

Character	Argument
!	Approximate length of file in kilobytes.
"	Type of file. (Table 10.4)
#	Creation date of file. (For example, 19940326 13:52:17) The seconds and time are optional, and the date and time are separated by exactly one space. As always, the sender should use the least ambiguous form possible, while the receiver should be tolerant of common variants, such as omission of the first two digits of the year.
$	File creator's name.
%	Name of account to which file should be charged.
&	Name of area to store file.
\	Password for above.
(	Block size.
)	How receiver should handle duplicate files. (Table 10.5)
*	Encoding. (Table 10.6)
+	Disposition. (Table 10.8)
,	Protection Code.
–	Generic Protection Code.
.	Originating system. (Table 10.10)
/	Data record format. (Table 10.9)
0	System-specific attributes.
1	Approximate file length in bytes.
2–@	Reserved.

Table 10.3   Kermit File Attributes

Argument	Description
A	Text, lines separated by CR/LF.
A*xx*	Like above, characters following A encode the control characters used to separate lines, for example, AMJ indicates CR/LF, AM indicates CR, etc.
B	Binary.
B8	Binary with eight bits per byte, same as B.
B36	Binary with 36 bits per word, with each word sent as four seven-bit values and one eight-bit value.
I	System-specific image file. A number may follow the I to indicate the number of bits per byte.

Table 10.4   Kermit File Type Attribute (") Arguments

(This string is *not* subject to normal prefix encoding.) Several packets can be used if the attributes won't all fit into a single packet, although this is unusual because the attributes are encoded fairly compactly.

An attribute string consists of any number of individual attributes, each specified as a *type* (a single ASCII character), a *length* (indicating the length of the following argument), and an ASCII *argument*. The length is encoded using Kermit's standard excess-32 encoding. For example, the string 1%12345."U1 contains two file attributes. The first is the file length in bytes (1), with a five-byte (%) argument 12345. The second is the type of system the file came from (.), with a two-byte (") argument U1, indicating the file originated on a Unix system (Table 10.10). Table 10.3 lists all of the currently defined file attributes and their encodings.

No Kermit implementation will support all of these attributes. Senders can only send attributes they support. For example, CP/M doesn't store the creation date of files; MS-DOS has no notion of a file owner; Unix files don't have a record format. Similarly, receivers can interpret only attributes that make sense for them.

For common microcomputer operating systems, the two file length attributes (! and 1), the file type ("), the encoding (*), and the creation date (#) are the most important attributes. The file type and encoding require some explanation.

The file types shown in Table 10.4 include a couple of options that may seem odd to programmers familiar with microcomputers. In particular, the option to specify the byte size is an artifact of systems such as the DECSYSTEM-20, which had a large memory word, with direct hardware support for a variety of different byte sizes. On such systems, the byte size of the data is an important attribute: text files could be variously stored with five, six, seven, or eight bits per byte, with these

Argument	Description
N	(New) Create a new file under this name.
S	(Supersede) Overwrite a preexisting file of the same name.
W	(Warn) Don't overwrite a preexisting file; rename this file if necessary.
A	(Append) If file already exists, add this to end of that file.

Table 10.5   Kermit File Management Attribute ( )) Arguments

Argument	Description
A	Normal Kermit prefix encoding, ASCII character set.
C$xxxx$	Normal Kermit prefix encoding, specified character set. (Table 10.7)
E	EBCDIC text file sent with normal Kermit prefix encoding.
X	Encrypted.
H	Hexadecimal encoding.
3	3-for-2 encoding, each two bytes are decomposed into three bytes in base 64.
4	4-for-3 encoding, like the original uuencode encoding described on page 41.

Table 10.6   Kermit Encoding Attribute (*) Arguments

bytes then packed into 36-bit words in various fashions. Again, microcomputer programs usually only need to support A and B, and should usually accept I as a synonym for B. Although the A file type allows the line separator to be given, for compatibility with old receivers and receivers that do not fully process this attribute, text files should *always* be sent with CR/LF line separators.

Like ZModem, Kermit allows the sender to suggest how file collisions should be handled. How these interact with any options the user has manually specified to the receiver depends on the implementation. The popular C-Kermit implementation takes the sender's specification when one is given, treating the user's instructions to the receiver as a default.

Most of the encodings specified in Table 10.6 have never been implemented, although if you're implementing both sides of a Kermit connection, you may want to consider using encoding type 4 for some binary files. The most important encoding is the C encoding that specifies the character set. With Kermit gaining

Code	Name and Description
I6	US ASCII.
I6/100	ISO 8859-1, Latin 1 (Danish, Dutch, English, Faeroese, Finnish, French, German, Icelandic, Irish, Italian, Norwegian, Portuguese, Spanish, Swedish).
I6/101	ISO 8859-2, Latin 2 (Albanian, Czech, English, German, Hungarian, Polish, Romanian, Croatian, Slovak, Slovene).
I6/109	ISO 8859-3, Latin 3 (Afrikaans, Catalan, Dutch, English, Esperanto, French, Galician, German, Italian, Maltese, Spanish, Turkish).
I6/110	ISO 8859-4, Latin 4 (Danish, English, Estonian, Finnish, German, Greenlandic, Lappish/Sami, Latvian, Lithuanian, Norwegian, Swedish).
I6/144	ISO 8859-5, Cyrillic (Bulgarian, Byelorussian, English, Macedonian, Russian, Serbian, Ukrainian).
I6/127	ISO 8859-6, Arabic.
I6/126	ISO 8859-7, Greek.
I6/138	ISO 8859-8, Hebrew.
I6/148	ISO 8859-9, Latin 5 (Danish, Dutch, English, Faeroese, Finnish, French, German, Irish, Italian, Norwegian, Portuguese, Spanish, Swedish, Turkish).
I14/13	JIS x 0201, Japanese Katakana.
I14/87/13	Japanese EUC, Japanese Katakana and Kanji.
I6/58	Chinese GB 2312-80, Chinese.
I6/149	KS C 5601 (1989), Korean.
I6/180	TCVN 5712:1993, Vietnamese.

Table 10.7   Kermit Character Set Codes

attention worldwide, problems have arisen with users transferring files between systems (such as Macintosh and MS-DOS) that use different encodings for letters other than the standard US ASCII characters. (In some cases, even those vary!) In any environment in which eight-bit or 16-bit characters are a possibility, the Kermit program should support US ASCII and at least one other character set from Table 10.7. For example, Macintosh and MS-DOS Kermit programs should support ISO Latin 1. Whenever files containing extended characters are transferred, the sender should convert into one of the standard character sets, and specify the character set used in the encoding attribute. For example, a Macintosh Kermit may

Argument	Description
M$xxxx$	Mail file to specified user.
O$xxxx$	Send the file as a message to the specified terminal, job, or user.
S$xxxx$	Submit the file as a batch job, with any specified options.
P$xxxx$	Print the file, with any specified options.
T	Type the file on the screen, equivalent to starting the file with a Text (X) packet.
L$xxxx$	Load the file into memory at the given decimal address.
X$xxxx$	Like L, except execute the file after loading.
A	Archive the file; save all Kermit attributes in some fashion so the file can be sent with identical attributes later.

Table 10.8   Kermit Disposition Attribute (+) Arguments

choose to translate extended characters into ISO Latin 1 and specify *'CI6/100 as one of the attributes. Then the receiver will be able to translate such characters as ÿ into whatever character encoding is in use on the receiving system.

The character set names in Table 10.7 have a simple structure. The first character is the *registration authority*. Right now, all of the standard character sets are ISO standards, but that may change in the future. For ISO eight-bit character sets, there are two numbers separated by a slash. The first number indicates the encoding for the "left half" (a 6 here indicates the lower 128 characters are identical to US ASCII), and the second number is the encoding for the "right half." Which character sets are supported by a given implementation will depend on the system and the country. Clearly, a version intended for use in Russia will need to support ISO Cyrillic, which may be impossible on a Mexican version that runs on a computer that does not support Cyrillic characters. Chapter 5 gives a more thorough discussion of character sets, character set translation, and other related issues.

Kermit implementations on large systems may allow a file to be conveniently redirected to a variety of system utilities. The disposition attributes listed in Table 10.8 allow the sender to request an unusual destination for the file. The most interesting is the A disposition, which is intended to allow files with complex attributes to be transferred through one or more intermediate systems before it arrives at a system that fully supports the specified attributes.

I'll briefly discuss some of the mainframe-oriented attributes, even though it's unlikely you'll encounter them. Many mainframe file systems treat files as databases. Unlike the Unix model, in which a file is simply a sequence of bytes, a

Argument	Description
Ax	Variable-length records with delimiters. Like A in Table 10.4.
Dn	Variable-length records preceded by a n-character decimal length; for example, 0005A indicates the one-character record "A," assuming D4.
Fn	Fixed-length records of n bytes each.
Rn	In conjunction with one of the above, each record begins with an n-byte file offset where the record is stored.
Mn	In conjunction with one of the above, indicates the maximum record length for variable-length records.

Table 10.9   Kermit Data Record Format Attribute (/) Arguments

mainframe file is a sequence of records. Sometimes, all records are the same size, and sometimes they are variably sized. Text files, for example, are often stored as variably sized records, each holding a single line of text, while binary files are often stored in fixed size records. In transferring such files, the file's format (fixed or variable length records, record separator, access method, and so on) must be preserved as closely as possible. The data record format attribute (/) specifies both the record format of the original file and how the sender will separate records in transit.

The system name attribute is arguably one of the least useful attributes, but it is widely implemented for two reasons. First, it is easy to implement (just add a constant four-character string to the sent attributes, for example, ."L1 for a Commodore PET implementation of Kermit). Second, Kermit implementors are often proud of the system they use and want to advertise it. Table 10.10 gives a list of the system types defined by Kermit. Additional codes can be obtained from Columbia University if they are needed.

Server Command Transactions

To simplify use for less computer-literate users, most mainframe and minicomputer implementations of Kermit support *server mode*, in which the Kermit implementation continuously waits for the next Kermit transaction. The local Kermit implementation can then present a simple, menu-driven interface to allow the user to do certain common tasks.

Note that each transaction begins with packet number zero. If appropriate, any transaction may begin with a Send-Init (S) packet to negotiate which features

Code	Name of System	Code	Name of System
A	Apple computer	J	Tandy microcomputer
A1	Apple II	K	Atari microcomputer
A2	Apple III	K1	Atari eight-bit computer
A3	Apple Macintosh	K2	Atari ST
A4	Apple Lisa	L	Commodore microcomputer
B	Sperry/Univac mainframe	L1	Commodore Pet
B1	Sperry/Univac 1100 series	L2	Commodore 64
B2	Sperry/Univac 9080, VS9	L3	Commodore Amiga
C	CDC Cyber mainframe	M	Misc. mainframe/mini
C1	CDC Cyber, NOS	M1	Gould/SEL mini, MPX
C2	CDC Cyber, NOS-BE	M2	Harris, VOS
C3	CDC Cyber, NOS-VE	M3	Perkin-Elmer mini, OS/32
C4	CDC Cyber, SCOPE	M5	Tandem, Nonstop
D	DEC computer	M6	Cray, CTSS
D1	DECSYSTEM-10/20, TOPS-10	M7	Burroughs
D2	DECSYSTEM-10/20, TOPS-20	M8	GEC4000, OS4000
D3	DECSYSTEM-10/20, TENEX	M9	ICL machines
D4	DECSYSTEM-10/20, ITS	MA	Norsk Data, Sintran III
D5	DECSYSTEM-10/20, WAITS	MB	Nixdorf machines
D6	DECSYSTEM-10/20, MAXC	MS	Soviet EC-1840
D7	DEC VAX-11, VMS	MV	Stratus VOS
D8	DEC PDP-11, RSX-11	N	Misc. micro/workstation
D9	DEC PDP-11, IAS	N1	Acorn BBS
DA	DEC PDP-11, RSTS/E	N2	Alpha Micro
DB	DEC PDP-11, RT-11	N3	Appolo Aegis
DC	DEC Professional-300, P/OS	N4	Convergent/Burroughs
DD	DEC Word Processor	N5	Corvus, CCOS
DE	DEC PDP-8, OS8, or RTS8	N6	Cromemco, CDOS
E	Honeywell mainframe	N7	Intel x86/3x9, iRMS-x86
E1	Honeywell MULTICS system	N8	Intel MDS, ISIS
E2	Honeywell DPS series, CP-6	N9	Luxor ABC-800, ABCDOS
E3	Honeywell DPS series, GCOS	NA	Perq
E4	Honeywell DTSS	NB	Motorola, Versados
F	Data General system	NC	Sinclair QL/QDOS
F1	Data General RDOS	U	Portable Operating System
F2	Data General AOS	U1	Unix and related systems
F3	Data General AOS/VS	U2	Software Tools
G	PR1ME, PRIMOS	U3	CP/M-80
H	Hewlett-Packard	U4	CP/M-86
H1	HP-1000, RTE	U5	CP/M-68k
H2	HP-3000, MPE	U6	MP/M
I	IBM 370 compatible systems	U7	Concurrent CP/M
I1	IBM 370, VM/CMS	U8	MS-DOS
I2	IBM 370, MVS/TSO	U9	UCSD p-System
I3	IBM 370, DOS/VSE	UA	MUMPS
I4	IBM 370, MUSIC	UB	LISP
I5	IBM 370, MVS/GUTS	UC	FORTH
I6	IBM 370, MTS	UD	OS-9
I7	IBM, CICS	UE	PICK
I8	IBM, WYLBUR	UO	OS/2
I9	IBM, ROSCOE		

Table 10.10   Kermit System Attribute (.) Arguments

should be used for that transaction. Any features negotiated are "forgotten" as soon as that transaction is complete.

The easiest transaction is sending a file. The server is normally waiting for packet 0 to arrive. The local Kermit can send a file as it normally would.

To get a file from a Kermit server, send a Receive-Init (R) packet with the name(s) of the file(s) the server should send. This is the one place in the Kermit protocol where the typical response to a packet will not be an acknowledgment (Y). Rather, the server will either respond with a Send-Init (S) packet (with packet number zero) to begin the transfer, an Error (E) packet if the Receive-Init was mangled, or a negative acknowledge (N) if the Receive-Init was totally lost.

Note that every file transfer in server mode begins with a Send-Init, just as a stand-alone transfer would. The catch is that since the sender begins the negotiation, there's no way for the local Kermit to request the server use windows or other features. To remedy this, the local Kermit can issue an Init (I) transaction. The Init packet contains an initialization string just as a Send-Init or its acknowledgment does, but the server interprets this string as a suggested configuration for future transfers. Note that the Init transaction is a separate transaction, and is merely a request by the receiver. Any subsequent file transfer still will start with a Send-Init (S), and the usual negotiation rules (and defaults) still apply.

Simply transferring files is often insufficient. Kermit provides several facilities that allow a client to request a variety of operations from the server. Often, an operation results in some text that needs to be displayed to the user. This text can be returned in the acknowledgment (Y) packet, or may be handled through a text transfer. A text transfer is identical to a file transfer except that the File (F) packet is replaced with a Text (X) packet.

The most general transactions are initiated by the Command (C) or Kermit-Command (K) packets. The argument to these packets are prefix-encoded strings containing a command for the server's host command interpreter or the server's own command interpreter, respectively. There are four responses the server might make:

- If the command was not received, the server will respond with a negative acknowledge (N) packet.

- If the command was received, but could not be executed, the server will respond with an error (E) packet containing a text error message.

- If the command was received and executed, and the output from the command is short enough, the server will respond with an acknowledgment (Y) containing a prefix-encoded string with the output of the command.

Code	Description
C	Change to specified directory.
D	Directory listing.
E	Erase specified files.
F	Finish. Server program terminates.
I	Login.
J	Control Journal logging of transactions.
K	Copy the file.
L	Logout.
M	Send short message to indicated user.
P	Execute named program; output is displayed to user.
R	Rename or relocate the file.
T	Type specified file.
U	Disk usage query.
V	Set or query a server variable.
W	List who is currently logged in.

Table 10.11   Kermit Generic Command Codes

- If the command was received and executed, but the output is too long for a single packet acknowledgment, the server will respond with a Send-Init (S) or Text (X) packet initiating the transfer of the full output of the command.

Unfortunately, the commands for the Command and Kermit-Command packets are in the server's language, which by definition will vary among servers. To avoid this dependency, the Generic-Command (G) packet was developed. The Generic-Command packet is used like the Command or Kermit-Command packets, but its argument is encoded in a special way. The argument to the Generic-Command packet has a single character command code from Table 10.11, followed by one or more strings for the command. As with the Attributes packet, each string is preceded by a length value, offset by 32. For example, E%file1 is the Erase command (E), with the five character (%) argument file1. Similarly, K%file1&file10 is the command to copy file1 to file10. Unlike the Attribute packet, however, the argument to the Generic-Command packet *is* prefix encoded after it is constructed.

Here's a more complete description of the generic commands and their arguments. Depending on the system, any of these can have a response. That response can be either a single acknowledge (Y) packet or a text transfer of any length. For example, the C command may respond with the name of the resulting directory, while the E command may respond with a list of files successfully erased.

C   The change directory command requires the first argument to be the name of the desired directory. An optional second argument can contain a password for the directory.

D   The directory command returns a list of files. An optional argument can specify which files to list. If possible, file sizes and creation dates should be included in the list.

E   The erase command has one argument, which specifies the files to be erased.

F   The finish command requires no arguments. After receiving this command, the server terminates.

I   A Kermit server can provide the primary access to a computer system. In that situation, the first transaction sent by a user will be a login command. The first argument specifies the user name, the second argument specifies a password, and an optional third argument specifies any additional account information. If no arguments are given, this is equivalent to a logout (L) command.

J   The journal command allows the client to control how the server records information. The first argument contains one of the characters + (begin/resume logging), - (suspend logging), C (suspend logging and close the log file), or S (list the log file to the user). The + option has an optional second argument specifying the name of the file to use for logging.

K   The copy command has two arguments specifying the source and destination, respectively.

L   On some systems, the logout command is synonymous with the finish (F) command.

M   The message command has two arguments, the user to whom to send the message, and the text of the message.

P   The program command executes a particular program and returns the output to the user. The first argument is the name of the program to run. The optional second argument specifies any commands or options to give to the program. On systems that have a notion of a "current" program, the first argument can have a zero length, in which case the current program is run.

R   The rename command accepts two arguments, the file to rename, and the new name. On some systems, this command may also allow a file to be moved from one directory to another.

T   The type command accepts a filename and returns the contents of that file to the user.

U   The usage command accepts one optional argument specifying the disk or file area to be queried. If omitted, the amount of space used and free in the "current" disk or file area is returned.

V   Many servers have internal variables that can be altered or queried. Many additional features can be added in this fashion, for example, a query for the value of "phone tony" may result in the server looking up and returning a phone number from a system database. The first argument to the V command is a letter specifying whether a variable is to be set (S) or queried (Q). If a variable is to be set, the second argument specifies the variable name, and the third the value. If the value is omitted, the variable is unset. To query a variable, the second argument specifies the variable to query. If the variable name is omitted, a list of all currently active variables and their values should be returned.

W   The who command allows the user to request information about other users on the same system. The optional first argument can specify a particular user or a particular host to be queried. A second argument can be used to provide additional options.

A few final notes about server transactions. Normally, the server is waiting for packet zero to arrive. In some older implementations, the server will periodically send a negative acknowledge (N) packet to prompt a response. These packets can be buffered at various points in the connection, as many as several hundred. Kermit implementations that provide server support should be careful not to become confused by a large number of these packets. A client, before starting a new server transaction, may need to carefully flush incoming data buffers and take other steps to clear these buffered packets. Because of these problems, newer server implementations do not send out these packets

Session Layer

As you might expect from the preceding discussion, Kermit's initial capabilities exchange has gained several new fields. The first nine fields shown in Table 10.12

Length	Description
1	Normal packet length.
1	Timeout.
1	Number of pad characters.
1	Pad Character.
1	End-of-packet character.
1	Control prefix.
1	Eighth-bit prefix.
1	Packet check.
1	Repeat prefix.
variable	Capabilities bitmap.
1	Window size, offset by 32.
2	Extended packet length.

Table 10.12   Kermit Extended Capabilities String

were discussed on page 120. As described there, a Kermit capabilities string contains three parts. The first part consists of the nine fields discussed earlier. The second part is a bitmap that allows specific capabilities to be enabled. The bitmap has a variable size which allows future capabilities to be added without restriction. The third section consists of fixed-size fields in fixed positions, but, because of the variable length of the capabilities bitmap, their positions in the capabilities string are not fixed.

The capabilities bitmap encodes five capabilities into each byte, which is then converted into a single printable character by adding 32. The value of the byte is obtained by adding together the capabilities codes as listed in Table 10.13. In addition, one is added if there is another byte in the bitmap. Note that even though there is currently only one byte in the capabilities bitmap, that may change, and implementations must be careful to correctly locate the end of the bitmap before reading any fields that follow the capabilities bitmap.

Attributes Capability   This bit indicates that attributes packets can be received.

Windowing Capability   If this bit is set, the first byte following the capabilities bitmap is used to specify the maximum window size that can be supported. The actual window size to be used will be the largest that both sides support. If either side fails to specify this bit, a window size of one will be used. Note that this bit must be checked before interpreting the window size value. Kermit

Value	Description
2	I can receive long packets.
4	I can support windowing.
8	I can receive Attributes packets.
16	I can receive extra-long packets.
32	I can send and receive locking shifts.

Table 10.13   Kermit Capabilities Bitmap

implementations that support long packet sizes but not windowing still have to put some value in the window size field to specify the packet size field that follows.

Locking Shifts   Locking shifts will be used only if both sides specify the capability and an eighth-bit prefix is successfully negotiated. This makes more sense if you keep in mind that an eighth-bit prefix should always be negotiated over seven-bit connections, and that locking shifts are of no use over eight-bit connections.

Extended Packets   If either extended packet bit is set, the extended length field specifies the longest packet that can be received. This field is always two characters representing a number in base 95. If extra-long packets are not supported, the value is taken as-is. If extra-long packets are supported, the value should be multiplied by 95 to obtain the actual maximum packet length supported. Note that this dual interpretation complicates the negotiation, because a Kermit implementation that does not support extra-long packets may interpret the extended length field as a much smaller size than was intended.

Analysis

The slowness of the original Kermit protocol has been addressed rather thoroughly by the addition of longer packets, full-duplex transfers, and relaxed encoding constraints.

When carefully tuned with large packets, a suitable window size, and minimal encoding, Kermit transfers are about the same speed as ZModem over good quality connections. When there are both channel delays and errors, Kermit is noticeably faster. This latter effect is because when an error occurs, the ZModem receiver must ignore data already in the channel, while the Kermit receiver can receive and store good packets already in transit when the error occurred, without requiring that data to be resent.

References

The best reference for the Kermit protocol is Frank da Cruz's book *Kermit: A File Transfer Protocol* [4]. Unfortunately, the book is a bit dated now, and many of the Kermit extensions described in this chapter do not appear there. Some discussion of these extensions is given in the manuals for C-Kermit [5] and MS-Kermit [8]. More detailed descriptions of the newer Kermit extensions are available from the archives at `kermit.columbia.edu`.

More information about Kermit can be obtained by contacting:

Office of Kermit Development and Distribution
Columbia University
612 West 115th Street
New York, New York 10025, USA
Voice: +1 212 854-3703
Fax: +1 212 663-8202
Email: kermit@columbia.edu
Web: http://www.columbia.edu/kermit/

Designing Your Own 11

If none of the protocols I've described so far meet your needs, you may have to design your own protocol from scratch. Paying careful attention to the pros and cons of existing protocol designs can help ensure the success of your protocol.

Existing protocols won't always meet your requirements. For example, none of the protocols I've discussed is particularly well suited to bi-directional data flow, such as is required by some games and productivity programs that allow two players on two different computers to interact. In embedded applications, the size of the implementation may be critical, leading you to devise your own protocol that can be effectively implemented in the small amount of memory available. Unusual channels, such as the use of broadcast radio to initially transfer data followed by a separate two-way error-correction phase, may also rule out existing protocols.

Regardless of your needs, all serial protocols rely on the same basic ideas. The five layers discussed in Chapter 2 cover the essential parts of any serial protocol, and the protocols described in the preceding chapters show some of the various ways those parts function in practice. Understanding them is the key to making your protocol as good as possible.

Defining Your Needs

The first step, of course, is to define what your protocol needs to accomplish. The better you can define your requirements, the easier it will be to develop a protocol to fit those needs. For starters, you need to know the type of channel you'll be using and what type of data you'll be transferring. These two are interrelated. If you'll only be transferring seven-bit text, it becomes much easier to build a protocol that works over seven-bit channels.

145

Protocol Considerations

One of the motivations behind the layered protocol model I've been using in this book is to isolate some of the different issues that arise in the design and analysis of serial protocols. Each different component attempts to deal with a very different set of issues.

Encoding Layer

The method used to encode your data depends heavily on the type of data and the transparency of your channel. Generally, for highly random binary data (such as compressed data), radix encoding provides less expansion at a slightly higher processing cost. The advantage of radix encoding over prefix approaches becomes dramatic when you consider transferring random binary data over seven-bit channels. On the other hand, if your data is relatively well suited to your channel, prefix encoding is faster and often easier to implement.

Packetization Layer

Even if you don't currently plan to run your protocol over seven-bit channels, there are some good reasons to design your packets using text encodings for the packet overhead.

The first is, of course, that someday you may need to adapt to a seven-bit channel, and that's much easier if you don't need to change your packet format. With a carefully-designed packet format, adapting to a seven-bit channel may only require altering the encoding used for the actual data.

A text format also simplifies debugging. When viewing packets in a debug log or data scope, it is usually easier to spot and understand packets that use text representations rather than binary numbers. For example, Kermit's Y and N packets are easier to understand than XModem's use of characters 0x06 and 0x15.

Two good examples of text-format packets are ZModem's hexadecimal packets and Kermit's packet format. Each exhibits different trade-offs. ZModem encodes numbers in a relatively easy-to-read hexadecimal encoding, while Kermit uses a more compact base 64 or base 95 encoding. Similarly, Kermit uses mnemonic letters for packet types, while ZModem uses numeric values.

Reliability Layer

Deciding between half-duplex and full-duplex reliability is difficult. If the typical channel has a short delay, it may be best to use a half-duplex reliability approach at first, adding full-duplex reliability later. Kermit shows that allowing for such an extension is not particularly difficult. If your protocol needs to carry a lot of data, and channels with long delays are going to be common, you may have no choice but to go with a full-duplex approach from the beginning. Even here, though, it is often wise to make the full-duplex aspect a negotiated feature. Doing so simplifies future implementations by allowing them to be written as half duplex initially, then tested and later extended to full duplex.

One way to simplify full-duplex is to use the same shortcut as ZModem and UUCP's G protocol. Both of these allow the receiver to ignore out-of-sequence data. This is a good approach when your channels will almost always be either error-free or have no delay. If both errors and delays are common, however, Kermit-style packet reassembly is the only way to maintain good throughput.

Transaction Layer

As I mentioned earlier, one of the reasons you may be developing your own protocol is that it requires transactions not available with existing protocols. Determining what types of transactions your protocol will need depends heavily on your application.

Session Layer

When designing custom protocols, the session-layer issues of starting, ending, and cancelling the protocol are often forgotten. Be careful to include an initial capabilities exchange at the beginning of the protocol. Even if it's simply empty now, it will serve as the cornerstone for future enhancements. Also think carefully about the impact of new packet types. The protocols described in this book often terminate immediately when they see a packet they don't understand. Depending on how you expect your protocol to evolve, it may be more appropriate to simply ignore unrecognized packet types.

Planning Ahead

Many people who design protocols expect that their protocol will never change. Not surprisingly, when it becomes necessary for those protocols to change, it's often more difficult than it should be. The bottom line is this: Every successful protocol changes. Protocols that can't change get replaced rather than extended.

Implementation

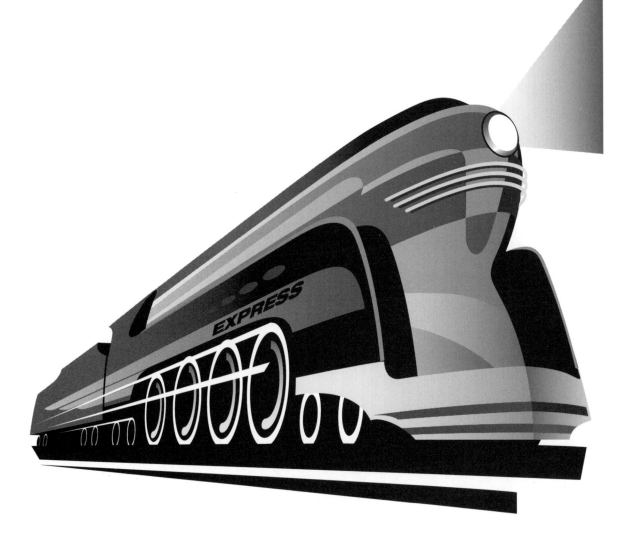

Coding Issues

12

Before delving into the nitty-gritty coding details, I'll go over some of the general concerns and techniques that you should keep in mind, both as you read my implementations and as you consider writing your own.

Why C?

One of the purposes of this book is to provide portable, easily understood implementations of the basic file transfer protocols. To provide portability, I've chosen to present those implementations in the C programming language. C is currently one of the most widely available languages, with implementations for nearly every system. With the ANSI/ISO standard gaining widespread acceptance, it's relatively easy to provide C code that will compile and be usable on a variety of platforms.

However, C is not as readable as some alternatives. Its terse notation sometimes confuses even experienced users. It also places strong restrictions on the order in which the program must appear (for example, identifiers must be declared before being used), which means that straight C program listings are not always in the best order to be *understood*.

To address these concerns, I've used a system called CWEB to format the source code in this book. The advantage of CWEB is that it allows the source code to be rearranged in a fashion that (hopefully) makes it easier to understand, while still allowing me to compile and test the code directly from the text of the book. The result should be easier for you to read and understand while providing the reassurance that the code hasn't been possibly altered by being retyped or copied. The source code on the accompanying disk was extracted from the text automatically.

The only change from standard C syntax is the use of named *scraps* of code, as in this example:

```
int SomeFunction(int someArg)
{
  ⟨ Some variables  152 ⟩
  ⟨ Some work  152 ⟩
  return returnVal;
}
```

The names ⟨ Some variables 152 ⟩ and ⟨ Some work 152 ⟩ refer to scraps of code that are defined on page 152. These page numbers make it easier to quickly find the definition of a scrap. Notice that after a scrap, there's a list of the pages where that scrap is used, as well as a list of pages where additional definitions appear:

⟨ Some variables 152 ⟩ ==
```
  int i1;
```
See also page 152.
This code is used on page 152.

Sometimes, it makes more sense to show how something is used before explaining what it is, such as `returnVal` in this scrap:

⟨ Some work 152 ⟩ ==
```
  i1 = someArg * 2;
  returnVal = sqrt(i1);
```
This code is used on page 152.

Scraps can be defined in pieces, which is especially useful for global variables, which in C often need to be defined early in the file, but make more sense to define near where they are used. Note that the page number refers only to the page where the first part of the scrap is defined.

⟨ Some variables 152 ⟩ +==
```
  int returnVal;
```

General Conventions

Every programmer has developed personal preferences for naming variables and functions, and structuring source code. To help you better understand my coding, here's a brief summary of some of my conventions:

- Variables and functions have mixed-case names. Variable names begin with a lower case letter (`variableName`), while function names begin with an upper case letter (`FunctionName`).

- The names of constants and `typedef` tags are in upper case with words separated by an underscore character (`NEW_TYPE`, `SOME_CONSTANT`).

- Pointer variables are prefixed with a p character (pCount).

- The source is broken into *modules*. Each module is defined by two files: a .h header file publishing the module interface and a .c source file with the module implementation. Similarly, all filenames are prefixed with ft (File Transfer) to reduce filename conflicts when merging these files into existing source code. For example, the disk module is defined in ftdisk.h and ftdisk.c.

- Function and global variables use the name of the module as a prefix; for example, functions in the Z module have Z as their first character (ZReceiveFile). This convention eases merging these modules into existing source code, and reduces the chance of naming conflicts. For similar reasons, functions and variables are declared static whenever possible.

- With only a few exceptions, module interfaces are handled through function calls rather than published variables or data structures. Publicly, most modules provide a data type that is made equivalent to void * in the header. This pointer points to a private structure that is only visible within the module. Among other benefits, this arrangement should simplify converting modules into classes in object-oriented languages.

- I do heavily use ANSI typing constructs, including function prototypes, const, and unsigned. These constructs have proven invaluable in detecting minor errors at compile-time. The code currently compiles with no warning or error messages under GCC versions 1.42 and 2.5.8.[1]

- The code assumes that short is at least 16 bits and long is at least 32 bits. These sizes are the minimum guaranteed by ANSI, and are common even in pre-ANSI compilers.

- Beyond the ANSI typing constructs mentioned above, I've avoided a number of ANSI features that are not available in all C compilers or which would make it more difficult to port the code to another language, including: token-pasting, stringizing, variable argument lists, floating point arithmetic, and global variables. I've also attempted to limit my use of unusual library calls.

---

[1] If your favorite compiler can find any nit in this source, please notify me and the error will be fixed in a later edition of the book. I can be contacted through the publisher.

- The core protocol implementations should be *completely* system independent. The protocols interface with serial, disk, and progress reporting capabilities through a set of small stub functions in each protocol implementation. Depending on the complexity of the interface, these can be modified to directly call the relevant system services. In the provided code, these are simply interface calls to functions in the `serial`, `progress`, and `disk` modules.

Overview of the Source

The source code on the accompanying disk consists of seven modules. These modules are explained in detail in the following chapters. Here's a quick overview:

debug   The `ftdebug.h` and `ftdebug.c` files provide a collection of debugging routines that I've found useful in developing and maintaining this code. The module allows debugging messages to be selectively enabled at run-time, and allows the messages to be redirected to a file for later perusal.

serial   The `ftserial.h` and `ftserial.c` files interface to the serial port. While the details are necessarily system-dependent, the description in Chapter 14 provides many suggestions for implementing this interface on specific systems.

disk   The `ftdisk.h` and `ftdisk.c` files provide additional file interfacing beyond what is normally found in C libraries. In particular, this module guesses the type of data in the file, and provides some system-dependent translation for text files.

progress   The `ftprog.h` and `ftprog.c` files provide a generic interface for reporting transfer progress. The implementation here simply displays a text summary of the progress, but it can be easily adapted to other types of display. (Unfortunately, `ftprogress.c` is too long for some systems.)

xy   The `ftxy.h` and `ftxy.c` files provide a combined implementation of XModem and YModem. The `xy` module can automatically adapt to the most common XModem and YModem dialects.

z   The `ftz.h` and `ftz.c` files implement the ZModem protocol, including command uploading and downloading.

k   The `ftk.h` and `ftk.c` files implement the Kermit protocol, including many of the more advanced features described in Chapter 10.

Error Handling

In one sense, the entire purpose of a serial protocol *is* error handling, so it's not surprising that this is a central concern. I've adopted several coding conventions specifically to simplify error handling.

- Every function that can possibly produce an error returns an integer that represents the error value. A value of zero means that no error occurred. Many function calls are immediately followed by `switch` statements to handle any error value returned.

- Each module defines its own symbolic error codes. If those error codes need to be exported, they're defined in the header file. Error codes always begin with the name of the module, to avoid cross-module naming conflicts.

- Two macros have been very useful. `StsRet` takes a single argument, a variable or expression. It evaluates that expression once and causes the current function to return its value if the value is an error value. `StsWarn` calls an error-reporting function that displays any error values to the screen, along with the file and line number where the error occurred. These macros are redefined in each module source.

```
#define StsRet(expr)  do {
        int tmpErrorVal = (expr);      /* Evaluate expr only once */
        if (tmpErrorVal != xyOK)      /* If an error was generated... */
            return StsWarn(tmpErrorVal);      /* ...return the error */
        } while (FALSE)      /* Require a semicolon after StsRet */
#define StsWarn(expr)  WarningFunction((expr),__FILE__,__LINE__)
    int WarningFunction(int errorVal, const char *fileName, int
        lineNumber);
        /* Generate a warning message if errorVal is non-zero */
```

Multitasking

Serial protocols can be time-consuming, but needn't be very CPU intensive. Users expect to be able to perform other tasks while file transfers are occurring. Even under non-multitasking operating systems, applications are often written in a multitasking fashion to provide a responsive user interface even while other operations are happening.

Good implementations of serial protocols must understand how the system or application handles multiple tasks, so the program responds quickly enough to incoming data. Real-time operating systems provide many features to ensure that waiting processes are notified quickly and predictably when outside events occur. These features allow programs such as serial protocols to simply wait for incoming data, assured that the operating system will awaken them promptly when data is available.

Unfortunately, most popular operating systems are not real-time. When real-time features are not available, serial protocol implementations need to interact closely with the operating system to ensure predictable response. Depending on the system, this may include juggling process priorities, locking the code into memory, or executing part of the serial protocol implementation in some privileged fashion, for example, as a device driver.

Another reason that good serial protocol implementations must be aware of the system's multitasking strategy is to minimize the system load. One extreme approach to guaranteeing fast response to arriving data is to take over the entire system. Such a heavy-handed approach doesn't permit other tasks to run.

To illustrate how different multitasking strategies require different approaches to balance the demands of fast response and low CPU load, I'll describe the three most popular multitasking approaches and their impact on implementing efficient file transfers.

Polling: Cooperative "From the Top"

The simplest way to implement multitasking from the system designer's point of view is to have each process be a single function. The operating system then alternately calls each process, which performs whatever task it can and returns immediately so that the next application function can have its chance.

While uncommon among operating systems, this approach is very common among applications that attempt to multitask internally. In fact, the first terminal program I wrote worked in this fashion. Its attraction lies in the simplicity with which it can be implemented. Only a single stack is needed, and the top-level handler needs only to maintain a list of processes. Each process is simply a function pointer.

Obtaining good protocol performance on this type of system requires considerable care. The protocol typically is implemented as a function that is called with newly received data or timeout events. The overhead of storing and restoring the current state is considerable, especially if the protocol function is called once for each byte. To reduce this overhead, protocol implementations for polling systems are typically implemented as state machines. If possible, you should also try to arrange to call the protocol function with chunks of received data rather than single bytes. Since the protocol function cannot be assured of being awakened promptly when data is available, interrupt-driven device drivers need to have ample buffering for received data. On some systems, you may be forced to augment or even replace the system device driver to get acceptable performance at higher speeds.

I've chosen not to implement the protocols in this book as state machines. You'll need to do some additional work to adapt them to a polled system. Instead of rewriting them as state machines, it may be possible to convert them from *subroutines* into *coroutines*, as described in [13] and many other computer science textbooks. This conversion involves adding some code at the top level to create a new stack, switching to this new stack, and executing the protocol as usual. The routines to read serial data should, if there is no data immediately available, switch back to the original stack, and return to the main loop. Subsequent calls will then switch to the protocol's stack and return into the serial read function.

Cooperative "From the Bottom"

In this multitasking approach, each process has its own stack, and the operating system provides a function to switch to the next process. Each process is responsible for calling this system function regularly to ensure that other processes have a chance to execute.

Compared to polling, this approach simplifies the coding of individual processes. It's not necessary for time-consuming operations to be able to completely save their internal state before they relinquish the CPU to another process. The system coding is still fairly simple, primarily because process switches can occur only at safe times. Many popular systems, including Macintosh, Windows, and multitasking Forth kernels, use this approach.

The primary impact on serial protocols is that the routine to wait for data to arrive should be polite and relinquish the processor if no data is immediately available. Depending on the system, it may even be possible to arrange that the system will not resume this process until more data is available. In that case, the protocol process does not use any CPU time during pauses in the transfer. Like polling, there is no guarantee that the protocol will be resumed promptly when data is available, so interrupt-driven device drivers with ample buffering are still a necessity.

Preemptive Multitasking

In preemptive multitasking, the system forcibly switches between tasks without the process specifically relinquishing the processor. Intuitively, it simply requires attaching the process switch routine described above to a periodic interrupt. In practice, certain routines must not be preempted, and the system must be carefully written to avoid synchronization problems.

Preemptive multitasking is becoming the favorite multitasking approach for two reasons. The first is that it places most of the burden on the system, and generally simplifies applications, which needn't return immediately nor remember to call a particular system function frequently. The second reason is that it is necessary for real-time operation, in which external events may require certain processes to awaken immediately without waiting for the current process to relinquish the CPU. Even non-real-time preemptive systems can often provide good performance by setting the critical processes to a very high priority and writing them to be very efficient. The efficiency means that they will not unduly burden the CPU, while the high priority makes them more likely to respond quickly when data becomes available.

Implementing protocols for preemptive systems is not entirely trivial, however. In particular, protocol implementations must be careful to exploit blocking system calls (which don't awaken the process until the operation is complete) rather than looping to repeatedly check the status of some serial operation. Unfortunately, even though almost all preemptive systems provide blocking serial I/O functions, you can't always use them because of the need to handle timeouts. A very few systems provide blocking I/O functions with timeout handling, but most require that you either:

- use a software interrupt (also called a *signal*) to interrupt the I/O function after a certain interval,

- ask the serial port for a software interrupt when data is available, and sleep until that interrupt awakens you, or

- alternately check the serial port status and the timeout interval.

This last option is often both the easiest to program and the worst in terms of CPU overhead. When it's necessary to do this type of iterative check, it may be possible to relinquish the processor for short intervals (such as 1/4 second) between checks, relying on buffering in the device driver to handle bursts of data that occur while you're asleep.

Debugging Tools
13

If you want to really understand how these protocols work, you'll need to watch them in action. You'll also find these tools useful as you adapt my code to your requirements.

The classic debugging approach is to have the program display messages about its current operation. Usually, this is done on an ad-hoc basis, with random `printf`'s scattered throughout the source. Such messages commonly are removed long before the program is shipped.

Especially as programs become larger, however, it's helpful to formalize this common practice somewhat. A good set of instrumentation tools allows run-time control over which messages are displayed, and provides the ability to direct the messages to a file for later perusal.

While the functions in this module do not provide a full set of such features, they do give a framework within which these features can be added. Displaying all debugging messages with this facility creates a deliberate bottleneck where these messages can be intercepted, filtered, saved, or otherwise manipulated. Because the protocols themselves are relatively small, there's no compelling reason for a more complex package at this point.

Public Interface

Every source file in this book has a header file with a similar structure. I'll go over this header file in detail this time only, so you'll see how it works.

⟨ftdebug.h   159⟩ ==

```
#ifndef FTDEBUG_H_INCLUDED
#define FTDEBUG_H_INCLUDED
```

```
    typedef void *DEBUG;
    void DebugInit(DEBUG *pDebugHandle);
    void DebugDestroy(DEBUG debugHandle);
    void DebugFile(DEBUG debugHandle, const char *filename);
    void DebugSetFilter(DEBUG debugHandle, int filter);
  #define DebugBegin(db, selector)DebugBeginInternal
    ((db), (selector), __FILE__, __LINE__)
    void DebugBeginInternal(DEBUG debugHandle, int selector, const
        char *file, int line);      /* Begin a new message */
    void DebugEnd(DEBUG debugHandle);     /* End a message */
    void DebugString(DEBUG, const char *);      /* String to debug log */
    void DebugStringCount(DEBUG, const char *, unsigned long);
        /* String to debug log */
    void DebugInt(DEBUG, long);      /* Integer */
    void DebugUInt(DEBUG, unsigned long);      /* Unsigned integer */
    void DebugIntHex(DEBUG, unsigned long);      /* Integer in hex */
    void DebugPtr(DEBUG, const void *);      /* Pointer */
    void DebugChar(DEBUG, char);      /* Single character */
  #endif      /* ! FTDEBUG_H_INCLUDED */
```

The first thing you'll notice is that the header file is surrounded by a "guard." The macro FTDEBUG_H_INCLUDED is used to prevent the file from being included more than once. If you're well versed in the ANSI standard, you'll recall that carefully-written header files can be safely included more than once, but older compilers may complain about multiple definitions, so it's easier and safer to consistently guard all header files in this fashion.

The header declares DEBUG as a pointer to void. Within the package, this DEBUG *handle* will be cast to a pointer to an appropriate structure. Clients will only see an abstract handle that they manipulate by calling functions in this module.

The rest of the header declares functions to create and destroy a debug handle and to manipulate it in various ways. Briefly, this debugging package is based on building debug *messages*. Each message has a *selector* that describes the significance of this particular message. This selector allows messages to be filtered and otherwise manipulated. Messages are generated by calling DebugBegin with the message selector, making calls to build the text of the message, and finally calling DebugEnd to finish the message.

Two of the functions in this package affect all subsequent debug messages. The first is DebugFile, which specifies a file to which messages will be appended. The second is DebugSetFilter, which specifies a *filter* for selecting only certain messages to be displayed. In this implementation, a filter is a bitmap; a message will be displayed only if the selector specifies one of the bits in the filter. The default filter has all bits set.

If your C compiler fully supports the ANSI/ISO C standard, you may want to add a DebugPrintF function, which accepts a `printf`-style argument list, and generates a single message from that list. Such a function would probably look something like the following:

```
void DebugPrintF(DEBUG, int selector, char *format, ...);
```

Implementation

Because debugging isn't the purpose of the book, I've deliberately kept this implementation simple. I just use the `<stdio.h>` library to dump messages to the standard error path.

```
#include "ftdebug.h"
#include <stddef.h>    /* size_t */
#include <stdio.h>
  int fprintf(FILE *, const char *, ...);
  char *sprintf(char *, const char *, ...);
  FILE *fopen(const char *, const char *);
  void fclose(FILE *);
  void fflush(FILE *);    /* int putc(int, FILE *); */
#include <stdlib.h>    /* malloc, free */
  void *malloc(size_t);
  void free(void *);
#include <time.h>    /* time_t, struct tm, time, localtime, ctime */
  time_t time(time_t *);
  struct tm *localtime(const time_t *);
  char *ctime(const time_t *);
#include <string.h>    /* strlen */
  int strlen(const char *);
```

Internally, a DEBUG_PRIVATE structure keeps just a handful of values: the filter parameter (0 by default), the selector for the current message, and the file to receive the messages.

```
typedef struct {
  unsigned int filter;    /* Currently active filter condition */
  int thisSelect;    /* Selector for this message */
  FILE *outputFile;    /* File to send messages to */
} DEBUG_PRIVATE;
```

Private Routines

The DebugPrint function is a deliberate bottleneck. It handles the filtering and display.

A slight modification of this function would make it quite useful even in production code. Allocate a block of memory and use it as a queue to save the most recent messages. A suitably hidden control can allow end users to dump that block of memory to a file, allowing post-mortem debugging of user problems.

```
static void DebugPrint(DEBUG_PRIVATE *pD, const char *msg, int
        length)
{
  if ((pD) && (pD -> thisSelect & pD -> filter)) {
    while (length -- > 0) putc(*msg ++, pD -> outputFile);
  }
}
```

Handle Management

Creating and destroying a handle is pretty simple, as long as you're careful to initialize the handle correctly.

```
void DebugInit(DEBUG *pdPublic)
{
  DEBUG_PRIVATE *pD;

  *pdPublic = NULL;
  pD = (DEBUG_PRIVATE *) malloc(sizeof (*pD));
  if (pD) {
    pD -> filter = 0xffff;
    pD -> thisSelect = 0;
    pD -> outputFile = stderr;     /* Default path for messages */
    *pdPublic = (void *) pD;
  }
}


void DebugDestroy(DEBUG dPublic)
{
  DEBUG_PRIVATE *pD = (DEBUG_PRIVATE *) dPublic;
  if (pD) {
    if (pD -> outputFile != stderr) fclose(pD -> outputFile);
    free(pD);
  }
}
```

Redirecting error messages to a file involves opening the file in append mode and writing an initial mark and timestamp so you can easily find the start of the debugging messages for this particular run.

```
void DebugFile(DEBUG dPublic, const char *filename)
{
  DEBUG_PRIVATE *pD = (DEBUG_PRIVATE *) dPublic;
  FILE *f;

  if (pD) {
    f = fopen(filename, "a");
    if (f != NULL) {
      time_t  t = time(NULL);

      pD -> outputFile = f;
      fprintf(f, "\n***********************␣%s\n", ctime(&t));
    }
  }
}
```

Message Selection

This filter approach is the simplest one that seems to meet the needs of this project. An alternative approach is to have the filter specify a *level*, and only display messages whose level is below that specified. A hybrid approach, which I've used on some projects, is to have each message specify both a *category* and a *level*. A message is displayed if its level is below the filter level for its category. This technique is useful in large projects, where each source file or package is assigned its own category. It's then possible, at run time, to choose which packages to trace and at which level.

```
void DebugSetFilter(DEBUG dPublic, int filter)
{
  DEBUG_PRIVATE *pD = (DEBUG_PRIVATE *) dPublic;

  if (pD) pD -> filter = filter;
}
```

The current time, to the nearest second, is printed at the beginning of each output message to aid in diagnosing timing-related problems.

```
void DebugBeginInternal(DEBUG dPublic, int select, const char
        *file, int line)
{
  DEBUG_PRIVATE *pD = (DEBUG_PRIVATE *) dPublic;

  if (pD) {
    time_t  t = time(NULL);
```

```
        struct tm *pNow = localtime(&t);
        char tmpString[10];

        pD -> thisSelect = select;      /* Set the selection mask */
        sprintf(tmpString, "%02d:%02d:%02d⌴",      /* Format the time */
        pNow -> tm_hour, pNow -> tm_min, pNow -> tm_sec);
        DebugPrint(pD, tmpString, 9);      /* Print the time */
        DebugPrint(pD, file, strlen(file));
        sprintf(tmpString, ":%d:", line);
        DebugPrint(pD, tmpString, strlen(tmpString));
    }
    return;
}


void DebugEnd(DEBUG dPublic)
{
    DEBUG_PRIVATE *pD = (DEBUG_PRIVATE *) dPublic;
    if (pD) {
        DebugPrint(pD, "\n", 1);
        if (pD -> outputFile == stderr) fflush(pD -> outputFile);
    }
}
```

Logging Specific Data Types

These routines are all very simple. They use `sprintf` to format their argument and display it through `DebugPrint`.

```
        void DebugString(DEBUG dPublic, const char *str)
        {
            DEBUG_PRIVATE *pD = (DEBUG_PRIVATE *) dPublic;
            DebugPrint(pD, str, strlen(str));
        }
```

`DebugStringCount` is used for dumping strings containing binary data. It makes some effort to provide a readable version of its argument, including dumping suitable C-style escapes as appropriate.

```
        void DebugStringCount(DEBUG dPublic, const char *str, unsigned
                long length)
        {
            DEBUG_PRIVATE *pD = (DEBUG_PRIVATE *) dPublic;
            char buff[10];
            int i;
```

```
  for (i = 0; i < length; i++) {
    if ((str[i] >= 0x20) && (str[i] <= 0x7e))
      DebugPrint(pD, str + i, 1);
    else
      switch (str[i]) {
      case 0x0d: DebugPrint(pD, "\\r", 2); break;
      case 0x0a: DebugPrint(pD, "\\l", 2); break;
      case 0x08: DebugPrint(pD, "\\b", 2); break;
      case 0x00: DebugPrint(pD, "\\0", 2); break;
      default: sprintf(buff, "\\x%02x", 255 & (int) (str[i]));
        DebugPrint(pD, buff, 4);
        break;
      }
  }
}


void DebugInt(DEBUG dPublic, const long l)
{
  DEBUG_PRIVATE *pD = (DEBUG_PRIVATE *) dPublic;
  char buff[20];
  sprintf(buff, "%ld", l);
  DebugString(pD, buff);
}


void DebugUInt(DEBUG dPublic, const unsigned long l)
{
  DEBUG_PRIVATE *pD = (DEBUG_PRIVATE *) dPublic;
  char buff[20];
  sprintf(buff, "%lu", l);
  DebugString(pD, buff);
}


void DebugIntHex(DEBUG dPublic, const unsigned long l)
{
  DEBUG_PRIVATE *pD = (DEBUG_PRIVATE *) dPublic;
  char buff[20];
  sprintf(buff, "0x%lX", l);
  DebugString(pD, buff);
}


void DebugPtr(DEBUG dPublic, const void *p)
{
  DEBUG_PRIVATE *pD = (DEBUG_PRIVATE *) dPublic;
```

```
      char buff[20];
      sprintf(buff, "%p", p);
      DebugString(pD, buff);
   }


   void DebugChar(DEBUG dPublic, const char c)
   {
      DebugString(dPublic, "'");
      DebugStringCount(dPublic, &c, 1);
      DebugString(dPublic, "'");
   }
```

Serial Interfacing

14

It's impossible for me to address the details of serial interfacing for every possible system. Instead, this chapter provides a framework from which you can build. Along the way, I'll point out some of the issues that you may encounter.

Unfortunately for this book, serial interfacing is inherently system-dependent. Nowhere does the ANSI/ISO C standard discuss "timeouts" or "parity errors." However, the principles and requirements are pretty common. The interface in this chapter is one I've refined over many years to be both easy to implement on different systems and easy for clients to use. With a little work, it could easily form the basis of a complete serial communications library.

Public Interface

The header file is similar to the header file I described in the previous chapter. The only major difference is a collection of error codes that are returned by the functions in the package.

```
⟨ftserial.h  167⟩ ==
#ifndef SERIAL_H_INCLUDED
#define SERIAL_H_INCLUDED
  typedef void *SERIAL_PORT;
  enum {    /* Error codes returned by functions in this package */
    serialOK = 0, serialTimeout, serialUserCancel, serialFrame,
       serialFatal
  };
#include <stddef.h>    /* size_t */
  ⟨ Port Creation and Configuration 168 ⟩
  ⟨ Basic I/O functions 169 ⟩
```

167

```
#endif     /* ! SERIAL_H_INCLUDED */
```

The interface for creating and configuring the serial port is shaped by the issues I've encountered while writing terminal programs that support file transfers. It's often necessary to alter the serial configuration temporarily and then restore it when done. For example, XModem requires an eight-bit connection with no parity or software flow control. If the original connection didn't satisfy this requirement, it's necessary to change the serial configuration, perform the transfer, and then restore the original configuration. Rather than asking clients to request and store the original configuration, I implement a stack discipline that allows clients to ask the serial port to save its configuration.

⟨ Port Creation and Configuration 168 ⟩ ==
```
    int SerialOpen(SERIAL_PORT *pPort, const char *name);
    int SerialClose(SERIAL_PORT port);
    int SerialSaveState(SERIAL_PORT port);
    int SerialRestoreState(SERIAL_PORT port);
    int SerialSetWord(SERIAL_PORT port, int wordLength);
    enum { parityNone = 0, parityEven, parityOdd };
    int SerialSetParity(SERIAL_PORT port, int parity);
    int SerialMakeTransparent(SERIAL_PORT port);
```
This code is used on page 167.

The `SerialOpen` and `SerialClose` functions create and destroy the serial object. `SerialSaveState` and `SerialRestoreState` implement the stack discipline described earlier. The remainder of these functions alter various parameters. In particular, `SerialMakeTransparent` disables any non-transparent flow control that may be in effect.

The most significant difference between serial I/O and devices such as disk drives or even terminals is the need for a *timeout*. File transfer protocols never simply read data from the port. As mentioned earlier, file transfers are largely an exercise in error handling, and the most likely error is that the data never arrives.

For this reason, the basic function for reading data from a serial port is suggestively called `SerialReadWithTimeout`. Some systems provide a call that satisfies this description, but there are two variants. In one variant, the timeout is an overall limit on the time for the call. In the second, it's an inter-byte timeout. At higher speeds, it doesn't matter. However, at slow speeds, the difference can be pronounced. Reading 1024 bytes of data at 300 baud will take over 30 seconds. It's preferable to have the timeout expire only if no character arrives for the indicated amount of time. For example, if a two second timeout is specified, ten bytes that arrive at one-second intervals can all be read with a single call.

Sending is split into two functions. The first, `SerialSend`, puts the data into a serial queue to be sent, while the second, `SerialWaitForSentBytes`, returns only when the serial queue is empty. This division allows protocols to do certain tasks during the "dead time" while the serial queue empties. Unfortunately, it's not possible to implement `SerialWaitForSentBytes` on all systems. In that case, `SerialSend` should return when the serial queue has emptied.

⟨ Basic I/O functions 169 ⟩ ≡
```
    int SerialReadWithTimeout(SERIAL_PORT port, int
        timeoutSeconds, void *pBuffer, size_t *pLength);
    int SerialSend(SERIAL_PORT port, const void *pBuffer, size_t
        length);
    int SerialWaitForSentBytes(SERIAL_PORT port);
```
See also page 169.

This code is used on page 167.

A handful of miscellaneous I/O functions are useful in certain situations. `SerialPause` simply delays for the indicated amount of time. I've placed it in the serial module for two reasons. First, as mentioned earlier, on some systems it may be necessary for the serial routines to be aware of the user interface, so that user actions (such as a request to cancel a transfer) are handled quickly. Second, on some systems it's necessary to poll the serial port occasionally to prevent low-level buffers from overflowing.

⟨ Basic I/O functions 169 ⟩ +≡
```
    int SerialSendBreak(SERIAL_PORT port);
    int SerialPause(SERIAL_PORT port, int seconds);
```

Note that this interface, while sufficient for the needs of this book, is not sufficient for most communications applications. However, the outline here should be clear enough to allow you to add whatever additional facilities are needed for your application.

External Dependencies

The implementation given here is necessarily sketchy, because of the many system dependencies. The comments should be taken as a rough guide for implementing this package on your particular system.

I start, as usual, by including whatever system headers are needed. Including `ftserial.h` helps to catch any inconsistencies between the public interface declared above and the implementation.

```
    #include "ftserial.h"
```

Most systems will require the inclusion of special headers in addition to the ones mentioned here.

```
#include <stdio.h>
  void fprintf(FILE *, const char *, ...);
#include <stddef.h>    /* size_t */
#include <stdlib.h>    /* malloc, free */
  void *malloc(size_t);
  void free(void *);
```
System-specific headers.

Managing the Serial Port

The save/restore discipline is implemented with a stack of PORT_PARAMS. Each PORT_PARAMS structure holds everything that can be queried and set about a port, including baud rate, parity, word length, and flow control. On many systems, a standard system structure can be put into PORT_PARAMS to hold this information. On other systems, you'll need to declare individual fields for each serial attribute.

On Unix-like systems, it may be appropriate to have two complete sets of such fields. This approach allows for the use of logically different ports for input and output, that is, input through stdin and output through stdout. Using two ports complicates some of the other functions, however, since they'll need to separately manipulate each one.

```
typedef struct PORT_PARAMS PORT_PARAMS;
struct PORT_PARAMS {
  PORT_PARAMS *pNext;
  System-specific fields to record port status.
};
```

The object manipulated by a client is called SERIAL_PORT in the header file, but internally is called a SERIAL_PORT_PRIVATE. A SERIAL_PORT_PRIVATE contains whatever is needed to identify a particular port to the system as well as a pointer to a list of PORT_PARAMS. Note that it's usually unnecessary to keep the current serial port configuration here. As long as the system allows you to query the serial port status, you should rely on the system to keep track of the current status. Relying on the system both simplifies your code and helps avoid the common error of failing to completely synchronize two different copies of the same data.

As above, some Unix-style systems may want to keep separate fields to identify input and output paths.

```
typedef struct {
  PORT_PARAMS *stack;
```
System-specific information to identify serial port.
```
} SERIAL_PORT_PRIVATE;
```

Opening the serial port requires first allocating the structure and then opening and initializing the port. It may be a good idea for `SerialOpen` to call `SerialSaveState` after the port is open, but before any configuration occurs, so that `SerialClose` can guarantee the port is correctly restored to its original state.

`SerialOpen` can be quite complex, depending on the details of the system. For this reason, it may make sense to split important parts out into separate functions. For example, some systems may use serial ports for both dial-in and dial-out purposes, and so you'll need to make sure the port is properly configured for the correct direction.

```
int SerialOpen(SERIAL_PORT *pPort, const char *name)
{
  SERIAL_PORT_PRIVATE *port;
  port = malloc(sizeof (*port));
  if (port == NULL) return serialFatal;
  port -> stack = NULL;
```
System-specific code to open serial port.
```
  *pPort = port;
  return serialOK;
}
```

Closing the port is usually a bit simpler. The one important piece of generic code here is to call `SerialRestoreState`, both to make sure the original port configuration is is restored and to free the stack storage.

```
int SerialClose(SERIAL_PORT portPublic)
{
  SERIAL_PORT_PRIVATE *port = portPublic;
  while (port -> stack) SerialRestoreState(portPublic);
```
System-specific code to close port.
```
  free(port);
  return serialOK;
}
```

If you're lucky, saving the port parameters on the internal stack will consist of a single system call to return all of the port parameters in a single structure which can be copied directly into pParams. If you're unlucky, you'll need to call a variety of functions to query as much information about the port as is likely to be changed and store each individual factlet in separate fields.

```
int SerialSaveState(SERIAL_PORT portPublic)
{
    SERIAL_PORT_PRIVATE *port = portPublic;
    PORT_PARAMS *pParams;

    pParams = malloc(sizeof (*pParams));
    if (pParams == NULL) return serialFatal;
```
System-specific code to query port.
```
    pParams -> pNext = port -> stack;
    port -> stack = pParams;
    return serialOK;
}
```

In restoring the serial port, I've chosen to treat an empty stack as a non-error, since I expect this function to be called as a safety check by the client.

```
int SerialRestoreState(SERIAL_PORT portPublic)
{
    SERIAL_PORT_PRIVATE *port = portPublic;
    PORT_PARAMS *pParams;

    pParams = port -> stack;      /* Get parameters to be restored */
    if (pParams == NULL) return serialOK;
    port -> stack = pParams -> pNext;
```
System-specific code to restore port state.
```
    free(pParams);
    return serialOK;
}
```

Setting the word length and parity is pretty routine. My personal preference is to combine these into one call, since there is a widespread convention that word length and parity change together. However, you may need to integrate this with an existing application which treats the two parameters separately, so I've left them as two separate functions.

```
int SerialSetWord(SERIAL_PORT portPublic, int wordLength)
{
    SERIAL_PORT_PRIVATE *port = portPublic;
```
System-specific code to set word length.
```
    return serialOK;
}
```

```
int SerialSetParity(SERIAL_PORT portPublic, int parity)
{
    SERIAL_PORT_PRIVATE *port = portPublic;
```
System-specific code to set the parity.
```
    return serialOK;
}
```

Protocols such as XModem and YModem are incompatible with software flow control, so this function is provided for the sole purpose of disabling any software flow control that may be in effect. Because of the stack discipline provided by `SerialSaveState` and `SerialRestoreState`, there's no need for a function to explicitly re-enable such flow control, although if this module is going to be fleshed out into a full general-purpose serial interface, functions will be needed for setting different types of flow control.

```
int SerialMakeTransparent(SERIAL_PORT portPublic)
{
    SERIAL_PORT_PRIVATE *port = portPublic;
```
System-specific code to disable software flow control.
```
    return serialOK;
}
```

Serial I/O

`SerialReadWithTimeout` is the single most important function in this entire module. The reason it's so important is that a well-written protocol will spend the majority of its time waiting for data from the serial port. This has two important implications.

The first is that `SerialReadWithTimeout` should interact nicely with the system multitasking. A poorly-written implementation can easily consume excessive CPU time, causing the system to be unnecessarily sluggish when file transfers are occurring. Users that expect to be able to perform other tasks while waiting on long transfers will appreciate the extra care required to ensure that `SerialReadWithTimeout` consumes minimal resources. This typically means using timed blocking I/O calls when they are available, or deliberately relinquishing the processor whenever the data is not immediately available. It also means that serial I/O should be performed in large blocks whenever possible. Many systems have considerable overhead for each system call, and there can be a significant difference in the time required for a single bulk read compared to a series of single-byte reads.

There's also an implication for the user interface. If the user decides to cancel the transaction for any reason, either by clicking a mouse or tapping a key, the odds are high that this function will be running. Quick user interface response requires that this function somehow be informed of the user's attempt to cancel, so that it can return `serialUserCancel` to the caller.

It's perfectly reasonable to return a `serialTimeout` error even if data was received. Some clients (such as the ZModem code in this book) will deliberately request more data than they need in an attempt to reduce the number of times they call this function. If a client does this, they're responsible for checking the returned count of bytes read. A `serialTimeout` error simply means that not all of the data was read. In addition, a timeout of zero is legitimate, it simply returns data that might have already been received. Many systems don't directly handle a zero timeout, or interpret it as a request with no timeout, so you may have to explicitly check for a zero timeout and handle it differently.

The value in `*pLength` is the number of bytes requested, and is used to return the number of bytes actually read. Most implementations will store `*pLength` in a local variable and then immediately set `*pLength` to zero, so that a valid value is returned if an error occurs.

```
int SerialReadWithTimeout(SERIAL_PORT portPublic, int
        timeout, void *pBuffer, size_t *pLength)
{
  SERIAL_PORT_PRIVATE *port = portPublic;
  System-specific code to read bytes with timeout.
  return serialOK;
}
```

Breaking the send routine into two parts enables certain optimizations that can greatly speed file transfers. When possible, `SerialSend` should return as soon as the data is queued to be sent. This allows the caller to overlap other operations. For example, the XYModem code sends the contents of a packet, and then computes the CRC while the data is being sent.

```
int SerialSend(SERIAL_PORT portPublic, const void
        *pBuffer, size_t length)
{
  SERIAL_PORT_PRIVATE *port = portPublic;
  System-specific code to send bytes.
  return serialOK;
}
```

The problem is that, at low baud rates, it can take a long time for the queue to empty. At 300 baud, a 1024-byte YModem packet can take over 30 seconds to finish sending. If the sending program queues such a long packet and then immediately begins to wait for a response with a typical ten-second timeout, then the sender will see a timeout error waiting for a response to a packet that hasn't yet been sent!

There are two ways to address this problem. One is to limit the amount of data that can be queued. At 300 baud, it makes sense to limit the queue to as little as 30 bytes, and have `SerialSend` return only after the last data is stored into the queue. In the previous example, `SerialSend` would feed data into the queue as it was sent, and not return until the last data was put into the queue, only one second before the last data was actually sent. The other way to address the problem is to provide an explicit call, `SerialWaitForSentBytes`, which does not return until the queue of data to send is empty.

In my experience, `SerialWaitForSentBytes` cannot be implemented on very many systems. Nonetheless, the protocol sources in this book do use it. If it cannot be implemented, it's quite reasonable to simply leave it empty, and try to restrict the send queue or otherwise take steps to keep `SerialSend` from returning too soon.

```
int SerialWaitForSentBytes(SERIAL_PORT portPublic)
{
    SERIAL_PORT_PRIVATE *port = portPublic;
    System-specific code to wait for outgoing data.
    return serialOK;
}
```

Miscellaneous Serial Operations

In addition to the 128 or 256 character values, there are some non-character conditions that can be signalled over a serial line. The most common is known as a *break* signal. The most common use of a break signal is as an interrupt. A break signal is usually 250–300 milliseconds, although a *long break* of 2 seconds or more is sometimes used to force a modem to disconnect. The following function should send a normal break signal when hardware supports it.

```
int SerialSendBreak(SERIAL_PORT port)
{
    System-specific code to send a break signal.
    return serialOK;
}
```

On systems with good serial input buffering, `SerialPause` may require no more than a call to a system `sleep` function. On the other hand, if serial input buffering is not what it should be, then you may need to watch the port so that data isn't lost during such a delay. It may also be necessary to have this function interact with the user interface so that the protocols can respond immediately if the user decides to cancel.

```
int SerialPause(SERIAL_PORT port, int seconds)
{
```

System-specific code to pause without losing serial data.

```
    return serialOK;
}
```

File Interfacing 15

Most serial protocols treat files in one of two different ways: Text *files are translated so that they can be used on the receiving system, while* binary *files are transferred strictly as-is. The problem is figuring out which is which.*

As discussed in Chapter 5, text files vary widely from system to system. To simplify the problems of converting text files across different systems, most file transfer protocols use a standard format for all text files. The sender of a text file converts the file into this common format, and the receiver then converts it into whatever format is appropriate on the receiving system. The most common standard format is:

- Lines are terminated by CR LF. (ZModem also allows lines to be terminated by a single LF.)

- Tabs are fixed to every eight characters.

It is usually helpful if text files end with an end-of-line; and XModem and YModem conventionally place a SUB (Control-Z) after the last character in the file.

Translating text files to and from this standard format is usually quite simple. The problem is figuring out when such translation is appropriate. Non-text files can be badly damaged by such translation. Generally, there are three ways to figure out the file type: you can ask the operating system, you can guess, or you can ask the user. The first method usually won't work; few systems track the type of a file. The other two approaches each have drawbacks: heuristics can fail in unusual cases, and users don't always have the knowledge to accurately specify the file type.

The best method, when the operating system doesn't provide file type information, is probably to combine the other two approaches, using heuristics to guess the type of each file and presenting that information in a way that is easy for the user to override.[1] Heuristics for distinguishing text from random binary files are simple, usually effective, and can actually help to educate users as they use the program.

Kermit supports more detailed file typing than many other protocols. A recent extension allows the Kermit sender to specify the character encoding used by a text file. Although the need for this extension may not be apparent to many American programmers, it is necessary for non-American users. For example, the character ê is character 144 on the Macintosh and character 136 on the IBM PS/2. A binary transfer of `raisons d'être` from the PS/2 to the Macintosh would give `raisons d'átre`. Kermit now allows the sender to translate from the local character set to some standard set, such as ISO Latin-1, and the receiver can then translate into the correct character set on the receiving end. This new Kermit feature has been rapidly adopted by users around the world.

Public Interface

The interface here is a bit more complex than in the previous chapters. This complexity is due to the number of attributes assigned to files on some systems, and the need to handle file typing.

```
⟨ftdisk.h   178⟩ ==
#ifndef DISK_H_INCLUDED
#define DISK_H_INCLUDED
#include <time.h>
  extern int diskDebug;     /* TRUE enables debug messages */
  typedef void *DISKFILE;
  ⟨ File Type Constants  179 ⟩
  ⟨ File I/O errors  179 ⟩
  ⟨ Functions for writing files  180 ⟩
  ⟨ Functions for reading files  180 ⟩
  ⟨ Functions for querying files  181 ⟩
#endif    /* ! DISK_H_INCLUDED */
```

Whenever a file is accessed, this module must determine the type of data in the file. If the file is binary, it is read or written exactly as-is. If it's a text file, some system-dependent transformations are applied. To simplify future additions to this

---

[1]Many programs only provide a single "text-mode" setting that transfers all files in text or binary mode. Unfortunately, a modal setting doesn't provide good support for protocols that can specify the type of each file, and can hence transfer a mixture of file types at one time.

list, I've adopted the convention that text types start with 100. This convention allows clients to test if a file is text by simply checking to see if the type is larger than `diskFileText`. Binary formats may also be added; for example, it may be appropriate to recognize special compressed formats and decompress them as they're received.

⟨ File Type Constants 179 ⟩ ==
```
enum {
  diskFileUnknown = 0,      /* File type is unknown */
  diskFileBinary,           /* File is not a text file */
  diskFileText = 100,       /* File is a text file */
  diskFileAscii,            /* File is US ASCII text file */
  diskFileLatin1            /* File is ISO Latin-1 text file */
};
```
This code is used on page 178.

There are only a handful of errors that actually mean anything to the client. Any other failure returns `diskError` if recovery is possible (such as a single file that couldn't be opened) or `diskFatal` if no further disk I/O is possible.

Because `diskEOF` is an error, it should not be returned if valid data is also being returned. A read request that results in `diskEOF` means that no data was available.

⟨ File I/O errors 179 ⟩ ==
```
enum {
  diskOK = 0, diskError,    /* Recoverable error */
  diskFatal,       /* Nonrecoverable error */
  diskNoSuchFile,        /* File can't be opened */
  diskCantRead,       /* No permission to read */
  diskEOF       /* Returned after end-of-file is read */
};
```
This code is used on page 178.

Opening a file for writing is a little involved, because I want to allow the client to specify many attributes of the resulting file. The first step in opening a file is to create a file handle with `DiskWriteInit`. The second step is to set the file attributes with `DiskWriteName`, etc. Attributes not explicitly set will default to reasonable values. (Except, of course, for the filename.) The last step is to actually open the file.

Opening the file is handled by one of three different functions, reflecting different goals in writing to the file. The function `DiskWriteOpen` is used by protocols such as XModem and YModem, and other protocols when special file handling isn't required. This version alters the filename as needed to avoid overwriting a preexisting file. By contrast, `DiskReplaceOpen` removes a preexisting file if possible (if not, it returns an error), while `DiskAppendOpen` opens the file for appending.

`DiskAppendOpen` has a risk that implementors should consider; the original file may have a different type than the material being appended. A type mismatch causes problems with "crash recovery" techniques on Unix-style operating systems that do not store any file type information. If the file was downloaded in text mode, and that transfer was interrupted, a user may attempt to resume the transfer by specifying crash recovery. Crash recovery is always handled in binary mode to avoid problems with text files changing size during transfer. The result is that the the initial part of the file receives text conversion and the latter is transferred raw, with some part in the middle being either omitted or duplicated.

⟨ Functions for writing files 180 ⟩ ==
```
    int DiskWriteInit(DISKFILE *pF);
    int DiskWriteName(DISKFILE f, const char *preferredName);
    int DiskWriteSize(DISKFILE f, long fileSize);
    int DiskWriteDate(DISKFILE f, struct tm *pFileDate);
    int DiskWriteMode(DISKFILE f, long fileMode);
    int DiskWriteType(DISKFILE f, int fileType);
    int DiskWriteOpen(DISKFILE f);
    int DiskAppendOpen(DISKFILE f);
    int DiskReplaceOpen(DISKFILE f);
    int DiskWrite(DISKFILE f, const void *buff, unsigned long size);
    int DiskWriteClose(DISKFILE f);
```
This code is used on page 178.

`DiskRead` returns the actual number of bytes read in `*pSizeRead`.

⟨ Functions for reading files 180 ⟩ ==
```
    int DiskReadOpen(DISKFILE *pF, const char *name, int fileType);
    int DiskRead(DISKFILE f, void *buff, unsigned long
        requestedSize, unsigned long *pSizeRead);
    int DiskReadClose(DISKFILE f);
```
This code is used on page 178.

You need to set file attributes before you open a file for writing. Similarly, you often need to check file attributes after you open a file for reading. The next group of functions return a variety of information about the currently open file. Most of them copy the data using the provided pointer; note that `DiskFileName` returns a pointer to the string. You must be careful not to modify the string. `DiskFileName` is sometimes used even for files that are being written. When a file is opened for writing, this package may actually open a different filename, either because the name provided is unusable on this system, or because a like-named file already exists.

⟨ Functions for querying files 181 ⟩ ==
```
int DiskFileType(DISKFILE f, int *pType);
int DiskFileMode(DISKFILE f, long *pMode);
int DiskFileDate(DISKFILE f, struct tm *pTm);
int DiskFileSize(DISKFILE f, long *pSize);
int DiskFileName(DISKFILE f, const char **pName);
```
This code is used on page 178.

Definitions

As usual, the implementation starts with a list of system headers and library functions that will be used. This list is mostly for the aid of people porting the code.

```
#include <stddef.h>     /* size_t */

#include <stdlib.h>     /* malloc, free */
  void *malloc(size_t);
  void free(void *);

#include <ctype.h>      /* isalpha, isdigit, isupper, tolower */
  int tolower(int c);

#include <time.h>       /* time_t, time */
  time_t time(time_t *);

#include <stdio.h>
      /* fprintf, fopen, fclose, fwrite, fread, putc */
  int fprintf(FILE *, const char *, ...);
  FILE *fopen(const char *, const char *);
  int fclose(FILE *);
  int fwrite(const void *, size_t, size_t, FILE *);
  int fread(void *, size_t, size_t, FILE *);

#include <string.h>     /* memset, memcpy, strcpy, strlen */
  void memset(void *, int, long);
  void *memcpy(void *dest, const void *src, size_t size);
  char *strcpy(char *s1, const char *s2);
  size_t strlen(const char *);

#ifndef FALSE
#define FALSE  (0)
#endif

#ifndef NULL
#define NULL ((void *) 0)
#endif

#define STATIC static
```

The only non-ANSI function I've used is the POSIX `access` function, which returns zero if the specified file exists. The `FileExists` macro here uses `access` to return TRUE if the specified file exists.

```
#define FileExists(fname)  (access(fname,0) == 0)
  int access(const char *name,int mode);
```

Including my own header helps guard against type mismatches.

```
#include "ftdisk.h"
```

All of the other packages use a debugging handle which was handed to them by their client. This package instead uses direct `fprintf` calls to dump debugging information to `stderr`. These messages are enabled by the global variable `diskDebug`. I chose this approach because it seemed a bit unwieldy to have the protocols pass a debug handle into every file open.

```
int diskDebug = 0;
```

Reading and writing operations store data temporarily in a buffer. This buffer reduces the frequency of low-level disk calls, and results in improved efficiency on some systems. However, it can be dangerous to set BUFFERSIZE too large. If too much time is spent reading or writing data, the protocol can time out or even fail completely. This problem appears primarily when dealing with slow media such as floppy disks.

Since the file type determination code is not invoked until the first time the buffer is flushed, the buffer size is artificially reduced initially. Using a smaller initial buffer causes the first flush to occur earlier, giving the user quicker feedback on the file type and reducing the likelihood of file type mixups from "padding" that protocols such as XModem and YModem add to the end of most files.

```
#define BUFFERSIZE  4096    /* Size of file buffer */
#define SHORTBUFF   1100    /* Size of output buffer at beginning */
```

Some of the various special characters used by file-type determination code are: NULL, HT, LF, CR, and SUB.

```
#define C_NULL  0x00    /* NULL character */
#define TAB  0x09    /* HT character */
#define LF  0x0a    /* LF character */
#define CR  0x0d    /* CR character */
#define SUB  0x1a    /* SUB character, Control-Z */
```

The DISKFILE structure seen by clients is really a pointer to this structure. Keeping it private to this package helps discourage clients from accessing it directly.

```
typedef struct {
  FILE *f;
  int fileType;
  long fileMode;
  struct tm fileDate;
  long fileSize;
  char *fileName;     /* name of file, NULL if name unknown */
  char lastChar;      /* used by text-conversion code */
  char *buffer;     /* buffer */
  unsigned bufferSize;    /* size of buffer */
  unsigned bufferLimit;    /* Current limit on buffer size */
  unsigned bufferBegin;    /* first byte in buffer */
  unsigned bufferEnd;    /* last byte in buffer */
} DISKFILE_PRIVATE;
```

Debugging

These debugging routines are explained on page 155.

```
#define StsRet(expr)
        do { int tmpErrorVal = (expr);
          if (tmpErrorVal != diskOK) return StsWarn(tmpErrorVal);
        } while (FALSE)
#define StsWarn(s)  DiskDebugWarn((s),__FILE__,__LINE__)
  STATIC int DiskDebugWarn(int s, const char *file, int line)
  {
    if (!diskDebug) return s;
    if (s != diskOK) fprintf(stderr, "!?:%s:%d:", file, line);
    switch (s) {
    case diskOK: break;
    case diskError: fprintf(stderr, "diskError\n"); break;
    case diskFatal: fprintf(stderr, "diskFatal\n"); break;
    case diskNoSuchFile: fprintf(stderr, "diskNoSuchFile\n");
      break;
    case diskCantRead: fprintf(stderr, "diskCantRead\n"); break;
    case diskEOF: fprintf(stderr, "diskEOF\n"); break;
    default: fprintf(stderr, "Disk Error %d\n", s); break;
    }
    return s;
  }
```

Utility Routines

The `DiskWriteEOL` macro writes an EOL sequence to a file opened in binary mode. It is necessarily system-specific. On ANSI-compliant systems, this macro could be avoided by opening text files in text mode, but since this module opens files before the file type is known, it seems just as easy to accept this small system dependency to avoid having to reopen files in different modes.

```
#define DiskWriteEOL_CR(f)  putc(CR,(f))      /* single CR */
#define DiskWriteEOL_LF(f)  putc(LF,(f))      /* single LF */
#define DiskWriteEOL_CRLF(f)  putc(CR,(f)); putc(LF,(f))
        /* CR/LF pair */
#define DiskWriteEOL(f)  DiskWriteEOL_CRLF(f)
        /* Define the right one */
```

One problem that arises in transferring files between systems is the variation in filenames. Ultimately, it is the receiver's responsibility to make sure the filename it uses is legal on the receiving system. This sample routine illustrates what may need to be done, but will clearly need to be adapted to the specific limitations of the system being used.

This routine does the following manipulations:

- Prepends `x_` to any filename that doesn't begin with a letter.

- Converts filenames to all lower case.

- Converts non-alphanumeric characters to underscores, and then removes any trailing underscores.

- Limits the name to 26 characters.

```
STATIC void DiskConvertName(char *resultName, const char
        *initialName)
{
  char *p = resultName;
  const char *q = initialName;
  if (!isalpha(*q)) {      /* Add x_ if needed */
    *p++ = 'x';
    *p++ = '_';
  }
  for ( ;  *q != '\0';  q++) {
    *p = isupper(*q) ? tolower(*q) : *q;      /* convert to lower case */
    if (!isalpha(*p) && !isdigit(*p) && (*p != '.'))
      *p = '_';      /* Convert illegal chars to underlines */
    p++;
```

```
    }
    while (*--p == '_')      /* remove trailing _ chars */
      ;
    *(++p) = '\0';      /* Terminate name */
    resultName[26] = '\0';      /* Chop name to 26 chars */
  }
```

Another problem arises when a file being received has the same name as a file that already exists. There are many ways to handle this situation. One way is to overwrite the preexisting file. While simple, such a heavy-handed approach can create problems for users. Another method is to rename the preexisting file. This function instead renames the file being received. Again, this version is only an example of what can be done. The best approach depends on your particular platform, and the expectations of the users on that platform.

This implementation of `DiskMakeNameUnique` alters the name of the file being written if there is already a file of that name. It places a decimal number at the end of the filename, overwriting the last characters in the filename as necessary. If the file has an extension that ends in one or more digits, those digits are treated as a decimal number to be incremented. When the digits overflow, a preceding character is converted into 1, for example, `file.ab9` becomes `file.a10`. For compatibility with MS-DOS, periods are skipped in this process, so that `file.999` becomes `fil1.000` rather than `file1000`. If the original filename lacks an extension, `.001` is added. If the existing extension does not end in a digit, the extension is filled with 0 digits to three characters, and the last character of the extension becomes 1, so that `file.c` becomes `file.c01`. This algorithm should be usable under many different operating systems, although certain operating systems (such as VAX/VMS) may offer other mechanisms.

```
    STATIC int DiskMakeNameUnique(char *fname)
    {
      char *p;
      char *dot = NULL;
      for (p = fname; *p; p++) {      /* Find the end of the string */
        if (*p == '.') dot = p;      /* Find extension */
      }
      p--;      /* Points to last character in string */
      while (FileExists(fname)) {      /* If file exists */
        if (!dot || !isdigit(*p)) {      /* Doesn't end in digit */
          if (!dot) {      /* Add extension */
            *++p = '.';
            dot = p;
          }
          while (p - dot < 3) *++p = '0';
```

```
        *p = '1';
        p[1] = 0;      /* NULL terminate */
    } else {      /* Increment decimal number at end */
        char *p1 = p;
        while ((*p1 == '9') && (p1 > fname)) *(p1--) = '0';
        if ((*p1 == '.') && (p1 > fname)) p1--;
        while ((*p1 == '9') && (p1 > fname)) *(p1--) = '0';
        if ((*p1 == '.') && (p1 > fname)) p1--;
        if ((p1 == fname) && ((*p1 == '.') || (*p1 == '9')))
            return StsWarn(diskError);
        if (!isdigit(*p1)) *p1 = '1';
        else (*p1)++;
    }
}
return diskOK;
}
```

DiskGuessType is the heart of this package. It is responsible for examining the data in a file and attempting to guess the type of the file based on that data. This version distinguishes between text and binary files based on the following assumptions:

- A text file consists only of seven-bit graphic characters, and the control codes CR, LF, TAB, SUB (Control-Z), and NULL. (The last two are included as possible pad characters.)

- No text file begins with a NULL or Control-Z character.

- If there is a Control-Z or NULL in a text file, it's padding, and will be repeated to the end of the file.

These criteria were initially developed for distinguishing random binary files (such as executables or compressed files) from seven-bit ASCII text files, and have proven fairly successful in practice. They'll require some modification if eight-bit text files are going to be used. The special consideration of NULL and Control-Z helps prevent incorrect classification of text files transferred by XModem or YModem, which commonly have padding characters appended to the end of the file.

Ideally, the initial guess generated by this function would be shown to the user (in a file browser, for example), who could then override it if it's incorrect. Notice that it's pretty much impossible to automatically determine the character set. That information will have to be obtained from the user or the operating system. Fortunately, it's uncommon for a single user on a single machine to use a variety of different character sets, so it makes sense to have a single modal setting for the default character set.

```
STATIC int DiskGuessType(const char *buff, unsigned long size)
{
  int i;
  const char *p;
  register int c;
  if (size == 0) return diskFileBinary;
  p = buff;
  i = size;
  c = ((int) *p) & 0xFF;
      /* First test: first byte can't be NULL or Control-Z */
  if ((c == C_NULL) || (c == SUB)) return diskFileBinary;
        /* Second test: check for illegal byte values */
  while (i -- > 0) {
    c = *p ++ & 0xff;
    if ((c >= 0x7f)        /* No high bit or DEL */
    || ((c < 0x20) && (c != CR) && (c != LF)      /* Odd Control char ? */
    && (c != TAB) && (c != SUB) && (c != C_NULL)))
        return diskFileBinary;      /* File is binary */
  }     /* Third test: Control-Z and NULL can only occur as padding */
  p = buff;
  i = size;
  while ((i > 0) && ((c = *p ++) != SUB) && (c != C_NULL)) {
    i -- ;     /* Find first occurence of Control-Z or NULL */
  }
  while ((i > 0) && (*p ++ == c)) {
    i -- ;     /* Find last pad char */
  }
  if (i > 0) return diskFileBinary;      /* If there's more, then binary */
  return diskFileText;     /* Passed all tests, assume it's text */
}
```

Writing Files

Once you can distinguish text and binary files, it's time to worry about converting data for this particular platform. The `DiskWriteText` function converts text data in the buffer as it's written to the file.

This version only handles generic text conversions: common end-of-line sequences (CR, LF, or CR/LF) are recognized and converted into the local end-of-line sequence, Control-Z and NULL characters are stripped from the data. If needed, this function can easily be extended to handle character-set conversion as well.

One shortcut is available on some systems. All of the file transfer protocols discussed in this book use a canonical text format with CR/LF pairs separating lines. If that is the standard text format on your system (as with MS-DOS), then it is faster to simply skip this step and write the data directly to the file. The only problem is with ZModem, which also allows text files to use a single LF to separate lines.

```
STATIC int DiskWriteText(DISKFILE fPublic)
{
  DISKFILE_PRIVATE *pF = (DISKFILE_PRIVATE *) fPublic;
  char *p = pF -> buffer;
  long num = pF -> bufferEnd;
  char lastChar = pF -> lastChar;
  register int c;
  for ( ;  num;  -- num) {
    c = *p ++;
    if ((c) && (c != LF) && (c != SUB) && (c != CR)) putc(c, pF -> f);
    else if (c == CR) {
      DiskWriteEOL(pF -> f);
    }
    else if ((c == LF) && (lastChar != CR)) {
      DiskWriteEOL(pF -> f);
    }
    lastChar = c;
  }
  pF -> lastChar = lastChar;
  return diskOK;
}
```

`DiskWriteFlush` is called whenever the buffer is full. It uses the file type to determine whether to write the data out raw (`diskFileBinary`), or to apply text conversions (`diskFileText`). If the file type is `diskFileUnknown`, it first calls `DiskGuessType` to determine the type of data in the file. If other types of binary or text files are to be handled, the `switch` statement here can be extended to call appropriate conversion functions.

```
STATIC int DiskWriteFlush(DISKFILE fPublic)
{
  DISKFILE_PRIVATE *pF = (DISKFILE_PRIVATE *) fPublic;
  int returnVal = diskOK;
  if (pF -> bufferEnd == 0) return (diskOK);
  if (pF -> fileType == diskFileUnknown)
    pF -> fileType = DiskGuessType(pF -> buffer, pF -> bufferEnd);
  if (diskDebug) fprintf(stderr,
      "Disk:␣Flushing␣%s␣file␣''%s''␣to␣disk:␣%d␣bytes.\n",
```

```
          (pF -> fileType >= diskFileText) ? "Txt" : "Bin",
          pF -> fileName, pF -> bufferEnd);
   switch (pF -> fileType) {
   case diskFileBinary: case diskFileUnknown:
     if (fwrite(pF -> buffer, 1, pF -> bufferEnd,
          pF -> f) != pF -> bufferEnd)
       returnVal = StsWarn(diskFatal);
     break;
   case diskFileText: case diskFileAscii: case diskFileLatin1:
     returnVal = StsWarn(DiskWriteText(pF));
     break;
   default:       /* Other text type? */
     returnVal = StsWarn(DiskWriteText(pF));
     break;
   }
   pF -> bufferEnd = 0;
   pF -> bufferLimit = pF -> bufferSize;
       /* After first flush, expand buffer for speed */
   return returnVal;
}
```

The client opens a file for writing by first creating a file handle, setting any needed file attributes, and then opening the file. Separating this process into multiple function calls simplifies file handling for protocols such as Kermit, which receives many separate pieces of file information up to the point where the file data is actually sent.

The `DiskWriteInit` function creates the file handle by allocating and initializing the `DISKFILE_PRIVATE` structure. One polishing touch here is to set `bufferLimit` small when the file is first opened. A small value of `bufferLimit` causes the file type determination to happen earlier, giving better feedback to the user and reducing file type errors from end-of-file padding added by XModem and YModem. (Some XModem and YModem senders fill the last packet with binary garbage, which can cause a text file to be incorrectly classified as binary.)

```
   int DiskWriteInit(DISKFILE *pFPublic)
   {
     DISKFILE_PRIVATE *pF;
     *pFPublic = NULL;       /* Initialize return values */
     if (diskDebug > 5) fprintf(stderr, "DiskWriteInit\n");
     pF = malloc(sizeof (*pF));
     if (pF == NULL) return StsWarn(diskFatal);
     memset(pF, 0, sizeof (*pF));
     pF -> buffer = malloc(BUFFERSIZE);
     if (pF -> buffer == NULL) {
```

```
      free(pF);
      return StsWarn(diskFatal);
  }
  {    /* Set default time */
    time_t  t = time(NULL);
    pF -> fileDate = *localtime(&t);
  }
  pF -> fileType = diskFileUnknown;
  pF -> fileMode = 0;
  pF -> fileSize = 0;
  pF -> bufferSize = BUFFERSIZE;
  pF -> bufferLimit = SHORTBUFF;
  pF -> bufferBegin = pF -> bufferEnd = 0;
  *pFPublic = pF;
  return diskOK;
}
```

Once the file handle is initialized, the client will call several of the following functions to set specific file attributes.

```
int DiskWriteName(DISKFILE fPublic, const char *preferredName)
{
  DISKFILE_PRIVATE *pF = (DISKFILE_PRIVATE *) fPublic;
  char fileName[256];

  if (diskDebug > 5)
    fprintf(stderr, "DiskWriteName(''%s'')\n", preferredName);
  DiskConvertName(fileName, preferredName);
  pF -> fileName = malloc(strlen(fileName) + 1);
  if (pF -> fileName == NULL) {
    return StsWarn(diskFatal);
  }
  strcpy(pF -> fileName, fileName);
  return diskOK;
}


int DiskWriteSize(DISKFILE fPublic, long fileSize)
{
  DISKFILE_PRIVATE *pF = (DISKFILE_PRIVATE *) fPublic;
  if (diskDebug > 5)
    fprintf(stderr, "DiskWriteSize(%ld)\n", fileSize);
  pF -> fileSize = fileSize;
  return diskOK;
}
```

```
int DiskWriteDate(DISKFILE fPublic, struct tm *pFileDate)
{
  DISKFILE_PRIVATE *pF = (DISKFILE_PRIVATE *) fPublic;
  if (diskDebug > 5) fprintf(stderr, "DiskWriteDate\n");
  pF -> fileDate = *pFileDate;
  return diskOK;
}


int DiskWriteMode(DISKFILE fPublic, long fileMode)
{
  DISKFILE_PRIVATE *pF = (DISKFILE_PRIVATE *) fPublic;
  if (diskDebug > 5)
    fprintf(stderr, "DiskWriteMode(0x%lX)\n", fileMode);
  pF -> fileMode = fileMode;
  return diskOK;
}


int DiskWriteType(DISKFILE fPublic, int fileType)
{
  DISKFILE_PRIVATE *pF = (DISKFILE_PRIVATE *) fPublic;
  if (diskDebug > 5)
    fprintf(stderr, "DiskWriteType(%d)\n", fileType);
  pF -> fileType = fileType;
  return diskOK;
}
```

As mentioned earlier, there are three different functions that open the file for writing. DiskWriteOpen is the usual one; it attempts to avoid overwriting an existing file. DiskAppendOpen and DiskReplaceOpen create the file if none exists, or open an existing file.

All three functions handle a few common chores. The name may need to be modified to suit the requirements of this system, and the file should be created with the other attributes specified. The fileMode, pFileDate, and fileSize variables all have special values to indicate that the default should be used. It may seem odd to specify a file size when creating a new file. This value is here only for the use of those systems (such as the UCSD p-System) that have difficulty extending files after they're created. Having the approximate file size available can make disk access much more efficient. The file size given by the client is not gauranteed, however; the final file can be either shorter or longer than this value.

DiskWriteOpen simply uses DiskMakeNameUnique to generate a unique name for the file, and then calls DiskReplaceOpen to actually open the file under the (possibly altered) name.

```
int DiskWriteOpen(DISKFILE fPublic)
{
  DISKFILE_PRIVATE *pF = (DISKFILE_PRIVATE *) fPublic;
  char fileName[256];      /* Avoid overwrites */
  strcpy(fileName, pF -> fileName);
  StsRet(DiskMakeNameUnique(fileName));
  free(pF -> fileName);
  pF -> fileName = malloc(strlen(fileName) + 1);
  if (pF -> fileName == NULL) {
    free(pF -> buffer);
    free(pF);
    return StsWarn(diskFatal);
  }
  strcpy(pF -> fileName, fileName);      /* Open the file */
  if (diskDebug) fprintf(stderr,
        "DiskWriteOpen:␣Opening␣file␣''%s''\n", pF -> fileName);
  return DiskReplaceOpen(fPublic);      /* Replace file */
}
```

`DiskReplaceOpen` and `DiskAppendOpen` are quite simple.

```
int DiskReplaceOpen(DISKFILE fPublic)
{
  DISKFILE_PRIVATE *pF = (DISKFILE_PRIVATE *) fPublic;
      /* Open the file */
  if (diskDebug)
    fprintf(stderr, "DiskReplaceOpen:␣Replacing␣file␣''%s''\n",
        pF -> fileName);
  pF -> f = fopen(pF -> fileName, "wb");
  if (pF -> f == NULL) {
    free(pF -> buffer);
    free(pF -> fileName);
    free(pF);
    return StsWarn(diskError);      /* Can't open this file */
  }
  return diskOK;
}

int DiskAppendOpen(DISKFILE fPublic)
{
  DISKFILE_PRIVATE *pF = (DISKFILE_PRIVATE *) fPublic;
      /* Open the file */
  if (diskDebug) fprintf(stderr,
        "DiskAppendOpen:␣Opening␣file␣''%s''\n", pF -> fileName);
```

```
    pF -> f = fopen(pF -> fileName, "wb+");
    if (pF -> f == NULL) {
      free(pF -> buffer);
      free(pF -> fileName);
      free(pF);
      return StsWarn(diskError);     /* Can't open this file */
    }
    return diskOK;
  }
```

DiskWrite simply copies data into the buffer and calls DiskWriteFlush if the buffer overflows. The only trick is correctly handling write requests that are too large for the buffer.

```
    int DiskWrite(DISKFILE fPublic, const void *buff, unsigned long
        cnt)
  {
    DISKFILE_PRIVATE *pF = (DISKFILE_PRIVATE *) fPublic;
    const char *pSource = (const char *) buff;
    unsigned long size;
    while (cnt > 0) {
      if ((pF -> bufferEnd + cnt) > pF -> bufferLimit)
        StsRet(DiskWriteFlush(pF));
      if ((pF -> bufferEnd + cnt) > pF -> bufferLimit)
        size = pF -> bufferLimit - pF -> bufferEnd - 1;
      else size = cnt;
      memcpy(pF -> buffer + pF -> bufferEnd, pSource, size);
      cnt -= size;
      pSource += size;
      pF -> bufferEnd += size;
    }
    return diskOK;
  }
```

Closing the file also requires freeing any allocated data.

```
    int DiskWriteClose(DISKFILE fPublic)
  {
    DISKFILE_PRIVATE *pF = (DISKFILE_PRIVATE *) fPublic;
    int returnVal = diskOK;
    returnVal = StsWarn(DiskWriteFlush(pF));
    if (diskDebug)
      fprintf(stderr, "Disk:␣Closing␣file␣''%s''\n", pF ->fileName);
    if ((returnVal == diskOK) && (fclose(pF -> f)))
      returnVal = StsWarn(diskError);
```

```
        if (pF -> buffer != NULL)
          free(pF -> buffer);
        if (pF -> fileName != NULL)
          free(pF -> fileName);
        free(pF);
        return returnVal;
    }
```

Reading Files

Text files are converted as they are read into the buffer. The `DiskCopyText` function performs this conversion in two slightly different situations. The first is when reading a file that is known to be text. The data is pulled from the file, and then converted into the buffer by this function. The second situation is when determing the file type. When the file is first opened, some portion of the file is analyzed by `DiskGuessType`. If the file is text, it's then copied into the buffer by `DiskCopyText` to perform text conversion. Without this two-step approach, I would need to rewind the file if it turned out to be text.

This function uses the same algorithm for detecting the end-of-line marker that was used in `DiskWriteText`. This means that regardless of the line separator actually in the file, it will be correctly converted before it is sent. This is only really important when 'foreign' text files are being handled (such as when sending an MS-DOS text file from a Unix system to a Macintosh; without this approach, the end-of-lines would end up doubled).

```
        STATIC void DiskCopyText(char *dest, unsigned *pDestSize, const
              char *source, unsigned sourceSize, char *pLastChar)
    {
      char lastChar = *pLastChar;
      const char *p = source;
      char *q = dest;
      int c;
      for ( ;  sourceSize;   -- sourceSize) {
        c = *p ++;
        if ((c) && (c != LF) && (c != SUB) && (c != CR))
          *q ++ = c;
        else if (c == CR) {
          *q ++ = CR;
          *q ++ = LF;
        } else if ((c == LF) && (lastChar != CR)) {
          *q ++ = CR;
          *q ++ = LF;
```

```
     }
     lastChar = c;
   }
   *pLastChar = lastChar;
   *pDestSize = q - dest;
 }
```

DiskReadFillBuffer is the analog of DiskWriteFlush. It reads data from the file and converts it as necessary into the buffer. Note that whether you're reading or writing, the file buffer always has data in the format used by the transfer. Any conversion occurs between the buffer and the file.

```
STATIC char diskReadBuff[BUFFERSIZE];

STATIC int DiskReadFillBuffer(DISKFILE fPublic)
{
  DISKFILE_PRIVATE *pF = (DISKFILE_PRIVATE *) fPublic;

  if (pF -> fileType >= diskFileText) {
    unsigned sizeRead;

    sizeRead = fread(diskReadBuff, 1, pF -> bufferSize / 2, pF -> f);
    pF -> bufferBegin = 0;
    if (sizeRead == 0) {
      pF -> bufferEnd = 0;
      return diskEOF;
    } else {
      DiskCopyText(pF -> buffer, &(pF -> bufferEnd), diskReadBuff,
          sizeRead, &(pF -> lastChar));
    }
  } else {
    pF -> bufferEnd = fread(pF -> buffer, 1, pF -> bufferSize, pF -> f);
    pF -> bufferBegin = 0;
    if (pF -> bufferEnd == 0)
      return diskEOF;
  }
  return diskOK;
}
```

Opening the file for reading requires first initializing the DISKFILE_PRIVATE structure, and then actually opening the file. Reasonable defaults for the file mode, size, and modification date are established just in case it's not possible to examine them.

```
int DiskReadOpen(DISKFILE *pFPublic, const char *name, int
       fileType)
{
  DISKFILE_PRIVATE *pF;

  *pFPublic = NULL;
  pF = malloc(sizeof (*pF));
  if (pF == NULL) return StsWarn(diskFatal);
  memset(pF, 0, sizeof (*pF));
  pF -> buffer = malloc(BUFFERSIZE);
  if (pF -> buffer == NULL) {
    free(pF);
    return StsWarn(diskFatal);
  }
  pF -> bufferSize = BUFFERSIZE;
  pF -> bufferLimit = SHORTBUFF;
  pF -> bufferBegin = pF -> bufferEnd = 0;      /* Open file */
  pF -> f = fopen(name, "rb");
  if (pF -> f == NULL) {
    free(pF);
    return StsWarn(diskNoSuchFile);
  }

  pF -> fileMode = -1;    /* Default fileMode is 'unknown' */
  pF -> fileSize = -1;    /* Default fileSize is 'unknown' */
  {     /* Default fileDate is 'now' */
    time_t t = time(NULL);

    pF -> fileDate = *localtime(&t);
  }

  pF -> fileName = malloc(strlen(name) + 1);
  if (pF -> fileName == NULL) {
    free(pF);
    return StsWarn(diskFatal);
  }
  strcpy(pF -> fileName, name);
  ⟨ Set fileType 197 ⟩
  ⟨ Get actual fileMode, fileDate, and fileSize 197 ⟩
  *pFPublic = pF;
  return diskOK;
}
```

When writing, it's necessary to wait for a write operation before there's any data available to use in guessing the file type. When reading a file, it should be possible to determine the file type immediately. Note that a file type specified by the client overrides everything else. Heuristics don't always work, and it's wise to allow some avenue for the user to double-check the result.

⟨ Set `fileType` 197 ⟩ ≡
```
pF -> fileType = fileType;
if (pF -> fileType == diskFileUnknown) {      /* Guess file type */
  unsigned sizeRead;
  sizeRead = fread(diskReadBuff, 1, pF -> bufferSize / 2, pF -> f);
  pF -> fileType = DiskGuessType(diskReadBuff, sizeRead);
  pF -> lastChar = 0;
  if (pF -> fileType >= diskFileText)
    DiskCopyText(pF -> buffer, &(pF -> bufferEnd), diskReadBuff,
        sizeRead, &(pF -> lastChar));
  else {
    memcpy(pF -> buffer, diskReadBuff, sizeRead);
    pF -> bufferEnd = sizeRead;
  }
}
```
This code is used on page 196.

I can't find anything in the ANSI/ISO standard that would provide a portable way to determine the actual mode, size, and modification date of the file. You'll have to add the appropriate code for your particular system.

⟨ Get actual `fileMode`, `fileDate`, and `fileSize` 197 ⟩ ≡
System-specific code to obtain file information.
This code is used on page 196.

```
int DiskRead(DISKFILE fPublic, void *buff, unsigned long
        requestedSize, unsigned long *pSizeRead)
{
  DISKFILE_PRIVATE *pF = (DISKFILE_PRIVATE *) fPublic;
  char *cbuff = buff;
  int err;
  *pSizeRead = 0;
  if (requestedSize == 0) return diskOK;
  while (requestedSize > 0) {
    unsigned bufferSize = pF -> bufferEnd - pF -> bufferBegin;
    if (requestedSize >= bufferSize) {
      memcpy(cbuff, pF -> buffer + pF -> bufferBegin, bufferSize);
      requestedSize -= bufferSize;
      *pSizeRead += bufferSize;
      cbuff += bufferSize;
      err = DiskReadFillBuffer(pF);
      if (err == diskEOF) break;
```

```
          if (err != diskOK) return err;
        } else {
          memcpy(cbuff, pF -> buffer + pF -> bufferBegin, requestedSize);
          *pSizeRead += requestedSize;
          pF -> bufferBegin += requestedSize;
          requestedSize = 0;
        }
      }
      if (*pSizeRead == 0) return diskEOF;
      return diskOK;
    }


    int DiskReadClose(DISKFILE fPublic)
    {
      DISKFILE_PRIVATE *pF = (DISKFILE_PRIVATE *) fPublic;
      int returnVal = diskOK;
      if (pF -> f != NULL)
        if (fclose(pF -> f)) returnVal = StsWarn(diskError);
      if (pF -> buffer != NULL) free(pF -> buffer);
      if (pF -> fileName != NULL) free(pF -> fileName);
      free(pF);
      return returnVal;
    }
```

File Queries

Clients of this package will need to query many different aspects of the file.

```
    int DiskFileType(DISKFILE fPublic, int *pType)
    {
      DISKFILE_PRIVATE *pF = (DISKFILE_PRIVATE *) fPublic;
      *pType = pF -> fileType;
      return 0;
    }
    int DiskFileMode(DISKFILE fPublic, long *pMode)
    {
      DISKFILE_PRIVATE *pF = (DISKFILE_PRIVATE *) fPublic;
      *pMode = pF -> fileMode;
      return 0;
    }
    int DiskFileDate(DISKFILE fPublic, struct tm *pTm)
    {
      DISKFILE_PRIVATE *pF = (DISKFILE_PRIVATE *) fPublic;
```

```
  *pTm = pF -> fileDate;
  return 0;
}
int DiskFileSize(DISKFILE fPublic, long *pSize)
{
  DISKFILE_PRIVATE *pF = (DISKFILE_PRIVATE *) fPublic;
  *pSize = pF -> fileSize;
  return 0;
}
int DiskFileName(DISKFILE fPublic, const char **pName)
{
  DISKFILE_PRIVATE *pF = (DISKFILE_PRIVATE *) fPublic;
  *pName = pF -> fileName;
  return 0;
}
```

Progress Reporting 16

Progress displays range from diminutive windows with a single progress bar to entire screens choked with flickering numbers. The best ones lie somewhere in the middle; informative, but without a lot of intimidating technical trivia.

To design an effective progress display, you have to think carefully about what questions the progress display should answer for the user. Here are some questions that the user might want answered:

Is it done yet?   This is probably the question the user asks most often. As such, the user should be able to find the answer quickly, even from far away. Simple graphical devices such as a thermometer bar or a pie display can help here.

How long will it take?   A graphical progress display also gives a partial answer to this question, because humans are quite accomplished at estimating when a moving object will reach a certain point. With some additional programming effort, it's possible to reinforce this. Measuring the actual transfer rate allows you to estimate the remaining time and display a reassuring second-by-second countdown.

Did it come out okay?   Once the transfer is complete, the user will want to verify the success of the operation. There should be some obvious record of the result.

How well did it go?   Transfer conditions vary from day to day and file to file. The final summary should include some indication of how fast the transfer was. Although this won't help the first-time user much, more experienced users will learn what speeds are common, and what indicates a significant deviation from the norm.

Based on these questions, I've developed a progress display that shows only the most important information to the user. During the transfer, the user sees the general status, filename, percentage progress, and file type (see the `disk` module for more explanation). After each file is transferred, a summary line indicates the final status, name, size, file type, and speed of the transfer.

Public Interface

The public interface consists of a function to create a "progress handle" (that is, a progress object), a set of functions to update the current progress, and a function to destroy the progress object when the transfer is done.

The file `ftdisk.h` is included to access the file type constants defined there.

```
⟨ftprog.h   202⟩ ==
#ifndef PROGRESS_H_INCLUDED       /* Protect against multiple inclusions */
#define PROGRESS_H_INCLUDED
#include "ftdisk.h"
#include "ftdebug.h"
  typedef void *PROGRESS;
  enum {
    progNegotiating,      /* figuring out what to do next */
    progSending,      /* Sending data */
    progReceiving,      /* Receiving data */
    progNewFile,      /* Just started file */
    progEOF,      /* Just finishing file (filename, etc., still valid) */
    progSkipped,       /* Like progEOF, but file not actually transferred */
    progEnding,      /* Finishing session */
    progDone,      /* Session ended successfully */
    progFailed,      /* Session failed for some reason */
    progCancelled      /* Local user terminated session */
  };
  int ProgressInit(PROGRESS *pProgress);
  void ProgressDestroy(PROGRESS progress);
  void ProgressSetDebug(PROGRESS progress,DEBUG debug);
  void ProgressProtocol(PROGRESS progress,const char *protocol);
  void ProgressFileName(PROGRESS progress,const char *fileName);
  void ProgressFileSize(PROGRESS progress,long fileSize);
  void ProgressFileType(PROGRESS progress,int fileType);
  void ProgressFilePosition(PROGRESS progress,unsigned long
      filePosition);
  void ProgressReport(PROGRESS progress,int progressCode);
  void ProgressSending(PROGRESS progress);
  void ProgressReceiving(PROGRESS progress);
```

```
#endif     /* ! PROGRESS_H_INCLUDED */
```

The `ProgressInit` and `ProgressDestroy` functions create and dispose of the progress object. `ProgressSetDebug` stores a debug handle that can be used to issue debug messages about the progress display. The next five functions allow the protocol to update various information about the transfer. `ProgressReport` actually updates the progress display. It accepts a code that indicates the general status of the transfer. The `ProgressSending` and `ProgressReceiving` functions notify the progress machinery of the direction of the current transfer. Many progress displays will alter their appearance accordingly. For example, a progress bar might grow from left to right when receiving and right to left when sending.

External Dependencies

After the usual list of system headers and library functions, I've defined symbolic constants for one million and one thousand. These are used for displaying large numbers with commas.

```
#include <stddef.h>    /* size_t */
#include <stdio.h>     /* fflush, fprintf */
  int fflush(FILE *);
  int fprintf(FILE *, const char *, ...);
#include <time.h>      /* time_t, time, difftime */
    /* double difftime(time_t, time_t); */
  time_t time(time_t *);
#include <stdlib.h>    /* malloc, free */
  void *malloc(size_t);
  void free(void *);
#include <string.h>    /* memset, strncpy, strcmp */
  void *memset(void *, int, int);
  char *strncpy(char *, const char *, size_t);
  int strcmp(const char *, const char *);

#ifndef FALSE
#define FALSE  (0)
#endif

#ifndef TRUE
#define TRUE  (1)
#endif

#define MILLION   (1000000)
#define THOUSAND  (1000)

#include "ftprog.h"
```

Progress Internal Data

Because actually drawing the screen display is usually a very time-consuming operation, it's a good idea to avoid it whenever possible. The following constants are used to track which parts of the current progress information have actually changed, so that screen updates can be minimized.

```
#define FILEPOSITION_CHANGED  (1)
#define FILESIZE_CHANGED  (2)
#define FILETYPE_CHANGED  (4)
#define PROTOCOL_CHANGED  (8)
#define FILENAME_CHANGED  (16)
#define FILEPERCENT_CHANGED  (32)
#define SOMETHING_CHANGED  (0xffff)
```

The PROGRESS_PRIVATE structure keeps all of the information about the current progress display.

```
#define MAX_PROTOCOL  32     /* Length of protocol name */
#define MAX_FILENAME  128     /* Length of filename */

typedef struct {
  int sending;     /* Are we sending or receiving? */
  int inFile;     /* Are we between files? */
  int progressCode;     /* Current status */
  long filePosition;     /* Current position in file */
  long fileSize;     /* Size of file */
  int fileType;     /* Type of file */
  int filePercent;     /* Percentage of file transferred */
  char protocol[MAX_PROTOCOL + 1];     /* Name of protocol */
  char fileName[MAX_FILENAME];     /* Name of file */
  time_t fileStartTime;     /* When transfer began */
  int changed;     /* What fields have changed? */
  DEBUG debug;
} PROGRESS_PRIVATE;
```

```
⟨ Initialize PROGRESS_PRIVATE 204 ⟩ ==
  pProgress -> debug = NULL;
  pProgress -> progressCode = −1;
  pProgress -> filePosition = 0;
  pProgress -> filePercent = −1;
  pProgress -> inFile = FALSE;
  pProgress -> changed = SOMETHING_CHANGED;     /* Force update */
```

This code is used on page 205.

Initialization and Termination

This `ProgressInit` function merely allocates and initializes the progress structure. In a version designed for a graphical environment, it would probably also create and display a window. Note that if you want to provide the user a convenient "Cancel" button as part of the progress display, you may need to have some communication between this module and the serial module. See page 174 for more information.

```
int ProgressInit(PROGRESS *ppProgress_public)
{
  PROGRESS_PRIVATE **ppProgress
   = (PROGRESS_PRIVATE **) ppProgress_public;
  PROGRESS_PRIVATE *pProgress;

  *ppProgress = NULL;
  pProgress = (PROGRESS_PRIVATE *) malloc(sizeof (*pProgress));
  if (pProgress == NULL) return -1;
  memset(pProgress, 0, sizeof (*pProgress));
  ⟨Initialize PROGRESS_PRIVATE 204⟩
  *ppProgress = pProgress;
  return 0;
}
```

The destructor is equally simple. Again, in a graphical version, this function would be responsible for destroying a window or other display objects.

```
void ProgressDestroy(PROGRESS progressPublic)
{
  PROGRESS_PRIVATE *pProgress
   = (PROGRESS_PRIVATE *) progressPublic;

  if (pProgress == NULL) return;
  free(pProgress);
}
```

Currently, the **progress** module doesn't generate any debugging messages. If you try to expand this into a more elaborate graphical display, you may want to use this handle to debug your changes.

```
void ProgressSetDebug(PROGRESS progressPublic, DEBUG debug)
{
  PROGRESS_PRIVATE *pProgress
   = (PROGRESS_PRIVATE *) progressPublic;

  if (pProgress == NULL) return;
  pProgress -> debug = debug;
```

```
    return;
}
```

Progress Information

The `ProgressSending` and `ProgressReceiving` functions are usually called at the beginning of a file transfer, so that the progress display can be adjusted accordingly. Having this state also removes the need to have two complete sets of status codes. For example, without this, it might be necessary to have two different `progNegotiating` codes, one to indicate you're negotiating to receive a file, another to indicate you're negotiating to send a file.

```
void ProgressSending(PROGRESS progressPublic)
{
  PROGRESS_PRIVATE *pProgress
   = (PROGRESS_PRIVATE *) progressPublic;

  if (pProgress == NULL) return;
  pProgress -> sending = 1;
  return;
}


void ProgressReceiving(PROGRESS progressPublic)
{
  PROGRESS_PRIVATE *pProgress
   = (PROGRESS_PRIVATE *) progressPublic;

  if (pProgress == NULL) return;
  pProgress -> sending = 0;
  return;
}
```

The next five functions update information about the transfer. These functions often are called repeatedly with exactly the same values. By testing the arguments to see if any change has actually occurred, the **changed** bitmap will accurately reflect which information has truly changed, which in turn allows the display update to be optimized.

```
void ProgressProtocol(PROGRESS progressPublic, const char
      *protocol)
{
  PROGRESS_PRIVATE *pProgress
   = (PROGRESS_PRIVATE *) progressPublic;
  if (pProgress == NULL) return;
  if ((protocol == NULL) && (pProgress -> protocol[0] != 0)) {
```

```
      pProgress -> protocol[0] = 0;
      pProgress -> changed |= PROTOCOL_CHANGED;
  } else if (strcmp(protocol, pProgress -> protocol) != 0) {
      strncpy(pProgress -> protocol, protocol, MAX_PROTOCOL);
      pProgress -> protocol[MAX_PROTOCOL] = 0;
      pProgress -> changed |= PROTOCOL_CHANGED;
  }
}

void ProgressFileName(PROGRESS progressPublic, const char
        *fileName)
{
  PROGRESS_PRIVATE *pProgress
   = (PROGRESS_PRIVATE *) progressPublic;

  if (pProgress == NULL) return;
  if ((fileName == NULL) && (pProgress -> fileName[0] != 0)) {
    pProgress -> fileName[0] = 0;
    pProgress -> changed |= FILENAME_CHANGED;
  } else if (strcmp(fileName, pProgress -> fileName) != 0) {
    strncpy(pProgress -> fileName, fileName, MAX_FILENAME);
    pProgress -> fileName[MAX_FILENAME] = 0;
    pProgress -> changed |= FILENAME_CHANGED;
  }
}

void ProgressFileSize(PROGRESS progressPublic, long fileSize)
{
  PROGRESS_PRIVATE *pProgress
   = (PROGRESS_PRIVATE *) progressPublic;

  if (pProgress == NULL) return;
  if (fileSize != pProgress -> fileSize) {
    pProgress -> fileSize = fileSize;
    pProgress -> changed |= FILESIZE_CHANGED;
  }
}

void ProgressFileType(PROGRESS progressPublic, int fileType)
{
  PROGRESS_PRIVATE *pProgress
   = (PROGRESS_PRIVATE *) progressPublic;

  if (pProgress == NULL) return;
  if (fileType != pProgress -> fileType) {
    pProgress -> fileType = fileType;
```

```
        pProgress -> changed |= FILETYPE_CHANGED ;
    }
}
```

Especially with basic Kermit, you need to avoid redrawing the progress display every time the protocol reports new progress. At higher baud rates, short Kermit packets can result in five to ten progress updates per second. If every update causes the progress display to be redrawn, performance can be reduced by 25 percent or more, simply due to the overhead from drawing the screen. `ProgressFilePosition` helps to reduce this overhead by updating two different variables. The sample `ProgressReport` function below doesn't redraw the display if only the file position (but *not* the `filePercent`) has changed. If the file size is known, there won't be more than 100 screen updates, one for each percentage of the file.

```
void ProgressFilePosition(PROGRESS progressPublic, unsigned
        long filePosition)
{
  PROGRESS_PRIVATE *pProgress
   = (PROGRESS_PRIVATE *) progressPublic;
  if (pProgress == NULL) return ;
  if (filePosition != pProgress -> filePosition) {
    pProgress -> filePosition = filePosition;
    pProgress -> changed |= FILEPOSITION_CHANGED ;
  }
  if (pProgress -> fileSize > 0) {
    int percent = filePosition * 100 / pProgress -> fileSize;
    if (percent > 100) percent = 100;
    if (percent != pProgress -> filePercent) {
      pProgress -> filePercent = percent;
      pProgress -> changed |= FILEPERCENT_CHANGED ;
    }
  }
}
```

Progress Display

At the end of each file, a summary line reports the success or failure of the transfer. This version of the summary line includes a speed estimate in bits per second. It's better to display the speed in bits per second rather than bytes per second, because modems are commonly rated in bits per second, which means that users will be better able to relate an estimate in bits per second to the stated speed of their modem. Any speed estimate is preferable to the "percentage efficiency" used by many programs, because the speed of the *transfer* can be measured, but computing percentage efficiency requires knowing the speed of the *channel*, which is rarely possible. New modems present different baud rates to the computer and phone line, and file transfers are increasingly occurring over networks, where the possible throughput varies depending on many factors.

The calculation of `transferBps` is arranged to round the result to the nearest multiple of 10. The timing here is not going to be precise, and there's no reason to lie to the user by feigning better precision than is actually available. In addition, numbers with few significant digits are easier to read and easier to remember. In fact, if `transferBps` is large, it should probably be rounded even further.

```
static void ProgressEndOfFile(PROGRESS_PRIVATE *pProgress, const
        char *label, int finished)
{
  long filePosition = pProgress -> filePosition;
  const char *fileName = pProgress -> fileName;

  if (!pProgress -> inFile) return;
  pProgress -> inFile = FALSE;
  fprintf(stderr, "%s:␣", label);
  if (filePosition >= MILLION) {
    fprintf(stderr, "%ld,%03ld,%03ld␣bytes",
        filePosition / MILLION, (filePosition % MILLION) / THOUSAND,
        filePosition % THOUSAND);
  } else if (filePosition >= THOUSAND) {
    fprintf(stderr, "%3ld,%03ld␣bytes", filePosition / THOUSAND,
        filePosition % THOUSAND);
  } else fprintf(stderr, "%7ld␣bytes", filePosition);
  if (!finished)
    fprintf(stderr, "␣(out␣of␣%ld␣bytes)", pProgress -> fileSize);
  if (finished) {     /* Throughput estimate */
    double transferSeconds    /* Use double for maximum accuracy */
      = difftime(time(NULL), pProgress -> fileStartTime);
    if (transferSeconds > 0) {
      long transferBps = (filePosition / transferSeconds) * 10;
      if (transferBps >= MILLION) {
        fprintf(stderr, "%ld,%03ld,%03ld", transferBps / MILLION,
            (transferBps % MILLION) / THOUSAND,
            transferBps % THOUSAND);
      } else if (transferBps >= THOUSAND) {
        fprintf(stderr, "%3ld,%03ld", transferBps / THOUSAND,
            transferBps % THOUSAND);
      } else fprintf(stderr, "%7ld", transferBps);
```

```
          fprintf(stderr, "␣bps␣");
        } else fprintf(stderr, "%7s␣␣␣␣␣", "␣");
    }
    switch (pProgress -> fileType) {
    case diskFileLatin1: fprintf(stderr, "Latin1"); break;
    case diskFileAscii: fprintf(stderr, "ASCII␣"); break;
    case diskFileText: fprintf(stderr, "Text␣␣"); break;
    case diskFileBinary: fprintf(stderr, "Binary"); break;
    default: fprintf(stderr, "?????␣");
      break;
    }
    fprintf(stderr, "␣%-37s", fileName);
    fprintf(stderr, "\n");
}
```

Finally, here's the function to actually display the information. The most interesting part is the code to determine if anything worthwhile has changed. If the display isn't going to change, then it's a good idea to not waste the time to update the screen. The one tricky point is that this display will display either the percent progress (if it can be calculated) or the file position, but not both. That makes it a bit more complicated to determine if the display needs to change.

```
void ProgressReport(PROGRESS progressPublic, int progressCode)
{
    PROGRESS_PRIVATE *pProgress
     = (PROGRESS_PRIVATE *) progressPublic;
    const char *statString;
    ⟨Declare and initialize local copies of progress variables 211⟩
    if (progressCode == pProgress -> progressCode) {
      if (pProgress -> changed == 0) return;
      if ((pProgress -> changed == FILEPOSITION_CHANGED) && (fileSize >
          0))      /* Position changed, but not percent */
        return;
    }
    pProgress -> changed = 0;
    pProgress -> progressCode = progressCode;
    ⟨Prepare to output line 212⟩
    ⟨Interpret progressCode, set up statString 211⟩
    ⟨Print output line 212⟩
    ⟨Finish the output line 213⟩
}
```

The local variables allow ProgressReport to "forget" certain values when they no longer apply, without actually altering the values stored in the pProgress structure. For example, if no file is being transferred, it makes no sense to display a filename. `ProgressReport` sets the local variable `fileName` to `NULL` if the filename should not be displayed, and similarly for the other local variables.

⟨ Declare and initialize local copies of progress variables 211 ⟩ ≡
```
const char *fileName, *protocol;
long fileSize, filePosition;
int filePercent, fileType;

if (pProgress == NULL) return;     /* No progress handle? */
fileName = pProgress -> fileName;     /* Copy everything over */
protocol = pProgress -> protocol;
fileSize = pProgress -> fileSize;
filePosition = pProgress -> filePosition;
filePercent = pProgress -> filePercent;
fileType = pProgress -> fileType;
```
This code is used on page 210.

The primary reason for the following `switch` statement is to select a string to display based on the `progressCode`. This is also a convenient place to handle certain chores that depend on the `progressCode`. For example, I clear `fileName` and related variables so they won't be displayed when there's no file being transferred.

⟨ Interpret progressCode, set up statString 211 ⟩ ≡
```
switch (progressCode) {
case progNegotiating: statString = "Negotiating..."; break;
case progSending: statString = "Sending..."; break;
case progReceiving: statString = "Receiving..."; break;
case progNewFile: statString = "New␣File...";
  pProgress -> inFile = TRUE;
  time(&(pProgress -> fileStartTime));     /* Store start time */
  break;
case progEOF: statString = "File␣Done...";
  if (pProgress -> sending)
    ProgressEndOfFile(pProgress, "Sent", TRUE);
  else ProgressEndOfFile(pProgress, "Received", TRUE);
  break;
case progSkipped: statString = "Skipping...";
  ProgressEndOfFile(pProgress, "Skipped", TRUE);
  break;
case progEnding: statString = "Finishing..."; break;
case progDone: statString = "Finished."; break;
case progFailed: statString = "Failed.";
  ProgressEndOfFile(pProgress, "Failed", FALSE);
  break;
```

```
case progCancelled: statString = "Cancelled.";
  ProgressEndOfFile(pProgress, "Cancelled", FALSE);
  break;
default: statString = "???";
  break;
}
if (! pProgress -> inFile) {      /* Invalidate file-specific vars */
  fileName = NULL;
  fileSize = -1;
  filePosition = -1;
  filePercent = -1;
  fileType = -1;
  protocol = NULL;
}
```

This code is used on page 210.

The total size of the file being transferred isn't always known, so it's not always possible to compute a percent progress. In this case, the number of bytes transferred is displayed instead.

⟨ Print output line 212 ⟩ ==
```
fprintf(stderr, "%-15s", statString);
fprintf(stderr, "%s␣", protocol);
if (filePercent >= 0)      /* Is percent valid? */
  fprintf(stderr, "␣␣␣␣␣%3d%%", filePercent);
else if (filePosition >= 0)      /* Can't do percent? Use bytes. */
  fprintf(stderr, "%8ld", filePosition);
else      /* No information available */
  fprintf(stderr, "%8s", "");
switch (fileType) {
case diskFileAscii: fprintf(stderr, "␣Asc"); break;
case diskFileText: fprintf(stderr, "␣Txt"); break;
case diskFileBinary: fprintf(stderr, "␣Bin"); break;
case diskFileUnknown: fprintf(stderr, "␣␣?␣"); break;
default: fprintf(stderr, "␣␣␣␣"); break;
}
fprintf(stderr, "␣%-37s", (fileName) ? fileName : "");
```

This code is used on page 210.

For text-only systems, it's nice to keep a current progress display on a single line. On some systems, this simply requires writing a single CR character to the output.

⟨ Prepare to output line 212 ⟩ ==
```
#if 0
```

```
    putchar('\r');
#endif
```

This code is used on page 210.

If it's not possible to use a CR or some similar mechanism to keep a single-line progress, then you need to finish the line.

⟨ Finish the output line 213 ⟩ ==
```
    fprintf(stderr, "\n");
    fflush(stderr);
```

This code is used on page 210.

Implementing XYModem *17*

The similarities between XModem and YModem make it possible to build a single implementation that automatically adapts to either one. The key aspects of this implementation are the techniques used to track which dialect is in use.

XModem and YModem are very similar protocols. They use the same packet structure and the same half-duplex reliability. The only differences are at the transaction and session layers. These similarities led me to build a single implementation that handles both. I've coined the name *XYModem* to refer to such a combined implementation. (I never use the name "XYModem" in end-user documentation, however. There are already too many confusing variations on the names XModem and YModem.)

Over the years, I've tinkered with XYModem implementations, and developed a number of heuristics for automatically detecting the protocol dialect to be used. While such heuristics are not 100 percent reliable, they simplify the use of these protocols considerably by making the user's protocol selection less critical. These heuristics will often allow the transfer to succeed even if the user sets the protocol incorrectly. By combining this approach with the file-type heuristics discussed in Chapter 15, I've produced XYModem implementations with essentially no user options. The implementation automatically negotiates the protocol to use, automatically detects the file type, and performs any needed file conversions.

Public Interface

The client of the XYModem package performs transfers by creating and manipulating a file transfer *handle*. The general outline is:

---

†This chapter is based on material previously published in [12].

215

- Create the handle by calling `XYModemInit`.

- Set the file transfer parameters. For example, to alter the default protocol, call `XYModemSetProtocol`.

- Perform a transfer with `XYModemSend` or `XYModemReceive`.

- Destroy the handle with `XYModemDestroy`.

The only parameter to `XYModemInit` is the `port` to be used during the transfer. Everything else adopts a suitable default. Those defaults can be overridden by modifying the handle before the transfer begins. Currently, the default protocol is YModem, from which this implementation can easily negotiate XModem-CRC.

```
⟨ftxy.h   216⟩ ==
#ifndef FTXY_H_INCLUDED
#define FTXY_H_INCLUDED
#include "ftserial.h"    /* Need SERIAL_PORT */
#include "ftprog.h"    /* Need PROGRESS */
#include "ftdebug.h"    /* Need DEBUG */
  typedef void *XYMODEM;
  enum {
    XMODEM = 0, XMODEMCRC = 1, XMODEMK = 2, YMODEM = 3, YMODEMG = 4
  };
  int XYModemInit(XYMODEM *pXY, SERIAL_PORT port);
  int XYModemDestroy(XYMODEM xy);
  int XYModemSetDebug(XYMODEM xy, DEBUG debug);
  int XYModemSetProgress(XYMODEM xy, PROGRESS progress);
  int XYModemSetFileType(XYMODEM xyPublic, int fileType);
  int XYModemSetProtocol(XYMODEM xy, int protocol);
  int XYModemSend(XYMODEM xy, const char *filenames[], int
      numFiles);
  int XYModemReceive(XYMODEM xy);
  int XYModemCancel(XYMODEM xy);
#endif    /* ! FTXY_H_INCLUDED */
```

External Dependencies

Here are all of the library functions used by the `xy` module. Besides including ANSI-standard headers, I've also provided prototypes so that the usage will be clear. These prototypes should be compatible with any ANSI-standard compiler, but may need to be altered slightly for older systems.

```
#include <stddef.h>    /* size_t */
#include <stdio.h>    /* sprintf */
  char *sprintf(char *, const char *, ... );
```

```
#include <string.h>     /* strcpy, strlen, memset */
  char *strcpy(char *s1, const char *s2);
  int strlen(const char *s1);
  void memset(void *, unsigned char, int);
#include <stdlib.h>      /* atoi, malloc, free */
  int atoi(const char *s);
  void *malloc(size_t);
  void free(void *);
#include <time.h>      /* struct tm, time_t, time(), localtime() */
  time_t time(time_t *);
  struct tm *localtime(const time_t *);
```

Now come the headers for each module used by this source. Including my own public header avoids duplicating those definitions, and helps check for typing inconsistencies.

```
#include "ftdebug.h"     /* Debugging messages */
#include "ftprog.h"      /* Progress reporting */
#include "ftdisk.h"      /* Disk interfacing */
#include "ftserial.h"     /* Serial interfacing */
#include "ftxy.h"      /* Our own public header */
```

Finally, a few useful constants that are defined in some C library headers, but not in others:

```
#ifndef TRUE
#define TRUE   (1)
#endif

#ifndef FALSE
#define FALSE  (0)
#endif

#ifndef NULL     /* NULL */
#define NULL ((void *) 0)
#endif

#define STATIC static
```

Definitions

A few character constants:

```
#define SOH  (0x01)     /* Start of 128-byte packet */
#define STX  (0x02)     /* Start of 1024-byte packet */
#define EOT  (0x04)     /* EOT packet */
#define ACK  (0x06)     /* ACK packet */
```

```
#define NAK  (0x15)    /* NAK packet */
#define CAN  (0x18)    /* Two to cancel a transfer */
#define SUB  (0x1A)    /* Used to pad last packet */
```

C programmers sometimes lose sight of the critical distinction between *bytes* of data transferred and the *characters* sometimes represented by those bytes. This distinction becomes especially important as computer software becomes increasingly international. The simple equivalence between bytes and characters that American programmers have enjoyed is lost when you have to deal with multiple character sets in an international setting.

Although I've tried to avoid them, there are probably a few places in the source that depend on BYTE being unsigned.

```
typedef unsigned char BYTE;
```

The XYMODEM_PRIVATE structure contains the current state of the transfer. By keeping all information about the transfer in a dynamically-allocated structure, we can allow multiple simultaneous transfers in a multi-threaded system. By convention, this structure is passed as the first argument to any function, and is referred to within the function as pXY. By rigidly following this convention, I can write macros that use values from this structure without having to pass the structure to every macro as well. This approach makes macros like StsWarn much easier to read.

⟨ Miscellaneous typedef 219 ⟩

```
typedef struct {
  ⟨XYModem variables  218⟩
} XYMODEM_PRIVATE;
```

Here are the basic protocol variables. I'll add more variables to this list as they become necessary.

⟨XYModem variables 218⟩ ≡

```
    int timeout;     /* Number of seconds timeout */
    int retries;     /* Number of times to retry a packet */
    volatile int userCancel;    /* Set when user asks for cancel */
    int packetNumber;    /* Current packet number */
    unsigned long transferred;    /* Number of bytes transferred so far */
    long fileSize;     /* Number of bytes to transfer */
```

See also pages 220, 222, 225, 228, and 232.

This code is used on page 218.

And here's the code to initialize these variables. Again, I'll add to this scrap as new variables are introduced.

⟨ Initialize XYModem variables 219 ⟩ ≡
```
  pXY -> timeout = 10;
  pXY -> retries = 10;
  pXY -> userCancel = 0;
  pXY -> packetNumber = 0;
  pXY -> transferred = 0;
  pXY -> fileSize = 0;
```
See also pages 220, 222, 225, 229, and 232.

This code is used on page 259.

A couple of variables also need to be reset at the beginning of each file transfer.
```
STATIC void XYNewFile(XYMODEM_PRIVATE *pXY)
{
  pXY -> fileSize = 0;
  pXY -> transferred = 0;
}
```

Automatically negotiating XModem and YModem dialects involves a couple of tricks.

The first one is to properly track the protocol variant currently in use. Tracking it in terms of the common names is tough; it's easier to define the dialects by a collection of CAPABILITY records. My first XYModem implementations simply used boolean variables, but occasionally failed because errors in the middle of the transfer would prompt the implementation to change its current capabilities rather than dealing with the problem as an error.

The solution is to keep two booleans for each capability: an enabled field tracks whether or not that capability is currently being used, and a certain field is used to freeze that capability once there's evidence that the guess is correct. For example, once any packet is successfully transferred, the error detection method can be frozen.

The biggest drawback is that errors early in the transfer can potentially cause the capabilities to be frozen incorrectly, leading to a failure. In this case, the solution is either to repeat the transfer and hope to avoid those errors the second time, or to have the user to specify the protocol.

⟨ Miscellaneous typedef 219 ⟩ ≡
```
  typedef struct {
    int enabled;
    int certain;
  } CAPABILITY;
```
See also page 233.

This code is used on page 218.

Dialect	crc	longPacket	batch	G
XModem				
XModem-CRC	*			
XModem-K	*	*		
YModem	*	*	*	
YModem-G	*	*	*	*
YModem-checksum		*	*	
XModem-1K-G	*	*		*

Table 17.1   XModem and YModem Dialects

The second trick is to decide which capabilities define the common XModem and YModem dialects. I use the following four:

crc   Is CRC error checking being used?

longPacket   Are long 1024-byte packets allowed in addition to the standard 128-byte packets?

batch   Is the current transfer a batch (YModem) or single-file transfer?

G   Is the current transfer a YModem-G transfer?

Table 17.1 shows how these capabilities describe the standard five XModem and YModem dialects, as well as some less common dialects.

The implementation here doesn't attempt to support every combination of capabilities. Attempting to do so would reduce the effectiveness of the dialect negotiation, which in turn complicates things for the user, since the user's dialect selection becomes more critical. Fortunately, there's no need to support every possible dialect. The important thing is to be able to transfer files with as many people as possible. By supporting the standard five XModem and YModem dialects, you retain maximum compatibility without drowning your users in a sea of unnecessary options.

⟨XYModem variables 218⟩ +==
```
    CAPABILITY crc, longPacket, batch, G;
```

The two most popular dialects are probably YModem and XModem-CRC. I set the default to YModem, and rely on the negotiation to handle the other protocols.

⟨Initialize XYModem variables 219⟩ +==
```
    pXY -> crc . enabled = TRUE;
```

```
pXY -> crc . certain = FALSE ;
pXY -> longPacket . enabled = TRUE ;
pXY -> longPacket . certain = FALSE ;
pXY -> batch . enabled = TRUE ;
pXY -> batch . certain = FALSE ;
pXY -> G . enabled = FALSE ;
pXY -> G . certain = FALSE ;
```

Utility Functions

A number of functions are pretty generic to all of the file transfer protocols, so you'll see many of these functions again in the **z** and **k** modules.

Error Handling

Every function returns a code to indicate the success or failure of the operation. Most of these codes are fairly self-explanatory, although there is one important convention regarding the use of xyFail versus xyFailed. Both mean that the transfer is ending abnormally, but xyFail carries the additional connotation that the cancel sequence should be sent. Thus, xyFailed is returned from a fatal serial port error (it may be impossible to send the cancel sequence), while xyFail is returned from a user cancel or a disk failure. The session-layer functions XYSend and XYReceive notice the xyFail error code and handle it by sending the cancel sequence and in turn returning xyFailed.

```
enum {
  xyOK = 0,      /* No error */
  xyFail,        /* Transfer failed; send cancel sequence */
  xyFailed,      /* Transfer failed; don't send cancel sequence */
  xyBadPacket,   /* Bad CRC/checksum or soft serial error */
  xyEOT,         /* Received EOT instead of data packet */
  xyEndOfSession,  /* No more files to transfer */
  xyEOF,         /* End-of-file on file read */
  xyTimeout      /* Timeout waiting for data */
};
```

The StsRet macro encapsulates a common and useful idiom. Because essentially every function returns an error code, it is quite common to pass any error we get from a function call back to our caller. This macro uses a few tricks to avoid evaluating expr more than once and to require a trailing semicolon, which makes StsRet behave syntactically more like a function. The only catch is that the expression e can't refer to tmpErrorVal.

```
#define StsRet(expr)
        do {
          int tmpErrorVal = (expr);
          if (tmpErrorVal != xyOK) return StsWarn(tmpErrorVal);
        } while (FALSE)
```

Debugging Support

Debug messages are displayed through a debug handle provided by the client. Having the client provide this handle allows the client (that is, the main application) decide how debug messages should be handled.

⟨XYModem variables 218⟩ +==
```
  DEBUG debug;
```

The debug module interprets a NULL handle as suppressing all debug output.

⟨Initialize XYModem variables 219⟩ +==
```
  pXY -> debug = NULL;
```

These constants are used to indicate the purpose of each debug message. See Chapter 13 for details about how these are used to select which debug messages are displayed.

```
#define debugWarn   (1)
#define debugPacket  (2)
#define debugAttr   (32)
#define debugInit   (64)
```

StsWarn is liberally sprinkled through the source (for example, StsRet calls it). When debugging is enabled, any unusual event will be reported to the debug stream, along with the file and line number where it was detected. Checking the debug variable first helps avoid the function call when debugging is disabled.

```
#define StsWarn(s)  ((pXY -> debug) ? XYDebugWarn(pXY, (s),
            __FILE__, __LINE__) : (s))
  STATIC int XYDebugWarn(XYMODEM_PRIVATE *pXY, const int s, const
          char *file, const int line)
  {
    const char *msg;
    if (s == xyOK) return s;
    DebugBeginInternal(pXY -> debug, debugWarn, file, line);
    DebugString(pXY -> debug, "!?!?!?:");
    switch (s) {
    case xyFail: msg = "xyFail"; break;
```

```
    case xyFailed: msg = "xyFailed"; break;
    case xyBadPacket: msg = "xyBadPacket"; break;
    case xyEOT: msg = "xyEOT"; break;
    case xyEndOfSession: msg = "xyEndOfSession"; break;
    case xyEOF: msg = "xyEOF"; break;
    case xyTimeout: msg = "xyTimeout"; break;
    default:     /* Unknown error code */
      DebugString(pXY -> debug, "Error␣");
      DebugInt(pXY -> debug, s);
      msg = "";
    }
    DebugString(pXY -> debug, msg);
    DebugEnd(pXY -> debug);
    return s;
}
```

CRC Calculation

A detailed discussion of this code appears in Chapter 4 on page 58.

```
    STATIC unsigned int xyCrcTable[256];
    STATIC void XYInitCrc16()
    {
      static int crcDone = 0;    /* Only compute it once */
      unsigned i, j, crc;
      if (crcDone) return;
      for (i = 0; i < 256; i++) {
        crc = (i << 8);
        for (j = 0; j < 8; j++)
          crc = (crc << 1) ^ ((crc & 0x8000) ? 0x1021 : 0);
        xyCrcTable[i] = crc & 0xffff;
      }
      crcDone = 1;
    }
```

There are two different CRC update functions. The first function accumulates the CRC over a block of data.

```
    STATIC unsigned XYCrc16(void *buff, unsigned int length, unsigned
        short crc)
    {
      unsigned char *p = buff;
      while (length -- > 0)
        crc = xyCrcTable[((crc >> 8) ^ *p++) & 0xFF] ^ (crc << 8);
      return crc & 0xFFFF;
```

```
          }
```

Packets are padded with a constant value. Rather than set up and explicitly fill a chunk of memory just to calculate the CRC, I've added the following function to compute the CRC of many copies of a single byte:

```
STATIC unsigned XYCrc16Constant(unsigned char c, unsigned int
        length, unsigned short crc)
{
  while (length -- > 0)
    crc = xyCrcTable[((crc >> 8) ^ c) & 0xFF] ^ (crc << 8);
  return crc & 0xFFFF;
}
```

Time Conversions

YModem represents the modification time of the file as the number of seconds since January 1, 1970. This representation must be converted to and from a more portable format. The following two functions convert times from the YModem format to the ANSI `struct tm`. These functions are explained in more detail in the next chapter (see page 278).

```
STATIC void XYTimeToTm(long s, struct tm *pT)
{
  long m, h;      /* minutes, hours */
  int d, M, y;    /* day, Month, year */
  if (s <= 0) {     /* If time undefined, just use current time */
    time_t t = time(NULL);

    *pT = *localtime(&t);
    return;
  }
  m = s / 60; h = m / 60; d = h / 24; y = d / 365;
  s %= 60; m %= 60; h %= 24; d %= 365;     /* Reduce everything */
  d -= (y + 1) / 4;     /* Correct for leap years since 1970 */
  if (d < 0) {
    y --;
    d += 365;
  }
  pT -> tm_sec = s; pT -> tm_min = m; pT -> tm_hour = h;
  pT -> tm_yday = d;
  if (((y - 2) % 4 != 0) && (d >= 59)) d++;
  if (d >= 60) d++;     /* day number if Feb has 30 days (see page 278) */
  M = (d > 214) ? 7 : 0 + ((d % 214) / 61) * 2 + ((d % 214) % 61) / 31;
      /* Jan is zero */
```

```
        d = ((d % 214) % 61) % 31 + 1;      /* day of month */
        pT -> tm_mday = d; pT -> tm_mon = M; pT -> tm_year = y + 70;
        pT -> tm_isdst = -1;      /* DST unknown */
        pT -> tm_wday = -1;       /* Day of week unknown */
    }
```

The function to convert from `struct tm` to YModem's time format is considerably simpler:

```
    STATIC long XYTime(struct tm *pT)
    {
        static const int mon[] = {0, 31, 60, 91, 121, 152, 182, 213, 244,
            274, 305, 335};
        int  y = pT -> tm_year - 70,  M = pT -> tm_mon;
        int  d = pT -> tm_mday - 1 + mon[M];
        if (((y + 2) % 4 != 0) & (M > 1)) d--;      /* Adjust for non-leap years */
        d += (y + 1) / 4;      /* Correct for leap years since 1970 */
        return ((((((long) y) * 365 + d) * 24 + pT -> tm_hour) * 60 + pT ->
            tm_min) * 60 + pT -> tm_sec;
    }
```

Interfaces to External Modules

These next few sections are a group of "sockets" where various services are plugged in. Because these services vary from system to system, the functions should be modified to fit whatever "plugs" are available.

Serial Interface

This section provides basic serial functions by interfacing to the `serial` module.

```
    ⟨XYModem variables 218⟩ +==
        SERIAL_PORT port;      /* Port to use */
```

```
    ⟨Initialize XYModem variables 219⟩ +==
        pXY -> port = NULL;
```

Because the `serial` module keeps all the information about the serial port status internally, only this one variable is necessary.

It's important that `XYSerialReadWithTimeout` accept an explicit `timeout` parameter rather than using the value in the `XYMODEM_PRIVATE` structure. At various points in the protocol, it's important to use a different timeout value.

Here are the errors that can be returned from this function:

xyFail is returned if pXY -> userCancel becomes set. Note that if the serial function indicates a user cancel, pXY -> userCancel is set first.

xyFailed is returned if there is a fatal serial port error—loss of carrier or some similar hardware-level failure—that prohibits future serial I/O.

xyTimeout is returned if there is a timeout.

xyBadPacket is returned if a framing or overflow error is detected.

xyOK is returned if the request is satisfied.

```
STATIC int XYSerialReadWithTimeout(XYMODEM_PRIVATE *pXY, int
        timeout, BYTE *pBuffer, size_t length)
{
  int s, returnVal;
  if (pXY -> userCancel) return StsWarn(xyFail);
  s = SerialReadWithTimeout(pXY -> port, timeout, pBuffer, &length);
  switch (s) {
  case serialOK: returnVal = xyOK;
    break;
  case serialTimeout: returnVal = xyTimeout;
    break;
  case serialUserCancel: pXY -> userCancel = TRUE;
    returnVal = xyFail;
    break;
  case serialFrame: returnVal = xyBadPacket;
    break;
  default: return StsWarn(xyFailed);
  }
  if (pXY -> userCancel) return StsWarn(xyFail);
  return returnVal;
}
```

Chapter 14 discusses the reason for dividing the routine to send bytes into the two functions XYSerialSend and XYSerialWaitForSentBytes. Page 174 discusses this in more detail.

Partly because sending takes less time than receiving, there are fewer errors to be considered:

xyFail is returned if pXY -> userCancel becomes set.

xyFailed is returned if there is a fatal serial port error.

xyOK is returned otherwise.

```
STATIC int XYSerialSend(XYMODEM_PRIVATE *pXY, const BYTE
      *pBuffer, unsigned int length)
{
  int s, returnVal;
  if (pXY -> userCancel) return StsWarn(xyFail);
  s = SerialSend(pXY -> port, pBuffer, length);
  switch (s) {
  case serialOK: returnVal = xyOK;
    break;
  case serialUserCancel: pXY -> userCancel = TRUE;
    returnVal = xyFail;
    break;
  default: return StsWarn(xyFailed);
  }
  if (pXY -> userCancel) return StsWarn(xyFail);
  return StsWarn(returnVal);
}
```

XYSerialWaitForSentBytes delays until the send queue is empty. This function is used by the protocol to exploit the time during which the outgoing serial queue is being emptied.

There are only a few errors that this function might return:

xyFail   is returned if pXY -> userCancel becomes set.

xyFailed   is returned if there is a fatal serial port error.

xyOK   is returned otherwise.

```
STATIC int XYSerialWaitForSentBytes(XYMODEM_PRIVATE *pXY)
{
  int s, returnVal;
  if (pXY -> userCancel) return StsWarn(xyFail);
  s = SerialWaitForSentBytes(pXY -> port);
  switch (s) {
  case serialOK: returnVal = xyOK;
    break;
  case serialUserCancel: pXY -> userCancel = TRUE;
    returnVal = xyFail;
    break;
  default: return StsWarn(xyFailed);
  }
  if (pXY -> userCancel) return StsWarn(xyFail);
  return StsWarn(returnVal);
}
```

It's convenient to have functions to read or send a single byte.

```
STATIC int XYSendByte(XYMODEM_PRIVATE *pXY, BYTE b)
{
  return StsWarn(XYSerialSend(pXY, &b, 1));
}


STATIC int XYSerialReadByte(XYMODEM_PRIVATE *pXY, int
        timeout, BYTE *pByte)
{
  return StsWarn(XYSerialReadWithTimeout(pXY, timeout, pByte, 1));
}
```

XYGobble simply reads characters from the serial port until a particular time-out occurs. It is used to skip over noise bursts when recovering from errors, and to swallow any dying gasp from the other end when the transfer is finished. As a special case, XYGobble(0) simply flushes the receive queue.

```
STATIC int XYGobble(XYMODEM_PRIVATE *pXY, int timeout)
{
  int err;
  BYTE junk[50];
  do {
    err = XYSerialReadWithTimeout(pXY, timeout, junk, sizeof
        (junk));
    if (err == xyBadPacket) err = xyOK;    /* Ignore soft errors */
  } while (err == xyOK);
  if (err == xyTimeout) return xyOK;
  return StsWarn(err);
}
```

Reading Files

The file interface consists of three functions for reading files and three for writing files. The read/write and close functions are pretty simple, but the open functions can be quite complex. Again, these versions just call the disk module.

The top-level XYModemSend function accepts a list of filenames to be sent and stashes it in these variables where XYFileReadOpenNext can access it. For simplicity, I've used an array of strings, although this can be replaced by another structure by changing XYModemSend and XYFileReadOpenNext.

```
⟨XYModem variables 218⟩ +==
  DISKFILE f;    /* Current file */
  const char **filenames;    /* Used by XYFileReadOpenNext */
  int currentFileName;
```

```
    int numFileNames;
    int fileType;
```

⟨ Initialize XYModem variables 219 ⟩ +==
```
    pXY -> f = NULL;
    pXY -> filenames = NULL;
    pXY -> currentFileName = 0;
    pXY -> numFileNames = 0;
    pXY -> fileType = diskFileUnknown;
```

XYFileReadOpenNext opens the next file to be sent. It attempts to open, in turn, each file in the list, silently skipping any files that can't be opened. It returns xyEndOfSession if there are no openable files.

```
    STATIC int XYFileReadOpenNext(XYMODEM_PRIVATE *pXY)
    {
      int err;
      while (1) {
        if (pXY -> currentFileName == pXY -> numFileNames)
          return xyEndOfSession;
        err = DiskReadOpen(&pXY -> f,
            pXY -> filenames [pXY -> currentFileName ++], pXY -> fileType);
        switch (err) {
        case diskOK: DiskFileSize(pXY -> f, &(pXY -> fileSize));
          return xyOK;
        case diskCantRead: break;
        case diskNoSuchFile: break;
        default: return xyFail;
        }
      }
    }


    STATIC int XYFileRead(XYMODEM_PRIVATE *pXY, BYTE
        *pBuffer, unsigned long *pLength)
    {
      int returnVal;
      switch (DiskRead(pXY -> f, pBuffer, *pLength, pLength)) {
      case diskOK: returnVal = xyOK; break;
      case diskEOF: returnVal = xyEOF; break;
      default: returnVal = xyFail; break;
      }
      return returnVal;
    }
```

```
STATIC int XYFileReadClose(XYMODEM_PRIVATE *pXY)
{
  int returnVal;

  switch (DiskReadClose(pXY -> f)) {
  case diskOK: returnVal = xyOK; break;
  default: returnVal = xyFail; break;
  }
  pXY -> f = NULL;
  return returnVal;
}
```

Writing Files

Rather than calling XYFileWriteOpen with a filename and other file attributes, I've opted to just pass the YModem batch header and have XYFileWriteOpen parse it directly.

Most of the hard work—making sure the filename is valid for this system and avoiding file collisions—is handled in the disk module.

```
STATIC int XYFileWriteOpen(XYMODEM_PRIVATE *pXY, BYTE
        *pBuffer, unsigned length)
{
  const char *fileName = (char *) pBuffer;
  long fileMode = −1;
  struct tm fileDate;

  ⟨ Set default fileName, fileDate 231 ⟩
  ⟨ Parse the YModem filename and file information 231 ⟩
  if (DiskWriteInit(&pXY -> f)) return StsWarn(xyFail);
  if (DiskWriteName(pXY -> f, fileName)) return StsWarn(xyFail);
  if (pXY -> fileSize >= 0)
    if (DiskWriteSize(pXY -> f, pXY -> fileSize))
      return StsWarn(xyFail);
  if (DiskWriteDate(pXY -> f, &fileDate)) return StsWarn(xyFail);
  if (DiskWriteMode(pXY -> f, fileMode)) return StsWarn(xyFail);
  if (DiskWriteType(pXY -> f, diskFileUnknown))
    return StsWarn(xyFail);
  if (DiskWriteOpen(pXY -> f)) return StsWarn(xyFail);
  return xyOK;
}
```

The previous function glosses over parsing the file information. The first step is to set up suitable defaults in case this is an XModem transfer with no filename. Here I simply set up a dummy YModem file header. The two NULL characters indicate empty attributes for the parsing code that follows. I also generate a suitable default file modification date.

⟨ Set default `fileName`, `fileDate` 231 ⟩ ==
```
if (fileName == NULL) fileName = "xymodem.000\0\0";
{      /* default file date is now */
  time_t  t = time(NULL);
  fileDate = *localtime(&t);
}
```
This code is used on page 230.

YModem sends a NULL-terminated filename, which is followed by a second NULL-terminated string with other file information. The three fields in this second string are the file size in decimal, the modification date as an octal number specifying seconds since January 1, 1970, and a Unix-style file mode. Any or all of these may be omitted, so this routine must be careful to watch for a truncated string.

⟨ Parse the YModem filename and file information 231 ⟩ ==
```
{
  const char *p = fileName;
  p += strlen(p) + 1;
  pXY -> fileSize = -1;      /* Initialize to default values */
  if (*p) {      /* Get the file size */
    pXY -> fileSize = atoi(p);
    while ((*p) && (*p != '␣')) p++;      /* Advance to next field */
    while (*p == '␣') p++;
  }
  if (*p) {      /* Get the mod date */
    long fileDateSeconds = 0;
    while ((*p) && (*p >= '0') && (*p <= '7')) {
      fileDateSeconds = fileDateSeconds * 8 + (*p) - '0';
      p++;
    }
    XYTimeToTm(fileDateSeconds, &fileDate);
    while ((*p) && (*p != '␣')) p++;      /* Advance to next field */
    while (*p == '␣') p++;
  }
  if (*p) {      /* Get the file mode */
    fileMode = 0;
    while ((*p) && (*p >= '0') && (*p <= '7')) {
      fileMode = fileMode * 8 + (*p) - '0';
      p++;
    }
```

```
        while ((*p) && (*p != '␣')) p++;        /* Advance to next field */
        while (*p == '␣') p++;
    }
}
```
This code is used on page 230.

Note that the file modification date is in UCT (Universal Coordinated Time, also known as Greenwich Mean Time). Depending on the file interface, it may be necessary to convert this date into local time. The `XYTimeToTm` and `XYTime` functions are probably the appropriate place to handle this conversion.

```
STATIC int XYFileWrite(XYMODEM_PRIVATE *pXY, const BYTE
        *pBuffer, unsigned length)
{
    switch (DiskWrite(pXY -> f, pBuffer, length)) {
    case diskOK: return xyOK;
    default: return xyFail;
    }
}


STATIC int XYFileWriteClose(XYMODEM_PRIVATE *pXY)
{
    int returnVal;
    switch (DiskWriteClose(pXY -> f)) {
    case diskOK: returnVal = xyOK;
        break;
    default: returnVal = xyFail;
        break;
    }
    pXY -> f = NULL;
    return returnVal;
}
```

Progress Reporting

The client provides a progress handle by calling `XYModemSetProgress` before the transfer begins. As always, if you don't want to use the machinery in `ftprog`, you can flesh out this section to do everything directly.

⟨ XYModem variables 218 ⟩ +≡
```
    PROGRESS progress;
```

⟨ Initialize XYModem variables 219 ⟩ +≡
```
    pXY -> progress = NULL;
```

Rather than using the constants from `ftprog` directly, I've defined aliases here. That way, if you do decide not to use the `ftprog` module, you can redefine these as appropriate.

⟨Miscellaneous `typedef` 219⟩ +≡
```
enum {
    stsNegotiating = progNegotiating, stsSending = progSending,
        stsReceiving = progReceiving, stsEnding = progEnding,
        stsDone = progDone, stsEOF = progEOF, stsNewFile = progNewFile,
        stsFailed = progFailed, stsCancelled = progCancelled
};
```

One interesting piece of progress information that's somewhat unique to this protocol implementation is the protocol dialect currently being used. I'll discuss the details of that in a moment.

```
STATIC void XYProgress(XYMODEM_PRIVATE *pXY, int status)
{
    const char *protocol;
    char protoName[15];

    ⟨Get name of current protocol in protocol 234⟩
    ProgressProtocol(pXY -> progress, protocol);
    if (pXY -> f) {
        const char *fileName = NULL;
        int fileType = 0;

        DiskFileName(pXY -> f, &fileName);
        ProgressFileName(pXY -> progress, fileName);
        DiskFileType(pXY -> f, &fileType);
        ProgressFileType(pXY -> progress, fileType);
    } else {
        ProgressFileName(pXY -> progress, NULL);
    }
    ProgressFileSize(pXY -> progress, pXY -> fileSize);
    ProgressFilePosition(pXY -> progress, pXY -> transferred);
    ProgressReport(pXY -> progress, status);
}
```

Determining the name of the current protocol based on the capbilities is a bit tricky. The approach used here will work for the standard dialects, but may need to be revised if you try to add other dialects.

To simplify debugging the protocol negotiation, the protocol name is generated differently if `pXY -> debug` is non-NULL. During debugging, the protocol name is replaced by a four-character string that encodes the four capabilities directly. This display is useful for debugging and for better understanding the negotiation techniques used. Each character represents one capability, according to the following tables:

Capability	Character
crc	C
longPacket	K
batch	B
G	G

	Enabled	Disabled
Certain	Upper case	dash
Uncertain	Lower case	blank

One point to watch for in this alternate display is that the `longPacket` capability is never both disabled and certain. (Think about it.) The `ChooseLetter` macro is an attempt to clarify this repetitive piece of code.

```
#define ChooseLetter(f,ec,eu,dc,du)
        ((f).enabled ? ((f).certain ? ec : eu) : ((f).certain ? dc :
        du))
```

⟨ Get name of current protocol in protocol 234 ⟩ ≡
```
if (pXY -> debug) {
    protoName[0] = ChooseLetter(pXY -> crc, 'C', 'c', '-', '␣');
    protoName[1] = ChooseLetter(pXY ->longPacket, 'K', 'k', '-', '␣');
    protoName[2] = ChooseLetter(pXY -> batch, 'B', 'b', '-', '␣');
    protoName[3] = ChooseLetter(pXY -> G, 'G', 'g', '-', '␣');
    protoName[4] = 0;
    protocol = protoName;
} else {
    if (pXY -> batch.enabled) {
        if (pXY -> G.enabled) protocol = "YModem-G";
        else protocol = "YModem";
    } else {
        if (pXY -> longPacket.enabled) protocol = "XModem-K";
        else if (pXY -> crc.enabled) protocol = "XModem-CRC";
        else protocol = "XModem";
    }
}
```
This code is used on page 233.

Packet Layer

One of biggest weaknesses of both XModem and YModem is the variety of different packets. Most control packets are single characters. I've taken a common approach and used single-byte I/O calls to read and write those packets directly throughout most of the implementation. This section deals primarily with sending and receiving data packets.

Sending Packets

One control packet does deserve it's own function. XYModem's Cancel packet consists of at least two consecutive CAN characters. This routine sends five (so that if any one is lost, two consecutive will still get through), and follows it with five BS (Backspace) characters. The BS characters are intended to erase the CANs from a command line in case the other end has already terminated.

The biggest problem with this approach is that since XYModem doesn't encode data, it's perfectly valid for two consecutive CAN characters to appear within a data packet. This can sometimes make it difficult to manually terminate a receiver; if the receiver is currently attempting to receive a data packet, it won't be watching for a cancel sequence.

```
STATIC int XYSendCAN(XYMODEM_PRIVATE *pXY)
{
  static const BYTE cancel[] = {CAN, CAN, CAN, CAN, CAN, 8, 8, 8, 8,
      8};
  XYSerialSend(pXY, cancel, sizeof (cancel) / sizeof (cancel[0]));
  if (pXY -> debug) {
    DebugBegin(pXY -> debug, debugWarn | debugPacket);
    DebugString(pXY -> debug, "Sent␣CAN␣CAN␣to␣cancel␣transfer.");
    DebugEnd(pXY -> debug);
  }
  return xyOK;
}
```

The XYSendPacket function actually sends an XYModem data packet. The length must be less than 1024. Packets shorter than 128 or longer than 128 but shorter than 1024 are padded with SUB characters.

```
STATIC int XYSendPacket(XYMODEM_PRIVATE *pXY, BYTE
        *pBuffer, unsigned length)
{
  int i;
  if (length <= 128) StsRet(XYSendByte(pXY, SOH));
  else StsRet(XYSendByte(pXY, STX));
  StsRet(XYSendByte(pXY, pXY -> packetNumber));
  StsRet(XYSendByte(pXY, ~pXY -> packetNumber));
  ⟨Send the data, pad to 128 or 1024 bytes 236⟩
  if (pXY -> crc . enabled) ⟨Accumulate and send CRC 237⟩
  else ⟨Accumulate and send checksum 237⟩
  if (pXY -> debug) {
    DebugBegin(pXY -> debug, debugPacket);
    DebugString(pXY -> debug, "Sent␣packet:␣Number:");
```

```
      DebugInt(pXY -> debug, pXY -> packetNumber);
      DebugString(pXY -> debug, "␣Length:");
      DebugUInt(pXY -> debug, length);
      DebugString(pXY -> debug, "␣''");
      if (length < 40) {
        DebugStringCount(pXY -> debug, (const char *)
            pBuffer, length);
        DebugString(pXY -> debug, "''");
      } else {
        DebugStringCount(pXY -> debug, (const char *) pBuffer, 39);
        DebugString(pXY -> debug, "...");
      }
      DebugEnd(pXY -> debug);
    }
    return xyOK;
  }
```

Some XModem and YModem implementations only insert a single SUB character (Control-Z) at the end of the file, and leave the remainder of the last packet with whatever garbage happened to be in the buffer. The problem is that XModem and YModem transfers regularly leave the padding as part of the received file; such padding can wreak havoc with certain applications, especially those that expect to find certain data at specific offsets from the end of the file. By filling the remainder of the last packet with the SUB character, it's easier to manually or automatically detect and remove this padding.

⟨ Send the data, pad to 128 or 1024 bytes 236 ⟩ ==
```
    StsRet(XYSerialSend(pXY, pBuffer, length));
    for (i = length; i < 128; i++) StsRet(XYSendByte(pXY, SUB));
    if (i > 128)
      for ( ;  i < 1024; i++) StsRet(XYSendByte(pXY, SUB));
```
This code is used on page 235.

The last three statements in this next section are quite critical. This code waits for the send buffer to clear, then flushes the receive queue, and only then sends the last byte of the packet. The reason for this approach is to dispose of any noise that was received while the packet was being sent. Since the receiver can't respond until the last byte of the packet is received, anything we receive before the last byte is sent must be noise. (The only exception is that the receiver or a remote user might send the cancel sequence. XYGobble checks for the cancel sequence for just this reason.) This effectively nullifies some "protocol cheating" schemes in which the receiver deliberately sends an ACK before it receives the packet in order to improve the throughput.

⟨ Accumulate and send CRC 237 ⟩ ==

```
{
  int crc = 0;      /* Accumulate CRC for data and padding */
  crc = XYCrc16(pBuffer,.length, 0);      /* Crc of data */
  if (length < 128)      /* Pad to 128 bytes */
    crc = XYCrc16Constant(SUB, 128 - length, crc);
  else if (length > 128)      /* Pad to 1024 bytes */
    crc = XYCrc16Constant(SUB, 1024 - length, crc);
  StsRet(XYSendByte(pXY, crc >> 8));
  StsRet(XYSerialWaitForSentBytes(pXY));
  StsRet(XYGobble(pXY, 0));      /* Clear receive queue */
  StsRet(XYSendByte(pXY, crc));
}
```

This code is used on page 235.

The same considerations apply to sending a checksum.

⟨ Accumulate and send checksum 237 ⟩ ==

```
{
  int checksum = 0;      /* Accumulate checksum for data and padding */
  for (i = 0; i < length; i++) checksum += pBuffer[i];
  if (i > 128) checksum += (1024 - i) * SUB;
  else checksum += (128 - i) * SUB;
  StsRet(XYSerialWaitForSentBytes(pXY));
  StsRet(XYGobble(pXY, 0));      /* Clear any garbage from receive queue */
  StsRet(XYSendByte(pXY, checksum));
}
```

This code is used on page 235.

Receiving Packets

Except for the initial startup handshake, the sender only needs to receive three kinds of packets:

- Acknowledgment packets, which consist of a single ACK character.
- Negative acknowledgment packets, which consist of a single NAK character.
- Cancel packets, which consist of two consecutive CAN characters.

```
STATIC int XYSendReadAckNak(XYMODEM_PRIVATE *pXY, BYTE
    *pResponse)
{
  int err;
  int canCount = 0;
```

```
   do {     /* Read ACK or NAK response */
    err = XYSerialReadByte(pXY, pXY -> timeout * 5, pResponse);
    switch (err) {
    case xyOK:     /* Got valid byte */
      if (*pResponse == CAN) {
        DebugBegin(pXY -> debug, debugWarn);
        DebugString(pXY -> debug, "Received␣CAN␣CAN␣wh\
            ile␣waiting␣on␣response␣to␣packet");
        DebugEnd(pXY -> debug);
        if (++ canCount >= 2) return StsWarn(xyFailed);
      } else canCount = 0;
      break;
    case xyBadPacket:     /* Soft serial error */
      *pResponse = 0;
      break;
    default: return StsWarn(err);
    }
  } while ((*pResponse != ACK) && (*pResponse != NAK));
  if (pXY -> debug) {
    DebugBegin(pXY -> debug, debugPacket);
    if (*pResponse == ACK)
      DebugString(pXY -> debug, "Received␣ACK␣for␣packet␣");
    else DebugString(pXY -> debug, "Received␣NAK␣for␣packet␣");
    DebugInt(pXY -> debug, pXY -> packetNumber);
    DebugEnd(pXY -> debug);
  }
  return StsWarn(err);
}
```

Similarly, the receiver cares about three types of packets:

- Data packets, which start with a recognizable 3-byte sequence.

- End-of-file packets, which consist of a single EOT character.

- Cancel packets, which consist of two consecutive CAN characters.

I've used a shorter timeout between bytes within a packet than between packets to speed error recovery.

```
STATIC int XYReceivePacket(XYMODEM_PRIVATE *pXY, int
      *pPacketNumber, BYTE *pBuffer, unsigned *pLength)
{
  BYTE startOfPacket = 0;
  BYTE packet = 0;
  BYTE packetCheck = 0;
```

```
    int err;
    ⟨ Search for packet start 239 ⟩
    ⟨ Receive the packet data 240 ⟩
    if (pXY -> crc . enabled)
        ⟨ Compare the CRC, return if it doesn't match 240 ⟩
    else ⟨ Compare the checksum, return if it doesn't match 240 ⟩
    ⟨ Debug message about received packet 241 ⟩
    *pPacketNumber = packet;
    pXY -> crc . certain = TRUE;        /* Checksum/crc mode is now known */
    if (*pLength > 128) {
        pXY -> longPacket . enabled = TRUE;
        pXY -> longPacket . certain = TRUE;
    }
    return xyOK;
}
```

Inter-packet noise is always a concern. Fortunately, XModem and YModem data packets have a check on the packet number, so I search incoming bytes for a three-byte sequence that matches the start of a valid packet. Such a sequence starts with either an SOH or STX for short or long packets, respectively. This byte is followed by the packet sequence number and its complement.

This code also notices and responds to end-of-file (EOT) and cancel packets (CAN CAN). Since end-of-file packets are a single byte, this loop deliberately does not look for an EOT character after the first byte. Otherwise, it might accidentally read the packet sequence number as an end-of-file packet. The cancel packet is pretty much immune from this problem.

```
⟨ Search for packet start 239 ⟩ ==
    do {      /* Ignore soft serial errors */
        err = XYSerialReadByte(pXY, pXY -> timeout, &packetCheck);
        if (err != xyBadPacket) StsRet(err);
    } while (err == xyBadPacket);
    if (packetCheck == EOT) return xyEOT;
    do {
        startOfPacket = packet;
        packet = packetCheck;
        err = XYSerialReadByte(pXY, pXY -> timeout, &packetCheck);
        if (err == xyBadPacket) {      /* Soft serial error resets search */
            startOfPacket = packet = packetCheck = 0;
        } else StsRet(err);
        if ((packetCheck == CAN) && (packet == CAN)) {
            DebugBegin(pXY -> debug, debugWarn | debugPacket);
            DebugString(pXY -> debug,
                "Received⎵CAN⎵CAN⎵while⎵waiting⎵for⎵packet");
```

```
        DebugEnd(pXY -> debug);
        return StsWarn(xyFailed);
    }
} while (((startOfPacket != SOH) && (startOfPacket !=
        STX)) || (((packet ^ packetCheck) & 0xFF) != 0xFF));
```
This code is used on page 239.

The next step is to receive the actual packet data. Notice that no attempt is made to watch for a cancel, because two consecutive **CAN** characters can legally appear within a packet. If the end of a data packet is lost, a cancel packet immediately following will be ignored. This is a fundamental restriction of the protocol, which explains why users sometimes have difficulty terminating an errant XModem or YModem transfer with the keyboard cancel sequence.

⟨ Receive the packet data 240 ⟩ ==
```
    if (startOfPacket == SOH) *pLength = 128;
    else *pLength = 1024;
    StsRet(XYSerialReadWithTimeout(pXY, 2, pBuffer, *pLength));
```
This code is used on page 239.

The next two scraps receive a CRC or checksum and verify the packet. The automatic negotiation could be carried one step further by adding code to these two scraps to try the other error check if the first one fails. This additional check would rapidly catch certain negotiation problems. If you decide to add this, be careful to do it only if the crc capability is still uncertain. Otherwise, you may compromise the error detection, accepting a damaged packet with an incorrect CRC because it happened to have a correct checksum.

⟨ Compare the CRC, **return** if it doesn't match 240 ⟩ ==
```
    {
        unsigned crc = XYCrc16(pBuffer, *pLength, 0);
        BYTE crcByte;
        int receivedCrc;
        StsRet(XYSerialReadByte(pXY, 2, &crcByte));
        receivedCrc = (crcByte & 0xFF) << 8;
        StsRet(XYSerialReadByte(pXY, 2, &crcByte));
        receivedCrc |= (crcByte & 0xFF);
        if (crc != receivedCrc) return StsWarn(xyBadPacket);
    }
```
This code is used on page 239.

⟨ Compare the checksum, **return** if it doesn't match 240 ⟩ ==
```
    {
        unsigned checksum = 0;
```

```
    BYTE receivedChecksum;
    int length = *pLength;
    while (length -- > 0)    /* Accumulate checksum */
      checksum += *pBuffer ++;
    checksum & = 0xFF;
    StsRet(XYSerialReadByte(pXY, 2, &receivedChecksum));
    if (checksum != receivedChecksum) return StsWarn(xyBadPacket);
  }
```
This code is used on page 239.

```
⟨ Debug message about received packet 241 ⟩ ==
  if (pXY -> debug) {
    DebugBegin(pXY -> debug, debugPacket);
    DebugString(pXY -> debug, "Received␣packet␣#");
    DebugInt(pXY -> debug, packet);
    DebugString(pXY -> debug, "␣length:");
    DebugUInt(pXY -> debug, *pLength);
    DebugEnd(pXY -> debug);
  }
```
This code is used on page 239.

Reliability Layer

For half-duplex protocols, sending a packet reliably simply means sending it until it is acknowledged. The only difference is for the YModem-G protocol, which doesn't require an acknowledgment (and hence cannot recover from errors).

You could add code here to attempt to recover from spurious ACKs. A spurious acknowledgment causes the sender to advance to the next packet, while the receiver is still waiting for this one. One solution is to fall back to the previous packet after a large number of NAKs. This approach requires saving an ACKed packet somewhere in the XYMODEM_PRIVATE structure, along with some additional bookkeeping information.

```
    STATIC int XYSendPacketReliable(XYMODEM_PRIVATE *pXY, BYTE
          *pBuffer, unsigned int length)
  {
    int err;
    BYTE response = ACK;
    do {
      StsRet(XYSendPacket(pXY, pBuffer, length));
      if (pXY -> G . enabled) return xyOK;
      err = XYSendReadAckNak(pXY, &response);
```

```
      if (err == xyTimeout) return StsWarn(xyFail);
      StsRet(err);
   } while (response != ACK);
   pXY -> crc . certain = TRUE;      /* Checksum/crc mode is now known */
   if (length > 128) {
     pXY -> longPacket . enabled = TRUE;
     pXY -> longPacket . certain = TRUE;
   }
   return xyOK;
}
```

One of the weaknesses of the original XModem protocol was its susceptibility
to a spurious EOT. An EOT character generated by noise would cause the receiver
to send an ACK and immediately terminate. To defend against a premature termination, newer implementations deliberately respond with a NAK to the first EOT,
expecting the sender to repeat it. If this fails, the receiver can reasonably assume
the EOT was a consequence of noise, and proceed with the transfer. This strategy,
discussed in [16], means that the sender must be careful to wait for an acknowledgment. Some older senders terminate prematurely, causing transfers to mysteriously
fail even after all of the data is correctly transferred.

```
STATIC int XYSendEOTReliable(XYMODEM_PRIVATE *pXY)
{
  BYTE b;
  int retries = pXY -> retries;
  int err;
  do {
    StsRet(XYSendByte(pXY, EOT));
    err = XYSerialReadByte(pXY, pXY -> timeout, &b);
    switch (err) {
    case xyOK:      /* Received valid byte */
      if (pXY -> debug) {
        DebugBegin(pXY -> debug, debugPacket);
        DebugString(pXY -> debug, "Response␣to␣EOT:␣");
        switch (b) {
        case ACK: DebugString(pXY -> debug, "ACK"); break;
        case NAK: DebugString(pXY -> debug, "NAK"); break;
        default: DebugChar(pXY -> debug, b); break;
        }
        DebugEnd(pXY -> debug);
      }
      if (b == ACK) return xyOK;
      else StsRet(XYGobble(pXY, 3));
      break;
```

```
    case xyTimeout:      /* Ignore timeout and soft serial errors */
      case xyBadPacket: break;
    default: return StsWarn(err);
    }
    if (retries -- == 0) return StsWarn(xyFail);
  } while (TRUE);
  return xyOK;
}
```

As mentioned before, the receiver must recognize three types of packets: data packets, EOT packets, and cancel packets. Unfortunately, each one has a different reliability concern.

Receiving data packets reliably simply requires responding with NAK to illegal packets or timeouts, until either the retry count is exceeded or a valid packet is received. Note that this layer does *not* send an ACK after receiving a good packet. The primary reason is to avoid overlapping serial and disk I/O. Not all computers can overlap I/O, so it's a good idea to make sure the other end won't have reason to send data until any disk I/O is complete. (Of course, if you know your system can safely overlap I/O, it is slightly faster to send the acknowledge before pausing to write to disk.)

Receiving EOT packets reliably is somewhat complicated. For YModem-G, any EOT packet must be assumed to be reliable (presumably, if spurious EOTs were possible, we wouldn't be using YModem-G). Otherwise, I follow the strategy described earlier of responding with a NAK and waiting for a repeat. The problem with this approach comes from older senders that don't wait for an acknowledgment. To handle such senders, I also treat an EOT followed by three successive timeouts as reliable. The trick is to keep a counter that is incremented by 3 for each EOT seen and by 1 for each timeout after an EOT. Once the counter reaches 6, there have either been two EOTs or an EOT followed by three timeouts.

Cancel packets (two CANs) are already reliable.

```
STATIC int XYReceivePacketReliable(XYMODEM_PRIVATE *pXY, int
    *pPacket, BYTE *pBuffer, unsigned *pLength)
{
  int err;
  int eotCount = 0;
  int retries = pXY -> retries;
  do {
    err = XYReceivePacket(pXY, pPacket, pBuffer, pLength);
    if (err == xyEOT) {      /* EOT packet seen */
      if (pXY -> G . enabled) return xyEOT;
      eotCount += 3;
    } else if (err == xyTimeout) {
```

```
            if (eotCount > 0) eotCount ++ ;     /* Timeout after EOT */
            else if (pXY -> G . enabled) return StsWarn(xyFail);
        } else if (err == xyBadPacket) {
            eotCount = 0;
            if (pXY -> G . enabled) return StsWarn(xyFail);
        } else return StsWarn(err);
        if (eotCount >= 6) return StsWarn(xyEOT);
        StsRet(XYSendByte(pXY, NAK));
    } while (retries -- > 0);
    return StsWarn(xyFail);
}
```

Transaction Layer

With the reliability functions described above, sending the actual file data is very
simple. The tricky part is handling the negotiation.

Sending Files

Sending a file requires first interpreting the receiver's handshake and determining
whether the receiver can accept a batch header. The first function simply builds
and sends a batch header for the current file. I've violated my layering conventions
by calling the file status functions in the disk module directly.

```
    STATIC int XYSendPacketZero(XYMODEM_PRIVATE *pXY)
    {
        const char *fileName = NULL;
        long fileSize = -1;
        int fileType = diskFileUnknown;
        long fileMode = -1;
        struct tm fileDate;
        BYTE data[1024];
        unsigned length = 128;
        char *p;      /* Try to get file information */
        if (pXY -> f) {
            DiskFileName(pXY -> f, &fileName);
            fileSize = pXY -> fileSize;
            DiskFileType(pXY -> f, &fileType);
            DiskFileMode(pXY -> f, &fileMode);
            DiskFileDate(pXY -> f, &fileDate);
        }
        memset(data, 0, sizeof (data));
        p = (char *) data;
```

```
    if (fileName && fileName[0]) {
      strcpy(p, fileName);
      p += strlen(p) + 1;
      if ((fileSize >= 0) && (fileType == diskFileBinary)) {
        sprintf(p, "%ld", fileSize);
        p += strlen(p);
        sprintf(p, " %lo", XYTime(&fileDate));
        p += strlen(p);
        if (fileMode >= 0) {
          sprintf(p, " %lo", fileMode);
          p += strlen(p);
        }
      }
    }
    if (p >= ((char *) data) + 128) length = 1024;
    pXY -> packetNumber = 0;
    return StsWarn(XYSendPacket(pXY, data, length));
}
```

Reading the receiver's handshake is a bit trickier. Besides the standard G, C, and NAK handshakes, the function to read a handshake also returns an ACK if it sees one, and watches for a cancel. The ACK is handled because errors can result in an ACK being sent during the negotiation for the second or later file in a batch.

```
STATIC int XYSendReadHandshake(XYMODEM_PRIVATE *pXY, int
        timeout, BYTE *pResponse)
{
  int err;
  int canCount = 0;

  while (TRUE) {        /* Read handshake */
    err = XYSerialReadByte(pXY, timeout, pResponse);
    if (err == xyBadPacket) continue;
    if (err != xyOK) return StsWarn(err);
    ⟨Check for CAN CAN 246⟩
    switch (*pResponse) {
    case 'G': ⟨Interpret G handshake 246⟩
    case 'C': ⟨Interpret C handshake 246⟩
    case NAK: ⟨Interpret NAK handshake 247⟩
    case ACK: return xyOK;
    default: break;
    }
  }
}
```

```
⟨ Check for CAN CAN 246 ⟩ ≡
  if (*pResponse == CAN) {
    if (++canCount >= 2) {
      DebugBegin(pXY -> debug, debugWarn | debugPacket);
      DebugString(pXY -> debug,
          "Received␣CAN␣CAN␣while␣waiting␣for␣startup␣handshake");
      DebugEnd(pXY -> debug);
      return StsWarn(xyFailed);
    }
  } else canCount = 0;
```
This code is used on page 245.

The code to handle each individual handshake is quite simple if you think
carefully about what might happen. For example, the user may have forced a
dialect incompatible with this handshake. Similarly, this file might be the second
file in a batch transfer, in which case certain capabilities will be already frozen. The
ordering of these checks is intended to catch situations in which frozen capabilities
mean this handshake should be ignored.

YModem-G always uses CRC error checking and batch session. If either of
those cannot be enabled, the G handshake should be ignored.

```
⟨ Interpret G handshake 246 ⟩ ≡
  if ((pXY -> crc . certain) && (! pXY -> crc . enabled)) break;
  if ((pXY -> batch . certain) && (! pXY -> batch . enabled)) break;
  if ((pXY -> G . certain) && (! pXY -> G . enabled)) break;
  pXY -> crc . enabled = TRUE;
  pXY -> batch . enabled = TRUE;
  pXY -> G . enabled = TRUE;
  return xyOK;
```
This code is used on page 245.

Unlike some YModem-G implementations, this logic does not accept a C handshake as a valid way to begin a YModem-G transfer. Returning quickly if crc is
already enabled allows this code to handle unusual dialects that were explicitly configured beforehand. Note that longPacket follows batch; YModem supports
long packets, but XModem-CRC does not. This convention does not provide the
best support for XModem-K; I send short packets to an XModem-K receiver unless the user has specifically configured otherwise. Some XModem-K receivers send
a two-character CK handshake; with some additional work, you could recognize
such a handshake and avoid this (admittedly minor) negotiation problem.

```
⟨ Interpret C handshake 246 ⟩ ≡
  if (! pXY -> G . certain) pXY -> G . enabled = FALSE;
  if (pXY -> G . enabled) break;
```

```
if (pXY -> crc . enabled) return xyOK;
if (! pXY -> crc . certain) pXY -> crc . enabled = TRUE ;
if (! pXY -> crc . enabled) break;
if (! pXY -> batch . certain) pXY -> batch . enabled = TRUE ;
if (! pXY -> longPacket . certain)
  pXY -> longPacket . enabled = pXY -> batch . enabled;
return xyOK;
```

This code is used on page 245.

A NAK handshake is incompatible with YModem or YModem-G. Although, technically, YModem can use a NAK handshake to indicate checksum error detection, it complicates automatic negotiation. Since it's an uncommon dialect, it seems worthwhile to disable it in order to simplify the negotiation.

⟨ Interpret NAK handshake 247 ⟩ ==
```
if (! pXY -> G . certain) pXY -> G . enabled = FALSE ;
if (pXY -> G . enabled) break;
if (! pXY -> crc . enabled) return xyOK;
if (! pXY -> crc . certain) pXY -> crc . enabled = FALSE ;
if (pXY -> crc . enabled) break;
if (! pXY -> batch . certain) pXY -> batch . enabled = FALSE ;
if (pXY -> batch . enabled) break;
if (! pXY -> longPacket . certain)
  pXY -> longPacket . enabled = FALSE ;
return xyOK;
```

This code is used on page 245.

The receiver's handshake does not always suffice to tell the sender what protocol to use. For example, both XModem-CRC and YModem begin with the same C handshake. The difference is that a YModem receiver will accept a file header packet and repeat its handshake, while an XModem-CRC receiver will either reject the packet zero, or will acknowledge it (as a duplicate) but fail to repeat the handshake. Handling this distinction requires the sender to simply try sending different packets and see how the receiver responds.

In the particular case where this side is configured for the default YModem but is talking to an XModem-CRC receiver, the negotiation can be lengthy. If the receiver acknowledges packet number zero (as a duplicate of the preceding packet), the only clue the sender has is the omission of the second handshake. Because the second handshake is a single character, it can get lost, so the sender should try several times before assuming it's talking to an XModem-CRC receiver. The result is that several timeouts must expire before the sender can safely fall back to XModem-CRC.

The buffer is passed into this routine as a parameter to reduce the stack requirements.

```
STATIC int XYSendFirstPacket(XYMODEM_PRIVATE *pXY,BYTE
        *pBuffer,int bufferLength)
{
  int err;
  int totalRetries = pXY -> retries;
  int retries = pXY -> retries / 3 + 1;
  BYTE firstHandshake;
  BYTE acknowledge;      /* Acknowledge received for packet */
  BYTE handshake;        /* Repeat handshake for YModem */
  int handshakeErr = xyOK;
  unsigned long dataLength = 0;
  ⟨ Get firstHandshake 248 ⟩
  do {
     ⟨ Send packet 0 or 1, depending on current batch mode 249 ⟩
     ⟨ Interpret response to first packet 249 ⟩
     ⟨ Count down number of retries, swap batch if necessary 250 ⟩
  } while ((acknowledge != ACK)
   || (pXY -> batch . enabled && (handshakeErr != xyOK)));
  pXY -> batch . certain = TRUE;      /* batch mode is known */
  pXY -> G . certain = TRUE;

  if (pXY -> packetNumber == 0) XYProgress(pXY, stsNewFile);
  ⟨ If we read the first packet but didn't send it, send it now 250 ⟩
  return xyOK;
}
```

Reading the first handshake from the receiver is just a minor elaboration on XYSendReadHandshake. The only two refinements are exaggerating the timeout in case the other end is slow to get started, and ignoring the ACK that XYSendReadHandshake might return.

```
⟨ Get firstHandshake 248 ⟩ ≡
  do {
    handshakeErr = XYSendReadHandshake(pXY, pXY -> timeout * 5,
        &firstHandshake);
    if (handshakeErr == xyTimeout) return StsWarn(xyFail);
    StsRet(handshakeErr);
    DebugBegin(pXY -> debug, debugPacket);
    DebugString(pXY -> debug, "Initial␣handshake␣");
    DebugChar(pXY -> debug, firstHandshake);
    DebugEnd(pXY -> debug);
  } while (firstHandshake == ACK);      /* Ignore spurious ACKs */
```
This code is used on page 248.

Once the first handshake is established, the next step is to send a packet and see what happens. The `dataLength` variable incidentally records whether or not the first packet of file data has already been read from the file.

⟨ Send packet 0 or 1, depending on current batch mode 249 ⟩ ≡
```
  if (pXY -> batch . enabled) {
    StsRet(XYSendPacketZero(pXY));
  } else {
    if (dataLength == 0) {      /* Get packet 1 */
      dataLength = (pXY -> longPacket . enabled) ? 1024 : 128;
      err = XYFileRead(pXY, pBuffer, &dataLength);
    }
    pXY -> packetNumber = 1;
    XYProgress(pXY, stsNewFile);
    StsRet(XYSendPacket(pXY, pBuffer, dataLength));
  }
```
This code is used on page 248.

The most interesting case is if you've just sent a YModem file data packet, in which case you might see any one of several different responses:

- The initial handshake might be repeated if the receiver didn't get the packet, or if an XModem receiver ignored it.

- An `ACK` followed by a repeated handshake indicates a YModem receiver accepted the file header and you should continue with the rest of the file.

- If an `ACK` is not followed by a handshake, you're probably talking to an XModem receiver that acknowledged packet zero as a duplicate packet. Or it might mean a YModem receiver, but the second handshake was lost in transit.

⟨ Interpret response to first packet 249 ⟩ ≡
```
  StsRet(XYSendReadHandshake(pXY, pXY -> timeout, &acknowledge));
  if ((acknowledge == ACK) && (pXY -> batch . enabled)) {
    DebugBegin(pXY -> debug, debugPacket);
    DebugString(pXY -> debug, "Received␣ACK␣for␣batch␣file␣header");
    DebugEnd(pXY -> debug);
    do {      /* Wait for error (timeout) or repeat handshake */
      handshakeErr = XYSendReadHandshake(pXY, pXY -> timeout,
          &handshake);
      if (handshakeErr == xyOK) {
        DebugBegin(pXY -> debug, debugWarn);
        DebugString(pXY -> debug, "Second␣handshake␣");
        DebugChar(pXY -> debug, handshake);
```

```
          if (handshake != firstHandshake) DebugString(pXY -> debug,
              "⎵doesn't⎵match⎵initial⎵handshake");
          DebugEnd(pXY -> debug);
        }
      }
      while ((handshakeErr == xyOK) && (handshake != firstHandshake));
      if ((handshakeErr != xyOK) && (handshakeErr != xyTimeout))
        return StsWarn(handshakeErr);
    } else if ((pXY -> G . enabled) && (acknowledge == 'G')) {
        /* YModem-G doesn't need an ACK */
      DebugBegin(pXY -> debug, debugPacket);
      DebugString(pXY -> debug, "Saw⎵second⎵'G'⎵handshake");
      DebugEnd(pXY -> debug);
      acknowledge = ACK;       /* So, pretend I got one anyway */
    } else {     /* Keep trying... */
      firstHandshake = acknowledge;
    }
```
This code is used on page 248.

If I've failed several times to transfer the first packet, it may be because I'm assuming the wrong `batch` mode. So I switch the `batch` mode and try again. Notice that `longPacket` follows `batch`, to avoid problems with XModem-CRC receivers.

⟨ Count down number of retries, swap `batch` if necessary 250 ⟩ ==
```
  if ((acknowledge != ACK)
  || (pXY -> batch . enabled && (handshakeErr != xyOK))) {
    if (retries -- == 0) {
      if (! pXY -> batch . certain)
        pXY -> batch . enabled = ! pXY -> batch . enabled;
      if (! pXY -> longPacket . certain)
        pXY -> longPacket . enabled = pXY -> batch . enabled;
      retries = 2;
    }
    if (totalRetries -- == 0) return StsWarn(xyFail);
  }
```
This code is used on page 248.

In the process of negotiating, I might have read the first packet from the file but not sent it because the other end (eventually) accepted the batch header packet. I need to send the first packet of file data before returning.

⟨ If we read the first packet but didn't send it, send it now 250 ⟩ ==
```
  if ((pXY -> packetNumber == 0) && (dataLength > 0)) {
    pXY -> packetNumber ++;
```

```
    StsRet(XYSendPacketReliable(pXY, pBuffer, dataLength));
    pXY -> transferred += dataLength;
  }
```

This code is used on page 248.

Once the first packet is sent successfully, the rest is pretty easy.

```
    STATIC int XYSendFile(XYMODEM_PRIVATE *pXY)
    {
      BYTE data[1024];
      unsigned long dataLength;
      int err = xyOK;

      XYProgress(pXY, stsNegotiating);
      StsRet(XYSendFirstPacket(pXY, data, sizeof (data) / sizeof
          (data[0])));
      while (err == xyOK) {
        unsigned packetLength;
        BYTE *p = data;

        dataLength = (pXY -> longPacket . enabled) ? 1024 : 128;
        err = XYFileRead(pXY, data, &dataLength);
        packetLength = (dataLength > 767) ? 1024 : 128;
        while ((err == xyOK) && (dataLength > 0)) {
          pXY -> packetNumber ++;
          XYProgress(pXY, stsSending);
          if (packetLength > dataLength) packetLength = dataLength;
          StsRet(XYSendPacketReliable(pXY, p, packetLength));
          pXY -> transferred += packetLength;
          dataLength -= packetLength;
          p += packetLength;
        }
      }
      if (err == xyEOF) {
        err = XYSendEOTReliable(pXY);
        XYProgress(pXY, stsEOF);
      }
      return StsWarn(xyOK);
    }
```

Receiving Files

When the receiver gets no response to its handshake, it tries a different handshake. The net effect of these gyrations is to cycle the handshake from G to C to NAK and back to G. Going back to G after NAK handles simple YModem or YModem-G senders that refuse to respond to NAK; completing the cycle guarantees that all three handshakes are attempted.

```
STATIC int XYReceiveFallback(XYMODEM_PRIVATE *pXY)
{
  if (pXY -> G . enabled) pXY -> G . enabled = FALSE;
  else if (pXY -> crc . enabled) pXY -> crc . enabled =
      pXY -> batch . enabled = pXY -> longPacket . enabled = FALSE;
  else pXY -> G . enabled = pXY -> batch . enabled =
      pXY -> longPacket . enabled = pXY -> crc . enabled = TRUE;
  return xyOK;
}
```

The XYReceiveSendHandshake function sends the correct handshake for the current capabilities. You may need to alter this function if you want to fully support some of the more esoteric dialects. For example, some implementations of XModem-K expect a two-character CK handshake to indicate CRC error detection and long packets.

```
STATIC int XYReceiveSendHandshake(XYMODEM_PRIVATE *pXY)
{
  BYTE handshake;
  if (pXY -> G . enabled) handshake = 'G';
  else if (pXY -> crc . enabled) handshake = 'C';
  else handshake = NAK;
  if (pXY -> debug) {
    DebugBegin(pXY -> debug, debugPacket);
    DebugString(pXY -> debug, "Sending handshake ");
    DebugChar(pXY -> debug, handshake);
    DebugEnd(pXY -> debug);
  }
  return StsWarn(XYSendByte(pXY, handshake));
}
```

Now comes the outline of XYReceiveFile. The first part is responsible for the negotiation; once the first packets have been transferred, the while loop handles the rest of the file transfer. If you know your system can safely overlap serial and disk I/O, you may be able to get a slight speed advantage by sending an ACK prior to writing the data to the file, rather than immediately after, as shown here.

```
STATIC int XYReceiveFile(XYMODEM_PRIVATE *pXY)
{
  BYTE data[1024];
  unsigned dataLength;
```

```
int err = xyOK;
int packetNumber;
int retries = pXY -> retries / 2 + 1;
int totalRetries = (pXY -> retries * 3) / 2 + 1;
XYNewFile(pXY);
XYProgress(pXY, stsNegotiating);
⟨ Get the first packet from the sender 253 ⟩
⟨ Update the capabilities 254 ⟩
⟨ Open the file and receive the first packet 255 ⟩
if ((err == xyOK) && (packetNumber == 1)) {
  ⟨ Write data to the file 255 ⟩
  ⟨ Receive the second packet 256 ⟩
}
while (err == xyOK) {
  if (packetNumber == (pXY -> packetNumber & 0xFF)) {
    ⟨ Write data to the file 255 ⟩
    if (! pXY -> G . enabled)       /* Ack correct packet */
      StsRet(XYSendByte(pXY, ACK));
  } else if (packetNumber == (pXY -> packetNumber - 1) & 0xFF)
    StsRet(XYSendByte(pXY, ACK));
        /* Ack repeat of previous packet */
  else        /* Fatal: wrong packet number! */
    return StsWarn(xyFail);
  err = XYReceivePacketReliable(pXY, &packetNumber, data,
    &dataLength);
}
if (err == xyEOT) {       /* ACK the EOT. Note that the Reliability layer
      has already handled a challenge, if necessary. */
  err = XYSendByte(pXY, ACK);
  DebugBegin(pXY -> debug, debugPacket);
  DebugString(pXY -> debug, "Acknowledging␣EOT");
  DebugEnd(pXY -> debug);
  XYProgress(pXY, stsEOF);
}
StsRet(XYFileWriteClose(pXY));
return StsWarn(err);
}
```

One way to think of the handshake is that the receiver is 'poking' the sender until it wakes up and sends something. Of course, different senders need to be poked in different places, so this code periodically rotates the handshake until the sender responds.

⟨ Get the first packet from the sender 253 ⟩ ≡

```
do {
```

```
        if (-- retries == 0) {
          XYReceiveFallback(pXY);
          XYProgress(pXY, stsNegotiating);
          retries = (pXY -> retries / 3);
        }
        if (totalRetries -- == 0) return StsWarn(xyFail);
        StsRet(XYReceiveSendHandshake(pXY));
        XYProgress(pXY, stsNewFile);
        err = XYReceivePacket(pXY, &packetNumber, data, &dataLength);
        if (err == xyEOT) {      /* EOT must be garbage... */
          StsRet(XYGobble(pXY, pXY -> timeout / 2));
          err = xyTimeout;       /* Treat as timeout */
        }
        if (err == xyBadPacket) {      /* garbaged packet */
          StsRet(XYGobble(pXY, pXY -> timeout / 3));
        }
        if ((packetNumber != 0) && (packetNumber != 1)) {
          err = xyBadPacket;      /* Only accept 0 or 1 */
        }
      } while ((err == xyTimeout) || (err == xyBadPacket));
      StsRet(err);
```

This code is used on page 253.

The first packet tells us the sender's batch mode. If this file is not the first, the batch mode is already frozen, and this packet had better be the right one.

This code only freezes the G capability if it's already enabled (the sender is responding to a G handshake) or batch mode is disabled (an XModem dialect is being used). The remaining possibility is that the sender responded to a C handshake with packet 0. Unfortunately, some YModem-G senders do respond to a C handshake. Because of this variation, the G capability must remain ambiguous for a little while.

⟨ Update the capabilities 254 ⟩ ==
```
      if (packetNumber == 0) {      /* Either batch . enabled is already TRUE or
              batch . certain is FALSE, so there's no need to check here for a batch
              mode mismatch. (Think about it.) */
        pXY -> batch . enabled = TRUE;
      } else {      /* packetNumber == 1 */
              /* If batch mode is certain, then a mismatch is fatal. */
        if (pXY -> batch . certain && pXY -> batch . enabled)
          return StsWarn(xyFail);
        pXY -> batch . enabled = FALSE;
        pXY -> G . enabled = FALSE;      /* Y-G is always batch */
      }
```

```
     pXY -> batch . certain = TRUE;
     if (pXY -> G . enabled || ! pXY -> batch . enabled)
       pXY -> G . certain = TRUE;
```
This code is used on page 253.

After this scrap of code, packet number one has been received and the file is open. If the first packet was packet zero, another packet has to be received.

⟨ Open the file and receive the first packet 255 ⟩ ==
```
     if (packetNumber == 0) {
       if (data[0] == 0) {
         if (! pXY -> G . enabled) StsRet(XYSendByte(pXY, ACK));
              /* Ack packet zero */
         return xyEndOfSession;
       }
       StsRet(XYFileWriteOpen(pXY, data, dataLength));
       if (! pXY -> G . enabled) StsRet(XYSendByte(pXY, ACK));
              /* Ack packet zero */
       StsRet(XYReceiveSendHandshake(pXY));
       err = XYReceivePacketReliable(pXY, &packetNumber, data,
           &dataLength);
     } else {
       StsRet(XYFileWriteOpen(pXY, NULL, 0));
     }
     pXY -> packetNumber = 1;
     pXY -> transferred = 0;
     XYProgress(pXY, stsReceiving);
```
This code is used on page 253.

⟨ Write data to the file 255 ⟩ ==
```
     if ((pXY -> fileSize > 0) && (dataLength + pXY -> transferred >
         pXY -> fileSize))
       dataLength = pXY -> fileSize − pXY -> transferred;
     StsRet(XYFileWrite(pXY, data, dataLength));
     pXY -> transferred += dataLength;
     pXY -> packetNumber ++;
     XYProgress(pXY, stsReceiving);
```
This code is used on page 253.

It may seem a little strange that I've put in special handling for the *second* packet of file data. This special handling deals with a very particular negotiation problem. The problem is that many YModem-G senders will begin sending data upon receipt of a C handshake. Although this approach violates the protocol, it is common, and the following code attempts to accommodate it. The strategy is: if you believe you're in a plain YModem session but the G parameter is still uncertain, don't immediately ACK the first packet. Instead, wait to see if the sender will send the second packet unprompted. If so, you're really in a YModem-G session.

Of course, this heuristic won't always work, since sometimes the first and second packets may have a long delay between them even if the sender is a YModem-G sender. However, this trick should catch most of the culprits.

```
⟨ Receive the second packet 256 ⟩ ≡
    if (pXY -> batch . enabled && ! pXY -> G . enabled && ! pXY -> G . certain) {
        int oldTimeout = pXY -> timeout;

        pXY -> timeout /= 3;      /* Temporarily shorten timeout */
        err = XYReceivePacketReliable(pXY, &packetNumber, data,
            &dataLength);
        pXY -> timeout = oldTimeout;      /* Restore timeout */
        if ((err == xyOK) && (packetNumber == 2)) {
            pXY -> G . enabled = TRUE;      /* Second packet came for free! */
            if (pXY -> debug) {
                DebugBegin(pXY -> debug, debugInit);
                DebugString(pXY -> debug, "Y-G␣sender␣detected");
                DebugEnd(pXY -> debug);
            }
        } else if (err == xyTimeout) {      /* No bonus second packet */
            StsRet(XYSendByte(pXY, ACK));      /* Ack packet one */
            err = XYReceivePacketReliable(pXY, &packetNumber, data,
                &dataLength);
        }
    } else {      /* skip special second-packet check */
        err = XYReceivePacketReliable(pXY, &packetNumber, data,
            &dataLength);
    }
```

This code is used on page 253.

Session Layer

A YModem sender ends the session by sending a packet zero with an empty filename. The XYSendSessionEnd function sends this end-of-session marker and waits for the response. It's used by XYSend.

```
STATIC int XYSendSessionEnd(XYMODEM_PRIVATE *pXY)
{
    int err;
    BYTE response;

    XYNewFile(pXY);
```

```
        XYProgress(pXY, stsEnding);
        do {    /* Read handshake */
          err = XYSendReadHandshake(pXY, pXY -> timeout, &response);
          if (err == xyTimeout) return StsWarn(xyFail);
          StsRet(err);
          DebugBegin(pXY -> debug, debugPacket);
          DebugString(pXY -> debug, "Initial␣handshake␣");
          DebugChar(pXY -> debug, response);
          DebugEnd(pXY -> debug);
        } while (response == ACK);
        do {
          StsRet(XYSendPacketZero(pXY));
          if (pXY -> G . enabled) return xyOK;
          do {      /* Read ACK or NAK response */
            err = XYSendReadHandshake(pXY, pXY -> timeout, &response);
            if (err == xyTimeout) return StsWarn(xyFail);
            StsRet(err);
          } while (err != xyOK);
          if (pXY -> debug) {
            DebugBegin(pXY -> debug, debugPacket);
            if (response == ACK) {
              DebugString(pXY -> debug,
                  "Received␣ACK␣for␣final␣YModem␣header");
            } else {
              DebugString(pXY -> debug, "Received␣");
              DebugChar(pXY -> debug, response);
              DebugString(pXY -> debug, "␣for␣final␣YModem␣header");
            }
            DebugEnd(pXY -> debug);
          }
        } while (response != ACK);
        return xyOK;
      }
```

All of the negotiation headaches handled above pay off here. The top-level send routine only needs to watch the `batch` capability to know whether the receiver can accept multiple files or only one. In particular, if the user specified several files, but the receiver only supports an XModem dialect, only the first file will be sent. This approach works well if the user interface manages a list of files to be sent, and removes files from the list whenever they are successfully sent. Then a user can send multiple files using XModem by first selecting the files to send and then repeatedly sending one file from the list.

```
STATIC int XYSend(XYMODEM_PRIVATE *pXY)
{
  int err;
  XYNewFile(pXY);
  do {
    err = XYFileReadOpenNext(pXY);
    if (err == xyOK) {
      err = XYSendFile(pXY);
      XYFileReadClose(pXY);
      XYNewFile(pXY);
    }
  } while ((err == xyOK) && (pXY -> batch . enabled));
  if (err == xyEndOfSession) {
    err = xyOK;
    if (pXY -> batch . enabled) err = XYSendSessionEnd(pXY);
  }
  if (err == xyFail) {
    XYSendCAN(pXY);
    err = xyFailed;
  }
  if (err == xyOK) XYProgress(pXY, stsDone);
  else if (pXY -> userCancel) XYProgress(pXY, stsCancelled);
  else XYProgress(pXY, stsFailed);
  return StsWarn(err);
}
```

The top-level receiver is quite similar.

```
STATIC int XYReceive(XYMODEM_PRIVATE *pXY)
{
  int err;
  do {
    err = XYReceiveFile(pXY);
  } while ((err == xyOK) && (pXY -> batch . enabled));
  if (err == xyEndOfSession) err = xyOK;
  if (err == xyFail) {
    XYSendCAN(pXY);
    err = xyFailed;
  }
  if (err == xyOK) XYProgress(pXY, stsDone);
  else if (pXY -> userCancel) XYProgress(pXY, stsCancelled);
  else XYProgress(pXY, stsFailed);
  XYGobble(pXY, 2);      /* Gobble any line garbage */
  return StsWarn(err);
}
```

Public Interface Layer

The following functions are the only public functions in this module. If you need to provide the client with additional control over some feature (for example, to set the timeout or number of retries), the appropriate approach is to add a function to this section, and have the client call that function to modify the XYModem handle prior to starting the actual transfer.

```
int XYModemInit(XYMODEM *pXYPublic, SERIAL_PORT port)
{
  XYMODEM_PRIVATE *pXY;

  XYInitCrc16();    /* Make sure the CRC table is computed */
  pXY = malloc(sizeof (*pXY));
  if (pXY == NULL) return 1;    /* non-zero indicates error */
  memset(pXY, 0, sizeof (*pXY));    /* Initialize structure */
  ⟨Initialize XYModem variables 219⟩
  pXY -> port = port;
  *pXYPublic = pXY;
  return xyOK;
}


int XYModemDestroy(XYMODEM xyPublic)
{
  free(xyPublic);
  return xyOK;
}


int XYModemSetProtocol(XYMODEM xyPublic, int protocol)
{
  XYMODEM_PRIVATE *pXY = xyPublic;
      /* Initialize them all to disabled */
  pXY -> G . enabled = FALSE;
  pXY -> crc . enabled = FALSE;
  pXY -> batch . enabled = FALSE;
  pXY -> longPacket . enabled = FALSE;    /* Conveniently, each of these
        implies all the capabilities of the lower ones. */
  switch (protocol) {
  case YMODEMG: pXY -> G . enabled = TRUE;
  case YMODEM: pXY -> batch . enabled = TRUE;
  case XMODEMK: pXY -> longPacket . enabled = TRUE;
  case XMODEMCRC: pXY -> crc . enabled = TRUE;
  case XMODEM: break;
  default: DebugBegin(pXY -> debug, debugWarn);
```

```
        DebugString(pXY -> debug,
            "XYModem initialized with illegal protocol");
        DebugEnd(pXY);
        return StsWarn(xyFailed);
    }
    return 0;
}
```

This function allows the client to specify a debug handle.

```
int XYModemSetDebug(XYMODEM xyPublic, DEBUG debug)
{
    XYMODEM_PRIVATE *pXY = (XYMODEM_PRIVATE *) xyPublic;
    pXY -> debug = debug;
    return xyOK;
}
```

This function allows the client to specify a progress handle.

```
int XYModemSetProgress(XYMODEM xyPublic, PROGRESS progress)
{
    XYMODEM_PRIVATE *pXY = (XYMODEM_PRIVATE *) xyPublic;
    pXY -> progress = progress;
    return xyOK;
}
```

If the client knows that all the files will have a specific type, it can specify that type by calling XYModemSetFileType. This type will be passed along to the disk module. If the client doesn't specify a type, diskFileUnknown will be used, which prompts the disk module to try to determine the file type from the file data.

```
int XYModemSetFileType(XYMODEM xyPublic, int fileType)
{
    XYMODEM_PRIVATE *pXY = (XYMODEM_PRIVATE *) xyPublic;
    pXY -> fileType = fileType;
    return xyOK;
}
```

If the user needs to cancel a transfer, there are two ways the protocol can be notified. The user interface could notify the serial routines, causing a pending serial call to return an appropriate error status. Alternatively, the user interface could call this function, which sets the userCancel flag and returns immediately. The protocol will terminate and return shortly afterward. For prompt user interface response, the first approach is best, since the userCancel flag may not be checked until after the next serial operation completes. Coordination between the user interface and the serial routines can prompt a pending serial operation to return prematurely.

```
int XYModemCancel(XYMODEM xyPublic)
{
  XYMODEM_PRIVATE *pXY = (XYMODEM_PRIVATE *) xyPublic;
  pXY -> userCancel = TRUE;
  return xyOK;
}
```

I've used an array of strings to hold the filenames to send. This data structure can easily be changed with minor modifications to `XYFileReadOpenNext` on page 229.

```
int XYModemSend(XYMODEM xyPublic, const char *filenames[], int
        count)
{
  XYMODEM_PRIVATE *pXY = (XYMODEM_PRIVATE *) xyPublic;
  int returnVal = 0;     /* No error */
  pXY -> currentFileName = 0;
  pXY -> filenames = filenames;
  pXY -> numFileNames = count;
  ProgressSending(pXY -> progress);
  if (XYSend(pXY) != xyOK) returnVal = 1;
  return returnVal;
}
```

Unlike many XModem implementations, `XYModemReceive` does not allow the client to specify a filename to use. Because of the auto-negotiation, I don't know whether or not the sender will provide a filename. If the sender does not provide one, I simply provide a generic default name (see page 231) and allow the user to change it after the transfer is done. On multithreaded systems, the protocol code could specify an empty filename to the disk interface, which would in turn pop up a dialog for the user. This is not a good approach on non-multithreaded systems, because you don't want to introduce a long delay just as the transfer is beginning.

```
int XYModemReceive(XYMODEM xyPublic)
{
  XYMODEM_PRIVATE *pXY = (XYMODEM_PRIVATE *) xyPublic;
  int returnVal = 0;
  ProgressReceiving(pXY -> progress);
  if (XYReceive(pXY) != xyOK) returnVal = 1;
```

```
    return returnVal;
}
```

Implementing ZModem 18

A ZModem implementation is largely an exercise in on-the-fly data processing. Sending and receiving very long data packets means that each layer must manage a steady flow of data.

According to the terms of the contract under which ZModem was originally developed, the ZModem protocol and implementation were to be public domain. The resulting implementation consisted of two programs, `rz` and `sz`, which have been used as the basis for including ZModem in many products.[1] To provide a different viewpoint, I've decided to present my own original ZModem code. If you're really interested in ZModem trivia, you should obtain a copy of the source code for the public domain versions of `rz` and `sz` and compare that to the implementation here.

Public Interface

The public interface uses a *handle*, which is essentially a ZModem object. Functions are provided for creating or destroying a handle, modifying the parameters of a handle, or performing a file transfer using a handle. Note that the client can use a handle only for a single session, and must create a new handle for each successive session. The client must also be careful not to attempt to modify a handle during a transfer.

One reason for this approach is to simplify extending the interface. Most extensions involve adding a function to set a new parameter. The addition of such a function breaks no old code, since the `ZModemInit` function will always initialize the handle with suitable defaults. Alternatives, such as including a large

---

[1] Only versions of `rz` and `sz` prior to 3.0 are actually public domain. Versions 3.0 and later incorporate proprietary extensions, and are copyrighted by Omen Technology.

number of arguments to the transfer functions, or having a large structure that the client initializes, both risk breaking old code when the interfaces need to be changed.

This handle approach also provides the client with a way to refer to a transfer in progress. The client can call the `ZModemCancel` function in response to a user request. This capability is only useful, of course, in multithreaded systems or systems that support signal interrupts.

These functions are actually defined at the end of this chapter, starting on page 347.

```
⟨ftz.h  264⟩ ==
#ifndef FTZ_H_INCLUDED     /* Protect against multiple inclusions */
#define FTZ_H_INCLUDED
#include "ftserial.h"     /* Defines SERIAL_PORT */
#include "ftprog.h"      /* Defines PROGRESS */
#include "ftdebug.h"     /* Defines DEBUG */
  typedef void *ZMODEM;
  int ZModemInit(ZMODEM *ppZ, SERIAL_PORT port);
  int ZModemDestroy(ZMODEM z);
  int ZModemSetDebug(ZMODEM z, DEBUG debug);
  int ZModemSetProgress(ZMODEM z, PROGRESS progress);
  int ZModemSetFileType(ZMODEM z, int fileType);
  int ZModemSend(ZMODEM z, const char *filenames[], int numFiles);
  int ZModemReceive(ZMODEM z);
  int ZModemSendCommand(ZMODEM z, const char *command);
  int ZModemCancel(ZMODEM z);
#endif     /* ! FTZ_H_INCLUDED */
```

External Dependencies

I've tried to isolate the references to other modules so that you can easily remove those references. If you're integrating this into a preexisting application, for instance, you probably already have your own code to handle serial interfacing and progress reporting. However, you may still want to skim through Chapters 13 through 16 for ideas.

```
#include "ftdisk.h"     /* Disk module */
#include "ftserial.h"     /* Serial module */
#include "ftdebug.h"     /* Debugging support */
#include "ftprog.h"     /* Progress reporting */
#include "ftz.h"     /* Your own public interface */
```

When porting code to different platforms, I've found it very helpful when the original author was careful to specify all of the system headers and library functions used in the code. As a result, I've listed below every C library function used in this module. After each header, I've listed all of the types and functions that are used from that header. I've also provided definitions for a few useful macros.

```
#include <stddef.h>     /* size_t */

#include <time.h>      /* struct tm, time_t, time, localtime */
  time_t time(time_t *);
  struct tm *localtime(const time_t *);

#include <stdio.h>      /* sprintf */
  char *sprintf(char *, const char *, ... );

#include <string.h>     /* strcpy, strlen, memset, memcpy */
  char *strcpy(char *s1, const char *s2);
  size_t strlen(const char *s1);
  void memset(void *, unsigned char, int);
  void *memcpy(void *, const void *, size_t);

#include <stdlib.h>     /* atoi, malloc, free, system */
  int atoi(const char *s);
  void *malloc(size_t);
  void free(void *);
  int system(const char *);
```

These constants aren't defined in all libraries, so I provide definitions here.

```
#ifndef TRUE
#define TRUE   1
#endif

#ifndef FALSE
#define FALSE  0
#endif

#ifndef NULL     /* NULL */
#define NULL ((void *) 0)
#endif
```

Since some compilers/debuggers can only provide debugging information for global symbols, I've declared local functions with STATIC rather than static. By simply redefining STATIC, you can make all such functions global if you need to.

```
#define STATIC static
```

System Dependencies

Different systems have different capabilities, and ZModem makes some concessions to these differences. These concessions have the greatest impact on the sender, which alters its transmission strategy based on the capabilities of the two sides. Generally, the receiver simply broadcasts these capabilities to the sender, who can then modify its strategy based on a knowledge of both its own and the receiver's restrictions.

The following constants define capabilities of your system, and may need to be altered. The serial module defined in Chapter 14 assumes this system can check for received data without blocking, so if you need to set I_CAN_SAMPLE to zero, you'll probably also need to examine the serial module. The other three can be changed as necessary.

```
#define I_CAN_SAMPLE   (1)
              /* I can check for received data without blocking */
#define I_CAN_FULL_DUPLEX   (1)
              /* I can send and receive simultaneously */
#define I_CAN_OVERLAP_DISK   (1)
              /* I can do serial and disk I/O simultaneously */
#define I_CAN_SEND_BREAK   (1)     /* I can send a break signal */
```

I just said that the sender is the one who modifies its behavior to accommodate restrictions on both sides. That's not quite true; there's one way in which the receiver modifies its behavior to accommodate the sender. Some senders can respond more quickly if they receive a certain sequence from the receiver. Typically, a break signal or special control code can be set to alert the sender (sometimes with the pleasant side effect of clearing network and modem buffers). Having the receiver send this *attention sequence* prior to an error notification allows the sender to respond more quickly. In some cases, the sender cannot sample for received data (and hence has I_CAN_SAMPLE disabled), and the attention sequence is necessary for it to respond to error packets at all.

The sender notifies the receiver of this sequence during the negotiation phase of the session, by including it as data following a ZSINIT packet. The Attention sequence is NULL-terminated, up to 32 bytes long, and can use character 0xDD to specify a break or character 0xDE to specify a 1-second delay. The default is to have no attention sequence.

```
#define ATTENTION   (NULL)     /* No attention sequence required */
```

Definitions

A few common characters are best referred to by their common ASCII names.

```
#define CR   (0x0d)
#define LF   (0x0a)
#define DLE  (0x10)
#define XON  (0x11)
#define XOFF (0x13)
#define CAN  (0x18)
#define DEL  (0x7F)
```

One subtle distinction that needs to be carefully considered in file transfer is the distinction between an uninterpreted BYTE and a char. I try to encourage this distinction by using BYTE for raw data being transferred to the serial port or a disk file, and char for text data such as filenames.

```
typedef unsigned char BYTE;
```

ZModem State Structure

This structure contains the current state of the transfer. By keeping all information about the transfer in a dynamically-allocated structure, I can allow multiple simultaneous transfers in a multi-threaded system. This approach also encourages efficient use of memory, because these variables do not take up memory space when there is no transfer in progress.

I've followed the convention that almost every function accepts a pointer to this structure as its first argument, and uses the name pZ to refer to the structure. This convention simplifies copying code between functions, and also simplifies a few macros, which can refer to variables in pZ without requiring an additional argument.

```
typedef struct {
  ⟨ ZModem variables 267 ⟩
} ZMODEM_PRIVATE;
```

There should be no surprises in these first few variables. I'll add more as necessary.

```
⟨ ZModem variables 267 ⟩ ==
  int crc32;      /* Does other end support CRC32? */
  int timeout;    /* Number of seconds timeout */
  int retries;    /* Number of times to retry a packet */
  int userCancel;    /* Set when user asks to cancel transfer */
  BYTE attention[40];    /* Attention sequence */
```

```
    unsigned long zrqinitFlags;      /* Argument from ZRQINIT */
    unsigned long senderFlags;       /* Flags from ZSINIT */
    unsigned long receiverFlags;     /* Flags from ZRINIT */
    unsigned long myZrqinitFlags;    /* Flags sent with ZRQINIT */
    unsigned long mySenderFlags;     /* Flags sent with ZSINIT */
    unsigned long myReceiverFlags;   /* Flags sent with ZRINIT */
    unsigned long fileFlags;
        /* Rx: current ZFILE opts, Tx: default ZFILE opts */
```

See also pages 269, 269, 270, 270, 276, 281, 288, 288, 295, 305, and 331.

This code is used on page 267.

I'll also extend this initialization as I add more variables.

⟨ Initialize ZModem variables, `return` if error 268 ⟩ ≡
```
    pZ -> crc32 = FALSE;
    pZ -> timeout = 10;
    pZ -> retries = 10;
    pZ -> userCancel = FALSE;
    pZ -> attention[0] = 0;
    pZ -> senderFlags = 0;
    pZ -> zrqinitFlags = 0;
    pZ -> receiverFlags = 0;
    pZ -> myZrqinitFlags = 0;
    pZ -> mySenderFlags = 0;
    pZ -> myReceiverFlags = KNOW_CRC32;
#if I_CAN_FULL_DUPLEX
    pZ -> myReceiverFlags |= CAN_FULL_DUPLEX;
#endif
#if I_CAN_OVERLAP_DISK
    pZ -> myReceiverFlags |= CAN_OVERLAP_DISK;
#endif
#if I_CAN_SEND_BREAK
    pZ -> myReceiverFlags |= CAN_SEND_BREAK;
#endif
    pZ -> fileFlags = 0;
```
See also pages 269, 270, 270, 276, 277, 282, 288, 288, 295, 298, 298, 305, and 331.

This code is used on page 347.

To quickly determine how to handle specific characters, I've mimicked the method used by the `ctype.h` macros. In particular, I need to know which characters should be encoded before being sent, and which should be ignored when received. The `classify` array details which characters require special handling. Notice that if a character is ignored by the receiver, it must be encoded by the sender, but not vice versa. The default for ZModem is to ignore only a few critical characters, which leaves the sender with a choice of how to send the remaining ones. It's reasonable for conservative senders to encode all control characters.

```
#define SetIgnore(c)   (pZ -> classify[c] |= 1)
#define TestIgnore(c)  (pZ -> classify[c] & 1)
#define SetEncode(c)   (pZ -> classify[c] |= 2)
#define TestEncode(c)  (pZ -> classify[c] & 2)
```
⟨ZModem variables 267⟩ +≡
```
    unsigned char classify[256];     /* How to handle special characters */
```

The defaults for encoding assume that software flow control uses `XON` and `XOFF` characters. This means that `XON` and `XOFF` characters are likely to be swallowed by the channel. It also means that `XON` and `XOFF` characters may be generated by the channel, which is why you ignore those values by default. By tradition, `DLE` and DLE_8 are also encoded.

⟨Initialize ZModem variables, `return` if error 268⟩ +≡
```
    {
        memset(pZ -> classify, 0, sizeof (pZ -> classify));
        SetEncode(CAN);
        SetEncode(XON); SetEncode(XON | 0x80);
        SetEncode(XOFF); SetEncode(XOFF | 0x80);
        SetEncode(DLE); SetEncode(DLE | 0x80);
        SetIgnore(XON); SetIgnore(XON | 0x80);
        SetIgnore(XOFF); SetIgnore(XOFF | 0x80);
    }
```

Unlike many protocols, ZModem packets can be arbitrarily large. In particular, there is no limit on the size of a `ZDATA` packet. Receiving or sending such large packets is done in pieces, and so some state must be maintained across those pieces.

This is primarily an issue when sending file data. Whenever I'm ready to send the next section of the file, I need to know whether I'm already in the process of sending a `ZDATA` packet. If so, I can simply send the data and a CRC escape. If not, I need to precede it with a `ZDATA` header.

⟨ZModem variables 267⟩ +≡
```
    int sendingCrc32;
    int txPacketType;     /* Set to -1 if no packet is open */
```

The corresponding variables for received packets are used primarily to save the most recently received packet header. One place this is useful is when a packet such as `ZRINIT` is received, which generally indicates the receiver thinks a transaction has ended. Lower layers aren't really prepared to deal with this, so it may be appropriate to let a higher layer try to handle it. One approach would be to allow many different functions to return the value of an unrecognized packet. Because this would bloat the function interfaces, I've chosen instead to store the packet in the `ZMODEM_PRIVATE` data structure, where it can be easily recovered as needed.

⟨ ZModem variables 267 ⟩ +==
```
   int receivingCrc32;
   int rxPacketType;
   unsigned long rxPacketArg;
```

⟨ Initialize ZModem variables, return if error 268 ⟩ +==
```
   pZ -> sendingCrc32 = FALSE;
   pZ -> txPacketType = -1;
   pZ -> receivingCrc32 = FALSE;
   pZ -> rxPacketType = -1;
   pZ -> rxPacketArg = 0;
```

The streaming transfer is driven by the two variables that hold the file positions of the sender and receiver. When receiving, they're generally the same, since the only way the receiver can know the sender's position is to successfully receive data. These variables occasionally get out of sync if the sender repeats data that was already correctly received. (This can happen, for example, when excessive noise or other problems cause the receiver to send duplicate `ZRPOS` packets.)

On send, however, these variables differ. The `receivePosition` indicates the last file position acknowledged by the receiver. This value sometimes will be considerably smaller than `sendPosition`, especially if there is a long delay. These variables have to maintain a few invariants:

- (`receivePosition` <= `sendPosition`) The sender shouldn't send data the receiver has already acknowledged.

- (`windowStart` <= `receivePosition`) The sender can't clear data from the window before it's acknowledged by the receiver.

- (`sendPosition` <= `windowEnd`) The sender can't send data that hasn't yet been read from disk.

When I discuss the windowing support, these variables will make more sense.

⟨ ZModem variables 267 ⟩ +==
```
   unsigned long sendPosition;      /* Sender's current file position */
   unsigned long receivePosition;    /* Receiver's current file position */
```

⟨ Initialize ZModem variables, return if error 268 ⟩ +==
```
   pZ -> sendPosition = 0;
   pZ -> receivePosition = 0;
```

ZModem Packet Types

ZModem uses small integers to indicate different packet types. The ZSTDERR packet type is defined in some of the early rz/sz sources, but is never used there.

```
#define ZRQINIT   (0)     /* Auto-send startup */
#define ZRINIT    (1)     /* Receiver's options */
#define ZSINIT    (2)     /* Sender's options */
#define ZACK      (3)
                  /* Acknowledge for ZData, ZCRC, ZChallenge, ZSInit */
#define ZFILE     (4)     /* File starts */
#define ZSKIP     (5)     /* Don't send this file */
#define ZNAK      (6)     /* Response to garbled or meaningless packet */
#define ZABORT    (7)     /* Receiver requests cancel */
#define ZFIN      (8)     /* End of the session */
#define ZRPOS     (9)     /* Reposition sender */
#define ZDATA     (10)    /* File data */
#define ZEOF      (11)    /* End-of-file */
#define ZFERR     (12)    /* File I/O error, equivalent to ZAbort */
#define ZCRC      (13)    /* Request file CRC */
#define ZCHALLENGE (14)   /* Security challenge */
#define ZCOMPL    (15)    /* Command completion status */
#define ZCAN      (16)    /* Emergency termination */
#define ZFREECNT  (17)    /* Request available disk space */
#define ZCOMMAND  (18)    /* Command for receiver to execute */
#define ZSTDERR   (19)    /* Error message for user (Unused) */
```

A common debugging requirement is to dump the contents of a packet. The DebugPacket macro dumps a packet by printing a string translation of the packet type together with the argument.

```
#define DebugPacket(debug, type, arg)
        DebugString((debug), zPacketName[(type)]);
        DebugString((debug), "(");
        DebugIntHex((debug), (arg));
        DebugString((debug), ")");
    const char *zPacketName[] = {"ZRQINIT", "ZRINIT", "ZSINIT",
        "ZACK", "ZFILE", "ZSKIP", "ZNAK", "ZABORT", "ZFIN", "ZRPOS",
        "ZDATA", "ZEOF", "ZFERR", "ZCRC", "ZCHALLENGE", "ZCOMPL",
        "ZCAN", "ZFREECNT", "ZCOMMAND", "ZSTDERR", NULL, NULL, NULL};
```

Other ZModem Constants

Clearly, the receiver ultimately determines the disposition of the file. For example, if a file being received has the same name as an already-existing file, the receiver can choose to overwrite the existing file, change the name of the incoming file, change the name of the existing file, or reject the incoming file. However, ZModem's automatic receive feature means that usually the sender is the side started by the user. So, it's convenient if the user can specify the file handling to the sender, which in turn relays it to the receiver. ZModem defines a variety of file options that allow the sender to suggest to the receiver how to deal with a particular file.

The first group of file handling options are the "conversion" options, which specify how the receiver should process the file data. Text files are presumed to consist of lines with CR/LF or LF separating successive lines. Note that because text files may require conversion at either end, resuming a text transfer is not generally possible, and is therefore prohibited.

```
#define CONV_BINARY   (0x01000000)
#define CONV_TEXT    (0x02000000)
#define CONV_RESUME   (0x03000000)      /* Implies file is binary */
#define CONV_MASK    (0xFF000000ᵤ)      /* Mask for file conversion options */
```

The mask for the conversion options is declared with a U to indicate to ANSI-compliant compilers that it's an unsigned value.

The next group of options specify how the receiver should store the file. In particular, they specify what the receiver should do if the file does or does not already exist. The first option, MAN_SKNOLOC can be ORed with any of the others to specify that the receiver should skip this file if it does not already exist. Clearly, this makes no sense with MAN_NONEXISTENT.

```
#define MAN_SKNOLOC   (0x00800000)
              /* skip if file does not already exist */
#define MAN_NEW_LONG   (0x00010000)
              /* Accept if file is newer or longer */
#define MAN_CRC_LENGTH   (0x00020000)
              /* Accept if CRC or length differs */
#define MAN_APPEND   (0x00030000)     /* Append to named file */
#define MAN_REPLACE   (0x00040000)      /* Replace named file */
#define MAN_NEW   (0x00050000)     /* Accept if newer */
#define MAN_DATE_LENGTH   (0x00060000)
              /* Accept if date or length differs */
#define MAN_NONEXISTENT   (0x00070000)     /* Accept if file doesn't exist */
#define MAN_MASK   (0x007F0000)     /* Mask for management options */
```

The "transport" options specify how the file is encoded for transport. Only one of these, TRAN_LZW, is defined in the basic ZModem protocol; the others are reserved for future extensions. The LZW format is defined to be compatible with Unix compress operating with 12-bit compression and VAX byte ordering.

```
#define TRAN_LZW   (0x00000100)     /* File is LZW compressed */
```

```
#define TRAN_CRYPT   (0x00000200)     /* File is encrypted */
#define TRAN_RLE   (0x00000300)     /* File is RLE compressed */
#define TRAN_MASK   (0x0000FF00)     /* Mask for transport options */
```

The final set of options allow for future extensions. The only one currently defined is EXTEN_SPARSE, which is reserved for a future extension where the sender relays only parts of a file.

```
#define EXTEN_SPARSE   (0x00000040)     /* Special sparse-file handling */
#define EXTEN_MASK   (0x000000FF)     /* Mask for extended options */
```

Initialization Flags

The initialization flags allow the sender and receiver to coordinate their capabilities. The first three are used by the receiver to specify its communications capabilities. The sender will modify its transmission strategy to satisfy the receiver's limitations. For example, if the receiver cannot do full-duplex serial I/O and cannot overlap disk and serial I/O, the sender can fall back to a half-duplex transmission strategy.

```
#define CAN_FULL_DUPLEX   (0x01000000)
#define CAN_OVERLAP_DISK   (0x02000000)
#define CAN_SEND_BREAK   (0x04000000)
```

The next three convey the receiver's implementation limits. This implementation, for example, does support the 32-bit CRC, but does not support LZW compression.

```
#define KNOW_CRYPT   (0x08000000)     /* Unused in standard ZModem */
#define KNOW_LZW   (0x10000000)
#define KNOW_CRC32   (0x20000000)
```

Finally, the last two flags are used to convey channel limitations. They are used in both ZSINIT and ZRINIT packets. The ESCAPE_CONTROLS bit has slightly different meanings depending on the context. In a ZSINIT packet, it instructs the receiver to ignore all control characters, while in a ZRINIT packet, it instructs the sender to encode all control characters.

```
#define ESCAPE_CONTROLS   (0x40000000)
#define ESCAPE_8BIT   (0x80000000)     /* Unused in standard ZModem */
```

Utility Functions

The following functions consist of a few general-purpose functions and a number of stubs to interface this module to serial, disk, and progress-reporting machinery.

Error Handling

Nearly every function returns a code that represents the success or failure of the operation. Note that I've explicitly defined zOK to be zero, since comparisons against zero are much more efficient on many compilers. You need enough error codes to cover the different things that can go wrong, but if you have too many error codes, error handling can become unwieldy. An early version of this code, for example, had a zBadCRC code that was different from zBadPacket. Further investigation revealed these two errors were always treated identically, so they were combined.

The distinction between zFail and zFailed deserves some attention. A transfer can fail for many reasons. One way to classify those reasons is based on whether or not this end should attempt to cancel the transfer. For example, if this end receives a cancel sequence, it's pointless to echo it back. On the other hand, a disk failure on this end merits at least an attempt to shut down the other end.

```
enum {
  zOK = 0,     /* No error */
  zFail,       /* Transfer failed; send cancel sequence */
  zFailed,     /* Transfer failed; don't send cancel sequence */
  zBadPacket,   /* Damaged packet or bad CRC */
  zEndOfSession,   /* No more files to transfer */
  zEOF,      /* end-of-file on file read */
  zTimeout,    /* Timeout waiting for data */
  zSkip     /* Don't send this file */
};
```

One common idiom is to test a return value and return it if it indicates an error. This idiom is encapsulated in the StsRet macro, which exploits C's do construction to declare a temporary variable, and to provide neater syntax. The while (FALSE) construction makes sure that StsRet requires a following semicolon, which makes such a macro call syntactically more like a function call.

```
#define StsRet(expr)  do { int tmpErrorVal = (expr);
        if (tmpErrorVal != zOK) return StsWarn(tmpErrorVal);
      } while (FALSE)    /* Do this loop exactly once */
```

Debugging Support

During development, it's convenient to track the origin of any unusual event. Fortunately, the return codes listed above define most of the unusual events. The StsWarn macro can be wrapped around a function call or return code variable to generate debug messages for any unusual values. The ANSI-standard __FILE__ and `__LINE__` macros pinpoint the position in the source where the event was detected.

By testing `pZ -> debug` before calling `ZDebugWarn`, the `StsWarn` macro becomes faster when debugging messages are disabled. This precaution makes it reasonable to leave these messages permanently within the code.

```c
#define StsWarn(s)
        ((pZ -> debug) ? ZDebugWarn(pZ, (s), __FILE__, __LINE__) : (s))


#define debugWarn   (1)
#define debugPacket   (2)
#define debugPacketErr   (4)
#define debugPacketLowLevel   (8)
#define debugCache   (16)
#define debugAttr   (32)
#define debugInit   (64)
#define debugEncoding   (256)
#define debugSerial   (512)


  STATIC int ZDebugWarn(ZMODEM_PRIVATE *pZ, const int s, const
          char *file, const int line)
  {
    const char *msg = NULL;
    if (s != zOK) {
      DebugBeginInternal(pZ -> debug, debugWarn, file, line);
      DebugString(pZ -> debug, "?!?!?!:");
    }
    switch (s) {
    case zOK: return zOK;
    case zFail: msg = "zFail"; break;
    case zFailed: msg = "zFailed"; break;
    case zBadPacket: msg = "zBadPacket"; break;
    case zEndOfSession: msg = "zEndOfSession"; break;
    case zEOF: msg = "zEOF"; break;
    case zTimeout: msg = "zTimeout"; break;
    }
    if (msg != NULL) DebugString(pZ -> debug, msg);
    else {
      DebugString(pZ -> debug, "Error ");
      DebugInt(pZ -> debug, s);
    }
    DebugEnd(pZ -> debug);
    return s;
  }
```

Of course, to display debug messages at all, there must be a debug stream to which to send them.

⟨ZModem variables 267⟩ +≡
```
DEBUG debug;        /* debug handle */
```

⟨Initialize ZModem variables, return if error 268⟩ +≡
```
pZ -> debug = NULL;
```

Between files, a few variables need to be reset.
```
STATIC void ZNewFile(ZMODEM_PRIVATE *pZ)
{
  pZ -> fileSize = -1;
  pZ -> sendPosition = 0;
  pZ -> receivePosition = 0;
}
```

CRC Calculation

The InitCRC function pre-computes two tables of constants, using a bitwise algorithm. These constants allow fast computation of the 16-bit and 32-bit CRCs. A detailed discussion of this code appears in Chapter 4 on page 58.

ZModem's 16-bit CRC is the CCITT CRC16. The generating polynomial is $x^{16} + x^{12} + x^5 + 1$, with binary representation 0x11021.

ZModem's 32-bit CRC generating polynomial is $x^{32} + x^{26} + x^{23} + x^{22} + x^{16} + x^{12} + x^{11} + x^{10} + x^8 + x^7 + x^5 + x^4 + x^2 + x + 1$, with binary representation 0x104c11db7. ZModem computes the 32-bit CRC 'backwards,' so it actually uses a binary representation of 0xedb88320 (the x^{32} bit is implied).

Note that ANSI C guarantees short int to be at least 16 bits and long int to be at least 32 bits.

```
STATIC unsigned short int zCrc16Table[256];
STATIC unsigned long int zCrc32Table[256];

STATIC void ZInitCrc()
{
  static int crcDone = 0;
  unsigned long i, j, crc;

  if (crcDone) return;       /* Only compute it once */
  for (i = 0;  i < 256;  i ++) {     /* Initialize 16-bit CRC table */
    crc = (i << 8);
    for (j = 0;  j < 8;  j ++)
      crc = (crc << 1) ^ ((crc & 0x8000) ? 0x1021 : 0);
    zCrc16Table[i] = crc & 0xffff;
```

```
      }
      for (i = 0;  i < 256;  i ++) {      /* Initialize 32-bit CRC table */
        crc = i;
        for (j = 0;  j < 8;  j ++)
          crc = (crc >> 1) ^ ((crc & 1) ? 0xEDB88320 U : 0);
        zCrc32Table[i] = crc & 0xffffffff U;
      }
      crcDone = 1;      /* Don't re-compute the CRC tables */
  }
```

⟨ Initialize ZModem variables, return if error 268 ⟩ +==
    `ZInitCrc();`   `/* Make sure the CRC table is computed */`

This basic CRC16 calculator actually computes the CRC of `message` $* x^{16}$.

```
    STATIC unsigned long ZCrc16(const BYTE *buff, unsigned int
          length, unsigned long crc)
  {
    const BYTE *p = buff;

    while (length -- > 0)
      crc = zCrc16Table[((crc >> 8) ^ *p ++) & 0xFF] ^ (crc << 8);
    return crc & 0xFFFF;
  }
```

For the 32-bit CRC, ZModem initializes the CRC register to all 1s, and uses the complement of the result. By complementing both before and after, I maintain consistent usage with the ZCrc16 routine (which is called with an initial value of zero) while still allowing for the CRC to be accumulated over multiple calls.

ZModem computes the 32-bit and 16-bit CRCs in opposite directions, so be careful comparing these two functions.

Like ZCrc16, this routine is actually computing the CRC of `message` $* x^{32}$.

```
    STATIC unsigned long ZCrc32(const BYTE *buff, unsigned int
          length, unsigned long crc)
  {
    const BYTE *p = buff;

    crc = ~ crc;
    while (length -- > 0)
      crc = zCrc32Table[(crc ^ *p ++) & 0xFF] ^ ((crc >> 8) & 0xFFFFFF);
    return ~ crc;
  }
```

A common idiom is to compute whichever CRC is appropriate for the packet being sent.

```
#define SendingCrc(pBuff,length,crc)
        ((pZ -> sendingCrc32) ? ZCrc32((pBuff),(length),
            (crc)) : ZCrc16((pBuff),(length),(crc)))
```

Time Conversions

ZModem preserves the modification date of a file even across time-zone boundaries, by storing the time using UCT (Universal Coordinated Time, also known as Greenwich Mean Time). Precisely, times are represented as the number of seconds since midnight, January 1, 1970.

Although some systems use this representation as their natural format, ANSI declined to specify the interpretation of `time_t`, so I provide a routine to convert between the ANSI-standard `struct tm` and ZModem's time representation. This particular version does not compensate for the time zone.

The algorithm rests on some nice arithmetic properties of a hyphothetical 367-day calendar. This calendar, which has 30 days in February, can be neatly split into two parts. The first consists of the 214 days from January 1 to July 31, and the second part consists of the remaining 153 days from August 1 to December 31. Within each part, the months alternate in length. Deciding the day of the month consists of converting the day number to a day in this hypothetical calendar, and then reducing modulo 214 (to get a day number within one of these partial years), then modulo 61 (day number in a pair of months), and finally modulo 31. The month number is computed similarly.

Table 18.1 may help to understand how this 367-day calendar works.

Month	Days	Month
January	31	August
February	30	September
March	31	October
April	30	November
May	31	December
June	30	
July	31	

Table 18.1   Months in 367-Day Calendar

Note that this function does not take into account any of the several minor adjustments to world time that have occurred since 1970.

```
STATIC void ZTimeToTm(long s, struct tm *pT)
```

```
{
  long m, h;       /* minutes, hours */
  int d, M, y;      /* day, Month, year */
  if (s <= 0) {      /* If time undefined, just use current time */
    time_t t = time(NULL);
    *pT = *localtime(&t);
    return;
  }      /* Reduce everything */
  m = s / 60; h = m / 60; d = h / 24; y = d / 365;
  s %= 60; m %= 60; h %= 24; d %= 365;
  d -= (y + 1) / 4;      /* Correct for leap years since 1970 */
  if (d < 0) { y -- ; d += 365; }
  pT -> tm_sec = s;      /* Save the time */
  pT -> tm_min = m;
  pT -> tm_hour = h;
  pT -> tm_yday = d;      /* Save the day number before destroying it */
  if (((y - 2) % 4 != 0) && (d >= 59)) d ++ ;
         /* Day number in leap year */
  if (d >= 60) d ++ ;      /* day number if Feb has 30 days */
  M = (d > 214) ? 7 : 0 + ((d % 214) / 61) * 2 + ((d % 214) % 61) / 31;
         /* Jan is zero */
  d = ((d % 214) % 61) % 31 + 1;      /* Day numbers start with 1 */
  pT -> tm_mday = d;
  pT -> tm_mon = M;
  pT -> tm_year = y + 70;
  pT -> tm_isdst = -1;      /* DST unknown */
  pT -> tm_wday = -1;      /* Day of week unknown */
}
```

Converting time from `struct tm` to a ZModem format time is considerably simpler. Like the previous function, ZTime doesn't handle time-zone conversion, nor does it take into account the minor time adjustments since 1970.

```
STATIC long ZTime(struct tm *pT)
{
  static const int mon[] = {0, 31, 60, 91, 121, 152, 182, 213, 244,
      274, 305, 335};
  int y = pT -> tm_year - 70, M = pT -> tm_mon;
  int d = pT -> tm_mday - 1 + mon[M];
  if (((y + 2) % 4 != 0) & (M > 1)) d -- ;      /* Adjust for non-leap years */
  d += (y + 1) / 4;      /* Correct for leap years since 1970 */
  return (((((long) y) * 365 + d) * 24 + pT -> tm_hour) * 60 + pT ->
      tm_min) * 60 + pT -> tm_sec;
}
```

Parsing of Special Packet Types

Several ZModem packets have bit-encoded arguments that need to be deciphered. These next two functions parse the startup packets used in the initial negotiation. Right now, the most important thing they handle is configuring the encoding array.

```
STATIC void ZParseZRINIT(ZMODEM_PRIVATE *pZ, unsigned long
        flags)
{
  pZ -> receiverFlags = flags;
  if (flags & KNOW_CRC32) pZ -> crc32 = TRUE;
  if (flags & ESCAPE_CONTROLS) {
    int i;
    SetEncode(DEL); SetEncode(DEL | 0x80);
    SetIgnore(DEL); SetIgnore(DEL | 0x80);
    for (i = 0;  i < 32;  i++) {
      SetEncode(i);
      SetIgnore(i);
    }
    for (i = 128;  i < 160;  i++) {
      SetEncode(i);
      SetIgnore(i);
    }
    pZ -> mySenderFlags |= ESCAPE_CONTROLS;
  }
}


STATIC void ZParseZSINIT(ZMODEM_PRIVATE *pZ, unsigned long
        flags)
{
  pZ -> senderFlags = flags;
  if (flags & ESCAPE_CONTROLS) {
    int i;
    SetEncode(DEL); SetEncode(DEL | 0x80);
    SetIgnore(DEL); SetIgnore(DEL | 0x80);
    for (i = 0;  i < 32;  i++) {
      SetEncode(i);
      SetIgnore(i);
    }
    for (i = 128;  i < 160;  i++) {
      SetEncode(i);
      SetIgnore(i);
    }
```

```
    pZ -> myReceiverFlags |= ESCAPE_CONTROLS;
  }
}
```

Interfaces to External Modules

Many people think of code reusability as reuse of *object code*. The goal of such reusability efforts seems to be to produce code that can be left in a library and simply linked when needed. My experience has been that such reuse is quite rare, and requires far more work than it's typically worth. What is more common, and usually more useful, is *source code* reuse.

Designing code for object reuse often involves passing complex function pointers to avoid dependencies on certain function interfaces. By focusing on source code reuse, such complexity can be avoided by simply isolating such dependencies where they can easily be modified by anyone with access to the source.

The next several sections describe functions that provide access to a variety of system and application capabilities. On some systems, it will make sense to expand these directly into system calls. In others, they simply will be wrappers for complex services implemented elsewhere. Although the versions presented here call the generic services discussed in previous chapters, they should be looked upon as "plugs" that can be freely altered to fit whatever socket is available.

Serial Interface

Packet-oriented protocols often include a packet size, which conveniently allows functions that read packets to make large I/O requests. By contrast, ZModem's approach requires the receiver to make a large number of single-byte calls to parse data and recognize the CRC escapes. For this reason, I've implemented a separate buffer here so that single-byte reads can be handled more efficiently.

Following the model of the ANSI C `<stdio.h>` library, single-byte reads are handled through a macro, `ZReadByteWithTimeout`, which first checks a buffer and only makes a function call when the buffer is empty. Multi-byte reads are handled through a function, `ZReadBytesWithTimeout`, which attempts to fill the buffer in addition to satisfying whatever explicit request is being made.

```
⟨ ZModem variables  267 ⟩ +≡
  SERIAL_PORT port;       /* Port to use */
  BYTE *serialBuffer;        /* Buffered data */
  int serialBufferSize;        /* Total size of buffer */
  BYTE *serialBufferRead;        /* Pointer to read from */
  BYTE *serialBufferLimit;        /* Pointer past last byte in buffer */
```

⟨ Initialize ZModem variables, `return` if error 268 ⟩ +==
```
    pZ -> port = NULL;
    pZ -> serialBuffer = malloc(256);
    if (pZ -> serialBuffer == NULL) return 1;
    pZ -> serialBufferSize = 256;
    pZ -> serialBufferRead = pZ -> serialBuffer;
    pZ -> serialBufferLimit = pZ -> serialBuffer;
```

`ZReadBytesWithTimeout` uses a three-stage approach to satisfy serial read requests:

1. It first tries to copy data out of the buffer, and hence avoid calling the low-level serial routines entirely.
2. It next makes a serial call with a zero timeout and a large size. Hopefully, this will both satisfy the request and pre-fill the buffer.
3. Finally, if the first two stages fail to fill the request, it makes another serial call with the specified timeout.

`ZReadBytesWithTimeout` accepts a timeout parameter rather than using the timeout value in the `ZMODEM_PRIVATE` structure, because different timeouts apply at different points in the protocol. These other timeouts are often computed from the timeout value in the `ZMODEM_PRIVATE` structure.

Because this may be implemented differently depending on the operating system and application services available, it's important to carefully detail the errors that can be returned.

`zFail` is returned if `pZ -> userCancel` becomes set.

`zFailed` is returned if there is a fatal serial port error, such as loss of carrier or a similar hardware failure. Such an error means that no more serial I/O can be performed.

`zTimeout` is returned if the timeout expires. Note that some data may have been read. The client should check the returned values if a partial response is meaningful. This error should never be returned if all of the data requested is returned.

`zBadPacket` is returned if a soft serial error occurs, such as a framing, parity, or overflow error. Such errors indicate that data has been damaged, but do not prevent future I/O calls from succeeding.

`zOK` is returned if the request was satisfied.

The outline of `ZReadBytesWithTimeout` is pretty simple:

```
STATIC int ZReadBytesWithTimeout(ZMODEM_PRIVATE *pZ, int
        timeout, BYTE *pBuffer, size_t *pLength)
{
  int err, returnVal = zOK;
  size_t lengthRead = 0;
  size_t lengthToRead = *pLength;
  ⟨ Try to partly fill request from buffered data 283 ⟩
  ⟨ Try to fill buffer with a zero timeout 283 ⟩
  ⟨ Try to finish filling request with correct timeout 284 ⟩
  if (pZ -> userCancel) return StsWarn(zFail);
  *pLength = lengthRead;
  return returnVal;
}
```

The first step in filling a serial read request is to try to satisfy it with already-buffered data, and so avoid a low-level serial call. However, on systems where the low-level serial routines are unreliable, this step may also attempt to fill the buffer, to help delay overrunning a lower-level serial buffer. If flow control is reliable, that should not be needed.

```
⟨ Try to partly fill request from buffered data 283 ⟩ ==
  if (pZ -> serialBufferRead < pZ -> serialBufferLimit) {
    lengthRead = pZ -> serialBufferLimit − pZ -> serialBufferRead;
    if (lengthRead > lengthToRead) lengthRead = lengthToRead;
    memcpy(pBuffer, pZ -> serialBufferRead, lengthRead);
    pZ -> serialBufferRead += lengthRead;
    pBuffer += lengthRead;
    lengthToRead −= lengthRead;
  }
```
This code is used on page 283.

If the buffer was emptied, try to fill the buffer and use that to satisfy the original request. As a concession to efficiency, this step is skipped if the request is larger than the buffer. In that case, it's more efficient to request the data directly into the client's buffer rather than storing it temporarily in pZ -> serialBuffer.

```
⟨ Try to fill buffer with a zero timeout 283 ⟩ ==
  if ((lengthToRead > 0) && (lengthToRead < pZ -> serialBufferSize)) {
    *pLength = pZ -> serialBufferSize;
    pZ->serialBufferRead = pZ->serialBufferLimit = pZ->serialBuffer;
    err = SerialReadWithTimeout(pZ -> port, 0, pZ -> serialBuffer,
        pLength);
    pZ -> serialBufferLimit += *pLength;
    switch (err) {
    case serialOK: returnVal = zOK;
```

```
        break;
      case serialTimeout: returnVal = zOK;
        break;
      case serialUserCancel: pZ -> userCancel = TRUE;
        returnVal = zFail;
        break;
      case serialFrame: returnVal = zBadPacket; break;
      default: return StsWarn(zFailed);
      }     /* If something was read into the buffer, use it to fill the request */
      if (pZ -> serialBufferRead < pZ -> serialBufferLimit) {
        lengthRead = pZ -> serialBufferLimit - pZ -> serialBufferRead;
        if (lengthRead > lengthToRead) lengthRead = lengthToRead;
        memcpy(pBuffer, pZ -> serialBufferRead, lengthRead);
        pZ -> serialBufferRead += lengthRead;
        pBuffer += lengthRead;
        lengthToRead -= lengthRead;
      }
    }
```

This code is used on page 283.

Finally, if the first two stages failed to fill the request, do a low-level call with the correct timeout. Note that the first two steps essentially required no time, so this third step provides correct timeout handling if the data is not available.

Happily, this last stage is not a performance penalty. Since the data wasn't immediately available, a wait was necessary anyway.

⟨ Try to finish filling request with correct timeout 284 ⟩ ==
```
    if ((lengthToRead > 0) && (returnVal == zOK)) {
      *pLength = lengthToRead;
      err = SerialReadWithTimeout(pZ->port, timeout, pBuffer, pLength);
      switch (err) {
      case serialOK: returnVal = zOK;
        break;
      case serialTimeout: returnVal = zTimeout;
        break;
      case serialUserCancel: pZ -> userCancel = TRUE;
        returnVal = zFail;
        break;
      case serialFrame: returnVal = zBadPacket;
        break;
      default: return StsWarn(zFailed);
      }
      lengthRead += *pLength;
    }
```

This code is used on page 283.

The functions to send data are considerably simpler than those to read data, simply because there can be no timeout. The errors are consequently fewer:

zFail   is returned if pZ -> userCancel becomes set.

zFailed   is returned if there is a fatal serial port error.

zOK   is returned otherwise.

```
STATIC int ZSendBytes(ZMODEM_PRIVATE *pZ, const BYTE
        *pBuffer, unsigned length)
{
  int err, returnVal;
  err = SerialSend(pZ -> port, pBuffer, length);
  switch (err) {
  case serialOK:
    returnVal = zOK;
    break;
  case serialUserCancel:
    pZ -> userCancel = TRUE;
    returnVal = zFail;
    break;
  default: return StsWarn(zFailed);
  }
  if (pZ -> userCancel) return StsWarn(zFail);
  return StsWarn(returnVal);
}
```

Page 174 describes the reasons for splitting the send operation into a non-blocking send and a blocking wait.

The possible errors are the same as with ZSendBytes:

zFail   is returned if pZ -> userCancel becomes set.

zFailed   is returned if there is a fatal serial port error (such as loss of carrier or similar hardware-level failure).

zOK   is returned otherwise.

```
STATIC int ZWaitForSentBytes(ZMODEM_PRIVATE *pZ)
{
  int err, returnVal;
  if (pZ -> userCancel) return StsWarn(zFail);
  err = SerialWaitForSentBytes(pZ -> port);
  switch (err) {
  case serialOK: returnVal = zOK;
```

```
          break;
       case serialUserCancel: pZ -> userCancel = TRUE;
         returnVal = zFail;
         break;
       default: return StsWarn(zFailed);
       }
       if (pZ -> userCancel) return StsWarn(zFail);
       return StsWarn(returnVal);
   }


   STATIC int ZSendByte(ZMODEM_PRIVATE *pZ, BYTE b)
   {
       return StsWarn(ZSendBytes(pZ, &b, 1));
   }
```

The ZReadByteWithTimeout is really just a convenience function for reading a single byte, except that because ZModem relies on it so heavily, I've optimized it as a macro.

The function version ZReadByteWithTimeoutFcn exists only to provide a local variable to swallow the count returned by ZReadBytesWithTimeout. Except for that detail, the ZReadByteWithTimeout macro simply checks the serial data buffered in the ZMODEM_PRIVATE structure and returns a byte immediately if it's available; otherwise it calls ZReadBytesWithTimeout.

```
   #define ZReadByteWithTimeout(pZ, timeout, pByte)
          (((pZ) -> serialBufferRead < (pZ) -> serialBufferLimit) ?
          (*(pByte) = *((pZ) -> serialBufferRead ++), zOK):
          (ZReadByteWithTimeoutFcn((pZ), (timeout), (pByte))))
     STATIC int ZReadByteWithTimeoutFcn(ZMODEM_PRIVATE *pZ, int
            timeout, BYTE *pByte)
     {
       size_t count = 1;
       return ZReadBytesWithTimeout(pZ, timeout, pByte, &count);
     }
```

ZGobble is used to handle noise in certain situations. Under extreme situations, error recovery is simpler if you just wait for silence on the line before responding. Calling ZGobble with the desired silence interval accomplishes this. ZGobble is also called at the end of the transfer in an attempt to swallow any "last gasp" from the other end. As a special case, ZGobble(0) simply flushes the receive queue.

```
     STATIC int ZGobble(ZMODEM_PRIVATE *pZ, int timeout)
     {
```

```
    int err;
    BYTE junk[50];
    size_t junkSize = sizeof (junk);
    do {
      err = ZReadBytesWithTimeout(pZ, timeout, junk, &junkSize);
      if (err == zBadPacket) err = zOK;        /* Ignore bad bytes */
    } while (err == zOK);
    if (err == zTimeout) return zOK;
    return StsWarn(err);
  }
```

A break signal is used as part of the attention sequence required by some senders.

```
    STATIC int ZSendBreak(ZMODEM_PRIVATE *pZ)
    {
      int returnVal;
      int err = SerialSendBreak(pZ -> port);

      switch (err) {
      case serialOK: returnVal = zOK;
        break;
      case serialUserCancel: pZ -> userCancel = TRUE;
        returnVal = zFail;
        break;
      default: return StsWarn(zFailed);
      }
      if (pZ -> userCancel) return StsWarn(zFail);
      return StsWarn(returnVal);
    }
```

I've treated this as part of the serial interface for two reasons: First, some serial drivers need to be 'baby-sat' to avoid losing data. Second, prompt user interface response means that lengthy operations (such as pauses) need special care. For reasons explained in Chapter 14, the `serial` module already needs to cooperate with the user interface, so this seems a suitable marriage.

```
    STATIC int ZPause(ZMODEM_PRIVATE *pZ)
    {
      int returnVal;
      int err = SerialPause(pZ -> port, 1);

      switch (err) {
      case serialOK: returnVal = zOK;
        break;
      case serialUserCancel: pZ -> userCancel = TRUE;
```

```
        returnVal = zFail;
        break;
    default: return StsWarn(zFailed);
    }
    if (pZ -> userCancel) return StsWarn(zFail);
    return StsWarn(returnVal);
}
```

Reading Files

The file interface splits into three pieces: functions to read data from files, functions to write data to files, and functions to handle miscellaneous chores.

The `disk` module keeps a variety of information about the current file in the `DISKFILE` structure. If the disk interface functions are replaced with functions that directly manipulate a `FILE` handle, this section needs to be fleshed out to maintain file information such as the filename, modification date, access permissions, and file type.

```
⟨ ZModem variables 267 ⟩ +==
    DISKFILE f;       /* Current file */
    long fileSize;      /* Size of file being transferred, -1 if not known */

⟨ Initialize ZModem variables, return if error 268 ⟩ +==
    pZ -> f = NULL;
    pZ -> fileSize = −1;
```

For simplicity, I use an array of `char *` to hold the names of files to be transferred. If you need a different data structure, you'll need to modify `ZModemSend` and `ZFileReadOpenNext` accordingly.

```
⟨ ZModem variables 267 ⟩ +==
    const char **filenames;       /* Used by ZFileReadOpenNext */
    int currentFileName;
    int numFileNames;
    int fileType;

⟨ Initialize ZModem variables, return if error 268 ⟩ +==
    pZ -> filenames = NULL;
    pZ -> currentFileName = 0;
    pZ -> numFileNames = 0;
    pZ -> fileType = diskFileUnknown;
```

This function tries to open each file in turn until it finds the next one that can be opened. It returns `zEndOfSession` if no files remain to be opened.

```
STATIC int ZFileReadOpenNext(ZMODEM_PRIVATE *pZ, int fileType)
{
  while (1) {
    if (pZ -> currentFileName == pZ -> numFileNames)
      return zEndOfSession;
    switch (DiskReadOpen(&pZ -> f,
          pZ -> filenames[pZ -> currentFileName ++], fileType)) {
    case diskOK: DiskFileSize(pZ -> f, &(pZ -> fileSize));
      return zOK;
    case diskCantRead: case diskNoSuchFile: break;
    default: return zFail;
    }
  }
}


STATIC int ZFileRead(ZMODEM_PRIVATE *pZ, BYTE *pBuffer, size_t
      *pLength)
{
  int returnVal;
  switch (DiskRead(pZ -> f, pBuffer, *pLength, pLength)) {
  case diskOK: returnVal = zOK;
    break;
  case diskEOF: returnVal = zEOF;
    break;
  default: returnVal = zFail;
    break;
  }
  return returnVal;
}
```

To support ZModem crash recovery, you need to be able to skip some part of the file. This implementation of **ZFileReadSkip** is crude but effective.

```
STATIC int ZFileReadSkip(ZMODEM_PRIVATE *pZ, size_t length)
{
  BYTE buff[500];
  while (length > 0) {
    size_t readSize = sizeof (buff);
    if (readSize > length) readSize = length;
    StsRet(ZFileRead(pZ, buff, &readSize));
    length -= readSize;
  }
  return zOK;
}
```

```
STATIC int ZFileReadClose(ZMODEM_PRIVATE *pZ)
{
  int returnVal;
  switch (DiskReadClose(pZ -> f)) {
  case diskOK: returnVal = zOK;
    break;
  default: returnVal = zFail;
    break;
  }
  pZ -> f = NULL;
  return returnVal;
}
```

Writing Files

The file writing interface, like file reading, consists of functions to open and close a file and do actual I/O. Also, like the file reading interface, the most complex function is the one to open a file, which has a myriad of responsibilities.

ZFileWriteOpen starts by parsing the ZModem file header. This file header contains a NULL-terminated filename, followed by a string with the file size and other file attributes.

The function then has a number of other duties. It must make sure the received filename is valid for this system. It should make sure the name provided is not too long. For systems such as MS-DOS, which have severe length restrictions on the filename, it may be necessary to use a phonetic algorithm (removing vowels, replacing "ph" with "f," "ch" with "c," and so on) to reduce the length of the filename. Filenames should be checked for illegal characters and format. (For example, VAX/VMS filenames can only have a single "." character.)

This function is also responsible for handling file collisions. In particular, pZ -> fileFlags has the coded file handling suggested by the sender. These considerations should be overridden by any options specified by the user of the local application. If the result is that the file should not be transferred, ZFileWriteOpen should return zSkip so that the sender will be notified.

```
STATIC int ZFileWriteOpen(ZMODEM_PRIVATE *pZ, BYTE
      *pBuffer, unsigned length)
{
  const char *fileName = (char *) pBuffer;
  long fileMode = -1;
  long fileSize = -1;
  struct tm fileDate;
  int fileType;
  int err;
```

```
⟨ Set defaults for fileName and fileDate 291 ⟩
⟨ Parse the file name and attributes string 291 ⟩
if (DiskWriteInit(&pZ -> f)) return StsWarn(zFail);
if (DiskWriteName(pZ -> f, fileName)) return StsWarn(zFail);
pZ -> fileSize = fileSize;
if (DiskWriteSize(pZ -> f, fileSize)) return StsWarn(zFail);
if (DiskWriteDate(pZ -> f, &fileDate)) return StsWarn(zFail);
if (DiskWriteMode(pZ -> f, fileMode)) return StsWarn(zFail);
⟨ Set file type 292 ⟩
⟨ Open file, store result in err 293 ⟩
if (err == diskError)      /* Error on this file */
  return StsWarn(zSkip);     /* Don't transfer it */
else if (err != diskOK)     /* Bad error */
  return StsWarn(zFail);     /* Kill entire session */
return zOK;
}
```

The default filename and file date are set here. Unlike YModem, which uses an empty filename to indicate the end-of-session, ZModem does not prohibit an empty filename. Many systems do not have a notion of file mode or file date, so those must be set to reasonable defaults.

```
⟨ Set defaults for fileName and fileDate 291 ⟩ ==
  if ((fileName == NULL) || (*fileName == 0))
    fileName = "zmodem.000\0\0";
  {    /* default file date is now */
    time_t t = time(NULL);
    fileDate = *localtime(&t);
  }
```
This code is used on page 291.

The first byte after the NULL-terminated filename begins a string with space-separated file attributes. ZModem defines four such fields: the file length in bytes, a file date, a Unix-style file access mode, and the serial number of the sending program. The first value is sent as an ASCII decimal number, the remainder are represented in octal. None of these are required, and the receiver must be careful to gracefully handle the case where some or all are omitted.

This implementation parses the first three; the serial number is not meaningful when programs from multiple vendors are intended to work together.

```
⟨ Parse the file name and attributes string 291 ⟩ ==
  {
    const char *p = fileName;
    p += strlen(p) + 1;
```

```
      if (*p) {
        fileSize = atoi(p);     /* Get the file size */
        while ((*p) && (*p != '␣')) p++;     /* Advance to next field */
        if (*p) p++;
      }
      if (*p) {     /* Get the modification date */
        long fileDateSeconds = 0;
        while ((*p) && (*p != '␣')) {
          fileDateSeconds = fileDateSeconds * 8 + (*p) — '0';
          p++;
        }     /* Note: fileDate is in UCT! */
        ZTimeToTm(fileDateSeconds, &fileDate);
        if (*p) p++;     /* Advance to next field */
      }
      if (*p) {     /* Get the file mode */
        fileMode = 0;
        while ((*p) && (*p != '␣')) {
          fileMode = fileMode * 8 + (*p) — '0';
          p++;
        }
        if (*p) p++;     /* Advance to next field */
      }     /* The next field is the serial number */
    }
```

This code is used on page 291.

The "conversion" options specify what conversions should be applied to the data as it is received.

```
⟨ Set file type  292 ⟩ ==
  fileType = pZ -> fileType;
  if (fileType == diskFileUnknown) {
    switch (pZ -> fileFlags & CONV_MASK) {
    case 0: break;
    case CONV_BINARY: fileType = diskFileBinary; break;
    case CONV_TEXT: fileType = diskFileText; break;
    case CONV_RESUME: fileType = diskFileBinary; break;
    default:     /* Unknown conversion option? */
      if (pZ -> debug) {
        DebugBegin(pZ -> debug, debugAttr);
        DebugString(pZ -> debug, "Unknown␣conversion␣option:␣");
        DebugIntHex(pZ -> debug, pZ -> fileFlags & CONV_MASK);
        DebugEnd(pZ -> debug);
      }
    }
  }
```

```
  if (DiskWriteType(pZ -> f, fileType)) return StsWarn(zFail);
```
This code is used on page 291.

The "management" options specify how the file should be opened, and how to decide if the file should be accepted.

⟨ Open file, store result in err 293 ⟩ ==
```
  if (pZ -> fileFlags & MAN_SKNOLOC) {      /* Skip if nonexistent */
    DISKFILE fTmp;

    err = DiskReadOpen(&fTmp, fileName, diskFileUnknown);
    if (err == diskNoSuchFile)      /* File doesn't exist */
      return StsWarn(zSkip);      /* Skip it */
    DiskReadClose(fTmp);
  }
  switch (pZ -> fileFlags & MAN_MASK) {
  case MAN_APPEND: err = DiskAppendOpen(pZ -> f); break;
  case MAN_REPLACE: err = DiskReplaceOpen(pZ -> f); break;
  default: err = DiskWriteOpen(pZ -> f); break;
  }
```
This code is used on page 291.

```
  STATIC int ZFileWrite(ZMODEM_PRIVATE *pZ, const BYTE
        *pBuffer, unsigned long length)
  {
    switch (DiskWrite(pZ -> f, pBuffer, length)) {
    case diskOK: return zOK;
    default: return zFail;
    }
  }
```

```
  STATIC int ZFileWriteClose(ZMODEM_PRIVATE *pZ)
  {
    int returnVal;
    switch (DiskWriteClose(pZ -> f)) {
    case diskOK: returnVal = zOK; break;
    default: returnVal = zFail; break;
    }
    pZ -> f = NULL;
    return returnVal;
  }
```

Miscellaneous File Functions

This function provides the size of the file.

```
STATIC long ZFileSize(ZMODEM_PRIVATE *pZ)
{
  long size;
  if (pZ -> f == NULL) return -1;
  else if (DiskFileSize(pZ -> f, &size)) return -1;
  else return size;
}
```

ZModem has a rarely-used feature that allows the sender to request the amount of free space remaining on the receiver. Like most implementations, this version returns a value of zero, which indicates an indefinite amount of free space.

```
STATIC unsigned long ZFileSystemFree(ZMODEM_PRIVATE
        *pZ, unsigned long *pFreeCount)
{
  *pFreeCount = 0L;
  return zOK;
}
```

One of ZModem's important features is that the sender can specify a number of different criteria that the receiver can use to accept or reject the file being transferred. One of those is that the receiver can use the file contents to judge whether the file should be transferred. At first glance, this approach seems circular. After all, how can the receiver compare file contents without first transferring the proposed substitute? The solution, of course, is for the sender to compute a signature of the file data and transfer that. This solution is implemented by allowing the receiver to request, prior to the file data transfer, a CRC of some or all of the file. The receiver can then use this to decide whether or not the file should be transferred (or, in the case of crash recovery, how much of the file should be transferred). The ZFileCRC function supports the sender's side of this functionality. One caveat, however: if the file being sent is being constructed on-the-fly, it may be impossible to scan the entire file to compute a CRC and then rewind to the beginning to carry out the actual transfer. Thus, if it's necessary to transfer files from a pipe, this function may need to save the piped data into an actual file and alter the already-opened file in pZ -> f to refer to that temporary file instead. ZFileCRC returns zFail if the attempt to accumulate a CRC fails for any reason.

```
STATIC int ZFileCRC(ZMODEM_PRIVATE *pZ, unsigned long
        numberBytes, unsigned long *pCrc)
{
  DISKFILE fTmp;
  BYTE buff[4096];
```

```
    unsigned long crc = 0;
    const char *fileName;
    int err;

    *pCrc = 0;
    DiskFileName(pZ -> f, &fileName);      /* Get name of current file */
    err = DiskReadOpen(&fTmp, fileName, diskFileBinary);
        /* Re-open it */
    if (err != diskOK) return StsWarn(zFail);
    while (numberBytes > 0) {      /* Accumulate CRC requested */
      size_t numberRead = numberBytes;

      if (numberRead > sizeof (buff)) numberRead = sizeof (buff);
      err = DiskRead(fTmp, buff, numberRead, &numberRead);
      if (err != diskOK) return StsWarn(zFail);
      crc = ZCrc32(buff, numberRead, crc);
      numberBytes -= numberRead;
    }
    DiskReadClose(fTmp);
    *pCrc = crc;
    return zOK;
  }
```

Progress Reporting

The client provides the progress handle, which allows the client to configure how the progress should be displayed. For example, an application may have an optional 'expert' display that can be enabled.

```
⟨ ZModem variables 267 ⟩ +≡
    PROGRESS progress;      /* Progress handle */
```

```
⟨ Initialize ZModem variables, return if error 268 ⟩ +≡
    pZ -> progress = NULL;
```

One interesting point here is that I've used `receivePosition` as the basis for reporting the progress. Other implementations use the sender's position when sending, but that approach results in strange gyrations when errors occur. It seems more honest to report only the progress to which both sides actually agree.

```
    enum {
      stsNegotiating = progNegotiating, stsNewFile = progNewFile,
          stsSending = progSending, stsReceiving = progReceiving,
          stsEnding = progEnding, stsEOF = progEOF, stsDone = progDone,
          stsFailed = progFailed, stsCancelled = progCancelled,
          stsSkipped = progSkipped
```

```
};

STATIC void ZProgress(ZMODEM_PRIVATE *pZ, int status)
{
  if (pZ -> f) {      /* Get file information */
    const char *fileName = NULL;
    int fileType = diskFileUnknown;

    DiskFileName(pZ -> f, &fileName);
    ProgressFileName(pZ -> progress, fileName);
    DiskFileType(pZ -> f, &fileType);
    ProgressFileType(pZ -> progress, fileType);
  } else {
    ProgressFileName(pZ -> progress, NULL);
  }
  ProgressFileSize(pZ -> progress, pZ -> fileSize);
  ProgressFilePosition(pZ -> progress, pZ -> receivePosition);
  ProgressReport(pZ -> progress, status);
}
```

Encoding Layer

ZModem uses two different encodings for its packets. Prefix encoded data is sent by the ZSendEncodedBytes function, while hexadecimal encoded data is sent by ZSendHexBytes.

Sending prefix encoded data is pretty simple. The only concession to efficiency here is that the data is encoded into a local buffer and then sent all at once, to minimize the number of calls into the serial routines.

```
STATIC int ZSendEncodeBytes(ZMODEM_PRIVATE *pZ, const BYTE
      *pBuffer, unsigned int length)
{
  BYTE buff[100];
  unsigned buffPos;
  int buffFree;
  if (pZ -> debug) {
    DebugBegin(pZ -> debug, debugPacketLowLevel | debugEncoding);
    DebugString(pZ -> debug, "ZSendEncodeBytes:␣encoding␣");
    DebugUInt(pZ -> debug, length);
    DebugString(pZ -> debug, "␣bytes:␣'‘");
    if (length > 30) {
      DebugStringCount(pZ -> debug, (const char *) pBuffer, 30);
      DebugString(pZ -> debug, "...");
    } else {
```

```
          DebugStringCount(pZ -> debug, (const char *)
              pBuffer, length);
          DebugString(pZ -> debug, "'''");
        }
        DebugEnd(pZ -> debug);
      }
      while (length > 0) {
        buffPos = 0;
        buffFree = sizeof (buff) - 5;
        while ((buffFree > 0) && (length > 0)) {
          int c = *pBuffer ++;

          length --;
          if (TestEncode(c)) {        /* Should character be encoded? */
            buff[buffPos ++] = CAN;
            if (c == 0x7F) buff[buffPos ++] = 'l';
            else if (c == 0xFF) buff[buffPos ++] = 'm';
            else buff[buffPos ++] = c | 0x40;
            buffFree -= 2;
          } else {
            buff[buffPos ++] = c;
            buffFree --;
          }
        }
        StsRet(ZSendBytes(pZ, buff, buffPos));
      }
      return zOK;
    }
```

This function is almost identical to the `Hexify` function on page 44.

```
    STATIC int ZSendHexBytes(ZMODEM_PRIVATE *pZ, BYTE *pBuffer, int
        length)
    {
      BYTE buff[100];
      unsigned buffPos;
      int buffFree;
      static const char digits[] = "0123456789abcdef";
      while (length > 0) {
        buffPos = 0;
        buffFree = sizeof (buff) - 2;
        while ((length -- > 0) && (buffFree > 0)) {
          int c = *pBuffer ++;

          buff[buffPos ++] = digits[(c >> 4) & 15];
          buff[buffPos ++] = digits[c & 15];
```

```
        buffFree −= 2;
      }
      StsRet(ZSendBytes(pZ, buff, buffPos));
    }
    return zOK;
}
```

Receiving and Decoding

To simplify the actual decoding of prefix-encoded data, some additional data structures are quite useful. The first of these is a way to quickly determine which bytes form valid prefix sequences. Since the classify array introduced earlier isn't fully utilized, it can hold this additional information.

```
#define SetDecode(c)   (pZ -> classify[c] |= 4)
#define TestDecode(c)  (pZ -> classify[c] & 4)

⟨ Initialize ZModem variables, return if error 268 ⟩ +==
    {
      int i;

      for (i = 0x40;  i < 0x60;  i ++) SetDecode(i);
      for (i = 0xc0;  i < 0xe0;  i ++) SetDecode(i);
      SetDecode('l');
      SetDecode('m');
    }
```

The other useful structure is an array that does the actual decoding.

```
STATIC BYTE zDecode[256];
```

Although I could simply list the contents of the zDecode array, I find it a bit more intelligible to describe the contents with the following short piece of code. Remember that ZModem encodes most control characters by setting bit six; decoding requires clearing that bit.

```
⟨ Initialize ZModem variables, return if error 268 ⟩ +==
    {
      int i;

      for (i = 0;  i < 256;  i ++) zDecode[i] = 0;
      for (i = 0x40;  i < 0x60;  i ++) zDecode[i] = i & 0xBF;
      for (i = 0xc0;  i < 0xe0;  i ++) zDecode[i] = i & 0xBF;
      zDecode['l'] = 0x7F;
      zDecode['m'] = 0xFF;
    }
```

ZReadDecodeBytes is the first of three similar-looking routines that do progressively more complex things with the data as they receive it. This first one simply reads and decodes prefix-encoded data. It's used by the routines for reading packets and CRC escapes. ZReadDataSubpacket adds the handling of the single CRC escape that follows certain types of packets, and ZReceiveStream adds the repositioning support and other tidbits needed to handle file data.

```
STATIC int ZReadDecodeBytes(ZMODEM_PRIVATE *pZ, int timeout, BYTE
        *pBuffer, int *pLength)
{
  BYTE byte;
  int sawCAN = FALSE;
  int lengthDesired = *pLength;
  int canCount = 0;

  while (1) {
    StsRet(ZReadByteWithTimeout(pZ, pZ -> timeout, &byte));
    if (TestIgnore(byte)) {      /* Ignore XON/XOFF chars */
    } else if (byte == CAN) {
      if (sawCAN) {      /* Count repeated CAN characters */
        canCount ++;
        if (canCount >= 5) return StsWarn(zFailed);
      } else {
        canCount = 1;
        sawCAN = TRUE;
      }
    } else if (sawCAN) {      /* Decode byte following CAN */
      sawCAN = FALSE;
      if (TestDecode(byte)) *pBuffer ++ = zDecode[byte];
      else {
        *pLength -= lengthDesired;
        return StsWarn(zBadPacket);
      }
      lengthDesired --;
    } else {
      *pBuffer ++ = byte;
      lengthDesired --;
    }
    if (lengthDesired == 0) return zOK;
  }    /* while (1) */
}
```

Reading and decoding hex data is similar. Note that ZModem ignores parity for hex data, but does restrict hex data to lower case letters.

```
STATIC int ZReadDecodeHexBytes(ZMODEM_PRIVATE *pZ, int
        timeout, BYTE *pBuffer, int *pLength)
{
  BYTE byte;
  int lengthDesired = *pLength;
  int evenOdd = 0;      /* 0 -> even digit, TRUE-> odd digit */
  while (1) {
    int digit = -1;
    StsRet(ZReadByteWithTimeout(pZ, timeout, &byte));
    byte &= 0x7F;
    if ((byte >= '0') && (byte <= '9')) digit = byte - '0';
    else if ((byte >= 'a') && (byte <= 'f')) digit = byte - 'a' + 10;
    else if (!TestIgnore(byte))     /* Illegal digit */
      return StsWarn(zBadPacket);
    if (digit >= 0) {
      if (evenOdd) {
        *pBuffer ++ |= digit;
        lengthDesired --;
      } else *pBuffer = digit << 4;
      evenOdd = ! evenOdd;
    }
    if (lengthDesired == 0) return zOK;
  }    /* while (1) */
}
```

ZModem uses a special encoding for one unusual situation. Because some senders cannot easily check for pending data, the sender can specify an *attention sequence* to the receiver. The receiver is expected to send this sequence before sending any "error packet." The NULL-terminated string is stored in pZ ->attention. Two special values are 0xDD, which specifies a break, and 0xDE, which specifies a 1-second delay. There is no way for the attention sequence to specify the characters 0x00, 0xDD, or 0xDE.

```
STATIC int ZSendAttention(ZMODEM_PRIVATE *pZ)
{
  BYTE *pB = pZ -> attention;
  while (TRUE) {
    switch (*pB) {
    case 0:     /* End of string */
      return zOK;
    case 0xDD:    /* Send break */
      ZSendBreak(pZ);
      break;
    case 0xDE:     /* Pause 1 second */
```

```
            ZPause(pZ);
            break;
        default:      /* Send any other value */
            StsRet(ZSendByte(pZ, *pB));
            break;
        }
        pB++;
    }
}
```

Packet Layer

Unlike XModem and YModem, ZModem is careful to include error checking on all control packets. This makes ZModem much more robust than XModem and YModem. ZModem packets have a fairly involved structure. Most packets consist only of a header, which can be sent in any of three different formats. A few packets require additional data, which is sent after the header. ZData file data packets can include any amount of data. The functions in this section don't attempt to send or receive an entire packet at one time, but rather provide tools that higher layers can use to construct these very large packets.

Sending Packets

This function sends a ZCAN packet, which has a unique format, designed to be easy for panicked users to quickly type. The packet itself is five Control-X characters. This function actually sends ten Control-X characters, and follows them with ten backspace characters. The backspace characters are intended to erase the Control-X characters in case the other end has already terminated. That way, the user will hopefully not find themselves staring at a command prompt that has mysteriously sprouted gibberish.

```
STATIC int ZSendCAN(ZMODEM_PRIVATE *pZ)
{
    static const BYTE cancel[] = {CAN,CAN,CAN,CAN,CAN,CAN,CAN,
        CAN,CAN,CAN,8,8,8,8,8,8,8,8,8,8};
    return ZSendBytes(pZ,cancel,sizeof (cancel) / sizeof
        (cancel[0]));
}
```

ZModem has three different packet formats that are handled by the following two functions. ZSendHexHeader sends a hexadecimal header with a 16-bit CRC.

Hexadecimal headers are used for almost every packet that doesn't require data. The reasoning is that hexadecimal headers contain no characters (except for the initial CAN) that could wreak havoc with a command prompt or terminal interface, and hence are safer to use. In addition, when there is no data, efficiency is less of a concern, so the longer hexadecimal headers do not significantly affect efficiency.

Because these headers might have to make their way through terminal interfaces, they are terminated with CR and LF. To help 'fix' flow control that may be stuck because of spurious XOFF characters, an XON is also appended to each packet. There are two cases where the trailing XON is deliberately omitted. ZACK packets are sent during the transfer of streaming data, and so must avoid tampering with the flow control. ZFIN packets are the very last things sent during the session, and hence might be sent or received when the terminal port is in an odd state.

Note the final call to ZWaitForSentBytes that helps ensure future timed reads will be accurate.

```
STATIC int ZSendHexHeader(ZMODEM_PRIVATE *pZ, int
        headerType, unsigned long arg)
{
  BYTE headerStart[] = {'*', '*', CAN, 'B'};
     /* CRC16 hex header */
  BYTE headerData[7];
  BYTE headerEnd[] = {CR, LF, XON};
  pZ -> txPacketType = headerType;
  if (pZ -> debug) {
    DebugBegin(pZ -> debug, debugPacket);
    DebugString(pZ -> debug, "Sending␣hex␣header␣");
    DebugPacket(pZ -> debug, headerType, arg);
    DebugEnd(pZ -> debug);
  }    /* ZCAN header is handled differently */
  if (headerType == ZCAN) return ZSendCAN(pZ);
        /* Build the header data with 16-bit CRC */
  headerData[0] = headerType;
  headerData[1] = arg & 0xFF;
  headerData[2] = (arg >> 8) & 0xFF;
  headerData[3] = (arg >> 16) & 0xFF;
  headerData[4] = (arg >> 24) & 0xFF;
  {
     short crc = ZCrc16(headerData, 5, 0);
     headerData[5] = (crc >> 8) & 0xFF;
     headerData[6] = crc & 0xFF;
  }    /* Send the complete header */
  StsRet(ZSendBytes(pZ, headerStart, sizeof (headerStart)));
  StsRet(ZSendHexBytes(pZ, headerData, sizeof (headerData)));
     /* Omit the trailing XON in two special cases */
```

```
    if ((headerType == ZACK) || (headerType == ZFIN))
      StsRet(ZSendBytes(pZ, headerEnd, 2));
    else StsRet(ZSendBytes(pZ, headerEnd, 3));
    StsRet(ZWaitForSentBytes(pZ));
    return zOK;
}
```

ZModem 'binary' headers (actually, they're prefix-encoded headers) come in two varieties, depending on the CRC size. This function sends either type, depending on the setting of pZ -> crc32. The bulk of the code is involved in disassembling numbers into individual bytes. This approach avoids any dependency on the "endianness" of the system.

For historical reasons, ZModem deals with 16-bit and 32-bit CRCs differently. They are computed in opposite directions and then stored in the opposite byte order.

```
        STATIC int ZSendHeader(ZMODEM_PRIVATE *pZ, int
              headerType, unsigned long arg)
{       /* Default to CRC16 binary header */
    BYTE headerStart[] = {'*', CAN, 'A'};      /* CRC16 binary header */
    BYTE headerData[9];
    unsigned headerLength = 7;      /* Data length for CRC16 */

    pZ -> txPacketType = headerType;
    if (pZ -> debug) {
      DebugBegin(pZ -> debug, debugPacket);
      DebugString(pZ -> debug, "Sending binary header ");
      DebugPacket(pZ -> debug, headerType, arg);
      DebugEnd(pZ -> debug);
    }

    if (headerType == ZCAN) return ZSendCAN(pZ);

    headerData[0] = headerType;
    headerData[1] = arg & 0xFF;
    headerData[2] = (arg >> 8) & 0xFF;
    headerData[3] = (arg >> 16) & 0xFF;
    headerData[4] = (arg >> 24) & 0xFF;
    if (pZ -> crc32) {
      unsigned long crc = ZCrc32(headerData, 5, 0);

      headerData[5] = crc & 0xFF;
      headerData[6] = (crc >> 8) & 0xFF;
      headerData[7] = (crc >> 16) & 0xFF;
      headerData[8] = (crc >> 24) & 0xFF;
      headerStart[2] = 'C';      /* CRC32 binary header */
      headerLength = 9;
```

```
      pZ -> sendingCrc32 = TRUE;
    } else {
      unsigned short crc = ZCrc16(headerData, 5, 0);
      headerData[5] = (crc >> 8) & 0xFF;
      headerData[6] = crc & 0xFF;
      pZ -> sendingCrc32 = FALSE;
    }
    StsRet(ZSendBytes(pZ, headerStart, sizeof (headerStart)));
    StsRet(ZSendEncodeBytes(pZ, headerData, headerLength));
    StsRet(ZWaitForSentBytes(pZ));
    return zOK;
  }
```

The handling of the `timeout` parameter requires some explanation. In this implementation, the `timeout` parameter is obeyed only for the beginning of the packet. Once the * character is seen, a fixed 2-second timeout is used for successive characters. A fixed timeout is used because this routine is often called with a timeout of 0 to check for a received packet. The strategy of only using the timeout for the first character ensures that it won't time out in the middle of a legitimate packet. On the other hand, a long timeout between characters seems unnecessary; headers are short, and they should not be unduly separated in transit.

The careful framing at the beginning means that inter-packet noise will be silently skipped. In particular, pad characters inserted after hex headers will be skipped when this routine looks for the next header.

```
    STATIC int ZReadHeader(ZMODEM_PRIVATE *pZ, int timeout)
    {
      BYTE pad = 0, sync = 0, headerType = 0;
      BYTE packet[15];
      int canCount = 0;
      int length;
      int err;
      unsigned long crc;
      unsigned long arg;
      int noiseCount = 0;
      ⟨Search for initial *; return any error 305⟩
      ⟨Get packet start in pad, sync, headerType 306⟩
      ⟨Read packet type, argument, and CRC 306⟩
      arg = ((packet[4]*256+packet[3])*256+packet[2])*256+packet[1];
      ⟨If debugging, dump packet contents 307⟩
      ⟨Check CRC and return zBadPacket if it fails 307⟩
      pZ -> rxPacketType = packet[0];     /* stash type, arg */
      pZ -> rxPacketArg = arg;
      if (pZ -> rxPacketType == ZABORT) return zFail;
```

```
        return zOK;
    }
```

The loop to search for the initial ∗ obeys the specified timeout. The only error that receives special handling is zBadPacket, indicating a damaged byte. Inter-packet noise shouldn't prevent the reception of otherwise valid packets. The noiseCount variable is used to generate an error if no legitimate packet is seen for too long.

```
⟨Search for initial *; return any error 305⟩ ==
  do {
    err = ZReadByteWithTimeout(pZ, timeout, &pad);
    if ((err != zOK) && (err != zBadPacket)) return err;
    if (err == zOK) {
      if (noiseCount ++ > pZ -> noiseLimit)
        return StsWarn(zBadPacket);
      if (pad == CAN) {
        if (++ canCount >= 5) {
          pZ -> rxPacketType = ZCAN;
          return StsWarn(zFailed);
        }
      } else canCount = 0;
    }
  } while (pad != '*');
```

This code is used on page 304.

The noiseLimit parameter has to balance two requirements. If it's set too low, the receiver will end up generating many redundant reposition requests as data stored in the channel prior to the error continues to be received. These redundant requests can significantly reduce the throughput. On the other hand, if it's set too high, it will take a long time before the receiver repeats a reposition request that may have been lost. The default 25000 here may seem high, especially given that the original 1986 version of **rz** used 1400, but considering that common modem speeds have increased from 2400 bps to 28,800 bps in the same interval, this value is probably quite reasonable for current applications.

```
⟨ZModem variables 267⟩ +==
  size_t noiseLimit;
```

```
⟨Initialize ZModem variables, return if error 268⟩ +==
  pZ -> noiseLimit = 25000;
```

Using the three variables pad, sync, headerType as a three-byte shift register lets the following code search for a legal packet start fairly quickly, skipping over pad characters generated by noise. It also checks for a ZCAN packet.

⟨ Get packet start in pad, sync, headerType 306 ⟩ ≡
```
headerType = '*';       /* Last character was a * */
do {
  pad = sync;
  sync = headerType;
  StsRet(ZReadByteWithTimeout(pZ, 2, &headerType));
  if (noiseCount ++ > pZ -> noiseLimit) return StsWarn(zBadPacket);
  if (headerType == CAN) {
    if (++ canCount >= 5) {
      pZ -> rxPacketType = ZCAN;
      return StsWarn(zFail);
    }
  } else canCount = 0;
} while ((pad != '*') || (sync != CAN) || ((headerType !=
    'A') && (headerType != 'B') && (headerType != 'C')));
```
This code is used on page 304.

As Table 8.1 on page 97 shows, the start-of-packet code in the headerType variable specifies the CRC type and the encoding method used by the header packet. The total length is one byte for the packet type, four for the packet argument, and either two or four for the CRC.

⟨ Read packet type, argument, and CRC 306 ⟩ ≡
```
switch (headerType) {
case 'A':       /* 16-bit CRC prefix-encoded header */
  pZ -> receivingCrc32 = FALSE;
  length = 1 + 4 + 2;
  StsRet(ZReadDecodeBytes(pZ, 2, packet, &length));
  break;
case 'B':       /* 16-bit CRC hex header */
  pZ -> receivingCrc32 = FALSE;
  length = 1 + 4 + 2;
  StsRet(ZReadDecodeHexBytes(pZ, 2, packet, &length));
  break;
case 'C':       /* 32-bit CRC prefix-encoded header */
  pZ -> receivingCrc32 = TRUE;
  length = 1 + 4 + 4;
  StsRet(ZReadDecodeBytes(pZ, 2, packet, &length));
  break;
default: return StsWarn(zBadPacket);
  break;
```

```
    }
```
This code is used on page 304.

⟨ If debugging, dump packet contents 307 ⟩ ≡
```
    if (pZ -> debug) {
      DebugBegin(pZ -> debug, debugPacket);
      DebugString(pZ -> debug, "Read␣packet:␣");
      switch (headerType) {
      case 'A': DebugString(pZ -> debug, "Bin16␣");
        break;
      case 'B': DebugString(pZ -> debug, "Hex16␣");
        break;
      case 'C': DebugString(pZ -> debug, "Bin32␣");
        break;
      }
      DebugPacket(pZ -> debug, packet[0], arg);
      if (pZ -> receivingCrc32) crc =
            ((packet[8]*256+packet[7])*256+packet[6])*256+packet[5];
      else crc = (packet[5] * 256 + packet[6]) & 0xFFFF;
      DebugString(pZ -> debug, "␣crc:");
      DebugIntHex(pZ -> debug, crc);
      DebugEnd(pZ -> debug);
    }
```
This code is used on page 304.

As mentioned earlier, ZModem stores the 16-bit and 32-bit CRCs in opposite orders.

⟨ Check CRC and return zBadPacket if it fails 307 ⟩ ≡
```
    if (pZ -> receivingCrc32) {
      crc = ((packet[8]*256+packet[7])*256+packet[6])*256+packet[5];
      if (crc != ZCrc32(packet, 5, 0)) {
        DebugBegin(pZ -> debug, debugPacketLowLevel | debugPacketErr);
        DebugString(pZ -> debug, "Computed␣CRC:␣");
        DebugIntHex(pZ -> debug, ZCrc32(packet, 5, 0));
        DebugEnd(pZ -> debug);
        return StsWarn(zBadPacket);
      }
    } else {
      crc = (packet[5] * 256 + packet[6]) & 0xFFFF;
      if (crc != ZCrc16(packet, 5, 0)) {
        DebugBegin(pZ -> debug, debugPacketLowLevel | debugPacketErr);
        DebugString(pZ -> debug, "Computed␣CRC:␣");
        DebugIntHex(pZ -> debug, ZCrc16(packet, 5, 0));
        DebugEnd(pZ -> debug);
```

```
        return StsWarn(zBadPacket);
    }
}
```

This code is used on page 304.

Receiving Data

Only four packet headers in ZModem have trailing data. Those are ZDATA, ZSINIT, ZCOMMAND, and ZFILE.

ZDATA packets can have arbitrary amounts of data. Because of the full-duplex issues involved, I'm going to wait to discuss how that's handled.

The other three are followed by a single chunk of data and a single CRC escape, which will always be CAN k. In data transfer, this CRC escape indicates both the end of the packet (which is appropriate) and a request for an acknowledgment (which doesn't make much sense, but that's the way it works).

The next two functions provide the basic support for data following a packet header. ZSendCrcEscape sends a CRC escape. ZReceivePacketData reads a single chunk of data following ZSINIT, ZCOMMAND, or ZFILE.

A CRC escape is a two-byte CAN sequence followed by a prefix-encoded CRC. The CAN sequence itself is included in the CRC, to safeguard this important piece of information. The sequences are shown in Table 8.2 on page 97.

```
STATIC int ZSendCrcEscape(ZMODEM_PRIVATE *pZ, unsigned long
        crc, int packetEnd, int needAck)
{
  unsigned char crcBuff[4];
  BYTE crcEscape;
  if (packetEnd) pZ -> txPacketType = -1;
      /* Send CRC escape sequence */
  if (needAck) {
    if (packetEnd) crcEscape = 'k';
    else crcEscape = 'j';
  } else {
    if (packetEnd) crcEscape = 'h';
    else crcEscape = 'i';
  }
  StsRet(ZSendByte(pZ, CAN));
  StsRet(ZSendByte(pZ, crcEscape));
  if (pZ -> sendingCrc32) {
    crc = ZCrc32(&crcEscape, 1, crc);
        /* Include crcEscape code in CRC */
    crcBuff[0] = crc & 0xFF;
    crcBuff[1] = (crc >> 8) & 0xFF;
```

```
      crcBuff[2] = (crc >> 16) & 0xFF;
      crcBuff[3] = (crc >> 24) & 0xFF;
      StsRet(ZSendEncodeBytes(pZ, crcBuff, 4));
   } else {
      crc = ZCrc16(&crcEscape, 1, crc);
         /* Include crcEscape code in CRC */
      crcBuff[0] = (crc >> 8) & 0xFF;
      crcBuff[1] = crc & 0xFF;
      StsRet(ZSendEncodeBytes(pZ, crcBuff, 2));
   }
   return StsWarn(ZWaitForSentBytes(pZ));
}
```

ZReadDecodeBytes on page 299 showed how to read data while decoding
the prefix sequences. ZReceivePacketData is similar, but adds code to handle
the CRC escape that follows. One simplifying factor is that it's used in situations
where only a limited amount of data must be handled.

```
STATIC int ZReceivePacketData(ZMODEM_PRIVATE *pZ, BYTE
      *pBuffer, unsigned int *pLength)
{
  BYTE byte;
  BYTE *pB = pBuffer;
  int sawCAN = FALSE;
  int canCount = 0;

  *pLength = 0;
  while (1) {
    StsRet(ZReadByteWithTimeout(pZ, pZ -> timeout, &byte));
    if (TestIgnore(byte)) {      /* Ignore XON/XOFF chars */
    } else if (byte == CAN) {
      if (sawCAN) {
        canCount ++;
        if (canCount >= 5) return StsWarn(zFailed);
      } else {
        canCount = 1;
        sawCAN = TRUE;
      }
    } else if (sawCAN) {
      sawCAN = FALSE;
      if (TestDecode(byte)) *pB ++ = zDecode[byte];
      else break;      /* must be CRC escape? */
      (*pLength) ++;
    } else {
      *pB ++ = byte;
      sawCAN = FALSE;
```

```
        (*pLength) ++;
      }
    if (*pLength > 1024) return StsWarn(zBadPacket);
  }    /* while (1) */
  switch (byte) {
  case 'h': case 'i': case 'j':
    if (pZ -> debug) {
      DebugBegin(pZ -> debug, debugEncoding | debugWarn);
      DebugString(pZ -> debug, "Non-conforming␣CRC␣escape:␣CAN␣");
      DebugChar(pZ -> debug, byte);
      DebugEnd(pZ -> debug);
    }    /* fall through to accept it anyway */
  case 'k': break;
  default:
    if (pZ -> debug) {
      DebugBegin(pZ -> debug, debugEncoding | debugWarn);
      DebugString(pZ -> debug, "Illegal␣CAN␣sequence:␣CAN␣");
      DebugChar(pZ -> debug, byte);
      DebugEnd(pZ -> debug);
    }
    return StsWarn(zBadPacket);
  }
  {
    unsigned long crc, txCrc;
    if (pZ -> receivingCrc32) {
      crc = ZCrc32(pBuffer, *pLength, 0);
      crc = ZCrc32(&byte, 1, crc);
    } else {
      crc = ZCrc16(pBuffer, *pLength, 0);
      crc = ZCrc16(&byte, 1, crc);
    }
    ⟨Read CRC into txCrc 311⟩
    if (crc != txCrc) return StsWarn(zBadPacket);
  }
  if (pZ -> debug) {
    DebugBegin(pZ -> debug, debugPacket);
    DebugString(pZ -> debug, "Received␣data␣following␣packet:␣");
    DebugUInt(pZ -> debug, *pLength);
    DebugString(pZ -> debug, "␣bytes");
    DebugEnd(pZ -> debug);
  }
  return zOK;
}
```

The code to collect the CRC is used both in the previous function, and in `ZReceiveStream`.

⟨ Read CRC into `txCrc` 311 ⟩ ≡

```
{
  BYTE crcBuff[4];
  int crcLength;
  if (pZ -> receivingCrc32) crcLength = 4;
  else crcLength = 2;
  StsRet(ZReadDecodeBytes(pZ, pZ -> timeout, crcBuff, &crcLength));
  if (pZ -> receivingCrc32)
    txCrc = ((crcBuff[3] * 256 + crcBuff[2]) * 256 + crcBuff[1]) *
        256 + crcBuff[0];
  else
    txCrc = crcBuff[0] * 256 + crcBuff[1];
}
```

This code is used on pages 309 and 313.

Reliability

The interesting part of ZModem is its streaming approach. Because the receiver is simpler, I'll start there.

Receiving Data Reliably

ZModem's decision to have the receiver ignore out-of-sequence data simplifies things considerably. Any data the receiver does receive is either ignored or can be written to the file immediately; there's no need to store data until the preceding data has been correctly received. The price is that error recovery can be slow when there are long delays. Whenever data is damaged, any following data in transit is now redundant, and must be ignored. ZModem streaming can be even slower than some half-duplex protocols when there are both long delays and high error rates.

The `ZReceiveStream` function is similar to the `ZReceivePacketData` function (page 309), but it also handles acknowledgments as requested by the sender. If an error is detected, `ZReceiveStream` sends a reposition request and returns `zBadPacket`.

This routine simply reads and decodes bytes and accumulates them in a buffer. When it hits a CRC escape, it computes the CRC of the buffered data for comparison, and returns `zBadPacket` if the CRCs fail to match.

```
STATIC int ZReceiveStream(ZMODEM_PRIVATE *pZ, BYTE *buff)
```

```
{
  BYTE *pBuff = buff;
  unsigned length = 0;
  int packetEnd, needAck;
  BYTE byte;
  int byteDecoded;
  int sawCAN = FALSE;
  int canCount = 0;
  while (length < 1025) {
    StsRet(ZReadByteWithTimeout(pZ, pZ -> timeout, &byte));
    byteDecoded = −1;
    if (TestIgnore(byte)) {       /* Ignore XON/XOFF */
    } else if (byte == CAN) {      /* Byte is CAN */
      if (sawCAN) {
        canCount ++;
        if (canCount >= 5) return zFailed;
      } else {
        canCount = 1;
        sawCAN = TRUE;
      }
    } else if (sawCAN) {      /* Byte follows CAN */
      sawCAN = FALSE;
      if (TestDecode(byte)) byteDecoded = zDecode[byte];
      else {
        ⟨ Decode CRC Escape and check for CRC error 313 ⟩
        ⟨ Write data to file and acknowledge if necessary 314 ⟩
        if (packetEnd) return zOK;
        length = 0;
        pBuff = buff;
      }
    } else {      /* Byte doesn't follow CAN */
      byteDecoded = byte;
      sawCAN = FALSE;
    }
    if (byteDecoded >= 0) {      /* Save byte received */
      *pBuff ++ = byteDecoded;
      length ++;
    }
  }
  if (pZ -> debug) {      /* Debug message about too-long packet */
    DebugBegin(pZ -> debug, debugPacketErr | debugWarn);
    DebugString(pZ->debug, "Data␣CRC␣not␣seen,␣buffer␣overflow");
    DebugEnd(pZ -> debug);
  }
```

```
      return StsWarn(zBadPacket);
  }
```

⟨ Decode CRC Escape and check for CRC error 313 ⟩ ==

```
  {
    unsigned long crc, txCrc;
    switch (byte) {      /* Is it a CRC escape? */
    case 'h': packetEnd = TRUE;  needAck = FALSE;  break;
    case 'i': packetEnd = FALSE; needAck = FALSE;  break;
    case 'j': packetEnd = FALSE; needAck = TRUE;   break;
    case 'k': packetEnd = TRUE;  needAck = TRUE;   break;
    default:
      if (pZ -> debug) {
        DebugBegin(pZ -> debug, debugEncoding | debugWarn);
        DebugString(pZ -> debug, "Illegal␣CAN␣sequence:␣CAN␣");
        DebugChar(pZ -> debug, byte);
        DebugEnd(pZ -> debug);
      }
      return StsWarn(zBadPacket);
    }
    if (pZ -> receivingCrc32) {
      crc = ZCrc32(buff, length, 0);
      crc = ZCrc32(&byte, 1, crc);
    } else {
      crc = ZCrc16(buff, length, 0);
      crc = ZCrc16(&byte, 1, crc);
    }
    ⟨ Read CRC into txCrc 311 ⟩
    if (crc != txCrc) {
      ⟨ Issue debug message about incorrect data 313 ⟩
      return StsWarn(zBadPacket);
    }
  }
```

This code is used on page 312.

This rather lengthy debugging message attempts to show enough information to explain why a received packet would have been considered wrong.

⟨ Issue debug message about incorrect data 313 ⟩ ==

```
  if (pZ -> debug) {
    DebugBegin(pZ -> debug, debugPacketLowLevel | debugPacketErr);
    DebugString(pZ -> debug, "Erroneous␣data:␣");
    DebugStringCount(pZ -> debug, (const char *) buff, length);
    DebugEnd(pZ -> debug);
```

```
        DebugBegin(pZ -> debug, debugPacketLowLevel | debugPacketErr);
        DebugString(pZ -> debug, "terminator:␣");
        DebugChar(pZ -> debug, byte);
        DebugString(pZ -> debug, "length␣of␣data:␣");
        DebugUInt(pZ -> debug, length);
        DebugString(pZ -> debug, ",␣CRC␣received:␣");
        DebugIntHex(pZ -> debug, txCrc);
        DebugString(pZ -> debug, ",␣CRC␣calculated:␣");
        DebugIntHex(pZ -> debug, crc);
        DebugEnd(pZ -> debug);
    }
```

This code is used on page 313.

Before writing the received data to the file, it's a good idea to calculate which part of the data belongs in the file, since a common ZModem error is for the sender to resend data already correctly received. You want to only write data that's not already in the file. The alternative (used by some naïve ZModem implementations) is to issue reposition requests to move the sender forward, but as discussed on page 111, that's not generally a good idea.

The order of writing to the file and acknowledging depends on whether or not disk I/O can be overlapped with serial I/O. If it can, there's a slight speed advantage to issuing the acknowledgment earlier. If not, the initial ZRINIT arguments will notify the sender of this fact, and the file transfer will proceed in half-duplex, with the sender pausing after each acknowledgment request until it receives the acknowledgment. In that case, issuing the acknowledgment early risks having the next data arrive during the disk I/O, so it's important to finish the disk I/O before acknowledging.

```
⟨ Write data to file and acknowledge if necessary 314 ⟩ ≡
    if (pZ -> sendPosition + length > pZ -> receivePosition) {
        BYTE *pDataBegin = buff + pZ -> receivePosition - pZ -> sendPosition;
        unsigned long dataLength = length - pZ -> receivePosition + pZ ->
            sendPosition;

        pZ -> receivePosition += dataLength;
#if I_CAN_OVERLAP_DISK
        if (needAck) ZSendHexHeader(pZ, ZACK, pZ -> receivePosition);
        StsRet(ZFileWrite(pZ, pDataBegin, dataLength));
#else
        StsRet(ZFileWrite(pZ, pDataBegin, dataLength));
        if (needAck) ZSendHexHeader(pZ, ZACK, pZ -> receivePosition);
#endif
    }
    pZ -> sendPosition += length;
```

```
    ZProgress(pZ, stsReceiving);
```
This code is used on page 312.

Sending Data Reliably

One of the biggest concessions ZModem makes to simplify the receiver is its decision to have the receiver simply ignore out-of-sequence data. Thus, it falls to the sender to track the "window" of outstanding data. Because managing this window is such an important part of the sender's job, I may as well jump right in and start explaining the code to maintain the window.

Window Management

Traditional ZModem implementations use the file itself to buffer the window, seeking to whatever file position was needed. Unfortunately, this requires that the source of data be a seekable file, which is not always a reasonable assumption. One implementation I've seen attempted to use this approach when the source of data was a dynamically-constructed archive. Rewinding the data source in this scheme was both difficult and slow, and the entire archive would sometimes have to be re-built from scratch in order to satisfy a seek request. To avoid this type of problem, I've implemented an explicit window data structure which holds some contiguous chunk of data to be transferred. The drawback over the conventional implementation is that the window is limited by the amount of data storage allocated. Usually, window sizes of 64k are quite adequate, although in extreme cases, full throughput can require a window size of a megabyte or more. (Corresponding to a 10 *minute* round-trip delay at 19,200 baud!)

Note that the size of the window data structure is simply one upper limit on the amount of outstanding data. There may be other factors.

```
    #define DEFAULT_WINDOW_SIZE  (100000)
                /* One hundred thousand bytes */
```

To reduce memory requirements, the window structure and its associated buffer are allocated only during the sending of a file. The memory is released as soon as the file is sent.

The window structure holds pointers to the first and last data in the queue and the corresponding file positions. The file positions are needed because ZModem identifies data by its byte position in the file. In fact, the file positions are much more important than the pointers, as you'll notice when you read the send code.

```
    typedef struct {
        int atEOF;     /* TRUE: window is at file EOF */
```

```
  BYTE *data;      /* Data that can be sent */
  size_t size;     /* Total possible size of window */
  size_t startFilePos;    /* File position of start of window */
  size_t endFilePos;      /* File position of end of window + 1 */
  BYTE *pStart;    /* First byte in window */
  BYTE *pEnd;      /* last byte in window + 1 */
} WINDOW;
```

Now comes the code to allocate the window. This function tries to allocate the given amount of memory, but falls back to a smaller size if it can't. That way, the send routine can be hard-coded to allocate a large window, but will be able to function even if the system cannot allocate the memory for such a window. Note that the lower limit here of 256 bytes represents an *extremely* small window. Hopefully, you'll never actually encounter this limit.

```
STATIC int ZInitWindow(ZMODEM_PRIVATE *pZ, WINDOW *pWindow, long
        size, long startPos)
{
  int err;
  pWindow -> startFilePos = startPos;
  pWindow -> endFilePos = startPos;
  pWindow -> atEOF = FALSE;
  pWindow -> data = NULL;
  err = ZFileReadSkip(pZ, startPos);
  if (err == zEOF) {
    pWindow -> atEOF = TRUE;
    return zOK;
  } else StsRet(err);    /* Return any real error */
  while ((pWindow -> data == NULL) && (size > 256)) {
    pWindow -> size = size;
    pWindow -> data = malloc(pWindow -> size);
    size /= 2;
    pWindow -> pStart = pWindow -> data;
    pWindow -> pEnd = pWindow -> data;
  }
  if (pWindow -> data == NULL) return zFail;
  else return zOK;
}
```

To simplify allocation, ZSendFileData keeps the WINDOW structure itself as a local variable, so destroying the window just means freeing the actual buffer.

⟨ Destroy window 316 ⟩ ==
```
  if (window . data) free(window . data);
```
This code is used on pages 322, 326, and 327.

Filling the window is a bit more subtle than it might seem. The problem that can arise is that for a very large window, it might take a long time to read the data from disk (imagine sending a file from floppy), causing undesirable delays when the file transfer starts. For that reason, this function accepts a number which limits the amount of data it will read, to reduce this delay.

```
STATIC int ZSendFillWindow(ZMODEM_PRIVATE *pZ, WINDOW
        *pWindow, size_t readLimit)
{
  int err = zOK;
  if (pZ -> debug) {
    DebugBegin(pZ -> debug, debugCache);
    DebugString(pZ -> debug, "Filling window: readLimit = ");
    DebugUInt(pZ -> debug, readLimit);
    DebugEnd(pZ -> debug);
  }
  if ((pWindow -> endFilePos - pWindow -> startFilePos) >=
        pWindow -> size) return zOK;
        /* Return immediately if window is already full */
  if (pWindow -> atEOF)
        /* Return immediately if window is already at EOF */
    return zEOF;
  if (pWindow -> pStart <= pWindow -> pEnd) {
        /* Buffer doesn't wrap */
    unsigned long readLength = pWindow -> size - (pWindow -> pEnd -
        pWindow -> data);
    if (readLength > readLimit) readLength = readLimit;
    if (readLength > 0) {
      err = ZFileRead(pZ, pWindow -> pEnd, &readLength);
      if (err == zOK) {
        pWindow -> endFilePos += readLength;
        pWindow -> pEnd += readLength;
        readLimit -= readLength;
        if ((pWindow -> pEnd - pWindow -> data) >= pWindow -> size)
          pWindow -> pEnd = pWindow -> data;
      }
    }
  }
  if ((err == zOK) && (pWindow -> pEnd < pWindow -> pStart)) {
        /* Buffer does wrap */
    unsigned long readLength = pWindow -> pStart - pWindow -> pEnd;
    if (readLength > readLimit) readLength = readLimit;
    if (readLength > 0) {
      err = ZFileRead(pZ, pWindow -> pEnd, &readLength);
```

```
        if (err == zOK) {
          pWindow -> endFilePos += readLength;
          pWindow -> pEnd += readLength;
        }
      }
    }
    if (err == zEOF) pWindow -> atEOF = TRUE;
    return StsWarn(err);
}
```

This routine is responsible for sending a chunk of data and a CRC escape from the current window. It's careful to not send data past the end of the window, and simplifies its task by not sending data that's broken across the end of the queue.

It also sends a ZDATA header if pZ -> txPacketType doesn't indicate that one has already been sent.

```
STATIC int ZSendFileDataPacket(ZMODEM_PRIVATE *pZ, WINDOW
        *pWindow, unsigned size, int endOfPacket, int needAck)
{
  unsigned long crc = 0L;
  unsigned packetLength = size;
  BYTE *packetStart;
  if (pZ -> txPacketType != ZDATA)
    StsRet(ZSendHeader(pZ, ZDATA, pZ -> sendPosition));
        /* Figure the start and size of the data to send */
  packetStart = pWindow -> pStart + (pZ -> sendPosition - pWindow ->
      startFilePos);
  if ((packetStart - pWindow -> data) >= pWindow -> size)
    packetStart -= pWindow -> size;
  if ((pZ -> sendPosition + packetLength) > pWindow -> endFilePos)
    packetLength = pWindow -> endFilePos - pZ -> sendPosition;
  if ((packetStart - pWindow->data+packetLength) >= pWindow->size)
    packetLength = pWindow -> data + pWindow -> size - packetStart;
  if (packetLength > 0) {      /* Send the data */
    StsRet(ZSendEncodeBytes(pZ, packetStart, packetLength));
    crc = SendingCrc(packetStart, packetLength, 0);
  }
  StsRet(ZSendCrcEscape(pZ, crc, endOfPacket, needAck));
  if (pZ -> debug) {
    DebugBegin(pZ -> debug, debugPacketLowLevel);
    DebugString(pZ -> debug, "Sent␣file␣data:␣");
    DebugUInt(pZ -> debug, packetLength);
    DebugString(pZ -> debug, "␣bytes␣starting␣at␣");
    DebugIntHex(pZ -> debug, pZ -> sendPosition);
```

```
        if (endOfPacket) DebugString(pZ -> debug, "␣(packetEnd)");
        if (needAck) DebugString(pZ -> debug, "␣(needAck)");
        DebugEnd(pZ -> debug);
    }
    pZ -> sendPosition += packetLength;
    return zOK;
}
```

Sending Streamed Data

Now I'm ready to delve into the actual send routine. As mentioned earlier, the
sender is responsible for adapting to channel and receiver restrictions. The parameters the sender juggles in accomplishing this are the *CRC interval*, *acknowledgment
interval*, *burst length*, and *window size*.

```
⟨ Sender variables 319 ⟩ ==
    unsigned crcInterval = 1024;        /* Current packet size */
    unsigned long ackInterval = 8192;       /* Interval between ack requests */
    unsigned long lastAck = 0;      /* File position of last Ack request */
    unsigned long burstLength = 0;      /* Maximum burst length */
    unsigned long lastBlock = 0;        /* File position of last block */
    unsigned long windowSize = 0;       /* Limit on outstanding data */
```
See also pages 319 and 320.

This code is used on page 320.

Each CRC escape indicates to the receiver whether or not the receiver should
acknowledge. (The receiver can, in theory, acknowledge at any time, although most
ZModem receivers simply follow the sender's cue.) There are several factors that the
sender must juggle to determine how frequently to request an acknowledgment.

When the sender does request an acknowledgment, it can do so in two ways.
The most common way is to request an acknowledgment in the middle of a packet
and continue sending. A more conservative action is to *block*, that is, to end the
packet and wait for either an acknowledgment indicating the receiver is completely
caught up, or a reposition. The burst length is how frequently you should block.
Note that if the burst length is less than the acknowledgment interval, then you're
operating in half-duplex, since every acknowledgment request will be a block.

```
⟨ Sender variables 319 ⟩ +==
    int block = FALSE;      /* block after sending next data */
    int blocked = FALSE;        /* already blocked */
```

In half-duplex protocols such as XModem or YModem, it's pretty clear what
an "error" is, and hence pretty easy to specify that the protocol should give up after

too many consecutive errors. For ZModem, it's a bit more subtle, since even when there are many reposition requests, the protocol may still be making progress. For ZModem, the important issue to notice is when the reposition requests always reposition to the same place. Hence you need two variables to keep track of the last reposition request and how many times you've revisited that file position.

⟨ Sender variables 319 ⟩ +≡

```
long lastReposition = 0;      /* File position of last ZRPOS */
int repositionCount = 0;
    /* How many times you repositioned to same place */
```

Now I'm ready to build the actual send routine. The only interesting point in this top level is the handling of the `block` and `blocked` variables. Copying `block` to `blocked` at the end of the loop converts a decision to `block` to an actual `blocked` situation at the top of the loop.

```
STATIC int ZSendFileData(ZMODEM_PRIVATE *pZ, long startPos)
{
    int err = zTimeout;
    size_t refillInterval = 4096;      /* How often to go to disk */
    WINDOW window;
    ⟨ Sender variables 319 ⟩
    StsRet(ZInitWindow(pZ, &window, DEFAULT_WINDOW_SIZE, startPos));
    pZ -> sendPosition = startPos;
    pZ -> receivePosition = startPos;
    ⟨ Set transmit parameters 320 ⟩
    while (TRUE) {
        ⟨ Check for and process any pending packets 322 ⟩
        ⟨ Refill the window 327 ⟩
        ⟨ Send more data 328 ⟩
        blocked = block;      /* Are you blocked? */
    }
}
```

I'll take a little time here to explain how the transmit parameters are initialized. This implementation is not very complex, but some of the reasoning behind it can be informative.

The window size sets a limit on how much data can be outstanding at any given time. One upper limit is, of course, how much data you can store.

⟨ Set transmit parameters 320 ⟩ ≡

```
    windowSize = window . size;
```

See also pages 321, 321, and 322.

This code is used on page 320.

In this implementation, transfer progress is based on receiver acknowledgments, which means that I'd like to set `ackInterval` fairly low to get good progress reporting. I've chosen to start with one percent of the file size in an effort to get good progress reporting, and then enforce some rather arbitrary upper and lower limits. The best values for the upper and lower limits are dependent on the channel speed. A too-low upper limit can cause too frequent acknowledgments over fast channels, resulting in reduced speed from excessive screen updating or from reduced efficiency of some high-performance modems. The value 16384 here corresponds to an acknowledgment roughly every second and a half at 115,200 baud. On the other hand, a too-large lower limit produces problems with slow channels; it's nice to have more frequent acknowledgments so that user progress is updated regularly. The value I've chosen corresponds to about one acknowledgment every two seconds at 2400 baud.

```
#define ACK_INTERVAL_MIN   512
#define ACK_INTERVAL_MAX   16384
```

⟨ Set transmit parameters 320 ⟩ +≡
```
  ackInterval = ZFileSize(pZ) / 100;
  if (ackInterval < ACK_INTERVAL_MIN)
    ackInterval = ACK_INTERVAL_MIN;
  if (ackInterval > ACK_INTERVAL_MAX)
    ackInterval = ACK_INTERVAL_MAX;
```

The burst length limit tries to accomodate receivers that can buffer large amounts of data, but can't necessarily process data at full speed. The receiver is supposed to use the lower 16 bits of the argument to ZRINIT to indicate how large a buffer it has.

It actually makes sense to set the burst length to force synchronization at least every 30 seconds or so, to ensure that severe errors do not go uncaught in long transfers. But setting the burst length to a particular *time* interval requires some estimate of the channel rate, which isn't always available.

If the receiver has communication limits, or you're unable to sample the I/O stream, then you use a half-duplex strategy. If the receiver hasn't specified a burst size to use, default to 1k, which will make the transfer function about as well as YModem.

```
#define HasLimits(flags)                                              \
        (!((flags)&(CAN_FULL_DUPLEX | CAN_OVERLAP_DISK)))
#define HALF_DUPLEX_BURST   1024     /* Default burst length limit */
```

⟨ Set transmit parameters 320 ⟩ +≡
```
  burstLength = pZ -> receiverFlags & 0xFFFF;
  if (HasLimits(pZ -> receiverFlags) || ! I_CAN_SAMPLE) {
    if (burstLength == 0) burstLength = HALF_DUPLEX_BURST;
```

```
        ackInterval = burstLength * 2;        /* No intermediate ACKs */
    }
```

The `crcInterval` limits the distance between CRC requests. To avoid the need for very large buffers, the ZModem protocol limits this to a maximum of 1024 bytes. Generally, a larger value results in slightly faster transfers from reduced overhead, while a smaller value can give better performance when there are errors, because smaller data packets are less likely to be damaged en route. Conventionally, ZModem senders set the `crcInterval` to about once per second. For example, 1024 bytes at 9600 baud, 256 bytes at 2400 baud, 128 bytes at 1200 baud, etc.

⟨ Set transmit parameters 320 ⟩ +≡
```
    crcInterval = 1024;
    if (crcInterval > ackInterval) crcInterval = ackInterval;
```

The next major section of the sender code is the code to read and process any packets from the receiver. One interesting point is the strategy used here to attempt to swallow and discard redundant errors. It's common for the ZModem receiver to generate multiple reposition requests. To avoid needlessly resending data, adopt a greedy approach: Whenever you see one error packet, go back and look for another one. In this case, a two second timeout is used when looking for a subsequent error packet.

```
    #define CloseDataPacket(pZ)                                    \
            if (pZ -> txPacketType == ZDATA)                       \
                StsRet(ZSendFileDataPacket(pZ, &window, 0, TRUE, FALSE))
```
⟨ Check for and process any pending packets 322 ⟩ ≡
```
    do {
      if (pZ -> debug) {
        if (block || blocked) {
          DebugBegin(pZ -> debug, debugPacket);
          DebugString(pZ -> debug,
              blocked ? "Window␣blocked" : "Window␣set␣to␣block");
          DebugEnd(pZ -> debug);
        }
      }
      err = StsWarn(ZReadHeader(pZ,
          blocked ? pZ -> timeout : block ? 2 : 0));
      switch (err) {
      case zTimeout: break;
      case zBadPacket: block = TRUE;
        break;
      case zOK: break;
      default: ⟨ Destroy window 316 ⟩
```

```
        return StsWarn(err);
}
if (err == zOK) {
  switch (pZ -> rxPacketType) {
  case ZRPOS:     /* Reposition request */
    if ((pZ -> rxPacketArg >= pZ -> receivePosition) && (pZ ->
          rxPacketArg <= window . endFilePos)) {
      ⟨ Handle ZRPOS 325 ⟩
    } else {     /* Bogus ZRPOS */
      block = TRUE;
      blocked = FALSE;
      DebugBegin(pZ -> debug, debugWarn);
      DebugString(pZ -> debug, "Bogus␣ZRPOS");
      DebugEnd(pZ -> debug);
    }
    break;
  case ZACK:     /* Acknowledgment */
    if ((pZ -> rxPacketArg >= pZ -> receivePosition) && (pZ ->
          rxPacketArg <= window . endFilePos)) {
      ⟨ Handle ZACK 326 ⟩
    } else {     /* Bogus ZACK */
      block = TRUE;
      blocked = FALSE;
      DebugBegin(pZ -> debug, debugWarn);
      DebugString(pZ -> debug, "Bogus␣ZACK");
      DebugEnd(pZ -> debug);
    }
    break;
  case ZRINIT:      /* Next transaction, Acknowledge a ZEOF */
    ZParseZRINIT(pZ, pZ -> rxPacketArg);
    if (window . atEOF && (pZ -> sendPosition >= window . endFilePos))
      {
      pZ -> receivePosition = pZ -> sendPosition;
      ZProgress(pZ, stsSending);
      ⟨ Destroy window 316 ⟩
      return zOK;
    } else {     /* Bogus ZRINIT */
      block = TRUE;
      blocked = FALSE;
      DebugBegin(pZ -> debug, debugWarn);
      DebugString(pZ -> debug, "Bogus␣ZRINIT");
      DebugEnd(pZ -> debug);
    }
    break;
```

```
        case ZNAK:     /* Receiver didn't get the last packet */
          CloseDataPacket(pZ);
          pZ -> sendPosition = pZ -> receivePosition;
          block = TRUE;
          blocked = FALSE;
          break;
        default:     /* Just plain bogus */
          block = TRUE;
          blocked = FALSE;
          break;
        }
        ZProgress(pZ, stsSending);
      }
      ⟨ Adjust transmit parameters 324 ⟩
      ⟨ See if you need to block 324 ⟩
    } while ((err == zOK) || (blocked));
```
This code is used on page 320.

In response to various packets from the receiver, the transmit parameters may
be adjusted. This scrap sanitizes those parameters to make sure they don't become
unreasonable. In particular, it makes sure that crcInterval stays smaller than
burstLength. (Otherwise, the transfer would lock up because no data could be
sent without violating the burstLength limit.)

```
⟨ Adjust transmit parameters 324 ⟩ ==
    if (crcInterval > 1024) crcInterval = 1024;
    if (crcInterval > ackInterval) crcInterval = ackInterval;
    if ((burstLength > 0) && (crcInterval > burstLength / 4))
      crcInterval = burstLength / 4;
```
This code is used on page 322.

Block whenever you hit the end of the data in the window or whenever you
hit the burst length limit.

```
⟨ See if you need to block 324 ⟩ ==
    if (pZ -> sendPosition − pZ -> receivePosition >= windowSize)
      block = blocked = TRUE;
    if ((burstLength > 0)
    && (pZ -> sendPosition + crcInterval > lastBlock + burstLength))
      block = blocked = TRUE;
```
This code is used on page 322.

A reposition request provides a surprisingly large amount of information. An
aggressive full-streaming sender operating under good conditions actually has very
little solid information about the conditions under which the transfer is occurring,

simply because it receives no information from the receiver. As soon as an error forces the receiver to send a reposition request, however, this situation changes dramatically. To begin with, the sender knows that the receiver has received everything prior to this point.

⟨ Handle `ZRPOS` 325 ⟩ ==
```
    pZ -> receivePosition = pZ -> rxPacketArg;
```
See also pages 325, 325, 326, and 326.
This code is used on page 322.

The reposition may leave a bunch of extraneous data in the channel, data that's already been sent but which the receiver is going to ignore as soon as it sees it. To compensate, I reduce `lastBlock` by the amount of extraneous data left dangling by the reposition request. The result is that the burst length calculation of `pZ -> sendPosition − lastBlock` still reflects the actual amount of data left in the channel. If there were a guaranteed way to flush this extraneous data from the channel, such a correction would be unnecessary.

⟨ Handle `ZRPOS` 325 ⟩ +==
```
    lastBlock -= (pZ -> sendPosition - pZ -> rxPacketArg);
```

You should start sending from this file position.

⟨ Handle `ZRPOS` 325 ⟩ +==
```
    CloseDataPacket(pZ);        /* Restart sending */
    pZ -> sendPosition = pZ -> rxPacketArg;
```

Finally, a reposition request provides information about the channel. A lot can be gleaned from carefully watching the pattern of reposition requests. Even though I'm not going to attempt an extensive analysis here, it's worth thinking about what a reposition request can tell you, because it does give insight into the next few adjustments. The distance between successive reposition requests depends on the error rate, so it makes sense to adjust the `crcInterval` so that a single packet of data is more likely to pass through unscathed. If there is a flow control problem, repositions will tend to occur about the same distance after a block—at the point where buffers begin to overflow—so it's reasonable to try to adjust `burstLength` based on the difference between `lastBlock` and the reposition request.[2] Finally, the difference between the current send position and the reposition request depends on the channel delay, so it makes sense to adjust `windowSize` based on this information.

This code only attempts to adjust the `crcInterval`. The `crcInterval` is reduced after successive repositions to the same location. (Think of this as an

---

[2]I would expect the standard deviation of the distance between successive errors to be useful in determining the optimum burst length.

attempt to make sure that `crcInterval` is less than the average distance between errors.) If the send becomes totally stuck, indicated by a long series of repositions to the same location, this routine eventually gives up.

⟨ Handle ZRPOS 325 ⟩ +≡
```
if (pZ -> sendPosition == lastReposition) repositionCount ++;
else repositionCount = 1;
lastReposition = pZ -> sendPosition;
if (repositionCount > 4) {
  if (crcInterval > 32) {
    crcInterval /= 2;
    repositionCount = 0;
  } else if (repositionCount > pZ -> retries) {
    ⟨ Destroy window 316 ⟩
    return StsWarn(zFail);
  }
}
```

After receiving a reposition request, the sender must unblock (otherwise, it cannot send the data to respond to the request). By blocking just after the next chunk of data is sent, the burst length is temporarily reduced. This specific behavior is described in the ZModem protocol description, but it's certainly possible for a more sophisticated implementation to dynamically determine the best burst length to provide better transfer without completely blocking after each reposition.

⟨ Handle ZRPOS 325 ⟩ +≡
```
block = TRUE;
blocked = FALSE;
```

Not too surprisingly, acknowledgments also provide useful information. The most obvious is that an acknowledgment communicates the receiver's current position.

⟨ Handle ZACK 326 ⟩ ≡
```
pZ -> receivePosition = pZ -> rxPacketArg;
```
See also pages 326 and 327.
This code is used on page 322.

If the receiver is completely caught up, then you need to clear any pending block.

⟨ Handle ZACK 326 ⟩ +≡
```
if (pZ -> receivePosition == pZ -> sendPosition) {
  if (blocked) lastBlock = pZ -> sendPosition;
  block = blocked = FALSE;
}
```

An acknowledgment says something about the error rate. This fairly simple code complements the response to ZRPOS above by increasing the `crcInterval` after a suitable number of acknowledgments.

```
⟨Handle ZACK 326⟩ +==
  if (repositionCount -- < −4) {
    crcInterval *= 2;
    repositionCount = 0;
  }
```

Deciding when to read more data into the window buffer is a little bit complex. The buffer should be kept full, but there should be no large disk operations that create delays. Frequent small disk operations can also slow down the transfer. The logic here reads more data into the window buffer whenever there's at least `refillInterval` free in the buffer and the `sendPosition` is close to the end of the buffer.

In operation, the effect is that the buffer starts out empty, and then another `refillInterval` bytes are read into the buffer at suitable intervals. Once the buffer is full, it never has more than `refillInterval` bytes of free space in it. The value 1500 was chosen at random. (The only significance is that it's larger than 1024, and hence larger than any legal value of `crcInterval`.)

```
#define BufferFree
        (window . size − (window . endFilePos − pZ -> receivePosition))
⟨Refill the window 327⟩ ==
  if ((! window . atEOF) && (pZ -> sendPosition + 1500 >
        window . endFilePos) && (BufferFree >= refillInterval)) {
      /* bump up start of window */
    window . pStart += (pZ -> receivePosition − window . startFilePos);
    if ((window . pStart − window . data) > window . size)
      window . pStart −= window . size;
    window . startFilePos = pZ -> receivePosition;
      /* Fill the window */
    err = ZSendFillWindow(pZ, &window, refillInterval);
    if ((err != zEOF) && (err != zOK)) {
      ⟨Destroy window 316⟩
      return StsWarn(err);
    }
  }
```

This code is used on page 320.

The logic used to decide when to request an acknowledgment is a bit obscure. The first consideration is that an acknowledgment should be requested every `ackInterval` bytes. The other consideration is that an acknowledgment should be requested before blocking. Notice that in either case, the packet is ended only just before a block.

⟨ Send more data 328 ⟩ ==
```
if (window . atEOF && (pZ -> sendPosition + crcInterval >=
        window . endFilePos)) ⟨Finish off end of file 328⟩
else {
  if (pZ -> sendPosition + crcInterval - lastAck >= ackInterval) {
    StsRet(ZSendFileDataPacket(pZ, &window, crcInterval, block,
        TRUE));
    lastAck = pZ -> sendPosition;      /* Save last Ack request */
  } else {
    StsRet(ZSendFileDataPacket(pZ, &window, crcInterval, block,
        block));
    if (block) lastAck = pZ -> sendPosition;
  }
}
```
This code is used on page 320.

When you hit the end of the file, you need to send the last data in the file, close the last ZDATA packet, and finally send a ZEOF. The loop here makes sure that the last data all gets sent. (Remember that ZSendFileDataPacket may decide to send less than crcInterval bytes on any one call.) In particular, note that no acknowledgment is needed for the last packet, since that would just duplicate the response to ZEOF.

⟨ Finish off end of file 328 ⟩ ==
```
{
  while (pZ -> sendPosition < window . endFilePos)
    StsRet(ZSendFileDataPacket(pZ, &window, crcInterval, TRUE,
        FALSE));
  if (pZ -> txPacketType == ZDATA)     /* Close last data packet */
    StsRet(ZSendCrcEscape(pZ, 0, TRUE, FALSE));
  StsRet(ZSendHeader(pZ, ZEOF, window . endFilePos));
  block = TRUE;
}
```
This code is used on page 328.

Miscellaneous Send-Side Reliability

Generally, ZModem exchanges can be looked upon as an attempt to solicit a particular response from the other end. For example, the sender begins by sending ZRQINIT packets in an attempt to squeeze a ZRINIT from the receiver.

```
STATIC int ZSendGetZRINIT(ZMODEM_PRIVATE *pZ)
```

```
{
  int timeout = 0;
  int retries = pZ -> retries;
  int err;
  do {
    err = ZReadHeader(pZ, timeout);
    timeout = pZ -> timeout;
    switch (err) {
    case zOK:
      if (pZ -> rxPacketType == ZRINIT) {
        ZParseZRINIT(pZ, pZ -> rxPacketArg);
        break;
      } else err = zBadPacket;
    case zTimeout: case zBadPacket:
      StsRet(ZSendHexHeader(pZ, ZRQINIT, pZ -> myZrqinitFlags));
      if (retries -- <= 0) return StsWarn(zFailed);
      break;
    default: return StsWarn(err);
    }
  } while (err != zOK);
  return StsWarn(err);
}
```

This function reliably sends the ZSINIT packet. Often, no ZSINIT packet is required, in which case this exchange can be skipped completely. Otherwise, repeat the ZSINIT until the receiver acknowledges.

```
STATIC int ZSendZSINIT(ZMODEM_PRIVATE *pZ)
{
  int retries = pZ -> retries;
  int err;      /* Maybe I don't need to send ZSINIT ? */
  if ((pZ -> mySenderFlags == 0) && (ATTENTION == NULL)) return zOK;
        /* Send ZSINIT as necessary until you get a ZACK response */
  do {
    StsRet(ZSendHexHeader(pZ, ZSINIT, pZ -> mySenderFlags));
    if (ATTENTION) {
      unsigned long crc;
      StsRet(ZSendEncodeBytes(pZ, ATTENTION, strlen(ATTENTION)));
      crc = SendingCrc(ATTENTION, strlen(ATTENTION), 0);
      StsRet(ZSendCrcEscape(pZ, crc, TRUE, TRUE));
    } else {
      StsRet(ZSendCrcEscape(pZ, 0, TRUE, TRUE));
    }
    err = ZReadHeader(pZ, pZ -> timeout);
```

```
     switch (err) {
     case zOK:
       if (pZ -> rxPacketType == ZACK) break;
       else err = zBadPacket;
     case zTimeout: case zBadPacket:
       if (retries -- <= 0) return StsWarn(zFail);
       break;
     default: return StsWarn(err);
     }
   } while (err != zOK);
   return StsWarn(err);
}
```

At the end of the session, a few tricks are used to prevent the user from seeing a burst of garbage after the transfer is ostensibly done.

After the sender sends a ZFIN packet and the receiver responds, the sender sends a seemingly gratuitous OO (Over and Out). It turns out that this final handshake serves a number of purposes. First of all, because it consists of two printable ASCII characters, it is reasonably safe to send even if the other end of the file transfer has already terminated. An OO appearing on the user's screen or standing at a command prompt is unlikely to cause any problems. Secondly, it gives the receiver a chance to make sure that the sender actually saw the final ZFIN packet. If the sender did not, it will repeat its own ZFIN, and the receiver will see a * pad character rather than the O it's expecting. (This also explains why hexadecimal headers have *two* * characters at the beginning of the packet.)

Error handling may seem a bit unusual here. Since this function is only called when all transactions have successfully completed, it makes little sense to return an error status that would misinform the user. Failure here doesn't really mean anything to the user, so this function always returns zOK.

```
   STATIC int ZSendEndSession(ZMODEM_PRIVATE *pZ)
   {
     int retries = pZ -> retries;
     int err;
     do {
       StsRet(ZSendHexHeader(pZ, ZFIN, 0));
       err = ZReadHeader(pZ, pZ -> timeout);
       switch (err) {
       case zOK:
         if (pZ -> rxPacketType == ZFIN) break;
         else err = zBadPacket;
       case zTimeout: case zBadPacket:
         if (retries -- < 0) return StsWarn(zOK);
```

```
      break;
    default: return StsWarn(zOK);
      break;
    }
} while (err != zOK);
ZSendBytes(pZ,(const BYTE *) "OO",2);
return zOK;
}
```

File/Transaction Layer

This layer is where user preferences really begin to have an effect. One of ZModem's most popular features is "crash recovery." This feature allows the sender to specify to the receiver that part of the file was previously received; the sender can skip ahead and avoid resending the first part of the file. This feature is usually used to complete a transfer that failed in the middle of a file.

⟨ ZModem variables 267 ⟩ +≡
```
    int crashRecovery;
```

As mentioned on page 180, there are some potential problems with crash recovery in general, so it's standard practice to leave it disabled by default.

⟨ Initialize ZModem variables, **return** if error 268 ⟩ +≡
```
    pZ -> crashRecovery = FALSE;
```

Sending Files

Sending the actual file data has been fairly thoroughly discussed. There are only a few minor issues that remain before you can actually send a file. The first of these is building and sending the ZFILE packet.

```
      STATIC int ZSendZFile(ZMODEM_PRIVATE *pZ)
      {
        const char *fileName = NULL;
        long fileSize = -1;
        int fileType = diskFileUnknown;
        long fileMode = -1;
        struct tm fileDate;
        BYTE data[1024];
        unsigned length = 128;
        unsigned long options = pZ -> fileFlags;
        char *p = (char *) data;
        ⟨ Get filename and information 332 ⟩
```

```
        if ((options & CONV_MASK) == 0)      /* Build file options */
          if ((fileType == diskFileBinary) || (fileType ==
              diskFileUnknown))
            if (pZ -> crashRecovery) options |= CONV_RESUME;
                /* Try to resume a binary transfer */
            else options |= CONV_BINARY;      /* Plain binary transfer */
          else options |= CONV_TEXT;
        StsRet(ZSendHeader(pZ, ZFILE, options));
        ⟨ Build filename and information strings in data 332 ⟩
        length = p − (char *) data;
        StsRet(ZSendEncodeBytes(pZ, data, length));     /* Send data */
        {     /* Compute crc and send CRC escape */
          unsigned long crc = SendingCrc(data, length, 0);

          return StsWarn(ZSendCrcEscape(pZ, crc, TRUE, TRUE));
        }
    }
```

I've simply called the `disk` module functions directly to obtain information
about the open file.

```
⟨ Get filename and information 332 ⟩ ==
  if (pZ -> f) {
    DiskFileName(pZ -> f, &fileName);
    fileSize = pZ -> fileSize;
    DiskFileType(pZ -> f, &fileType);
    DiskFileMode(pZ -> f, &fileMode);
    DiskFileDate(pZ -> f, &fileDate);
  }
```
This code is used on page 331.

ZModem uses the same format for the filename and attributes as YModem.
The one important difference is that the sender doesn't guarantee the file size. The
sender can and should send a file size estimate even if the file size is not precisely
known. This estimate allows the receiver to build a progress display or (tentatively)
allocate buffers or disk storage. The receiver is responsible for making sure that all
data received is correctly stored, regardless of the sender's initial file size estimate.

```
⟨ Build filename and information strings in data 332 ⟩ ==
  memset(data, 0, sizeof (data));
  if (fileName && fileName[0]) {
    strcpy(p, fileName);
    p += strlen(p) + 1;
    if (fileSize >= 0) {
      sprintf(p, "%ld", fileSize);
      p += strlen(p);
```

```
    sprintf(p, "␣%lo", ZTime(&(fileDate)));
    p += strlen(p);
    if (fileMode >= 0) {
      sprintf(p, "␣%lo", fileMode);
      p += strlen(p);
    }
  }
}
```

This code is used on page 331.

There are three valid responses to the sender's ZFILE packet. The receiver may request more information about the file through a ZCRC request. The receiver may ask the sender not to send this file by responding with a ZSKIP. If the receiver does wish to receive this file, it responds to the ZFILE with a ZRPOS specifying the file offset at which the transfer should begin. This ZRPOS normally specifies a zero offset, but it may be larger if the receiver is attempting to perform crash recovery.

```
STATIC int ZSendFile(ZMODEM_PRIVATE *pZ)
{
  int err = zOK;
  long startPosition = 0;
  ZProgress(pZ, stsNewFile);
  ⟨Solicit a ZRPOS, ZCRC, or ZSKIP 333⟩
  if (pZ -> rxPacketType == ZCRC)
    ⟨Respond to ZCRC request 334⟩      /* Send the file */
  ZProgress(pZ, stsSending);
  StsRet(ZSendFileData(pZ, startPosition));
  ZProgress(pZ, stsEOF);
  return StsWarn(err);
}
```

Actually obtaining one of these three responses may require some juggling, however. In particular, if the ZFILE isn't received, the receiver may repeat its previous ZRINIT.

```
⟨Solicit a ZRPOS, ZCRC, or ZSKIP 333⟩ ==
  do {
    StsRet(ZSendZFile(pZ));
    err = ZReadHeader(pZ, pZ -> timeout * 5);
    if (err == zOK) {
      switch (pZ -> rxPacketType) {
      case ZSKIP: ZProgress(pZ, stsSkipped);
        return zOK;      /* Finished with this file */
      case ZRPOS: startPosition = pZ -> rxPacketArg;
```

```
      break;      /* Ready to send file */
    case ZCRC: break;      /* Compute requested CRC below */
    case ZRINIT: ZParseZRINIT(pZ, pZ -> rxPacketArg); break;
    case ZNAK: break;
    default: break;
    }
  } else if ((err != zTimeout) && (err != zBadPacket))
    return StsWarn(err);
} while ((err != zOK) || ((pZ -> rxPacketType !=
    ZRPOS) && (pZ -> rxPacketType != ZCRC)));
```

This code is used on page 333.

The ZCRC request is optional. The receiver specifies how much of the file should be included in the CRC, and the sender responds with its own ZCRC packet containing the requested CRC. After the ZCRC exchange, if any, the only valid responses are ZSKIP to reject the file or ZRPOS to accept it.

```
⟨ Respond to ZCRC request 334 ⟩ ==
  {
    unsigned long crc;

    err = ZFileCRC(pZ, pZ -> rxPacketArg, &crc);
      /* Compute the file CRC */
    if (err == zFail) crc = 0;
    do {
      StsRet(ZSendHexHeader(pZ, ZCRC, crc));
      err = ZReadHeader(pZ, pZ -> timeout * 5);
      if (err == zOK) {
        switch (pZ -> rxPacketType) {
        case ZSKIP: return zOK;
          break;      /* Finished with this file */
        case ZRPOS: startPosition = pZ -> rxPacketArg;
          break;      /* Ready to send file data */
        case ZCRC: break;      /* Receiver didn't see the reponse */
        case ZNAK: break;      /* Receiver timed-out */
        default: break;
        }
      } else if ((err != zTimeout) && (err != zBadPacket))
        return StsWarn(err);
    } while ((err != zOK) || (pZ -> rxPacketType != ZRPOS));
  }
```

This code is used on page 333.

Receiving Files

Like ZSendFile, most of the work for ZReceiveFile has already been done. The arguments to ZReceiveFile provide the string argument that came with the ZFILE packet that started this transaction. This string is passed along to ZFileWriteOpen, which extracts the filename and file attributes from it.

```
STATIC int ZReceiveFile(ZMODEM_PRIVATE *pZ, BYTE *buff, unsigned
        fileInfoLength)
{
  int err = zOK;
  unsigned length;
  int repositionCount;
  size_t lastReposition;

  ZNewFile(pZ);
  pZ -> receivePosition = 0;
  ⟨ Issue debug message with ZFILE argument 335 ⟩
  err = StsWarn(ZFileWriteOpen(pZ, buff, fileInfoLength));
  if (err == zSkip) {      /* Ask sender to not send file */
    ZProgress(pZ, stsSkipped);
    ZSendHexHeader(pZ, ZSKIP, 0);
    return zOK;
  }
  if (err != zOK) {      /* File I/O error */
    StsWarn(ZSendHexHeader(pZ, ZFERR, 0));
    return zOK;
  }
  StsRet(ZSendHexHeader(pZ, ZRPOS, pZ -> receivePosition));
  ZProgress(pZ, stsNewFile);

  ⟨ Receive and process packets 336 ⟩
}
```

The ZFILE packet essentially carries three arguments: a bit-mapped set of flags indicating how the transfer should proceed, the filename, and a string encoding certain file attributes.

```
⟨ Issue debug message with ZFILE argument 335 ⟩ ==
  if (pZ -> debug) {
    char *p = (char *) buff;

    DebugBegin(pZ -> debug, debugPacket);
    DebugString(pZ -> debug, "Read␣ZFILE␣Data:␣options:␣");
    DebugIntHex(pZ -> debug, pZ -> fileFlags);
    DebugString(pZ -> debug, "␣filename:␣''");
    DebugString(pZ -> debug, p);
```

```
    DebugString(pZ -> debug, "''␣File␣attributes:␣");
    DebugString(pZ -> debug, p + strlen(p) + 1);
    DebugEnd(pZ -> debug);
  }
```

This code is used on page 335.

There are really only three packets that make any sense. A ZFILE received here is just a duplicate of the one already received. Besides that possibility, only ZDATA and ZEOF packets are meaningful.

One interesting point is the handling of damaged data. Whenever a timeout or a damaged packet is detected, four things must be done. The first is to send the Attention sequence, in case the sender needs an interrupt to detect the error packet. Then, the input queue is flushed so that no time will be wasted processing data that's no longer of interest. Then the actual reposition request is sent. Finally, a count is maintained of identical reposition requests. At the bottom of the loop, this count is used to cancel the transfer if no progress is being made. Error situations that do not involve damaged data usually omit the Attention sequence and the flush, since the sender is probably already waiting for a response.

⟨ Receive and process packets 336 ⟩ ==

```
  lastReposition = pZ -> receivePosition;
  repositionCount = 0;
  while (1) {
    err = StsWarn(ZReadHeader(pZ, pZ -> timeout));
    if ((err == zTimeout) || (err == zBadPacket)) {
      ZSendAttention(pZ);
      ZGobble(pZ, 0);
      ZSendHexHeader(pZ, ZRPOS, pZ -> receivePosition);
      if (pZ -> receivePosition == lastReposition)
        repositionCount ++;
      else {
        lastReposition = pZ -> receivePosition;
        repositionCount = 1;
      }
    } else if (err != zOK) {
      return StsWarn(err);
    } else {      /* err == zOK */
      switch (pZ -> rxPacketType) {
      case ZFILE: length = 1024;
        StsWarn(ZReceivePacketData(pZ, buff, &length));
        ZSendHexHeader(pZ, ZRPOS, pZ -> receivePosition);
        break;
      case ZEOF:
        if (pZ -> rxPacketArg == pZ -> receivePosition) {
```

```
            ZProgress(pZ, stsEOF);
            StsRet(ZFileWriteClose(pZ));
            ZSendHexHeader(pZ, ZRINIT, pZ -> myReceiverFlags);
            return zOK;
        } else {      /* lost data prior to end-of-file */
            ZSendHexHeader(pZ, ZRPOS, pZ -> receivePosition);
            if (pZ -> receivePosition == lastReposition)
                repositionCount ++;
            else {
                lastReposition = pZ -> receivePosition;
                repositionCount = 1;
            }
        }
        break;
    case ZDATA: pZ -> sendPosition = pZ -> rxPacketArg;
        err = StsWarn(ZReceiveStream(pZ, buff));
        if (err == zOK) break;
        if ((err != zBadPacket) && (err != zTimeout))
            return StsWarn(err);
                /* if err is zBadPacket or zTimeout, fall through */
        ZSendAttention(pZ);
    default:       /* Unknown packet type */
        ZGobble(pZ, 0);       /* Flush input queue */
        ZSendHexHeader(pZ, ZRPOS, pZ -> receivePosition);
        if (pZ -> receivePosition == lastReposition)
            repositionCount ++;
        else {
            lastReposition = pZ -> receivePosition;
            repositionCount = 1;
        }
        break;
    }
}
if (repositionCount > 2 * pZ -> retries) {
    if (pZ -> debug) {
        DebugBegin(pZ -> debug, debugWarn);
        DebugString(pZ -> debug,
            "No␣progress,␣terminating␣transfer...");
        DebugEnd(pZ -> debug);
    }
    return StsWarn(zFail);
}
}
```

This code is used on page 335.

Session Layer

A few things are common to both the sender and receiver. In particular, the final cleanup and progress update are the same. The distinction mentioned on page 274 between zFail and zFailed becomes concrete here.

⟨ Handle final cleanup and return err 338 ⟩ ==

```
if (err == zFail) {
  ZSendHeader(pZ, ZCAN, 0);
  ZGobble(pZ, 2);
  err = zFailed;
}
if (err == zOK) ZProgress(pZ, stsDone);
else if (pZ -> userCancel) ZProgress(pZ, stsCancelled);
else ZProgress(pZ, stsFailed);
return StsWarn(err);
```

This code is used on pages 338, 339, and 347.

Sender Session

One interesting convention that's implemented here is the convention of typing rz before the session starts. Because the standard Unix ZModem program is called rz, and many bulletin board systems also use this command to initiate a ZModem upload, this allows many users to upload files using ZModem without having to manually initiate the receive.

```
STATIC int ZSendFiles(ZMODEM_PRIVATE *pZ)
{
  int err = zOK;      /* Initialize */
  ZNewFile(pZ);
  ZProgress(pZ, stsNegotiating);
  ZSendBytes(pZ, (const BYTE *) "rz\r", 3);
  err = ZSendGetZRINIT(pZ);     /* Get Receiver's capabilities */
  if (err == zOK) err = ZSendZSINIT(pZ);
        /* Inform receiver of your capabilities */
  while (err == zOK) {      /* Send Files */
    err = ZFileReadOpenNext(pZ, pZ -> fileType);
    if (err == zOK) {
      err = ZSendFile(pZ);
      ZFileReadClose(pZ);
      ZNewFile(pZ);
    }
  }
  ZProgress(pZ, stsEnding);
```

```
    if (err == zEndOfSession)        /* If end of session */
      err = ZSendEndSession(pZ);
    ⟨ Handle final cleanup and return err 338 ⟩
}
```

Receiver Session

ZModem sessions are master-slave sessions in which the sender is the master. As slave, the receiver simply processes requests from the sender. Note that ZRINIT doubles both as a receiver capabilities notification and as a request for the next transaction. In the latter role, it's repeated after most transactions to signal that I'm ready for another one.

To reduce memory requirements, you allocate a 1200-byte buffer here and pass it to ZReceiveFile as a parameter. This buffer suffices because the protocol dictates that CRC escapes cannot be spaced less often than every 1024 bytes. Hence, packets such as ZFILE and ZSINIT cannot have more than 1024 bytes of data.

```
#define ZSendZRINIT(pZ)
        ZSendHexHeader(pZ, ZRINIT, pZ -> myReceiverFlags)
  STATIC int ZReceive(ZMODEM_PRIVATE *pZ)
  {
    BYTE buff[1200];
    int retries = pZ -> retries;
    int err;

    err = ZSendZRINIT(pZ);
    while (err == zOK) {
      ZProgress(pZ, stsNegotiating);
      err = ZReadHeader(pZ, pZ -> timeout);
      if ((err == zTimeout) || (err == zBadPacket)) {
        retries --;
        if (retries == 0) err = zFail;       /* Fail if too many retries */
        else err = ZSendZRINIT(pZ);
               /* The previous line incidentally resets "err." */
      } else if (err == zOK) {
        retries = pZ -> retries;       /* Reset retry count */
        switch (pZ -> rxPacketType) {
          ⟨ Session startup and initialization packets 340 ⟩
          ⟨ File transaction packets 340 ⟩
          ⟨ Free space transaction packets 341 ⟩
          ⟨ Command transaction packets 341 ⟩
          ⟨ Session termination packets 342 ⟩
          default: err = ZSendHexHeader(pZ, ZNAK, 0);
```

```
            break;
        }
      }
    }
    if (err == zEndOfSession) err = zOK;
    ⟨Handle final cleanup and return err 338⟩
}
```

The function above does not yet specify how to handle the different packet types that might be received. I've divided the packet types into several different categories to simplify the discussion.

When the session starts, you might see ZRQINIT (the sender is just starting), an echo of your own ZRINIT (the sender hasn't yet started), or ZSINIT.

```
⟨Session startup and initialization packets 340⟩ ==
case ZRQINIT: err = ZSendZRINIT(pZ);
  break;
case ZRINIT:      /* Echo of your ZRINIT, pause */
  err = ZGobble(pZ, 2);
  break;
case ZSINIT: ZParseZSINIT(pZ, pZ -> rxPacketArg);
  err = ZSendHexHeader(pZ, ZACK, 0);
  break;
```
This code is used on page 339.

The transfer of a particular file begins with ZFILE. This layer might also see a repeated ZEOF after a file transfer is over.

ZReceiveFile is responsible for sending the ZRINIT or ZSKIP packet that ends the transaction.

```
⟨File transaction packets 340⟩ ==
case ZFILE: pZ -> fileFlags = pZ -> rxPacketArg;
  {
    unsigned length;

    err = ZReceivePacketData(pZ, buff, &length);
    if (err == zOK) err = ZReceiveFile(pZ, buff, length);
    else err = ZSendZRINIT(pZ);
  }
  break;
case ZEOF: err = ZSendZRINIT(pZ);
  break;
```
This code is used on page 339.

Although rarely used, it's possible for the sender to ask the receiver if it has enough space to store the files. Most receivers simply respond with an indefinite zero argument.

⟨ Free space transaction packets 341 ⟩ ==
```
case ZFREECNT:
  {
    unsigned long freeCount = 0;
    StsRet(ZFileSystemFree(pZ, &freeCount));
    err = ZSendHexHeader(pZ, ZACK, freeCount);
  }
  break;
```
This code is used on page 339.

The next case handles a command transaction. ZModem restricts command transactions to occur only in a session that contains one transaction. Because of this restriction, after a command, the session has to end, so this code simply waits to receive a ZFIN packet and then falls through to the end-of-session dance below.

⟨ Command transaction packets 341 ⟩ ==
```
case ZCOMMAND:
  {
    unsigned length;
    unsigned completion = 0;
    err = ZReceivePacketData(pZ, buff, &length);
    if (err == zOK) {
      char *command = (char *) buff;
      command[length] = 0;      /* Force NULL termination */
      ⟨ Process command 343 ⟩
    } else if ((err == zTimeout) || (err == zBadPacket)) {
      err = ZSendHexHeader(pZ, ZNAK, 0);
      break;
    } else return StsWarn(err);
    ⟨ Wait for ZFIN 341 ⟩
  }      /* Fall through after receiving ZFIN */
```
This code is used on page 339.

The flush takes care of any packets the sender may have sent while waiting for the command to finish.

⟨ Wait for ZFIN 341 ⟩ ==
```
  ZGobble(pZ, 0);      /* Flush input queue */
  do {
    StsRet(ZSendHexHeader(pZ, ZCOMPL, completion));
    err = ZReadHeader(pZ, pZ -> timeout);
```

```
        if ((err != zOK) && (err != zBadPacket) && (err != zTimeout))
          return StsWarn(err);
      } while ((err != zOK) || (pZ -> rxPacketType != ZFIN));
```
This code is used on page 341.

The sender ends the session with a ZFin. After the receiver responds, the sender is supposed to send a gratuitous OO. The catch is that if the receiver's response is lost, the sender will instead repeat the ZFin. The loop below watches for either the final OO or a * indicating a new header is coming (which will probably be the repeated ZFin). If neither comes, then the easy thing is to assume that the OO was lost, and just end. (Page 330 discusses this in more detail.)

```
⟨ Session termination packets 342 ⟩ ==
case ZFIN: err = ZSendHexHeader(pZ, ZFIN, 0);
  {
    BYTE overAndOut;
    int oCount = 0;
    while (err == zOK) {
      err = ZReadByteWithTimeout(pZ, pZ -> timeout, &overAndOut);
      if (err == zTimeout) err = zEndOfSession;
      else if (err == zOK) {
        if (overAndOut == 'O') {
          if (++oCount >= 2) err = zEndOfSession;
        } else if (overAndOut == '*') break;
        else oCount = 0;
      } else if (err == zBadPacket) {
        err = zOK;      /* Ignore minor serial errors */
      } else return StsWarn(err);
    }
  }
  break;
case ZCAN: err = zFailed;
  break;
case ZABORT: err = zFail;
  break;
```
This code is used on page 339.

Receiving a Command

One detail that was not completely filled in above was the processing of a received command. It's impossible to completely implement command processing in a system-independent fashion, because the methods of interfacing to the application or system command interpreter can differ pretty widely. The code here is typical, but should be modified to fit the requirements of your particular system.

ZModem has a convention that operating-system commands should be pre-fixed with a ! character to distinguish them from application commands. This convention is not rigidly observed, however. In particular, `rz` does not obey it; because `rz` has no application commands, it passes all commands to the system command interpreter. Although such an approach is quite reasonable for `rz`, this laxness has probably crept into other implementations as well, where it may not be as appropriate.

⟨ Process command 343 ⟩ ==
```
{
  if (pZ -> rxPacketArg & (0x01000000)) {
    if (pZ -> debug) {
      DebugBegin(pZ -> debug, debugPacket);
      DebugString(pZ -> debug, "Immediate␣command:␣");
      DebugString(pZ -> debug, command);
      DebugEnd(pZ -> debug);
    }        /* Delay command until after session or execute in background */
  } else {
    if (pZ -> debug) {
      DebugBegin(pZ -> debug, debugPacket);
      DebugString(pZ -> debug, "Normal␣command:␣");
      DebugString(pZ -> debug, command);
      DebugEnd(pZ -> debug);
    }
    if (command[0] == '!') {
      ⟨ Handle operating system command 343 ⟩
    } else {
      ⟨ Handle application command 344 ⟩
    }
  }
}
```
This code is used on page 341.

Operating system commands can often just be handed to the ANSI `system` function. For many applications, it may be necessary to pre-parse the command to limit the commands made available to the remote. (For example, a program that allowed anonymous users to dial in and download files from a public area should be careful to make sure that remote users cannot exploit this mechanism to access or alter data outside of the public area.)

⟨ Handle operating system command 343 ⟩ ==
```
completion = system(command + 1);      /* Ignore ! */
```
This code is used on page 343.

As an example of processing application commands, this simple parser accepts commands of the form **sz** *filenames* to allow the remote to initiate a file download. This parsing generally should be handled by the application's script language to provide more complete interaction. As above, applications that are designed to run without access limits may need to carefully restrict the commands that can be executed in this fashion.

```
#define IsWhitespace(c)
        ((c == '␣') || (c == '\t') || (c == '\r') || (c == '\n') || (c == '\f'))
⟨ Handle application command 344 ⟩ ==
  if ((command[0] == 's') && (command[1] == 'z') && (command[2] == '␣'))
    {
    char *p = command + 2;
    char *names[32];     /* Limit of 32 names */
    int numberNames = 0;

    while (*p) {      /* Parse list of names */
      while (IsWhitespace(*p))      /* Skip whitespace */
        p++;        /* Skip whitespace */
      if (*p)      /* Save this name */
        names[numberNames++] = p;
      while (*p && ! IsWhitespace(*p))      /* Skip name */
        p++;
      if (*p)      /* NULL-terminate name */
        *p++ = 0;
    }
    err = ZModemSend((ZMODEM) pZ, (const char **)
        names, numberNames);      /* Send files */
    if (err) completion = 1;      /* Unsuccessful completion */
    else completion = 0;      /* Successful completion */
  } else {      /* Unknown command, return error code */
    completion = 1;
  }
```

This code is used on page 343.

Send Command Session

The core of a command session is really just a reliability loop. The ZCOMMAND packet is repeatedly sent until a reasonable response is seen. The only place where special care is required is if the command is **sz** *filename*, in which case a ZRQINIT will come back, prompting this function to recursively call ZReceive to receive a file. After the receive is over, a number of minor problems may arise. The most common is that one or more ZFIN packets may be pending from the recursive session.

```
STATIC int ZSendZCommand(ZMODEM_PRIVATE *pZ, int immediate, const
        char *cmd)
{
  int err;
  int retries = pZ -> retries;
  size_t cmdLength = strlen(cmd) + 1;
  unsigned long crc = SendingCrc((const BYTE *)
      cmd, cmdLength, 0);

  do {
    StsRet(ZSendHeader(pZ, ZCOMMAND, (immediate) ? 1u : 0u));
    StsRet(ZSendEncodeBytes(pZ, (const BYTE *) cmd, cmdLength));
    StsRet(ZSendCrcEscape(pZ, crc, TRUE, TRUE));
    err = ZReadHeader(pZ,
        (immediate) ? (pZ -> timeout) : (pZ -> timeout * 5));
    if ((err == zTimeout) || (err == zBadPacket)) {
      retries --;
      if (retries == 0)      /* Fail if too many retries */
        return StsWarn(zFail);
    } else if (err != zOK)      /* Return other errors */
      return StsWarn(err);
    else {      /* err == zOK */
      retries = pZ -> retries;
      switch (pZ -> rxPacketType) {
      case ZCOMPL: return zEndOfSession;      /* All done */
      case ZRINIT: break;      /* ZCOMMAND not received */
      case ZNAK: break;      /* ZCOMMAND not received */
      case ZRQINIT:      /* recursive send beginning */
        if ((pZ -> rxPacketArg >> 24) & 0xFF == ZCOMMAND) {
            /* Can't have a recursive Command!! */
          StsRet(ZSendHeader(pZ, ZNAK, 0));
        } else {      /* Save the packet across the receive */
          int packetType = pZ -> rxPacketType;
          int packetArg = pZ -> rxPacketArg;

          err = ZReceive(pZ);
          pZ -> rxPacketType = packetType;
          pZ -> rxPacketArg = packetArg;
          if (err != zOK) return StsWarn(err);
          ZProgress(pZ, stsEnding);
        }
        break;
      default:      /* Other packet type?? */
        if (pZ -> debug) {
          DebugBegin(pZ -> debug, debugWarn);
```

```
                   DebugString(pZ -> debug,
                       "Unexpected␣response␣to␣ZCOMMAND␣:");
                   DebugPacket(pZ -> debug, pZ -> rxPacketType,
                       pZ -> rxPacketArg);
                   DebugEnd(pZ -> debug);
               }
               break;
           }
       }
   } while ((err != zOK) || (pZ -> rxPacketType != ZRQINIT));
       /* Finished recursive receive */
   while (TRUE) {
     err = ZReadHeader(pZ,
         (immediate) ? (pZ -> timeout) : (pZ -> timeout * 5));
     if ((err == zTimeout) || (err == zBadPacket)) {
       retries --;
       if (retries == 0)       /* Fail if too many retries */
         return StsWarn(zFail);
     } else if (err != zOK)      /* Return other errors */
       return StsWarn(err);
     else {      /* err == zOK */
       retries = pZ -> retries;
       switch (pZ -> rxPacketType) {
       case ZCOMPL: return zEndOfSession;      /* All done */
       case ZFIN:      /* Repeated ZFIN from recursive session */
         StsRet(ZSendHexHeader(pZ, ZFIN, 0));
         break;
       default:      /* Other packet type?? */
         if (pZ -> debug) {
           DebugBegin(pZ -> debug, debugWarn);
           DebugString(pZ -> debug,
               "Unexpected␣packet␣after␣recursive␣receive:");
           DebugPacket(pZ -> debug, pZ -> rxPacketType,
               pZ -> rxPacketArg);
           DebugEnd(pZ -> debug);
         }
         break;
       }
     }
   }
 }
```

The actual command session looks a lot like a normal send session. Except for the different ZRQINIT flags, this code is essentially identical to ZSendFiles.

```
STATIC int ZSendCommand(ZMODEM_PRIVATE *pZ, int immediate, const
        char *cmd)
{
  int err = zOK;

  pZ -> myZrqinitFlags = ZCOMMAND << 24;
  ZNewFile(pZ);
  ZProgress(pZ, stsNegotiating);
  ZSendBytes(pZ, (const BYTE *) "rz\r", 3);
  err = ZSendGetZRINIT(pZ);
  if (err == zOK) err = ZSendZSINIT(pZ);

  err = ZSendZCommand(pZ, immediate, cmd);

  ZProgress(pZ, stsEnding);
  if (err == zEndOfSession) err = ZSendEndSession(pZ);
  ⟨ Handle final cleanup and return err 338 ⟩
}
```

Public Interface Layer

One reason for limiting the public interface to the following functions is to simplify maintainance. Maintainers can be assured that no other function is used outside of this module. To keep this organization, you should be careful to add new public functions only in this section. For example, I did not provide a function to enable crash recovery. Such a function could be declared and used like ZModemSetFileType.

```
int ZModemInit(ZMODEM *ppZ, SERIAL_PORT port)
{
  ZMODEM_PRIVATE *pZ;

  pZ = malloc(sizeof (*pZ));
  if (pZ == NULL) return 1;        /* Non-zero indicates error */
  memset(pZ, 0, sizeof (*pZ));      /* Initialize structure */
  ⟨ Initialize ZModem variables, return if error 268 ⟩
  pZ -> port = port;
  *ppZ = pZ;
  return 0;     /* Return success */
}
```

Even though a ZModem handle is only intended to be used for a single session, the actual transfer functions do not consume the handle. The ZModemCancel function may be called from a separate execution thread from the actual transfer. If the transfer function consumed the handle when it was done, that would create a situation in which the ZModemCancel function could be called after the handle was destroyed, but before the transfer function had returned. Having the client explicitly destroy the handle allows the client to ensure this scenario doesn't happen.

```
int ZModemDestroy(ZMODEM zPublic)
{
  ZMODEM_PRIVATE *pZ = (ZMODEM_PRIVATE *) zPublic;
  if (pZ -> serialBuffer) free(pZ -> serialBuffer);
  free(zPublic);
  return zOK;
}
```

Once the handle is created, the client will probably need to configure the handle prior to performing the transfer. The next several functions allow the client to specify various aspects of the transfer.

```
int ZModemSetDebug(ZMODEM zPublic, DEBUG debug)
{
  ZMODEM_PRIVATE *pZ = (ZMODEM_PRIVATE *) zPublic;
  pZ -> debug = debug;
  return zOK;
}
```

ZModemSetProgress specifies the progress handle to use.

```
int ZModemSetProgress(ZMODEM zPublic, PROGRESS progress)
{
  ZMODEM_PRIVATE *pZ = (ZMODEM_PRIVATE *) zPublic;
  pZ -> progress = progress;
  return zOK;
}
```

```
int ZModemSetFileType(ZMODEM zPublic, int fileType)
{
  ZMODEM_PRIVATE *pZ = (ZMODEM_PRIVATE *) zPublic;
  pZ -> fileType = fileType;
  return zOK;
}
```

ZModemCancel is only really useful in multi-threaded environments, in which the user interface can actually run separately from the transfer itself. In that case, a user interface element to cancel the transfer can call this function. It may also be necessary to interrupt a serial wait; see the comments on page 174.

```
int ZModemCancel(ZMODEM zPublic)
{
```

```
  ZMODEM_PRIVATE *pZ = (ZMODEM_PRIVATE *) zPublic;
  pZ -> userCancel = TRUE;
  return zOK;
}


int ZModemReceive(ZMODEM zPublic)
{
  ZMODEM_PRIVATE *pZ = (ZMODEM_PRIVATE *) zPublic;
  int returnVal = 0;
  ProgressReceiving(pZ -> progress);
  if (ZReceive(pZ) != zOK) returnVal = 1;
  return returnVal;
}


int ZModemSend(ZMODEM zPublic, const char *filenames[], int
        count)
{
  ZMODEM_PRIVATE *pZ = (ZMODEM_PRIVATE *) zPublic;
  int returnVal = 0;
  pZ -> currentFileName = 0;
  pZ -> filenames = filenames;
  pZ -> numFileNames = count;
  ProgressSending(pZ -> progress);
  if (ZSendFiles(pZ) != zOK) returnVal = 1;
  return returnVal;
}


int ZModemSendCommand(ZMODEM zPublic, const char *command)
{
  ZMODEM_PRIVATE *pZ = (ZMODEM_PRIVATE *) zPublic;
  int returnVal = 0;      /* Default: successful return */
  ProgressSending(pZ -> progress);
  if (ZSendCommand(pZ, 0, command) != zOK) returnVal = 1;
  return returnVal;
}
```

Implementing Kermit 19

Kermit's windowing is the most complex feature of modern Kermit to implement. Fortunately, Kermit's cleanly layered design means this complexity only affects a small part of the total implementation.

As you probably realized while reading Chapter 10, the Kermit protocol has a number of features that are rarely, if ever, implemented. It follows that an important first step in implementing Kermit is to determine which parts are important for your application. The implementation in this chapter focuses on the more difficult parts of the core protocol, while omitting many features that are less common or are relatively easy to add. For example, it fully supports windowing and long packets, but only supports the rough outline of host mode. It shouldn't be too difficult to fill in any missing features that you need.

Public Interface

In good object-oriented style, the clients of this package see only an opaque Kermit *handle*, which is manipulated by functions in this package.

```
⟨ftk.h  351⟩ ==
#ifndef FTK_H_INCLUDED          /* Protect against multiple inclusions */
#define FTK_H_INCLUDED
#include "ftserial.h"    /* Defines SERIAL_PORT */
#include "ftprog.h"     /* Defines PROGRESS */
#include "ftdebug.h"     /* Defines DEBUG */
  typedef void *KERMIT;
  int KermitInit(KERMIT *pK, SERIAL_PORT port);
  int KermitDestroy(KERMIT k);
  int KermitSetFast(KERMIT k, int speed);
  int KermitSetDebug(KERMIT k, DEBUG debug);
```

```
      int KermitSetProgress(KERMIT k, PROGRESS progress);
      int KermitSetFileType(KERMIT k, int fileType);
      int KermitSend(KERMIT k, const char *filenames[], int numFiles);
      int KermitReceive(KERMIT k);
      int KermitServer(KERMIT k);
      int KermitCancel(KERMIT k);
   #endif    /* ! FTK_H_INCLUDED */
```

External Dependencies

The Kermit implementation depends on a number of external modules, ranging
from standard C library calls to modules for disk and serial I/O. For starters, this
implementation relies on several of the modules developed in previous chapters:

```
   #include "ftdisk.h"    /* Disk module */
   #include "ftserial.h"   /* Serial module */
   #include "ftdebug.h"    /* Debugging support */
   #include "ftprog.h"    /* Progress reporting */
   #include "ftk.h"     /* Your own public interface */
```

It's a simple fact of life that not all C compilers are created equal. While the
ANSI/ISO C Standard has done much to correct that, there are still many non-
standard systems. To simplify porting, I've listed all C library functions in this
section. This list should make it easier to identify potential problems. The explicit prototypes here may need to be adjusted for non-standard implementations.
They're provided for the benefit of systems that lack the standard headers, and to
point out any inconsistencies between their implementation on a particular system
and the way I've used them.

```
   #include <stddef.h>    /* size_t */

   #include <string.h>    /* strlen, memset, memcpy */
     size_t strlen(const char *s1);
     void memset(void *, unsigned char, size_t);
     void *memcpy(void *, const void *, size_t);

   #include <stdlib.h>    /* malloc, free */
     void *malloc(size_t);
     void free(void *);     /* A few macros that aren't defined in all libraries */
   #ifndef TRUE
   #define TRUE  1
   #endif

   #ifndef FALSE
   #define FALSE  0
   #endif
```

```
#ifndef NULL     /* NULL */
#define NULL ((void *) 0)
#endif
#define STATIC static
```

Definitions

One subtle distinction that needs to be carefully considered in file transfer is the distinction between an uninterpreted BYTE and a `char`. I try to encourage this distinction by using BYTE for raw data being transferred to the serial port or a disk file, and `char` for text data such as filenames.

> `typedef unsigned char BYTE;` ⟨Other definitions 385⟩

Kermit State Structure

The Kermit handle is really a pointer to a KERMIT_PRIVATE structure. The KERMIT_PRIVATE structure is organized into variables used for receiving and sending, and a collection of generic variables that apply to both sides.

```
typedef struct {
  ⟨General Kermit variables 353⟩
  struct {
    ⟨Kermit receive and send variables 365⟩
  } my, your;
} KERMIT_PRIVATE;
```

I'll define the individual variables that belong in this structure incrementally throughout the chapter. The first two are a simple flag to indicate whether I'm sending or receiving (which is used only in a very few locations) and a flag that is set when the user requests a cancel.

> ⟨General Kermit variables 353⟩ ==
> ```
>   int sending;
>   int userCancel;
> ```
> See also pages 356, 357, 361, 361, 363, 364, 365, 366, 366, 366, 368, 371, 374, 385, 386, 387, 387, 391, 391, and 424.
>
> This code is used on page 353.

For every variable, I'll also specify how it's initialized (and, in a few cases, how it's destroyed).

> ⟨Initialize Kermit variables 353⟩ ==
> ```
>   pK -> sending = TRUE;
> ```

```
pK -> userCancel = 0;
```

See also pages 356, 357, 357, 361, 361, 363, 364, 365, 366, 371, 374, 386, 386, 387, 387, 391, 391, 410, and 425.

This code is used on page 426.

Utility Functions

The next several sections describe functions that provide access to a variety of system and application capabilities. On some systems, it will make sense to expand these functions directly into system calls. On other systems, they simply will be wrappers for complex services implemented elsewhere. Although the versions presented here just call the generic services discussed in previous chapters, they should be looked upon as "plugs" that can be freely altered to fit whatever socket is available.

Error Handling

Nearly every function returns a code that represents the success or failure of the operation. Note that I've explicitly defined kOK to be zero, because comparisons against zero are much more efficient on many compilers. You need enough error codes to cover all of the different things that can go wrong, but too many error codes can make error handling unwieldy.

Two common idioms arise in this approach to error handling. The first is the idiom of testing a return value and returning it if it indicates an error. This idiom is encapsulated in the StsRet macro, which exploits C's do construction to declare a temporary variable, and to provide neater syntax. The while (FALSE) construction makes sure that StsRet requires a following semicolon, which makes such a macro call syntactically more like a function call. The second common idiom is that of a function call followed by a switch statement to handle a possible error return.

```
#define StsRet(expr)  do { int tmpErrorVal = (expr);
        if (tmpErrorVal != kOK) return StsWarn(tmpErrorVal);
      } while (FALSE)    /* Do this loop exactly once */
  enum {
    kOK = 0,     /* No error */
    kFail,      /* Transfer failed; send cancel sequence */
    kFailed,     /* Transfer failed; don't send cancel sequence */
    kBadPacket,     /* Damaged packet or bad CRC */
    kEndOfSession,     /* No more files to transfer */
    kEOF,      /* End-of-file on file read */
```

```
    kTimeout        /* Timeout waiting for data */
};
```

Debugging Support

During development, it's convenient to track the origin of any unusual event. Fortunately, the return codes defined above pretty much define what the unusual events are. By wrapping StsWarn around a function call or return code variable, you can be notified of all error values. The ANSI-standard __FILE__ and __LINE__ macros pinpoint the position in the source where any unusual event was detected.

By testing pK -> debug before calling KDebugWarn, the StsWarn macro becomes faster when debugging messages are disabled. This approach allows you to leave such messages permanently within the code, without incurring a serious performance penalty.

```
    #define StsWarn(s)
            ((pK -> debug) ? KDebugWarn(pK, (s), __FILE__, __LINE__) : (s))
    STATIC int KDebugWarn(KERMIT_PRIVATE *pK, const int s, const
            char *file, const int line)
    {
      const char *msg = NULL;
      if (s != kOK) {
        DebugBeginInternal(pK -> debug, debugWarn, file, line);
        DebugString(pK -> debug, "?!?!?!:");
      }
      switch (s) {
      case kOK: return kOK;
      case kFail: msg = "kFail"; break;
      case kFailed: msg = "kFailed"; break;
      case kBadPacket: msg = "kBadPacket"; break;
      case kEndOfSession: msg = "kEndOfSession"; break;
      case kEOF: msg = "kEOF"; break;
      case kTimeout: msg = "kTimeout"; break;
      }
      if (msg != NULL) DebugString(pK -> debug, msg);
      else {
        DebugString(pK -> debug, "Error␣");
        DebugInt(pK -> debug, s);
      }
      DebugEnd(pK -> debug);
      return s;
    }
```

Of course, to display debug messages at all, I need a debug handle.

⟨ General Kermit variables 353 ⟩ +==
```
   DEBUG debug;      /* debug handle */
```

The default is no debug stream. The `debug` module in this source accepts a NULL pointer and treats it as the null stream.

⟨ Initialize Kermit variables 353 ⟩ +==
```
   pK -> debug = NULL;
```

I've defined a collection of codes to specify the significance of certain messages, so they can be selectively enabled. See Chapter 13 for information on how messages are selectively displayed.

```
#define debugWarn   (1)
#define debugPacket   (2)
#define debugPacketErr   (4)
#define debugPacketLowLevel   (8)
#define debugCache   (16)
#define debugAttr   (32)
#define debugInit   (64)
#define debugEncoding   (256)
```

CRC Calculation

The `InitCRC` function pre-computes a table of constants, using a bitwise algorithm. These constants allow fast computation of the CRC. A detailed discussion of this code appears in Chapter 4, see page 58.

Kermit uses the CCITT CRC16. The generating polynomial is $x^{16} + x^{12} + x^5 + 1$, with binary representation 0x11021. This CRC is computed "backwards," so the constant used here is 0x8408.

```
STATIC unsigned short int kCrc16Table[256];
STATIC void KInitCrc()
{
    static int crcDone = 0;      /* Only do it once */
    unsigned long i, j, crc;
    if (crcDone) return;
    for (i = 0;  i < 256;  i ++) {
        crc = i;
        for (j = 0;  j < 8;  j ++) crc = (crc >> 1) ^ ((crc & 1) ? 0x8408 : 0);
        kCrc16Table[i] = crc & 0xffff;
    }
    crcDone = 1;      /* All done */
```

```
    }
```

The CRC table must be properly initialized. The `crcDone` variable helps avoid repeatedly initializing the CRC table.

⟨ Initialize Kermit variables 353 ⟩ +==
```
    KInitCrc();      /* Make sure the CRC table is computed */
```

This basic CRC calculator actually computes the CRC of `message` $* x^{16}$. It accepts a CRC and returns the CRC updated to reflect the additional data. The initial CRC value should be zero.

```
    STATIC unsigned short KCrc16(const BYTE *buff, unsigned int
            length, unsigned short crc)
    {
      const BYTE *p = buff;
      while (length -- > 0)
        crc = kCrc16Table[(crc ^ *p ++) & 0xff] ^ (crc >> 8);
      return crc & 0xffff;
    }
```

Interfaces to External Modules

These next few sections are a group of "sockets" where various services are plugged in. Because these services vary from system to system, the functions should be modified to fit whatever "plugs" are available.

Serial Interface

The `serial` module provides all of the basic serial operations you'll need. This section provides a thin interface to that module.

⟨ General Kermit variables 353 ⟩ +==
```
    SERIAL_PORT port;      /* Port to use */
```

⟨ Initialize Kermit variables 353 ⟩ +==
```
    pK -> port = NULL;
```

`KReadBytesWithTimeout` accepts a timeout parameter rather than using a value from the `KERMIT_PRIVATE` structure because different timeouts apply at different points in the protocol.

A variety of different errors can be returned from this function:

`kFail`   is returned if `pK -> userCancel` becomes set.

`kFailed` is returned if there is a fatal serial port error, such as loss of carrier or a similar hardware failure. Such an error means that no more serial I/O can be performed.

`kTimeout` is returned if the timeout expires. Note that some data may have been read. The client should check the returned values if a partial response is meaningful. This error should never be returned if all of the data requested is returned.

`kBadPacket` is returned if a soft serial error occurs, such as a framing, parity, or overflow error. Such errors indicate that data has been damaged, but do not prevent future I/O calls from succeeding.

`kOK` is returned if the request was satisfied.

```
STATIC int KReadBytesWithTimeout (KERMIT_PRIVATE *pK, int
        timeout, BYTE *pBuffer, size_t *pLength)
{
  int s, returnVal = kOK;
  s = SerialReadWithTimeout (pK -> port, timeout, pBuffer, pLength);
  switch (s) {
  case serialOK: returnVal = kOK;
    break;
  case serialTimeout: returnVal = kTimeout;
    break;
  case serialUserCancel: pK -> userCancel = TRUE;
    returnVal = kFail;
    break;
  case serialFrame: returnVal = kBadPacket;
    break;
  default: return StsWarn (kFailed);
  }
  if (pK -> userCancel) return StsWarn (kFail);
  return returnVal;
}
```

The functions to send data are simpler than those to read data, simply because there can be no timeout. The errors are consequently fewer:

`kFail` is returned if `pK -> userCancel` becomes set.

`kFailed` is returned if there is a fatal serial port error.

`kOK` is returned otherwise.

This function is best implemented as a non-blocking write; that is, the function queues the outgoing data and returns immediately. The reason is that you can exploit the multitasking inherent in common queued serial drivers to overlap such tasks as computing CRCs. To send data followed by a CRC, you first queue the data, then compute the CRC, queue the CRC, and finally wait for the send to complete. This process lets you begin the send slightly earlier than if you waited to compute the CRC prior to sending the data.

```
STATIC int KSendBytes(KERMIT_PRIVATE *pK, const BYTE
        *pBuffer, unsigned int length)
{
  int s, returnVal;
  if (length == 0) return kOK;
  s = SerialSend(pK -> port, pBuffer, length);
  switch (s) {
  case serialOK: returnVal = kOK;
    break;
  case serialUserCancel: pK -> userCancel = TRUE;
    returnVal = kFail;
    break;
  default: return StsWarn(kFailed);
  }
  if (pK -> userCancel) return StsWarn(kFail);
  return StsWarn(returnVal);
}
```

This next function complements KSendBytes by waiting until the outgoing data queue is empty. It's impossible to implement on some systems, but extremely useful when it can be implemented, because file transfers rely heavily on timed read calls to implement proper timeout handling. If you fail to wait for the previous send to complete, you risk the following scenario: The sender queues some data to be sent and starts to wait for a response from the sender. At low baud rates, the sender could timeout waiting for a response before it has finished sending the data that causes the response. Thus, there's a need to know when a queued send has actually completed. As you might expect, there's less need for such a function at high baud rates because the delay between queueing the data and the completion of the send is necessarily smaller.

If this function cannot be implemented, it can be left as a stub, but there are a few things that can be done to help compensate for its lack. The easiest way on many systems is to restrict the size of the outgoing data queue. That prevents KSendBytes from returning immediately, but does allow it to return before the send is actually complete. The optimal size varies with the data rate; it usually should be about one full second long; for example, 30 bytes at 300 bps or 11k at 115,200bps.

There are only a few errors that can be returned:

kFail   is returned if pK -> userCancel becomes set.

kFailed   is returned if there is a fatal serial port error (such as loss of carrier or similar hardware-level failure).

kOK   is returned otherwise.

```
STATIC int KWaitForSentBytes(KERMIT_PRIVATE *pK)
{
  int s, returnVal;
  if (pK -> userCancel) return StsWarn(kFail);
  s = SerialWaitForSentBytes(pK -> port);
  switch (s) {
  case serialOK: returnVal = kOK;
    break;
  case serialUserCancel: pK -> userCancel = TRUE;
    returnVal = StsWarn(kFail);
    break;
  default: return StsWarn(kFailed);
  }
  if (pK -> userCancel) return StsWarn(kFail);
  return StsWarn(returnVal);
}
```

The next two functions are just convenience functions for sending or reading a single byte. For performance reasons, they're used sparingly.

```
STATIC int KSendByte(KERMIT_PRIVATE *pK, BYTE b)
{
  return StsWarn(KSendBytes(pK, &b, 1));
}

STATIC int KReadByteWithTimeout(KERMIT_PRIVATE *pK, int
      timeout, BYTE *pByte)
{
  size_t count = 1;
  return KReadBytesWithTimeout(pK, timeout, pByte, &count);
}
```

Reading Files

The file interface splits into three pieces: functions to read data from files, functions to write data to files, and functions to handle miscellaneous chores.

The disk module keeps a variety of information about the current file in the DISKFILE structure. If the disk interface functions are replaced with functions that directly manipulate a FILE handle, this section will need to be fleshed out to maintain file information such as the filename, modification date, access permissions, and file type.

⟨ General Kermit variables 353 ⟩ +≡
```
DISKFILE f;      /* Current file */
long fileSize;      /* Size of file being transferred, -1 if not known */
```

⟨ Initialize Kermit variables 353 ⟩ +≡
```
pK -> f = NULL;
pK -> fileSize = −1;
```

For simplicity, I just use an array of char * to hold the names of files to be transferred. Using a different data structure only requires modifying KermitSend to accept different information, and KFileReadOpenNext to process a different type of list.

⟨ General Kermit variables 353 ⟩ +≡
```
const char **filenames;      /* Used by KFileReadOpenNext */
int currentFileName;
int numFileNames;
int fileType;
```

⟨ Initialize Kermit variables 353 ⟩ +≡
```
pK -> filenames = NULL;
pK -> currentFileName = 0;
pK -> numFileNames = 0;
pK -> fileType = diskFileUnknown;
```

This function tries to open each file in turn until it finds the next one that can be opened. It returns kEndOfSession if no files remain to be opened.

```
STATIC int KFileReadOpenNext(KERMIT_PRIVATE *pK, int fileType)
{
  while (1) {
    if (pK -> currentFileName == pK -> numFileNames)
      return kEndOfSession;
    switch (DiskReadOpen(&pK -> f,
          pK -> filenames[pK -> currentFileName ++], fileType)) {
    case diskOK: DiskFileSize(pK -> f, &(pK -> fileSize));
      return kOK;
    case diskCantRead: case diskNoSuchFile: break;
    default: return StsWarn(kFail);
```

```
        }
      }
   }

   STATIC int KFileRead(KERMIT_PRIVATE *pK, BYTE *pBuffer, unsigned
        long *pLength)
   {
     int returnVal;
     switch (DiskRead(pK -> f, pBuffer, *pLength, pLength)) {
     case diskOK: returnVal = kOK; break;
     case diskEOF: returnVal = kEOF; break;
     default: returnVal = StsWarn(kFail); break;
     }
     return returnVal;
   }

   STATIC int KFileReadClose(KERMIT_PRIVATE *pK)
   {
     int returnVal;
     switch (DiskReadClose(pK -> f)) {
     case diskOK: returnVal = kOK;
       break;
     default: returnVal = StsWarn(kFail);
       break;
     }
     pK -> f = NULL;
     return returnVal;
   }
```

Writing Files

The file writing interface, like file reading, consists of functions to open and close a file and do actual I/O. Also like the file reading interface, the most complex function is the one to open a file.

KFileWriteOpen has a number of duties. The most important is to ensure that the received filename is valid for this system.

```
   STATIC int KFileWriteOpen(KERMIT_PRIVATE *pK, const char
        *fileName, int length, int fileType)
   {
     pK -> fileSize = -1;
     if (DiskWriteInit(&pK -> f)) return StsWarn(kFail);
     if (DiskWriteName(pK -> f, fileName)) return StsWarn(kFail);
```

```
    if (DiskWriteType(pK -> f,fileType)) return StsWarn(kFail);
    if (DiskWriteOpen(pK -> f)) return StsWarn(kFail);
    return kOK;
}


STATIC int KFileWrite(KERMIT_PRIVATE *pK,const BYTE
        *pBuffer,unsigned long length)
{
  switch (DiskWrite(pK -> f,pBuffer,length)) {
  case diskOK: return kOK;
  default: return StsWarn(kFail);
  }
}


STATIC int KFileWriteClose(KERMIT_PRIVATE *pK)
{
  int returnVal;
  switch (DiskWriteClose(pK -> f)) {
  case diskOK: returnVal = kOK; break;
  default: returnVal = StsWarn(kFail); break;
  }
  pK -> f = NULL;
  return returnVal;
}
```

Progress Reporting

The progress reporting in this module is very simple. I'm just interfacing to the
`progress` module discussed in Chapter 16. If you want to provide an 'expert'
display with more detailed statistics about the transfer, you'll need to consider how
those statistics should be gathered and relayed to the progress machinery.

```
⟨ General Kermit variables 353 ⟩ +≡
   PROGRESS progress;    /* Progress handle */


⟨ Initialize Kermit variables 353 ⟩ +≡
  pK -> progress = NULL;
```

I've defined separate status codes, rather than use the ones defined in the
`progress` module. The primary reason for this redundancy is to document what
codes are used in this module. A secondary reason is to make it simpler to modify
this progress interface.

```
    enum {
```

```
        stsNegotiating = progNegotiating, stsNewFile = progNewFile,
          stsSending = progSending, stsReceiving = progReceiving,
          stsEnding = progEnding, stsEOF = progEOF, stsDone = progDone,
          stsSkipped = progSkipped, stsFailed = progFailed,
          stsCancelled = progCancelled
    };
```

⟨ General Kermit variables 353 ⟩ +≡
```
  unsigned long filePosition;
```

⟨ Initialize Kermit variables 353 ⟩ +≡
```
  pK -> filePosition = 0;

  STATIC void KProgress(KERMIT_PRIVATE *pK, int status)
  {
    if (pK -> f) {
      const char *fileName = NULL;
      int fileType = diskFileUnknown;

      DiskFileName(pK -> f, &fileName);
      ProgressFileName(pK -> progress, fileName);
      DiskFileType(pK -> f, &fileType);
      ProgressFileType(pK -> progress, fileType);
    } else {
      ProgressFileName(pK -> progress, NULL);
    }
    ProgressFileSize(pK -> progress, pK -> fileSize);
    ProgressFilePosition(pK -> progress, pK -> filePosition);
    ProgressReport(pK -> progress, status);
  }
```

Encoding Layer

If you've read the XYModem and ZModem source, you probably have the impression that the encoding functions layer on top of the serial I/O functions. After all, the goal of encoding is to compensate for lack of transparency in the channel, right? Kermit, however, takes a slightly different approach to satisfy this need. Remember that one of the goals of Kermit was to transfer files through mainframe terminal ports. Because of line-length limitations, packets in this environment must often be less than 80 bytes long. Such a restriction makes it difficult to encode a packet as it is sent; the protocol has to know how big the *encoded* data will be. For this reason, Kermit encodes and decodes data as it is read from or written to the file.

Thus, if the protocol knows that a packet has room for 64 bytes of encoded data, the encoding layer can read sufficient data from the file to accommodate that need.

One of the implications of this approach is that I need to buffer file I/O, since I'll be examining data from the file one byte at a time.

⟨ General Kermit variables 353 ⟩ +≡

```
BYTE *pFileBuffer;
int fileBufferSize;
BYTE *pFileThisChar;
BYTE *pFileBufferLimit;
int eofFlag;
```

The buffer needs to be allocated at the beginning of the transfer.

```
#define FILE_BUFFER_SIZE    (8000)
```

⟨ Initialize Kermit variables 353 ⟩ +≡

```
{
    pK -> pFileBuffer = (BYTE *) malloc(FILE_BUFFER_SIZE);
    if (pK -> pFileBuffer == NULL) return 1;
    pK -> fileBufferSize = FILE_BUFFER_SIZE;
    pK -> pFileThisChar = pK -> pFileBuffer;
    pK -> pFileBufferLimit = pK -> pFileBuffer;
    pK -> eofFlag = 0;
}
```

And destroyed at the end...

⟨ Destroy Kermit variables 365 ⟩ ≡

```
free(pK -> pFileBuffer);
```

This code is used on page 427.

⟨ Per-file Initialization 365 ⟩ ≡

```
pK -> eofFlag = 0;
```

See also pages 368 and 371.

This code is used on pages 404 and 409.

Kermit allows the sender and receiver to have different control prefixes. Even though the two sides must agree on the eighth-bit and repeat prefixes, having separate variables for the two sides does simplify the negotiation somewhat.

⟨ Kermit receive and send variables 365 ⟩ ≡

```
BYTE prefixControl;
BYTE prefix8bit;
BYTE prefixRepeat;
```

See also pages 374 and 410.

This code is used on page 353.

⟨ General Kermit variables 353 ⟩ +==
```
  int lockingShift;
```

The unusual initialization of the eighth-bit prefix here is explained on page 417.

⟨ Initialize Kermit variables 353 ⟩ +==
```
  pK -> your . prefixControl = '#';
  pK -> my . prefixControl = '#';
  pK -> your . prefix8bit = 'N';
  pK -> my . prefix8bit = 'Y';
  pK -> your . prefixRepeat = '~';
  pK -> my . prefixRepeat = '~';
  pK -> lockingShift = FALSE;
```

A number of arrays and macros simplify the actual encoding and decoding. The first is a bit-mapped array used to quickly determine which bytes require prefixing.

```
  #define SetControl(b)   (pK -> classify[b] |= 1)
  #define NeedsControl(b)   (pK -> classify[b] & 1)
```
⟨ General Kermit variables 353 ⟩ +==
```
  char classify[256];
```

It's also useful to keep arrays to perform encoding and decoding of control-prefixed values. An array is useful because different byte values are encoded in different ways. Control codes are prefixed and encoded by toggling bit six, while other values (such as the control prefix itself) are prefixed but not altered; for example, if # is the control prefix, the control prefix itself is encoded as ##.

⟨ General Kermit variables 353 ⟩ +==
```
  unsigned char encode[256];
  unsigned char decode[256];
```

Encoding

I'll worry about initializing these arrays a little later. Right now, to demonstrate how they're used, here's the code to actually do the prefix encoding. This scrap assumes that b holds the byte to be encoded, and `repeatCount` is the number of repeats of this byte. Note in particular that the combination of `NeedsControl` and the `encode` array make it unnecessary to manually determine how this character should be encoded.

⟨ Encode b into buffer pointed to by pBuffer 366 ⟩ ==
```
  if (repeatCount > 1) {
    *pBuffer ++ = pK -> my . prefixRepeat;
```

```
        *pBuffer ++ = repeatCount + 32;
        length -= 2;
    }
    if ((b & 0x80) && (pK -> my . prefix8bit)) {
        *pBuffer ++ = pK -> my . prefix8bit;
        length --;
        b &= 0x7f;
    }
    if (NeedsControl(b)) {
        *pBuffer ++ = pK -> my . prefixControl;
        length --;
        b = pK -> encode[b];
    }
    *pBuffer ++ = b;
    length -- ;
```

This code is used on page 369.

Now it's time to delve into locking shift encoding. As you'll recall from page 40, Kermit's locking shift works like the normal eighth-bit prefix, except that it alters all succeeding bytes until it is explicitly undone. Locking shifts can be done in conjunction with eighth-bit prefix encoding. In this case, each of them is considered a 'toggle;' the eighth-bit prefix doesn't *set* the eighth bit, but rather *toggles* the eighth bit. This approach allows a single seven-bit character to be compactly encoded within a long run of eight-bit characters by surrounding the whole sequence with locking shifts and using the eighth-bit prefix on the single seven-bit character.

The problem is figuring out when to use locking shifts, which are comparatively expensive (four bytes total assuming control prefixing must be done for those characters), but apply to many characters, and when to use the eighth-bit prefix, which is cheap (one byte) but only applies to a single character. Unfortunately, it's unreasonable to even try to do this encoding optimally,[1] but it is possible to do pretty well. The key point is to notice that locking shifts reduce the size of the encoded data by removing one character from each repeat group that would otherwise require an eighth-bit prefix. Assuming control prefixing is in effect, the shift-out and shift-in pair requires four bytes, so the encoder should shift whenever there are five repeat groups that would benefit. Notice that this approach requires that repeat encoding be done first.

---

[1] It's not too difficult to come up with two very long files that differ only in the last few bytes where one is optimally encoded with a single pair of locking shifts (shift-out at the beginning, shift-in near the end) and the other is optimally encoded with no locking shifts at all. The point is that it may not be possible to decide whether or not to insert a locking shift without first analyzing the rest of the file, which is impractical.

So, I've set up a circular queue to hold the next few repeat groups. If repeat-count encoding is disabled, the repeat counts in this array will all be one, but most Kermit receivers do support repeat counts.

⟨ General Kermit variables 353 ⟩ +==
```
    int repeatStart;
    int repeatEnd;
    int num8bit;
    BYTE repeatByte[6];
    int repeatCount[6];
```

⟨ Per-file Initialization 365 ⟩ +==
```
    pK -> repeatStart = 0;      /* Buffer has something in it at start */
    pK -> repeatEnd = 1;
    pK -> num8bit = 0;
    pK -> repeatByte[0] = 0;
    pK -> repeatCount[0] = 0;     /* Initial contents */
```

This queue needs to be kept filled in order to be effective. As with any circular queue, it's important to disambiguate empty and full buffers. Since the buffer will almost always be full, I've chosen to interpret the ambiguous state as full. This choice does require some footwork to straighten out end-of-file. The `eofFlag` is set to one when end-of-file is encountered, and two when the repeat queue is no longer full as a result.

⟨ Fill repeat group queue 368 ⟩ ==
```
    while ((pK -> repeatEnd != pK -> repeatStart) && (eofFlag < 2)) {
        if (pDiskBuffer >= pK -> pFileBufferLimit) {
            if (eofFlag == 0) {      /* Not at end-of-file */
                unsigned long bufferSize = pK -> fileBufferSize - 1;
                err = KFileRead(pK, pK -> pFileBuffer, &bufferSize);
                pDiskBuffer = pK -> pFileBuffer;
                if (bufferSize > 0)      /* Store marker byte */
                  pDiskBuffer[bufferSize] = ~pDiskBuffer[bufferSize - 1];
                pK -> pFileBufferLimit = pDiskBuffer + bufferSize;
                pK -> pFileThisChar = pDiskBuffer;
                if (err == kEOF) eofFlag = 1;
                else StsRet(err);
            } else eofFlag ++;
            if (eofFlag) break;
        }
        b = *pDiskBuffer;
        pK -> repeatByte[pK -> repeatEnd] = b;
        if (b ^ lockingFlip) pK -> num8bit ++;
        repeatCount = 1;
```

```
    if ((pDiskBuffer[1] == b) && (pK -> my . prefixRepeat)) {
      while (pDiskBuffer[repeatCount] == b) repeatCount ++;
      if (repeatCount > 94) repeatCount = 94;
      if ((repeatCount == 2) && (! NeedsControl(b))) repeatCount = 1;
    }
    pDiskBuffer += repeatCount;
    pK -> repeatCount[pK -> repeatEnd] = repeatCount;
    pK -> repeatEnd ++;
    if (pK -> repeatEnd >= (sizeof (pK -> repeatByte) / sizeof
          (pK -> repeatByte[0]))) pK -> repeatEnd = 0;
  }
```

This code is used on page 369.

With the preceding preliminaries, the rest of the function to read file data and encode it is pretty reasonable. I've taken one shortcut here: I've simply reduced the length requested by four rather than include a test to see if the next prefix group will fit in the packet. The last prefix group may overrun the reduced length, but it will still fit within the original request. This shortcut will result in slightly less efficient use of packets when extensive encoding is being done.

```
STATIC int KFileReadEncode(KERMIT_PRIVATE *pK, BYTE
        *pBuffer, unsigned long *pLength, unsigned long
        *pRawLength)
{
  int err;
  long length = (*pLength) -= 4;      /* Some room for slop */
  BYTE b;
  int repeatCount = 1;
  BYTE *pDiskBuffer = pK -> pFileThisChar;
  int eofFlag = pK -> eofFlag;
  int lockingFlip = pK -> lockingFlip;
  int quoteNext = pK -> quoteNext;
  if ((eofFlag > 1) && (pK -> repeatStart == pK -> repeatEnd))
    return StsWarn(kEOF);
  *pRawLength = 0;
  DebugBegin(pK -> debug, debugEncoding);
  DebugString(pK -> debug,
      "Beginning␣to␣encode␣for␣packet␣length␣");
  DebugInt(pK -> debug, length);
  DebugEnd(pK -> debug);
  while (length > 0) {
    ⟨ Fill repeat group queue 368 ⟩
    if ((eofFlag > 1) && (pK -> repeatStart == pK -> repeatEnd))
      break;
```

```
        b = pK -> repeatByte[pK -> repeatStart];
        repeatCount = pK -> repeatCount[pK -> repeatStart];
        if (pK -> lockingShift) {
          b ^= lockingFlip;
          if (quoteNext) {
            quoteNext = FALSE;
            pK -> repeatStart ++;
            if (b ^ lockingFlip) pK -> num8bit --;
            (*pRawLength) += repeatCount;
          } else {
            switch (b) {      /* Quote SI, SO, DLE */
            case 14: case 15: case 16: quoteNext = TRUE;
              b = 16;       /* Insert DLE */
              repeatCount = 1;
              break;
            default:
              if ((pK -> num8bit > 4) && (b & 0x80)) {
                pK -> num8bit = 6 - pK -> num8bit;
                lockingFlip ^= 0x80;
                b = (lockingFlip) ? 14 : 15;
                repeatCount = 1;
              } else {
                pK -> repeatStart ++;
                if (b ^ lockingFlip) pK -> num8bit --;
                (*pRawLength) += repeatCount;
              }
              break;
            }
          }
        } else {
          pK -> repeatStart ++;
          if (b ^ lockingFlip) pK -> num8bit --;
          (*pRawLength) += repeatCount;
        }
        if (pK -> repeatStart >= (sizeof (pK -> repeatByte) / sizeof
              (pK -> repeatByte[0]))) pK -> repeatStart = 0;
        if (repeatCount > 0) {
          ⟨ Encode b into buffer pointed to by pBuffer 366 ⟩
        }
      }
    }
    DebugBegin(pK -> debug, debugEncoding);
    DebugString(pK -> debug, "Done␣encoding␣packet");
    DebugInt(pK -> debug, length);
    DebugEnd(pK -> debug);
```

```
        pK -> pFileThisChar = pDiskBuffer;
        *pLength -= length;
        pK -> lockingFlip = lockingFlip;
        pK -> quoteNext = quoteNext;
        pK -> eofFlag = eofFlag;
        return kOK;
    }
```

Unlike normal prefixing, locking shifts can apply across many packets. The `lockingFlip` and `quoteNext` variables used above maintain the state of the locking shift encoding across packets. Unlike the normal prefix encoding, locking shifts are performed across the entire file. The `lockingFlip` variable holds the most recent shift state; 0x80 indicates that the locking shift is in effect. The `quoteNext` variable indicates that the last byte added to the last packet was a DLE which is escaping the first byte of the next packet.

⟨ General Kermit variables 353 ⟩ +≡
```
    int lockingFlip;
    int quoteNext;
```

⟨ Initialize Kermit variables 353 ⟩ +≡
```
    pK -> lockingFlip = 0;
    pK -> quoteNext = 0;
```

⟨ Per-file Initialization 365 ⟩ +≡
```
    pK -> lockingFlip = 0;
    pK -> quoteNext = 0;
```

Decoding

Decoding is quite similar. The only difference is the use of a small buffer to avoid generating many single-byte write requests.

```
        STATIC int KFileWriteDecode(KERMIT_PRIVATE *pK, const BYTE
                *pBuffer, size_t length)
    {
      BYTE buff[500];
      unsigned buffLength = 0;
      int mask = 0xff;
      int flip = 0;
      int repeatCount = 0;
      int lockingFlip = pK -> lockingFlip & 0x80;
      int quoteNext = pK -> quoteNext;
      BYTE b = 0;
```

```
if (pK -> your . prefix8bit) mask = 0x7f;
while (length > 0) {
  b = ((unsigned) (*pBuffer ++)) & mask;
  length --;
  repeatCount = 1;
  flip = 0;
  if ((pK -> your . prefixRepeat) && (b == pK -> your . prefixRepeat))
    {
    repeatCount = (((unsigned) (*pBuffer ++)) & 0x7f) - 32;
    b = ((unsigned) (*pBuffer ++)) & mask;
    length -= 2;
  }
  if ((pK -> your . prefix8bit) && (b == pK -> your . prefix8bit)) {
    flip ^= 0x80;
    b = ((unsigned) (*pBuffer ++)) & mask;
    length --;
  }
  if (b == pK -> your . prefixControl) {
    b = pK -> decode[((unsigned) (*pBuffer ++)) & mask];
    length --;
  }
  b ^= flip;
  if (pK -> lockingShift) {
    if (! quoteNext) {
      switch (b) {
      case 14: lockingFlip = 0x80;
        repeatCount = 0;
        break;
      case 15: lockingFlip = 0;
        repeatCount = 0;
        break;
      case 16: quoteNext = TRUE;
        repeatCount = 0;
        break;
      }
    } else quoteNext = FALSE;
  }
  b ^= lockingFlip;
  while (repeatCount > 0) {
    buff[buffLength ++] = b;
    repeatCount --;
    pK -> filePosition ++;
    if (buffLength >= sizeof (buff)) {
      StsRet(KFileWrite(pK, buff, buffLength));
```

```
            buffLength = 0;
        }
    }
}
StsRet(KFileWrite(pK, buff, buffLength));
pK -> lockingFlip = lockingFlip;
pK -> quoteNext = quoteNext;
return kOK;
}
```

Now, I'll finish the look at encoding by showing how the different encoding arrays are initialized. Since the encoding details depend on the negotiation, this function is not called until shortly after the session begins.

```
STATIC void KInitEncoding(KERMIT_PRIVATE *pK)
{
    int i;
    ⟨ Build classify array 373 ⟩
    ⟨ Build encode and decode arrays 373 ⟩
}
```

All control codes need to be prefixed, as do the control, eighth-bit, and repeat count prefixes themselves.

```
⟨ Build classify array 373 ⟩ ==
    for (i = 0;  i < 256;  i ++) pK -> classify[i] = 0;
    for (i = 0;  i < 32;  i ++) {
        SetControl(i);
        SetControl(i | 0x80);
    }
    SetControl(0x7f);
    SetControl(0xff);
    SetControl(pK -> my . prefixControl);
    if (pK -> my . prefix8bit) SetControl(pK -> my . prefix8bit);
    if (pK -> my . prefixRepeat) SetControl(pK -> my . prefixRepeat);
```
This code is used on page 373.

```
⟨ Build encode and decode arrays 373 ⟩ ==
    for (i = 0;  i < 256;  i ++) pK -> encode[i] = pK -> decode[i] = i;
    for (i = 0;  i < 32;  i ++) pK -> encode[i] = i ^ 0x40;
    pK -> encode[0x7f] = 0x7f ^ 0x40;
    for (i = 128;  i < 160;  i ++) pK -> encode[i] = i ^ 0x40;
    pK -> encode[0xff] = 0xff ^ 0x40;
    for (i = 0;  i < 32;  i ++)
        pK -> decode[((unsigned) (pK -> encode[i])) & 0xff] = i;
```

```
pK -> decode[((unsigned) (pK -> encode[0x7f])) & 0xff] = 0x7f;
for (i = 128;  i < 160;  i++)
   pK -> decode[((unsigned) (pK -> encode[i])) & 0xff] = i;
pK -> decode[((unsigned) (pK -> encode[0xff])) & 0xff] = 0xff;
```
This code is used on page 373.

Packet Layer

Kermit has three different packet formats, three different error checks, and a variety of options that control how different parts of the packet are handled.

⟨ General Kermit variables 353 ⟩ +==
```
char packetCheck;
```

Both sides of a Kermit transfer use the same packet check. However, most of the other packet parameters can differ.

⟨ Kermit receive and send variables 365 ⟩ +==
```
char preferredPacketCheck;
BYTE sopCharacter;
long maxPacketSize;
int timeout;
int padCount;
BYTE padByte;
BYTE packetTerminator;
```

The initialization of my . sopCharacter and your . sopCharacter may seem a bit odd. In order to remove one configuration headache, the receive packet routine allows any control character to serve as the start-of-packet character; see page 381 for details. Setting the sopCharacter fields to the illegal value of 0xff prompts the receive packet routine to set these fields from the first valid packet it receives. The send packet routine replaces an illegal sopCharacter value with the most common value of 0x01.

⟨ Initialize Kermit variables 353 ⟩ +==
```
pK -> your . preferredPacketCheck = '1';
pK -> my . preferredPacketCheck = '1';
pK -> packetCheck = '1';
pK -> your . sopCharacter = 0xff;
pK -> my . sopCharacter = 0xff;
pK -> your . maxPacketSize = 90;
pK -> my . maxPacketSize = 80;
pK -> my . timeout = 30;
pK -> your . timeout = 10;
```

```
pK -> your . padCount = 0;
pK -> my . padCount = 0;
pK -> your . padByte = 0;
pK -> my . padByte = 0;
pK -> your . packetTerminator = 0x0d;
pK -> my . packetTerminator = 0x0d;
```

The next function computes any of Kermit's four different error checks. Since there can be no error, this function simply returns the value of the error check. To allow error checks to be accumulated across several calls, the client can provide a pointer to an accumulator that will be used to store any intermediate computation. This is needed for the type 1 error check, which is based on a checksum, but the actual error check is mangled to create a six-bit result. In this case, the value stored in *pCheckValue is the unmangled checksum. For convenience in cases where there's no need to accumulate an error check over multiple calls, pCheckValue can be set to NULL.

```
STATIC int KCheckValue(KERMIT_PRIVATE *pK, char
        packetCheck, const BYTE *pData, unsigned int length, int
        *pCheckValue)
{
  int checkAccumulator;
  int finalCheck = 0;
  int i;
  if (pCheckValue) checkAccumulator = *pCheckValue;
  else checkAccumulator = 0;
  switch (packetCheck) {
  case '1':     /* Single-byte checksum */
    for (i = 0;  i < length;  i ++) checkAccumulator += pData[i];
    finalCheck = checkAccumulator;
    finalCheck += (finalCheck >> 6) & 3;
    finalCheck &= 63;
    break;
  case 'B':     /* 12-bit checksum without blanks */
  case '2':     /* 12-bit checksum */
    for (i = 0;  i < length;  i ++) checkAccumulator += pData[i];
    finalCheck = checkAccumulator & 0xfff;
    break;
  case '3':     /* CRC-CCITT16 */
    checkAccumulator = KCrc16(pData, length, checkAccumulator);
    finalCheck = checkAccumulator;
    break;
  default:
    if (pK -> debug) {
```

```
          DebugBegin(pK -> debug, debugWarn);
          DebugString(pK -> debug,
              "Internal␣error:␣illegal␣packet␣check␣");
          DebugChar(pK -> debug, packetCheck);
          DebugInt(pK -> debug, packetCheck);
          DebugEnd(pK -> debug);
        }
      break;
    }
    if (pCheckValue) *pCheckValue = checkAccumulator;
    return finalCheck;
  }
```

Sending Packets

Unlike XModem or YModem, where some packets are single control characters, or ZModem, which builds very long packets from raw encoded data, Kermit uses explicit packets for everything. In some ways, this approach greatly simplifies the implementation, because it's unnecessary for other layers to explicitly construct packets. The only variation that will have to be handled at higher layers is how the data field is encoded.

Note that the data argument to KSendPacket is already encoded.

```
    STATIC int KSendPacket(KERMIT_PRIVATE *pK, int sequence, BYTE
            type, const BYTE *pData, unsigned long dataLength)
    {
      int checkAccumulator = 0;
      int checkValue;
      int packetCheckLength = pK -> packetCheck — '0';
      if (pK -> packetCheck == 'B') packetCheckLength = 2;
      ⟨Send padding 376⟩
      if (dataLength + packetCheckLength > 9024)
        ⟨Send extra-long packet header 379⟩
      else if (dataLength + packetCheckLength + 2 > 95)
        ⟨Send long packet header 378⟩
      else ⟨Send normal packet header 378⟩
      ⟨Send packet data 377⟩
      ⟨Issue debug message about packet sent 377⟩
      StsRet(KWaitForSentBytes(pK));
      return kOK;
    }

  ⟨Send padding 376⟩ ==
    {
```

```
    int i;
    for (i = 0; i < pK -> my . padCount; i ++) {
      StsRet(KSendByte(pK, pK -> my . padByte));
    }
  }
```

This code is used on page 376.

The important facts about a packet are the sequence number, type, and length.
To avoid swamping the debug log, I've chosen to print only the first part of long
packets.

```
⟨ Issue debug message about packet sent 377 ⟩ ==
  if (pK -> debug) {
    DebugBegin(pK -> debug, debugPacket);
    DebugString(pK -> debug, "Sent␣#");
    DebugInt(pK -> debug, sequence);
    DebugString(pK -> debug, "␣type:");
    DebugChar(pK -> debug, type);
    DebugString(pK -> debug, "␣length:");
    DebugUInt(pK -> debug, dataLength);
    DebugString(pK -> debug, "␣check:");
    DebugInt(pK -> debug, checkValue);
    DebugString(pK -> debug, "␣''");
    if (dataLength < 40) {
      DebugStringCount(pK -> debug, (const char *)
          pData, dataLength);
      DebugString(pK -> debug, "''");
    } else {
      DebugStringCount(pK -> debug, (const char *) pData, 37);
      DebugString(pK -> debug, "...");
    }
    DebugEnd(pK -> debug);
  }
```

This code is used on page 376.

Normal, long, and extra-long packets differ only in the header. Basically, normal packets have a single-character length field, and are thus limited to 94 bytes.
Long and extra-long packets have two- and three-character length fields, allowing them to handle packets up to $95^2 - 1 = 9024$ and $95^3 - 1 = 857374$,
respectively.[2] The data and trailing check value are handled identically, however.

```
⟨ Send packet data 377 ⟩ ==
  StsRet(KSendBytes(pK, pData, dataLength));
```

---

[2]Actually, the negotiation only allows extra-long packet sizes of $95^3 - 95$ to be specified.

```
checkValue = KCheckValue(pK, pK -> packetCheck, pData, dataLength,
    &checkAccumulator);
switch (pK -> packetCheck) {
case '3': StsRet(KSendByte(pK, ((checkValue >> 12) & 15) + 32));
case '2': StsRet(KSendByte(pK, ((checkValue >> 6) & 63) + 32));
case '1': StsRet(KSendByte(pK, (checkValue & 63) + 32));
  break;
case 'B': StsRet(KSendByte(pK, ((checkValue >> 6) & 63) + 33));
  StsRet(KSendByte(pK, (checkValue & 63) + 33));
}
StsRet(KSendByte(pK, pK -> my . packetTerminator));
```

This code is used on page 376.

Normal packets have a simple four-byte header. Because the length field includes the two bytes for the sequence and type as well as the packet check, the length field will never be less than three. See page 374 for details about the odd handling of header [0] here.

⟨ Send normal packet header 378 ⟩ ==
```
{
  BYTE header[4];
  header[0] = pK -> my . sopCharacter;
  if (header[0] == 0xff) header[0] = 0x01;
  header[1] = dataLength + 2 + packetCheckLength + 32;
  header[2] = (sequence % 64) + 32;
  header[3] = type;
  StsRet(KSendBytes(pK, header, 4));
  KCheckValue(pK, pK->packetCheck, header+1, 3, &checkAccumulator);
}
```

This code is used on page 376.

The fact that normal packets never have lengths less than three was exploited to create long and extra-long packets. Long packets are indicated by a length field of zero. They add an extended two-character length field and a checksum for the header.

⟨ Send long packet header 378 ⟩ ==
```
{
  BYTE header[7];
  header[0] = pK -> my . sopCharacter;
  if (header[0] == 0xff) header[0] = 0x01;
  header[1] = '␣';
  header[2] = (sequence % 64) + 32;
  header[3] = type;
  header[4] = (dataLength + packetCheckLength) / 95 + 32;
```

```
          header[5] = (dataLength + packetCheckLength) % 95 + 32;
          header[6] = KCheckValue(pK, '1', header + 1, 5, NULL) + 32;
          StsRet(KSendBytes(pK, header, 7));
          KCheckValue(pK, pK->packetCheck, header+1, 6, &checkAccumulator);
      }
```
This code is used on page 376.

The extra-long packets use a length field of one to indicate the packet format. The rest of the header is identical to a long packet, except for the length of the size field.

⟨ Send extra-long packet header 379 ⟩ ==
```
      {
        BYTE header[8];

        header[0] = pK -> my . sopCharacter;
        if (header[0] == 0xff) header[0] = 0x01;
        header[1] = 1 + 32;
        header[2] = (sequence % 64) + 32;
        header[3] = type;
        header[4] = (dataLength + packetCheckLength) / 9025 + 32;
        header[5] = ((dataLength + packetCheckLength) / 95) % 95 + 32;
        header[6] = (dataLength + packetCheckLength) % 95 + 32;
        header[7] = KCheckValue(pK, '1', header + 1, 6, NULL) + 32;
        StsRet(KSendBytes(pK, header, 8));
        KCheckValue(pK, pK->packetCheck, header+1, 6, &checkAccumulator);
      }
```
This code is used on page 376.

There's an obvious additional extension for a packet with a four-character extended length field, using a length of two to indicate this packet format. Thus far, however, there's been no apparent need for packet sizes beyond the 800k supported by the extra-long packet format. In practice, packet sizes beyond 4k are rarely used, and few Kermit implementations bother to implement even extra-long packets.

Receiving Packets

Packet checks are from one to three digits in base 64. This function identifies the error check and returns its value given a pointer to the end of the data.

```
      STATIC int KFindCheckValue(KERMIT_PRIVATE *pK, BYTE *buffer, long
            *pCheckValue, char packetCheck)
      {
        BYTE *check;
        int i;
```

```
        long checkValue = 0;
        int checkLength = packetCheck - '0';

        if (packetCheck == 'B') checkLength = 2;
        check = buffer - checkLength;
        for (i = 0; i < checkLength; i++) {
          int thisValue = (check[i] & 0x7f) - 32;

          if (packetCheck == 'B') thisValue -= 1;
          if ((thisValue > 63) || (thisValue < 0)) {
            if (pK -> debug) {
              DebugBegin(pK -> debug, debugPacketErr);
              DebugString(pK -> debug,
                  "Received␣illegal␣check␣character␣");
              DebugInt(pK -> debug, check[i]);
              DebugChar(pK -> debug, check[i]);
              DebugEnd(pK -> debug);
            }
            return StsWarn(kBadPacket);
          }
          checkValue = (checkValue << 6) + thisValue;
        }
        *pCheckValue = checkValue;
        return kOK;
      }
```

Notice that all packet formats share the first four bytes of the header.

```
    STATIC int KReceivePacket(KERMIT_PRIVATE *pK, int timeout, BYTE
        *pBuffer, size_t *pDataLength, BYTE *pType, int
        *pSequence)
  {
    BYTE header[10];
    size_t headerLength = 3;
    int length, checkAccumulator = 0;
    size_t rxDataLength;
    int packetCheckLength = pK -> packetCheck - '0';

    if (pK -> packetCheck == 'B') packetCheckLength = 2;
    ⟨Receive common header 381⟩
    length = header[1] - 32;
    *pSequence = header[2] - 32;
    *pType = header[3];
    switch (length) {
    case 0:    /* Long packet */
    case 1:    /* Extra-long packet */
      ⟨Receive long packet headers 383⟩
```

```
      break;
   case 2:     /* Illegal */
      return StsWarn(kBadPacket);
   default:     /* Normal packet */
      ⟨ Receive normal packet header 383 ⟩
      break;
   }
   ⟨ Receive packet data and packet check, return if check fails 382 ⟩
   *pDataLength = rxDataLength;
   ⟨ Issue debug message about packet received 384 ⟩
   if (pK -> your . sopCharacter > 31)
      pK -> your . sopCharacter = header[0];
   if (pK -> my . sopCharacter > 31)
      pK -> my . sopCharacter = header[0];
   return kOK;
}
```

The normal header is four bytes long: the start-of-packet character, length field, sequence number, and packet type. Control information in Kermit packets always uses seven-bit values, so I'm careful to strip parity here before testing anything. (C-Kermit goes a step further. It checks the parity on these first four bytes to discover if this is actually a seven-bit connection. If parity is being used, it can proceed to negotiate an eighth-bit prefix.)

These first four bytes must satisfy certain general restrictions. The start-of-packet character is always a control character; the length field will always be between 32 and 126, inclusive; the sequence number will always be between 32 and 95, inclusive; and the packet type is always an upper case alphabetic character. The odds of four random bytes satisfying these conditions is less than two percent. It's reasonable, then, to use a shift-register approach like that used in the XYModem and ZModem source to locate the start of a packet without being specific to a particular start-of-packet character. This method removes one end-user configuration headache. A more conservative approach would only use such a general search until several packets were successfully transferred. Restricting after that point to the particular start-of-packet character actually in use would reduce the odds of a false header to less than 0.1 percent.

⟨ Receive common header 381 ⟩ ==
```
   {
   BYTE mark;
   int err;
   int i = 0;
   for (i = 0; i < 4; i ++) header[i] = 0xff;
   do {
```

```
    err = KReadByteWithTimeout(pK, timeout, &mark);
    switch (err) {
    case kOK:     /* I did get a character */
      mark &= 0x7f;
      header[0] = header[1];
      header[1] = header[2];
      header[2] = header[3];
      header[3] = mark;
      break;
    case kBadPacket:      /* Damaged character */
      header[3] = 0xff;
      break;
    default: return StsWarn(err);
    }
  } while ((header[0] > 31)
  || (header[1] < 32) || (header[1] > 126)
  || (header[2] < 32) || (header[2] > 95)
  || (header[3] < 'A') || (header[3] > 'Z') || (err != kOK));
}
```

This code is used on page 380.

Just as with KSendPacket, the actual packet data and packet check are handled the same regardless of the packet type.

⟨ Receive packet data and packet check, return if check fails 382 ⟩ ==

```
  {
    long myCheck, rxCheck;
    unsigned checkLength = pK -> packetCheck - '0';

    if (pK -> packetCheck == 'B') checkLength = 2;
    StsRet(KReadBytesWithTimeout(pK, 3, pBuffer, &rxDataLength));
    if (rxDataLength < checkLength) return StsWarn(kBadPacket);
    myCheck = KCheckValue(pK, pK -> packetCheck, pBuffer,
        rxDataLength - checkLength, &checkAccumulator);
    StsRet(KFindCheckValue(pK, pBuffer + rxDataLength, &rxCheck,
        pK -> packetCheck));
    if (myCheck != rxCheck) {
      if (pK -> debug) {
        DebugBegin(pK -> debug, debugPacketErr);
        DebugString(pK -> debug, "Wrong␣packet␣check:␣received:␣");
        DebugInt(pK -> debug, rxCheck);
        DebugString(pK -> debug, "␣computed:␣");
        DebugInt(pK -> debug, myCheck);
        DebugEnd(pK -> debug);
      }
      return StsWarn(kBadPacket);
```

```
        }
        rxDataLength −= checkLength;
    }
```

This code is used on page 380.

The normal packet header has really already been received. This scrap just interprets the header values and includes the header in the error check.

⟨ Receive normal packet header 383 ⟩ ==

```
    {
        if (length < 2) return StsWarn(kBadPacket);
        rxDataLength = length − 2;
        if (pK -> debug) {
            DebugBegin(pK -> debug, debugPacketLowLevel);
            DebugString(pK -> debug, "Receiving␣normal␣packet␣#");
            DebugInt(pK -> debug, *pSequence);
            DebugString(pK -> debug, "␣data␣length:␣");
            DebugUInt(pK -> debug, rxDataLength);
            DebugString(pK -> debug, "␣type:␣");
            DebugChar(pK -> debug, *pType);
            DebugEnd(pK -> debug);
        }
        checkAccumulator = 0;       /* Restart packet check */
        KCheckValue(pK, pK->packetCheck, header+1, 3, &checkAccumulator);
    }
```

This code is used on page 380.

Long and extra-long packets are the same except for the extended length field, which is two or three bytes. The `length` variable holds the value of the normal length field, which indicates which type of packet this is: zero if this is a long packet or one if this is an extra-long packet.

⟨ Receive long packet headers 383 ⟩ ==

```
    {
        headerLength = 3 + length;       /* Length of rest of header */
        StsRet(KReadBytesWithTimeout(pK, 3, header + 4, &headerLength));
        headerLength += 4;
        {    /* Strip parity */
          int i = 0;
          for ( ;  i < headerLength; i++) header[i] &= 0x7f;
        }
        {    /* Verify header check */
          int headerCheck = KCheckValue(pK, '1', header + 1,
              headerLength − 2, NULL);
          if (headerCheck != header[headerLength − 1] − 32) {
```

```
        if (pK -> debug) {
          DebugBegin(pK -> debug, debugPacketErr);
          DebugString(pK ->debug, "Wrong␣header␣check:␣received:␣");
          DebugInt(pK -> debug, header[headerLength − 1] − 32);
          DebugString(pK -> debug, "␣computed:␣");
          DebugInt(pK -> debug, headerCheck);
          DebugEnd(pK -> debug);
        }
        return kBadPacket;
      }
    }
    checkAccumulator = 0;      /* Restart packet check */
    KCheckValue(pK, pK -> packetCheck, header + 1, headerLength − 1,
        &checkAccumulator);
    rxDataLength = (header[4] − 32) * 95 + (header[5] − 32);
    if (length == 1)
      rxDataLength = rxDataLength * 95 + (header[6] − 32);
    if (pK -> debug) {
      DebugBegin(pK -> debug, debugPacketLowLevel);
      DebugString(pK -> debug,
          "Receiving␣extended␣packet,␣length:␣");
      DebugUInt(pK -> debug, rxDataLength);
      DebugEnd(pK -> debug);
    }
  }
```

This code is used on page 380.

⟨ Issue debug message about packet received 384 ⟩ ==
```
  if (pK -> debug) {
    DebugBegin(pK -> debug, debugPacket);
    DebugString(pK -> debug, "Rcvd␣#");
    DebugInt(pK -> debug, *pSequence);
    DebugString(pK -> debug, "␣Type:");
    DebugChar(pK -> debug, *pType);
    DebugString(pK -> debug, "␣length:");
    DebugUInt(pK -> debug, *pDataLength);
    DebugString(pK -> debug, "␣‘ ");
    if (*pDataLength < 40) {
      DebugStringCount(pK -> debug, (char *) pBuffer, *pDataLength);
      DebugString(pK -> debug, "’’");
    } else {
      DebugStringCount(pK -> debug, (char *) pBuffer, 37);
      DebugString(pK -> debug, "...");
    }
```

```
        DebugEnd(pK -> debug);
    }
```

This code is used on page 380.

Reliability Layer

Kermit's reliability scheme has the receiver sending an Acknowledge (Y) or Negative acknowledge (N) for each packet. In half-duplex (window size of one), the sender repeats each packet until it is acknowledged. In full-duplex (window size larger than one), the sender may continue sending packets until it receives an acknowledgment. Clearly, full-duplex requires that the sender and receiver cache packets. The sender must store packets until they've been acknowledged; the receiver must store packets that may have been received out of sequence until all preceding packets are also received. What may not be as obvious is that even in half-duplex, some packet caching is needed. In particular, if the receiver's acknowledgment is lost, the sender may repeat the packet, and the receiver should respond with the same acknowledgment it used before. (Remember that Kermit acknowledgements often carry data.) The receiver must store the data used in the last acknowledgment.

Window Management

The easiest way to keep track of packets sent and received is to keep an array with 64 entries, one for each possible packet sequence number. Each array entry holds the information about a packet sent and responded to.

⟨ General Kermit variables 353 ⟩ +==
```
    EXCHANGE exchange[64];
```

One obvious approach is for each exchange to contain two buffers, each big enough to hold any possible packet. Unfortunately, in addition to wasting memory, that approach would also waste considerable time, copying the data into the cache buffers. Instead, I've allocated pointers to two buffers. The cache management will be arranged so that caching a buffer of data usually requires only storing the pointer to that buffer in the appropriate slot.

Besides the actual data, I also need to know the data length, packet type, and packet check in effect when that packet was sent. It also turns out to be useful to track the "real" sequence number here.

⟨ Other definitions 385 ⟩ ==
```
    typedef struct {
        BYTE *myPacket;
        BYTE *yourPacket;
```

```
      unsigned long myPacketLength;
      size_t yourPacketLength;
      long sequence;
      char packetCheck;
      BYTE myPacketType;
      BYTE yourPacketType;
   } EXCHANGE;
```

This code is used on page 353.

⟨ Initialize Kermit variables 353 ⟩ +==
```
   {
     int i;
     pK -> exchange[0] . sequence = 0;        /* Set up slot 0 */
     pK -> exchange[0] . packetCheck = '1';
     pK -> exchange[0] . myPacket = NULL;
     pK -> exchange[0] . myPacketLength = 0;
     pK -> exchange[0] . myPacketType = 0;
     pK -> exchange[0] . yourPacket = NULL;
     pK -> exchange[0] . yourPacketLength = 0;
     pK -> exchange[0] . yourPacketType = 0;
     for (i = 1; i < 64; i++) {       /* Copy to other slots */
       pK -> exchange[i] = pK -> exchange[0];
       pK -> exchange[i] . sequence = i;
     }
   }
```

To isolate higher layers from the details of cache management, the `txPacket`
variables provide a place for new packets to be constructed, and the `rxPacket`
variables hold information about the packet just received.

⟨ General Kermit variables 353 ⟩ +==
```
   BYTE *txPacket;
   unsigned long txPacketLength;
   BYTE *rxPacket;
   unsigned long rxPacketLength;
   int rxPacketSequence;
   BYTE rxPacketType;
```

The cache buffers are set up during the Kermit negotiation phase, so the initialization becomes pretty simple.

⟨ Initialize Kermit variables 353 ⟩ +==
```
   pK -> rxPacket = NULL;
   pK -> rxPacketLength = 0;
   pK -> rxPacketType = 0;
```

```
pK -> txPacket = NULL;
pK -> txPacketLength = 0;
```

Because the window size varies during a Kermit transaction—only the data transfer can use a window size larger than one—I need separate variables for the currently active window size and the window size used for data transfer.

⟨General Kermit variables 353⟩ +≡

```
int currentWindowSize;     /* What I'm using now */
int windowSize;       /* Negotiated window size */
```

⟨Initialize Kermit variables 353⟩ +≡

```
pK -> currentWindowSize = 1;
pK -> windowSize = 1;
```

Besides the window size, I need variables to keep track of where the window is, that is, what packets are currently cached. The `minUsed` and `maxUsed` variables indicate the exchanges that have actual packets stored in them. The exchanges between `minCache` and `minUsed` hold buffers that can be reused for incoming packets.

⟨General Kermit variables 353⟩ +≡

```
int minCache;
int maxUsed;
int minUsed;
int sequence;
int retries;
```

⟨Initialize Kermit variables 353⟩ +≡

```
pK -> minCache = 0;
pK -> maxUsed = 0;
pK -> minUsed = 0;
pK -> sequence = 0;
pK -> retries = 10;
```

Now that I've shown you all of the cache variables, I'll explain them by developing the basic cache-manipulating code.

The first function is a debug function to dump the current cache status and do some sanity checking on the cache itself.

```
STATIC void KDumpCache(KERMIT_PRIVATE *pK)
{
  int i;
  char c[2];
  c[0] = 0;
```

```
c[1] = 0;
DebugBegin(pK -> debug, debugCache);
DebugString(pK -> debug, "␣␣␣minCache␣=␣");
DebugInt(pK -> debug, pK -> minCache);
DebugString(pK -> debug, "␣␣␣minUsed␣=␣");
DebugInt(pK -> debug, pK -> minUsed);
DebugString(pK -> debug, "␣␣␣sequence␣=␣");
DebugInt(pK -> debug, pK -> sequence);
DebugString(pK -> debug, "␣␣␣maxUsed␣=␣");
DebugInt(pK -> debug, pK -> maxUsed);
DebugEnd(pK -> debug);
DebugBegin(pK -> debug, debugCache);
DebugString(pK -> debug, "␣␣␣");      /* 3 spaces */
for (i = 0;  i < 64;  i++) {
  c[0] = (i % 10) + '0';
  if ((pK -> maxUsed & 63) == i) DebugString(pK -> debug, "M");
  else if ((pK -> minCache & 63) == i)
    DebugString(pK -> debug, "m");
  else if ((pK -> minUsed & 63) == i)
    DebugString(pK -> debug, "U");
  else if ((pK -> sequence & 63) == i)
    DebugString(pK -> debug, "S");
  else if ((i % 5) == 0) DebugString(pK -> debug, c);
  else DebugString(pK -> debug, ".");
}
DebugEnd(pK -> debug);
DebugBegin(pK -> debug, debugCache);
DebugString(pK -> debug, "Tx:");
for (i = 0;  i < 64;  i++) {
  c[0] = '␣';
  if (pK -> exchange[i] . myPacketType != 0) {
    c[0] = pK -> exchange[i] . myPacketType;
    if (pK -> exchange[i] . myPacket == NULL) c[0] = c[0] + 32;
  } else if (pK -> exchange[i] . myPacket) c[0] = '.';
  DebugString(pK -> debug, c);
}
DebugString(pK -> debug, ":");
DebugEnd(pK -> debug);
DebugBegin(pK -> debug, debugCache);
DebugString(pK -> debug, "Rx:");
for (i = 0;  i < 64;  i++) {
  c[0] = '␣';
  if (pK -> exchange[i] . yourPacketType != 0) {
    c[0] = pK -> exchange[i] . yourPacketType;
```

```
      if (pK -> exchange[i] . yourPacket == NULL) c[0] = c[0] + 32;
    } else if (pK -> exchange[i] . yourPacket) c[0] = '.';
    DebugString(pK -> debug, c);
  }
  DebugString(pK -> debug, ":");
  DebugEnd(pK -> debug);
  {     /* Some sanity tests */
    BYTE *pThisBuffer = pK -> rawBuffer;
    int buffersRemaining = pK -> rawBufferLength / pK ->
        rawBufferPacketSize;

    while (buffersRemaining > 0) {
      int j, count = 0;
      if (pThisBuffer == pK -> spareExchange . myPacket) count ++;
      if (pThisBuffer == pK -> spareExchange . yourPacket) count ++;
      for (j = 0; j < 64; j++) {
        if (pThisBuffer == pK -> exchange[j] . myPacket) count ++;
        if (pThisBuffer == pK -> exchange[j] . yourPacket) count ++;
      }
      if (count == 0) {
        DebugBegin(pK -> debug, debugWarn);
        DebugString(pK -> debug, "Cache buffer lost: address ");
        DebugPtr(pK -> debug, pThisBuffer);
        if (pThisBuffer == pK -> rxPacket)
          DebugString(pK -> debug, " == pK->rxPacket");
        DebugEnd(pK -> debug);
      } else if (count > 1) {
        DebugBegin(pK -> debug, debugWarn);
        DebugString(pK -> debug,
            "Cache buffer duplicated: address ");
        DebugPtr(pK -> debug, pThisBuffer);
        DebugEnd(pK -> debug);
      }
      pThisBuffer += pK -> rawBufferPacketSize;
      buffersRemaining --;
    }
  }
}
```

The easiest way to avoid copying packet data is just to move pointers. This macro provides an easy way to make sure no exchanges are lost.

```
#define SwapSlots(p1, p2)
        {
          EXCHANGE e = pK -> exchange[(p1) & 63];
```

```
    pK -> exchange[(p1) & 63] = pK -> exchange[(p2) & 63];
    pK -> exchange[(p2) & 63] = e;
}
```

At the beginning of a transfer, the sequence number is zero. Especially during server operation, the sequence number is reset to zero regularly. Because altering the sequence number affects the window, I need to reset the cache whenever I reset the sequence number. Resetting the cache means moving all of the buffers to the bottom of the cache.

```
STATIC void KResetSequence(KERMIT_PRIVATE *pK)
{
  int low = 0, high = 63;
  if (pK -> debug) {
    KDumpCache(pK);
    DebugBegin(pK -> debug, debugCache);
    DebugString(pK -> debug, "Resetting␣cache...");
    DebugEnd(pK -> debug);
  }
  while (low < high) {
    while (pK -> exchange[low] . myPacket != NULL) low++;
    while (pK -> exchange[high] . myPacket == NULL) high--;
    if (low < high) SwapSlots(low, high);
  }
  pK -> maxUsed = -1;
  pK -> minCache = 0;
  pK -> minUsed = 0;
  pK -> sequence = 0;
  KDumpCache(pK);
}
```

The packet cache buffers are actually allocated during the Kermit startup nego-tiation, by the following function. The two tricky parts are figuring out how many cache buffers to allocate, and degrading if there's not enough memory available. I'll discuss the second problem first: If there's not enough memory, file transfer is still possible, but I need to know what can be allocated to complete the startup negoti-ation. The allocation needs to be done during the negotiation, rather than waiting until the buffers are actually needed. Contrast this with ZModem, where the sender can allocate its storage whenever it likes, since the receiver does no caching and hence there's no need for the sender and receiver caches to be similarly sized.

Given a fast enough version of `malloc()`, it would be possible to allocate individual cache buffers during the transfer. Such an approach has the advantage of using less memory when the full window size is never actually used (the receiver can always acknowledge before the sender gets to the end of its window). Throughput will degrade if the receiver is unable to allocate memory when it needs to, but the transfer will still succeed. (The receiver never acknowledges a packet until it has been successfully cached. Simply receiving a packet is not sufficient if you are forced to immediately discard it because you cannot store it.) If the sender cannot allocate the full window size, it will be forced to block the window.

Because the initialization is performed twice (once before the negotiation starts and once during negotiation), I need to keep track of the blocks of memory allocated so they can be correctly freed.

⟨ General Kermit variables 353 ⟩ +==
```
BYTE *rawBuffer;
long rawBufferLength;
long rawBufferPacketSize;
```

⟨ Initialize Kermit variables 353 ⟩ +==
```
pK -> rawBufferLength = 0;
pK -> rawBuffer = NULL;
pK -> rawBufferPacketSize = 0;
```

I'll also need one extra exchange that's not part of the window. This exchange is used to hold received packets before they are placed into the window, and to hold packets that are being constructed before they are sent.

⟨ General Kermit variables 353 ⟩ +==
```
EXCHANGE spareExchange;
```

⟨ Initialize Kermit variables 353 ⟩ +==
```
pK -> spareExchange = pK -> exchange[0];
```

You can reduce your memory requirements by noticing that when long packets are selected, they will only be used for file data. The receiver's responses will always be short packets. Each exchange only needs one buffer to be larger than the 94-byte maximum for short packets. Keeping the other buffer small saves a lot of memory when large packets are selected.

```
STATIC int KInitWindow(KERMIT_PRIVATE *pK)
{
  unsigned long packetLimit;
  unsigned long packetCount = pK -> windowSize + 1;
  if (pK -> rawBuffer) {     /* If there's a previous allocation... */
    int i;
    free(pK -> rawBuffer);
    pK -> txPacket = NULL;
```

```
      pK -> rxPacket = NULL;
      pK -> spareExchange . myPacket = NULL;
      pK -> spareExchange . myPacketLength = 0;
      pK -> spareExchange . myPacketType = 0;
      pK -> spareExchange . yourPacket = NULL;
      pK -> spareExchange . yourPacketLength = 0;
      pK -> spareExchange . yourPacketType = 0;
      for (i = 0;  i < 64;  i ++)
        pK -> exchange[i] = pK -> spareExchange;
    }
    packetLimit = pK -> my . maxPacketSize;
    if (packetLimit < pK -> your . maxPacketSize)
      packetLimit = pK -> your . maxPacketSize;
    packetLimit += 100;      /* Size of both buffers */
    pK -> rawBuffer = malloc(packetLimit * packetCount);
    while (pK -> rawBuffer == NULL) {      /* Try a smaller allocation */
      if (packetLimit > 200) packetLimit = (packetLimit * 2) / 3;
      else if (packetCount > 2) packetCount --;
      else return StsWarn(kFailed);
      pK -> rawBuffer = malloc(packetLimit * packetCount);
    }
    pK -> rawBufferLength = packetLimit * packetCount;
    pK -> rawBufferPacketSize = packetLimit;
    {      /* Split rawBuffer into individual buffers */
      BYTE *pNextBuffer = pK -> rawBuffer;
      int i = 0;
      int offset = (pK -> sending ? packetLimit - 100 : 100);

      pK -> spareExchange . myPacket = pNextBuffer;
      pK -> spareExchange . yourPacket = pNextBuffer + offset;
      for (i = 0;  i < packetCount - 1;  i ++) {
        pNextBuffer += packetLimit;
        pK -> exchange[i] . myPacket = pNextBuffer;
        pK -> exchange[i] . yourPacket = pNextBuffer + offset;
        pK -> exchange[i] . sequence = i;
      }
      pK -> maxUsed = pK -> minUsed;
      pK -> txPacket = pK -> spareExchange . myPacket;
      pK -> txPacketLength = 0;
    }
    packetLimit -= 100;      /* Actual packet size limit */
    if (packetLimit < pK -> my . maxPacketSize)
      pK -> my . maxPacketSize = packetLimit;
    if (packetLimit < pK -> your . maxPacketSize)
      pK -> your . maxPacketSize = packetLimit;
```

```
    if ((pK -> sending) && (pK -> your . maxPacketSize > 95))
      pK -> your . maxPacketSize = 95;
    if (!(pK -> sending) && (pK -> my . maxPacketSize > 95))
      pK -> my . maxPacketSize = 95;
    if (packetCount <= pK -> windowSize)
      pK -> windowSize = packetCount - 1;
    if (pK -> debug) {
      DebugBegin(pK -> debug, debugCache);
      DebugString(pK -> debug, "Allocated␣");
      DebugUInt(pK -> debug, packetCount);
      DebugString(pK -> debug, "␣cache␣buffers␣of␣");
      DebugUInt(pK -> debug, packetLimit);
      DebugString(pK -> debug, "␣bytes␣each.");
      DebugEnd(pK -> debug);
      KDumpCache(pK);
    }
    return kOK;
  }
```

A packet is received directly into the cache by storing it into the buffer held by the `spareExchange`, and then moving it into the correct slot in the window.

```
    STATIC int KReceivePacketCache(KERMIT_PRIVATE *pK, int timeout)
    {
      int slot;
      int sequence;
      StsRet(KReceivePacket(pK, timeout, pK->spareExchange.yourPacket,
          &(pK -> spareExchange . yourPacketLength),
          &(pK -> spareExchange . yourPacketType), &sequence));
      slot = sequence & 63;
      ⟨ Compute actual sequence number from slot 395 ⟩
      pK -> rxPacketSequence = pK -> spareExchange . sequence = sequence;
      pK -> rxPacket = pK -> spareExchange . yourPacket;
      pK -> rxPacketLength = pK -> spareExchange . yourPacketLength;
      pK -> rxPacketType = pK -> spareExchange . yourPacketType;
      ⟨ Add new slot to window 395 ⟩
      if (pK -> exchange[slot] . yourPacket) {
        BYTE *pTmp;
        if (pK -> debug) {
          DebugBegin(pK -> debug, debugCache);
          DebugString(pK -> debug,
              "Putting␣received␣packet␣into␣slot␣");
          DebugInt(pK -> debug, slot);
          DebugEnd(pK -> debug);
        }
```

```
                pTmp = pK -> spareExchange . yourPacket;
                pK->spareExchange.yourPacket = pK->exchange[slot].yourPacket;
                pK -> exchange[slot] . yourPacket = pTmp;
                pK -> exchange[slot] . yourPacketLength =
                    pK -> spareExchange . yourPacketLength;
                pK -> exchange[slot] . yourPacketType =
                    pK -> spareExchange . yourPacketType;
                pK -> exchange[slot] . sequence = pK -> spareExchange . sequence;
                pK -> exchange[slot] . packetCheck = pK -> packetCheck;
                pK -> spareExchange . yourPacketLength = 0;
                pK -> spareExchange . yourPacketType = 0;
            } else {
                if (pK -> debug) {
                    DebugBegin(pK -> debug, debugCache | debugWarn);
                    DebugString(pK -> debug, "Received␣packet␣");
                    DebugInt(pK -> debug, pK -> spareExchange . sequence);
                    DebugChar(pK -> debug, pK -> spareExchange . yourPacketType);
                    DebugString(pK -> debug, "␣out␣of␣current␣window␣[");
                    DebugInt(pK -> debug, pK -> minUsed);
                    DebugString(pK -> debug, ",");
                    DebugInt(pK -> debug, pK -> maxUsed);
                    DebugString(pK -> debug, "]");
                    DebugEnd(pK -> debug);
                }
                if (pK -> spareExchange . sequence > pK -> minUsed) {
                    return StsWarn(kBadPacket);
                } else {      /* Problem: if before window, may need to synthesize ACK */
                    return StsWarn(kBadPacket);
                }
            }
        }
        return kOK;
    }
```

The following calculation explains why Kermit must limit the window size to 32. Each received packet carries only the six least significant bits of the packet sequence number, from which the receiver must reconstruct the full sequence number. Not all Kermit implementations do this explicitly, but the process of determining where a packet belongs in the window implicitly computes this value. Besides the lower six bits of the sequence number, the only information the receiver has is that the packet is within the window. In particular, it cannot be more than 32 behind the highest packet in the window, nor can it be more than 32 ahead of the lowest packet in the window. In particular, if this side currently has no packets in the window—for example, if this side is the receiver and there have been no errors—this range covers all 64 possible values. If Kermit allowed window sizes larger than 32, there would be situations under which the actual packet sequence number could not be unambiguously reconstructed.

⟨ Compute actual sequence number from `slot` 395 ⟩ ==

```
sequence = ((pK -> maxUsed - 32) & (~ 63)) | slot;
if (sequence < pK -> maxUsed - 32) sequence += 64;
if (sequence > pK -> minUsed + 32) return StsWarn(kBadPacket);
```

This code is used on page 393.

⟨ Add new slot to window 395 ⟩ ==

```
if ((pK->minCache < pK->minUsed) && (pK->exchange[slot].yourPacket ==
        NULL)) {
  if (pK -> debug) {
    DebugBegin(pK -> debug, debugCache);
    DebugString(pK -> debug, "Adding␣new␣slot␣to␣window");
    DebugEnd(pK -> debug);
  }
  SwapSlots(pK -> minCache, slot);
  pK -> minCache ++;
  if (pK -> spareExchange . sequence > pK -> maxUsed)
    pK -> maxUsed = pK -> spareExchange . sequence;
}
```

This code is used on page 393.

Sending a packet from the cache is pretty simple. The real reason why this function exists (instead of simply calling `KSendPacket` explicitly) is to provide a convenient place to issue debug messages as packets are sent.

```
STATIC int KSendPacketFromCache(KERMIT_PRIVATE *pK, int slot)
{
  slot &= 63;
  if ((pK -> exchange[slot] . myPacketType ==
        0) || (pK -> exchange[slot] . myPacket == NULL))
    {
    if (pK -> debug) {
      DebugBegin(pK -> debug, debugWarn | debugCache);
      DebugString(pK -> debug,
          "Can't␣send␣packet␣from␣cache␣slot␣");
      DebugInt(pK -> debug, slot);
      DebugEnd(pK -> debug);
    }
    return kOK;
  }
  if (pK -> debug) {
```

```
        DebugBegin(pK -> debug, debugCache);
        DebugString(pK -> debug, "Sending␣packet␣from␣cache␣slot␣");
        DebugInt(pK -> debug, slot);
        DebugEnd(pK -> debug);
    }
    return StsWarn(KSendPacket(pK, slot,
        pK -> exchange[slot] . myPacketType,
        pK -> exchange[slot] . myPacket,
        pK -> exchange[slot] . myPacketLength));
}
```

Sending Data Reliably

Kermit uses the same half-duplex reliability scheme everywhere[3] except during actual data transfer. The scheme is: The sender sends a packet, and the receiver responds with an Acknowledge (Y) if it was received and a Negative acknowledge (N) otherwise.

The complicating factor here is the support for full-duplex operation. When the window size is greater than one, this function will check for a returned packet, but won't block unless the window is full.

```
        STATIC int KSendPacketReliable(KERMIT_PRIVATE *pK, BYTE
                type, const BYTE *pSendData, unsigned long
                sendDataLength)
    {
      int retries = pK -> retries;
      int blocked = FALSE;      /* Is window blocked? */
      int err;
      int slot = pK -> sequence & 63;
      EXCHANGE *pThisExchange = &(pK -> exchange[slot]);
      ⟨ Add new slot to send window 398 ⟩
      if (pSendData == pK -> spareExchange . myPacket) {
        BYTE *pTmp = pThisExchange -> myPacket;

        pThisExchange -> myPacket = pK -> spareExchange . myPacket;
        pK -> spareExchange . myPacket = pTmp;
      } else {
        memcpy(pThisExchange -> myPacket, pSendData, sendDataLength);
      }
      if (pK -> sequence > pK -> maxUsed) pK -> maxUsed = pK -> sequence;
      pThisExchange -> sequence = pK -> sequence;
      pThisExchange -> myPacketLength = sendDataLength;
```

---

[3] Well, almost everywhere. The one exception is the Receive-Init (R) packet used to request the server to send a file. The response to that packet is the Send-Init (S) of the actual file transfer, not an acknowledge.

```
pThisExchange -> myPacketType = type;
pK -> txPacket = pK -> spareExchange . myPacket;
pK -> txPacketLength = 0;
StsRet(KSendPacketFromCache(pK, slot));
KDumpCache(pK);
if (pK -> minUsed <= pK -> minCache) blocked = 1;
if (pK -> maxUsed - pK -> minUsed + 1 >= pK -> currentWindowSize)
  blocked = (pK -> maxUsed - pK -> minUsed + 1) - pK ->
      currentWindowSize + 1;
if (pK -> debug) {
  if (blocked) {
    DebugBegin(pK -> debug, debugCache);
    DebugString(pK -> debug, "Window␣is␣blocked:␣");
    DebugInt(pK -> debug, blocked);
    DebugEnd(pK -> debug);
  }
}
do {
  err = KReceivePacketCache(pK, blocked ? pK -> my . timeout : 0);
  switch (err) {
  case kOK:     /* Received a response */
    ⟨Handle response to packet 399⟩
    KDumpCache(pK);
    break;
  case kBadPacket:      /* Messed-up packet */
  case kTimeout:      /* no response read */
    StsRet(KSendPacketFromCache(pK, pK -> minUsed));
        /* Send oldest packet in window */
    retries --;
    break;
  default: return StsWarn(err);
  }
  if (retries <= 0) {
    if (pK -> debug) {
      DebugBegin(pK -> debug, debugWarn);
      DebugString(pK -> debug, "Too␣many␣retries");
      DebugEnd(pK -> debug);
    }
    return StsWarn(kFail);
  }
} while (blocked || (err == kOK));
if (pK -> exchange[pK -> sequence & 63] . yourPacketType && (pK ->
      exchange[pK -> sequence & 63] . sequence == pK -> sequence)) {
    /* If pK -> sequence rec'd, put into rxPacket vars */
```

```
        pK -> rxPacket = pK -> exchange [pK -> sequence & 63] . yourPacket;
        pK -> rxPacketType = pK -> exchange [pK -> sequence & 63] .
            yourPacketType;
        pK -> rxPacketLength = pK -> exchange [pK -> sequence & 63] .
            yourPacketLength;
    }
    pK -> sequence ++;
    if (err == kTimeout) return kOK;
    if (err == kBadPacket) return kOK;
    return StsWarn(err);
}
```

This scrap moves the window forward by swapping a slot at the front of the window which doesn't contain a buffer for one at the back of the window.

```
⟨ Add new slot to send window 398 ⟩ ==
    if (pThisExchange -> myPacket == NULL) {
        if (pK -> minCache < pK -> minUsed) {
            if (pK -> debug) {
                DebugBegin(pK -> debug, debugCache);
                DebugString(pK -> debug,
                    "Adding␣new␣slot␣to␣window␣for␣packet␣to␣send");
                DebugEnd(pK -> debug);
            }
            SwapSlots(pK -> minCache, slot);
            pK -> minCache ++;
            pThisExchange -> yourPacketType = 0;
        } else {
            if (pK -> debug) {
                DebugBegin(pK -> debug, debugWarn | debugCache);
                DebugString(pK -> debug, "Fatal␣Internal␣Erro\
                    r:␣window␣blocked␣before␣packet␣sent");
                DebugEnd(pK -> debug);
                KDumpCache(pK);
            }
            return StsWarn(kFail);
        }
    }
```

This code is used on page 396.

There are only three valid responses to a packet. An Acknowledge (Y) means a packet was received correctly. A Negative acknowledge (N) indicates a packet that wasn't received correctly. The last possibility is an Error (E) packet, which cancels the entire transfer.

Note that the receiver will always request the first packet it has not already received, so a Negative Acknowledge (N) implies an Acknowledgment (Y) for the preceding packet. If the negative acknowledge is for a packet within the window, the indicated packet is resent. (Note that you might get a request for the first packet beyond the window.)

Anytime a packet is acknowledged (which includes one implicitly acknowledged by a negative acknowledge), the window must be adjusted. If a packet from the start of the window was acknowledged, the window has been reduced, and you may be able to `return`.

```
⟨ Handle response to packet 399 ⟩ ==
  switch (pK -> rxPacketType) {
  case 'N':      /* Negative acknowledge */
    retries --;
    pK -> exchange[(pK -> rxPacketSequence − 1) & 63] . yourPacketType =
        'Y';
    if (pK -> exchange[pK -> rxPacketSequence & 63] . myPacketType != 0)
        /* Look up and re-send cached packet */
      StsRet(KSendPacketFromCache(pK, pK -> rxPacketSequence));
  case 'Y':      /* Acknowledgment */
    while ((pK -> exchange[pK -> minUsed & 63] . yourPacketType == 'Y') &&
        (pK -> exchange[pK -> minUsed & 63] . sequence == pK -> minUsed))
    {
      pK -> minUsed ++;
      if (blocked > 0) {
        blocked --;
        if (pK -> debug) {
          DebugBegin(pK -> debug, debugCache);
          DebugString(pK -> debug, "Window␣is␣blocked:␣");
          DebugInt(pK -> debug, blocked);
          DebugEnd(pK -> debug);
        }
      }
    }
    break;
  case 'E':      /* Error packet */
    ⟨ Debug message about error packet 400 ⟩
    return StsWarn(kFailed);
  default:       /* Unknown packet type */
    return StsWarn(kFail);
  }
```

This code is used on page 396.

The data portion of an error packet contains a text string. For many implementations, this text string will be echoed to the user. I've chosen here to dump it to the debug log instead.

⟨ Debug message about error packet 400 ⟩ ==
```
if (pK -> debug) {
  DebugBegin(pK -> debug, debugWarn);
  DebugString(pK -> debug, "Transfer␣terminated␣by␣remote:␣'‘");
  DebugStringCount(pK -> debug, (const char *) pK -> rxPacket,
      pK -> rxPacketLength);
  DebugString(pK -> debug, "'’");
  DebugEnd(pK -> debug);
}
```

This code is used on pages 399 and 400.

Receiving Data Reliably

Reading a packet reliably involves receiving a packet and responding with a Negative Acknowledge (N) if there is an error. This function cannot acknowledge a successfully received packet, because the acknowledgment frequently carries data that depends on the packet received, so a higher layer has to interpret the packet before it can be acknowledged.

```
STATIC int KReceivePacketReliable(KERMIT_PRIVATE *pK)
{
  int retries = pK -> retries;
  int err;
  int thisSlot = pK -> sequence & 63;
  int timeout = (pK -> my . timeout >= 0) ? pK -> my . timeout : 10;
  ⟨ If already received packet, return it immediately 401 ⟩
  while (TRUE) {
    err = KReceivePacketCache(pK, timeout);
    switch (err) {
    case kTimeout:     /* no packet */
      if (pK -> my . timeout < 0)      /* Server wait, don't NAK!! */
        break;
    case kBadPacket:     /* Damaged packet */
      StsRet(KSendPacket(pK, pK -> sequence, 'N', NULL, 0));
      break;
    case kOK:     /* Did read something */
      if (pK -> rxPacketType == 'E') {
        ⟨ Debug message about error packet 400 ⟩
        return StsWarn(kFailed);
      }
      if ((pK -> rxPacketSequence & 63) == (pK -> sequence & 63)) {
```

```
        return kOK;
      } else {      /* Get response from cache */
        int slot = pK -> rxPacketSequence & 63;

        if (pK -> exchange[slot] . myPacketType == 0) {
          pK -> exchange[slot] . myPacketType = 'Y';
          pK -> exchange[slot] . myPacketLength = 0;
          pK -> exchange[slot] . myPacket = NULL;
          if (pK -> debug) {
            DebugBegin(pK -> debug, debugCache);
            DebugString(pK -> debug,
                "Synthesizing␣ACK␣for␣packet␣#");
            DebugInt(pK -> debug, pK -> exchange[slot] . sequence);
            DebugEnd(pK -> debug);
          }
        }
        KSendPacketFromCache(pK, slot);
      }
      break;
    default: return StsWarn(err);
    }
    if (retries -- <= 0) return StsWarn(kFail);
  }
}
```

The first thing KReceivePacketReliable does is to check to see if the requested packet is already in the cache. If it is, then there's no need to wait to receive a packet.

⟨ If already received packet, return it immediately 401 ⟩ ==
```
  if ((pK -> exchange[thisSlot] . yourPacketType !=
          0) && (pK -> exchange[thisSlot] . sequence = pK -> sequence)) {
    pK -> rxPacket = pK -> exchange[thisSlot] . yourPacket;
    pK -> rxPacketLength = pK -> exchange[thisSlot] . yourPacketLength;
    pK -> rxPacketType = pK -> exchange[thisSlot] . yourPacketType;
    pK -> rxPacketSequence = pK -> exchange[thisSlot] . sequence;
    return kOK;
  }
```
This code is used on page 400.

A packet isn't reliably received until you've responded to it. Rather than call KSendPacket directly, higher layers use this function, which caches the sent packet and handles window management bookkeeping. Note that the window management here is much simpler than in KSendPacketReliable, because KReceivePacketReliable has already set up the current exchange.

```
STATIC int KSendResponse(KERMIT_PRIVATE *pK,BYTE type,const
        BYTE *pResponse,unsigned long responseLength)
{
  int slot = pK -> sequence & 63;
  EXCHANGE *pThisExchange = &(pK -> exchange[slot]);
  if (pResponse == pK -> spareExchange . myPacket) {
    BYTE *pTmp = pThisExchange -> myPacket;
    pThisExchange -> myPacket = pK -> spareExchange . myPacket;
    pK -> spareExchange . myPacket = pTmp;
  } else
    memcpy(pThisExchange -> myPacket, pResponse, responseLength);
  pThisExchange -> myPacketLength = responseLength;
  pThisExchange -> myPacketType = type;
  StsRet(KSendPacketFromCache(pK, slot));
  pK -> sequence ++;
  pK -> minUsed = pK -> sequence;
  pK -> txPacket = pK -> spareExchange . myPacket;
  return kOK;
}
```

Transaction Layer

Kermit transactions are pretty much stand-alone. In particular, a single Kermit transaction can transfer any number of files in one direction.

Sending One File

Sending a file begins with the sender's File-Header (F) packet with the sending filename. After this packet is acknowledged, the sender sends the file attributes in Attribute (A) packets, the file contents in Data (D) packets, and finally concludes with an End-Of-File (Z) packet. The KSendFile function assumes that the file has already been opened.

Notice that windowing only has a minor impact at this level. The only concession is to set currentWindowSize to the negotiated value prior to sending the file data and resetting it to one at the end of the file.

```
STATIC int KSendFile(KERMIT_PRIVATE *pK)
{
  int err = kOK;
  {   /* Send 'F' packet */
    const char *fileName;
    DiskFileName(pK -> f, &fileName);
```

```
      pK -> filePosition = 0;
      KProgress(pK, stsNewFile);
      StsRet(KSendPacketReliable(pK, 'F', (const BYTE *)
          fileName, strlen(fileName)));
   }
   ⟨ Send file attributes 403 ⟩
   pK -> currentWindowSize = pK -> windowSize;
   do {      /* Send file data */
     unsigned long dataLength = pK -> my . maxPacketSize;
     unsigned long rawLength;
     BYTE *txBuffer = pK -> txPacket;

     err = KFileReadEncode(pK, txBuffer, &dataLength, &rawLength);
     if (err == kOK) {
       StsRet(KSendPacketReliable(pK, 'D', txBuffer, dataLength));
       pK -> filePosition += rawLength;
       KProgress(pK, stsSending);
       if (pK -> rxPacketLength > 0) {
         if (pK -> rxPacket[0] == 'X') {
           pK -> currentWindowSize = 1;
           err = KSendPacketReliable(pK, 'Z', (const BYTE *)
               "D", 1);
           KProgress(pK, stsSkipped);
           return kOK;
         } else if (pK -> rxPacket[0] == 'Z') err = kFail;
       }
     }
   } while (err == kOK);
   pK -> currentWindowSize = 1;
   if (err == kEOF) {
     err = KSendPacketReliable(pK, 'Z', NULL, 0);
     KProgress(pK, stsEOF);
   } else {      /* Discard this file */
     err = KSendPacketReliable(pK, 'Z', (const BYTE *) "D", 1);
   }
   return StsWarn(err);
}
```

This needs to be implemented ...

```
⟨ Send file attributes 403 ⟩ ==
   if (pK -> your . capabilities[0] & 8) {      /* Send file attributes */
   }
```

This code is used on page 402.

Sending Multiple Files

Sending multiple files just requires opening each file and calling KSendFile. I'll discuss the initial negotiation in the next section.

```
STATIC int KSendInitiate(KERMIT_PRIVATE *);
STATIC int KSendFiles(KERMIT_PRIVATE *pK)
{
  int err;
  KResetSequence(pK);
  err = StsWarn(KSendInitiate(pK));
  while (err == kOK) {
    ⟨Per-file Initialization 365⟩
    err = KFileReadOpenNext(pK, diskFileUnknown);
    if (err == kOK) {
      err = KSendFile(pK);
      KFileReadClose(pK);
    }
  }
  if (err == kEndOfSession) {
    err = KSendPacketReliable(pK, 'B', NULL, 0);
  }
  if (err == kOK) KProgress(pK, stsDone);
  else if (pK -> userCancel) KProgress(pK, stsCancelled);
  else KProgress(pK, stsFailed);
  return StsWarn(err);
}
```

Receiving One File

Receiving a file involves only three packet types: file attribute packets, data packets, and end-of-file packets. Because of the caching that's handled at the reliability layer, this is pretty straightforward.

```
STATIC int KReceiveFileData(KERMIT_PRIVATE *pK)
{
  pK -> filePosition = 0;
  pK -> fileSize = -1;
  while (TRUE) {
    StsRet(KReceivePacketReliable(pK));
    switch (pK -> rxPacketType) {
    case 'A':     /* File attribute packet */
      ⟨Dump attribute packet contents 406⟩
      ⟨Process attribute packet contents 405⟩
      StsRet(KSendResponse(pK, 'Y', NULL, 0));
```

```
      break;
   case 'D':     /* File data packet */
      StsRet(KFileWriteDecode(pK, pK -> rxPacket,
          pK -> rxPacketLength));
      KProgress(pK, stsReceiving);
      if (pK -> userCancel)
         StsRet(KSendResponse(pK, 'Y', (const BYTE *) "Z", 1));
      else StsRet(KSendResponse(pK, 'Y', NULL, 0));
      break;
   case 'Z':     /* End-of-File packet */
      if ((pK -> rxPacketLength > 0) && (pK -> rxPacket[0] == 'D')) {
         KProgress(pK, stsSkipped);     /* Discard file */
      } else {
         KProgress(pK, stsEOF);
      }
      StsRet(KSendResponse(pK, 'Y', NULL, 0));
      return kOK;
      break;
   }
   }
   return kOK;
}
```

The only odd point in processing the file attributes is that since there are two different attributes for the file size, a temporary variable is needed to hold the file size so far. The two file size attributes are handled slightly differently, so the 1 attribute will be preferred in case both appear in the attribute string.

⟨ Process attribute packet contents 405 ⟩ ≡
```
   {
      const BYTE *p = pK -> rxPacket;
      BYTE attribute;
      int length = pK -> rxPacketLength;
      int attrLength;
      long fileSize = -1;
      const char *attrValue;
      while (length > 0) {
         attribute = *p++;
         length--;
         attrLength = *p++ -32;
         length--;
         attrValue = (const char *) p;
         p += attrLength;
         length -= attrLength;
         DebugBegin(pK -> debug, debugAttr);
```

```
switch (attribute) {
case '!':     /* File size in K */
  {
    long num = 0;
    int i = 0;

    for ( ;  i < attrLength;  i ++)
       num = num * 10 + attrValue[i] − '0';
    if (fileSize == −1) fileSize = num;
  }
  break;
case '1':     /* Exact file size */
  {
    long num = 0;
    int i = 0;

    for ( ;  i < attrLength;  i ++)
       num = num * 10 + attrValue[i] − '0';
    fileSize = num;
  }
  break;
default:     /* Ignore other attributes */
  break;
  }
}
pK -> fileSize = fileSize;
}
```

This code is used on page 404.

The primary reason for doing such a careful dump of the Attribute (A) packet contents is simply to document the most common attributes. Most of these will be ignored on most systems.

```
⟨ Dump attribute packet contents  406 ⟩ ==
  if (pK -> debug) {
    const BYTE *p = pK -> rxPacket;
    BYTE attribute;
    int length = pK -> rxPacketLength;
    unsigned int attrLength;
    const char *attrValue;

    while (length > 0) {
      attribute = *p ++;
      length --;
      attrLength = *p ++ −32;
      length --;
      attrValue = (const char *) p;
```

```
        p += attrLength;
        length -= attrLength;
        DebugBegin(pK -> debug, debugAttr);
        DebugString(pK -> debug, "Attribute:␣");
        switch (attribute) {
        case '!': DebugString(pK -> debug, "Length␣in␣K:"); break;
        case '"': DebugString(pK -> debug, "Type:"); break;
        case '#': DebugString(pK -> debug, "Creation␣date:"); break;
        case '$': DebugString(pK -> debug, "Creator:"); break;
        case '%': DebugString(pK -> debug, "Account␣to␣charge:");
          break;
        case '&': DebugString(pK -> debug, "Area␣to␣store␣file:");
          break;
        case '\'':
          DebugString(pK -> debug, "Password␣for␣file␣storage␣area:");
          break;
        case '(': DebugString(pK -> debug, "Block␣size:"); break;
        case ')': DebugString(pK -> debug, "Access:"); break;
        case '*': DebugString(pK -> debug, "Encoding:"); break;
        case '+': DebugString(pK -> debug, "Disposition:"); break;
        case ',': DebugString(pK -> debug, "Protection␣Code:");
          break;
        case '-':
          DebugString(pK -> debug, "Generic␣Protection␣Code:"); break;
        case '.': DebugString(pK -> debug, "Originating␣system:␣");
          ⟨Decode originating system in attrValue 408⟩
          break;
        case '/': DebugString(pK -> debug, "Data␣format:"); break;
        case '0':
          DebugString(pK -> debug, "System-specific␣parameters:");
          break;
        case '1': DebugString(pK -> debug, "Length␣in␣bytes:");
          break;
        default: DebugString(pK -> debug, "Attribute␣");
          DebugChar(pK -> debug, attribute);
          break;
        }
        if (attrValue)
          DebugStringCount(pK -> debug, attrValue, attrLength);
        DebugEnd(pK -> debug);
      }
    }
```

This code is used on page 404.

The first character of the system code indicates the vendor; the second identifies a specific type of machine. The system code simplifies transfers between like systems by allowing them to skip certain translations, and transfer special attributes that other systems may not be able to handle.

The table here uses a zero value as a wildcard. The search simply finds the first system that matches; hence a wildcard should follow any more specific system identifiers. If nothing else matches, the final entry contains two wildcards. I've omitted most of this table in the interest of space. The full table can be found on page 136.

```
⟨ Decode originating system in attrValue 408 ⟩ ==
   {
     static struct {
       char vendor;
       char system;
       const char *name;
     } systems[] = {
     {'A',0,"Apple␣computer"},
     {'B',0,"Sperry/Univac␣mainframe"},
     {'C',0,"CDC␣mainframe"},
     {'D',0,"DEC␣system"},
     {'E',0,"Honeywell␣mainframe"},
     {'F',0,"Data␣General"},
     {'G',0,"PR1ME"},
     {'H',0,"Hewlett-Packard"},
     {'I',0,"IBM␣mainframe"},
     {'J',0,"Tandy␣microcomputer,␣TRSDOS"},
     {'K',0,"Atari␣microcomputer"},
     {'L',0,"Commodore"},
     {'M',0,"Miscellaneous␣mainframe"},
     {'N',0,"Microcomputer␣or␣workstation"},
     {'U','1',"Unix"},
     {'U','8',"MS-DOS"},
     {'U',0,"Portable␣O/S"},
     {0,0,"Unrecognized␣system"}    /* Must be last */
     };
     int i = 0;
     while (TRUE) {
       if (systems[i].vendor == 0) break;
       if (systems[i].vendor == attrValue[0]) {
         if (systems[i].system == 0) break;
         if ((systems[i].system == attrValue[1]) && (attrLength > 1))
           break;
       }
```

```
      i ++;
    }
    DebugString(pK -> debug, systems[i] . name);
    DebugString(pK -> debug, ":␣code␣");
  }
```

This code is used on page 406.

Receiving Multiple Files

The KReceiveFiles function handles the entire transaction to receive multiple files, except for the initial negotiation, which I'll discuss later.

```
STATIC int KReceiveFiles(KERMIT_PRIVATE *pK)
{
  KProgress(pK, stsNegotiating);
  while (TRUE) {      /* Should muck timeout */
    StsRet(KReceivePacketReliable(pK));
    switch (pK -> rxPacketType) {
    case 'F':      /* File header packet */
      pK -> rxPacket[pK -> rxPacketLength] = 0;
          /* NULL-terminate filename */
      StsRet(KFileWriteOpen(pK, (const char *) pK -> rxPacket, 0,
          diskFileUnknown));
      KProgress(pK, stsNewFile);
      ⟨ Per-file Initialization 365 ⟩
      StsRet(KSendResponse(pK, 'Y', NULL, 0));
      StsRet(KReceiveFileData(pK));
      StsRet(KFileWriteClose(pK));
      break;
    case 'B':      /* End-of-transmission packet */
      StsRet(KSendResponse(pK, 'Y', NULL, 0));
      KProgress(pK, stsDone);
      return kOK;
      break;
    }
  }
}
```

Session Layer

In Kermit, there's very little difference between a "session" and a "transaction." In order to keep to the outline I'm using for all protocols, I'm going to discuss initiation as a session-layer issue, even though it was originally defined as a transaction-layer issue in Frank da Cruz's book [4]. The only proper "session" that differs from a Kermit transaction is the "host mode," in which one end simply sits and receives multiple transactions (possibly from multiple clients!).

Session Initiation

After windowing, Kermit negotiation is the most involved part of a Kermit implementation. During the negotiation, the two sides must establish a large number of parameters. While no one parameter has a particularly complex negotiation, the number of different parameters can be a bit overwhelming at first.

The parameters string consists of three distinct sections. The first section is a collection of single-byte fields in specific locations. The second section is a variable-length capabilities bitmap. The third section consists of additional fields in specific locations. Because of the variable length of the capabilities bitmap, it's necessary to carefully locate the beginning of the third section before parsing the fields, and also necessary to assemble the string carefully.

The capabilities bitmap consists of six bits in each byte. Bit zero (the least-significant bit) is set in all bytes except the last one. As this is written (in early 1995), there are only five bits defined, so the capabilities bitmap contains only a single byte. But Kermit is an evolving protocol, and this bitmap will continue to be extended in the future.

⟨ Kermit receive and send variables 365 ⟩ +≡
```
BYTE capabilities[5];      /* Decoded capabilities bitmap */
```

The Kermit initialization string can be truncated, and all missing fields will assume reasonable defaults. The default capabilities bitmap is to have all bits clear, that is, no special capabilities enabled.

⟨ Initialize Kermit variables 353 ⟩ +≡
```
{
  int i;
  for (i = 0; i < 5; i ++) {
    pK -> your . capabilities[i] = 0;
    pK -> my . capabilities[i] = 0;
  }
}
```

To explain the initialization string and negotiation process, I'll start with a function to dump an initialization string to the debug path. I'll expand the scrap ⟨ Dump initialization string 413 ⟩ as I discuss each field in the string.
```
STATIC void KDumpInitString(KERMIT_PRIVATE *pK, BYTE
        *initString, unsigned initLength)
```

```
    {
      BYTE *pExtended = NULL;
      int extendedLength = 0;
      BYTE capabilities[5] = {0,0,0,0,0};
      ⟨Dump initialization string 413⟩
    }
```

The next two functions handle most of the negotiation chores. The first, KParseYourInit, parses a received initialization string, updating the values in pK -> your. The function KBuildMyInit creates an initialization string based on the current values in pK -> my. The order in which these two functions are called depends on whether this end is sending or receiving. Regardless of the order, however, KParseYourInit handles most of the negotiation chores. (If it's called first, it handles the negotiation by comparing the default values with the received values.)

```
    STATIC void KParseYourInit(KERMIT_PRIVATE *pK,BYTE
          *yourInit,unsigned yourInitLength)
    {
      BYTE *pYourExtended;
      int yourExtendedLength;
      long maxPacketSize;
      ⟨Parse your initialization string 413⟩
    }

    STATIC void KBuildMyInit(KERMIT_PRIVATE *pK,BYTE
          *myInit,unsigned *pMyInitLength)
    {
      BYTE *pMyExtended;
      int myInitLength = 0;
      ⟨Build my initialization string 413⟩
      *pMyInitLength = myInitLength;
    }
```

The outline for the send side negotiation is not too difficult. The only subtle point is that I've chosen to build the window at the end, after the negotiation is finished. The reason this simplification is acceptable is that the negotiation only establishes upper bounds on the window and packet sizes. If the sender uses a smaller window or packet size, nothing is compromised.

```
    STATIC int KSendInitiate(KERMIT_PRIVATE *pK)
    {
      BYTE *myInit = pK -> txPacket;
      unsigned myInitLength;
```

```
      KBuildMyInit(pK,myInit,&myInitLength);
      if (pK -> debug) KDumpInitString(pK,myInit,myInitLength);
      StsRet(KSendPacketReliable(pK, 'S',myInit,myInitLength));
      if (pK -> debug)
         KDumpInitString(pK,pK -> rxPacket,pK -> rxPacketLength);
      KParseYourInit(pK,pK -> rxPacket,pK -> rxPacketLength);
      StsRet(KInitWindow(pK));
      if (pK -> my . preferredPacketCheck ==
            pK -> your . preferredPacketCheck)
        pK -> packetCheck = pK -> my . preferredPacketCheck;
      else pK -> packetCheck = '1';
      pK -> lockingShift = pK -> your . capabilities[0] & pK -> my .
         capabilities[0] & 32;
      KInitEncoding(pK);
      return kOK;
    }
```

The receiver negotiation is similar, except that a couple of settings need to be adjusted before the response can be built.

```
      STATIC int KReceiveNegotiate(KERMIT_PRIVATE *pK, BYTE
            *yourInit, unsigned yourInitLength)
    {
      BYTE myInit[100];
      unsigned myInitLength;

      if (pK -> debug) KDumpInitString(pK,yourInit,yourInitLength);
      KParseYourInit(pK,yourInit,yourInitLength);
      StsRet(KInitWindow(pK));
      ⟨Adjust settings before responding 415⟩
      KBuildMyInit(pK,myInit,&myInitLength);
      if (pK -> debug) KDumpInitString(pK,myInit,myInitLength);
      StsRet(KSendResponse(pK, 'Y',myInit,myInitLength));
      pK -> packetCheck = pK -> my . preferredPacketCheck;
      pK -> lockingShift = pK -> your . capabilities[0] & pK -> my .
         capabilities[0] & 32;
      KInitEncoding(pK);
      return kOK;
    }
```

Negotiating Parameters

The following sections describe each field in the Kermit initialization string and show how that field is parsed, constructed, and negotiated.

Maximum Packet Length

The first byte is the old maximum packet length. Originally, Kermit only supported the "normal" packet format, and this field was used to indicate the maximum length. In more modern implementations, there are extended fields that allow larger packet sizes to be specified. It's still important, however, to set and interpret this field, because old or simple Kermit implementations do not use the extended initialization fields.

```
⟨ Dump initialization string 413 ⟩ ≡
  if (initLength > 0) {
    DebugBegin(pK -> debug, debugInit);
    DebugString(pK -> debug, "␣␣␣1:");
    DebugChar(pK -> debug, initString[0]);
    DebugString(pK -> debug, "␣Max␣Packet␣Length␣=");
    DebugInt(pK -> debug, initString[0] − 32);
    DebugEnd(pK -> debug);
  }
```
See also pages 414, 415, 416, 416, 417, 418, 419, 420, 422, and 423.
This code is used on page 410.

This is the largest packet size I want you to send. Note that this field can never be larger than 94, even if long or extra-long packets are going to be used. If the other end doesn't understand long or extra-long packets, it will use this value instead.

```
⟨ Build my initialization string 413 ⟩ ≡
  myInit[0] = ((pK -> your . maxPacketSize > 94) ? 94 :
      pK -> your . maxPacketSize) + 32;
```
See also pages 414, 415, 416, 417, 417, 418, 419, and 421.
This code is used on page 411.

The `maxPacketSize` variable refers to the maximum amount of *data* in a packet, while the negotiated value refers to the maximum value of the length field in a packet. The length field in a normal packet includes the sequence and type bytes and a one- to three-byte packet check. Thus, I've chosen to reduce the negotiated value by five to obtain a limit on the data size. I also enforce an arbitrary lower limit of twenty bytes on the packet size. Note that because Kermit doesn't allow breaking prefix-encoded sequences across packets, a packet size less than five will create problems.

```
⟨ Parse your initialization string 413 ⟩ ≡
  maxPacketSize = 89;
  if (yourInitLength > 0) {
    maxPacketSize = yourInit[0] − 32 − 5;
```

```
        if (maxPacketSize < 20) maxPacketSize = 20;
    }
```

See also pages 414, 415, 416, 417, 418, 418, 419, 421, 422, 423, and 424.

This code is used on page 411.

Timeout

The second field is the timeout to be used. For XModem, YModem, and ZModem, there is a convention that the receiver uses a timeout, but the sender either does not time out at all, or uses a very long timeout. Kermit tries not to assume that the receiver can time out, so it may be necessary for the sender to time out. Traditionally, Kermit uses very small timeouts; C-Kermit defaults to five seconds for the receiver and ten seconds for the sender. While adequate for local connections, longer timeouts are needed for use over packet-switched networks. It's also important to make sure that the timeouts are sufficiently different that the two ends will not time out simultaneously.

```
⟨ Dump initialization string 413 ⟩ +≡
    if (initLength > 1) {
      DebugBegin(pK -> debug, debugInit);
      DebugString(pK -> debug, "␣␣␣2:");
      DebugChar(pK -> debug, initString[1]);
      DebugString(pK -> debug, "␣Timeout␣=");
      DebugInt(pK -> debug, initString[1] − 32);
      DebugEnd(pK -> debug);
    }
```

The value I send is the value I want you to use.

```
⟨ Build my initialization string 413 ⟩ +≡
    myInit[1] = pK -> your . timeout + 32;
```

Similarly, the value you send is the value you want me to use.

```
⟨ Parse your initialization string 413 ⟩ +≡
    if (yourInitLength > 1) pK -> my . timeout = yourInit[1] − 32;
    else pK -> my . timeout = 10;
```

To keep the two sides from timing out simultaneously, I request the other side use a timeout which is both:

- at least five seconds longer than the timeout it asked me to use, and

- at least twice the timeout it asked me to use.

⟨ Adjust settings before responding 415 ⟩ ≡
```
    if (pK -> your . timeout < pK -> my . timeout + 5)
      pK -> your . timeout = pK -> my . timeout + 5;
    if (pK -> your . timeout < 2 * pK -> my . timeout)
      pK -> your . timeout = 2 * pK -> my . timeout;
```
See also pages 419, 420, and 422.

This code is used on page 412.

Pad Character

Kermit allows the specification of a certain number of pad characters prior to each packet sent. This padding compensates for two common channel problems. The first is that some mainframes require a delay before they can accept the next line of data. Padding with NULL characters gives these systems a chance to recover between packets. The second is that some channels, especially some error-correcting modems, consistently drop bytes when the direction of data flow reverses. Again, padding prior to each packet allows for such loss.

⟨ Dump initialization string 413 ⟩ +≡
```
    if (initLength > 2) {
      DebugBegin(pK -> debug, debugInit);
      DebugString(pK -> debug, "␣␣␣3:");
      DebugChar(pK -> debug, initString[2]);
      DebugString(pK -> debug, "␣Number␣Pad␣Characters␣=");
      DebugInt(pK -> debug, initString[2] - 32);
      DebugEnd(pK -> debug);
    }
    if (initLength > 3) {
      DebugBegin(pK -> debug, debugInit);
      DebugString(pK -> debug, "␣␣␣4:");
      DebugChar(pK -> debug, initString[3]);
      DebugString(pK -> debug, "␣Pad␣Character␣=");
      DebugInt(pK -> debug, initString[3] ^ 0x40);
      DebugChar(pK -> debug, initString[3] ^ 0x40);
      DebugEnd(pK -> debug);
    }
```

I tell you what padding I want you to send me.

⟨ Build my initialization string 413 ⟩ +≡
```
    myInit[2] = pK -> your . padCount + 32;
    myInit[3] = pK -> your . padByte ^ 0x40;
```

You tell me the padding you want me to send you.

⟨ Parse your initialization string 413 ⟩ +≡

```
if (yourInitLength > 2) pK -> my . padCount = yourInit[2] − 32;
else pK -> my . padCount = 0;
if (yourInitLength > 3) pK -> my . padByte = yourInit[3] ^ 0x40;
else pK -> my . padByte = 0;
```

End-of-Packet Character

Line-oriented mainframes often require a CR following each 'line' of input data. Even on systems that don't always require this, simple Kermit implementations sometimes take advantage of 'line input' routines that require a CR following each packet.

⟨Dump initialization string 413⟩ +==
```
if (initLength > 4) {
  DebugBegin(pK -> debug, debugInit);
  DebugString(pK -> debug, "␣␣␣5:");
  DebugChar(pK -> debug, initString[4]);
  DebugString(pK -> debug, "␣Packet␣Terminator␣=");
  DebugInt(pK -> debug, initString[4] − 32);
  DebugEnd(pK -> debug);
}
```

I tell you what terminator to send me.

⟨Build my initialization string 413⟩ +==
```
myInit[4] = pK -> your . packetTerminator + 32;
```

You tell me what terminator to send you.

⟨Parse your initialization string 413⟩ +==
```
if (yourInitLength > 4)
  pK -> my . packetTerminator = yourInit[4] − 32;
else pK -> my . packetTerminator = 0x0D;
```

Control Prefix Character

For many parameters, the value is a request to the other side, for example, the timeout parameter specifies the timeout I want you to use. This value, in contrast, is the control prefix that I will use.

⟨Dump initialization string 413⟩ +==
```
if (initLength > 5) {
  DebugBegin(pK -> debug, debugInit);
  DebugString(pK -> debug, "␣␣␣6:");
  DebugChar(pK -> debug, initString[5]);
  DebugString(pK -> debug, "␣Control␣prefix␣=");
```

```
        DebugInt(pK -> debug, initString[5]);
        DebugChar(pK -> debug, initString[5]);
        DebugEnd(pK -> debug);
    }
```

I tell you the control prefix I will use.

⟨ Build my initialization string 413 ⟩ +≡
```
    myInit[5] = pK -> my . prefixControl;
```

You tell me the control prefix you will use.

⟨ Parse your initialization string 413 ⟩ +≡
```
    if (yourInitLength > 5) pK -> your . prefixControl = yourInit[5];
    else pK -> your . prefixControl = '#';
```

Eighth-Bit Prefix Character

The eighth-bit prefix can be specified as Y by either side, indicating that eighth-bit prefixing is supported without requesting that it be used. The reason this is necessary here (and not elsewhere) is that the receiver may know of channel limitations of which the sender is unaware. So, the sender must be able to indicate its willingness to do eighth-bit prefixing even if it believes such prefixing is unnecessary.

⟨ Dump initialization string 413 ⟩ +≡
```
    if (initLength > 6) {
        DebugBegin(pK -> debug, debugInit);
        DebugString(pK -> debug, "␣␣␣7:");
        DebugChar(pK -> debug, initString[6]);
        DebugString(pK -> debug, "␣eighth-bit␣prefix␣=");
        DebugInt(pK -> debug, initString[6]);
        DebugChar(pK -> debug, initString[6]);
        DebugEnd(pK -> debug);
    }
```

Usually, pK ->my . prefix8bit will be initialized to Y. If a seven-bit channel is being used, however, it should be initialized to &.

⟨ Build my initialization string 413 ⟩ +≡
```
    if (pK -> my . prefix8bit) myInit[6] = pK -> my . prefix8bit;
    else myInit[6] = 'N';
```

Parsing the eighth-bit negotiation is a bit more complex, because of the special handling of Y. Recall that if one side specifies Y and the other specifies a legal prefix, then eighth-bit prefixing will be done. On the other hand, if both sides specify Y, eighth-bit prefixing will not be done. Notice that after this negotiation, the `prefix8bit` fields are zeroed (*not* set to Y) if no eighth-bit prefixing will be used.

```
⟨Parse your initialization string 413⟩ +≡
    if (yourInitLength > 6) {      /* eighth-bit prefix */
      char mine = pK -> my . prefix8bit;
      char yours = yourInit[6];

      if (mine == 'Y') mine = yours;      /* I will if you will */
      if (yours == 'Y') yours = mine;     /* You will if I will */
      if (mine == yours) {      /* We agree, check for validity */
        if (mine < '!') yours = 0;
        if ((mine > '>') && (mine < '‘')) yours = 0;
        if (mine > '&') yours = 0;
      } else yours = 0;      /* We disagree */
      pK -> my . prefix8bit = yours;
      pK -> your . prefix8bit = yours;
    } else {
      pK -> my . prefix8bit = 0;
      pK -> your . prefix8bit = 0;
    }
```

Packet Check Type

The packet check is a single character. Until recently, the only characters used were 0, 1, and 2, so it's tempting to store the packet check as an integer. But the addition of the B packet check means that the packet check should be stored internally as a character.

```
⟨Dump initialization string 413⟩ +≡
    if (initLength > 7) {
      DebugBegin(pK -> debug, debugInit);
      DebugString(pK -> debug, "␣␣␣8:");
      DebugChar(pK -> debug, initString[7]);
      DebugString(pK -> debug, "␣Packet␣check␣type␣=");
      DebugInt(pK -> debug, initString[7] - '0');
      DebugEnd(pK -> debug);
    }
```

```
⟨Build my initialization string 413⟩ +≡
    myInit[7] = pK -> my . preferredPacketCheck;
```

Because the check type negotiation is so simple (either we agree or we both use type 1), I just echo the sender's suggestion, checking only to make sure it's a packet check that I understand.

⟨ Parse your initialization string 413 ⟩ +==
```
if (yourInitLength > 7) {
  switch (yourInit[7]) {
  case '1': default: pK -> your . preferredPacketCheck = '1';
    break;
  case '2': case '3': case 'B':
    pK -> your . preferredPacketCheck = yourInit[7];
    break;
  }
} else {      /* No packet check specified, default to '1' */
  pK -> your . preferredPacketCheck = '1';
  pK -> my . preferredPacketCheck = pK -> your . preferredPacketCheck;
}
```

⟨ Adjust settings before responding 415 ⟩ +==
```
pK -> my . preferredPacketCheck = pK -> your . preferredPacketCheck;
```

Repeat Prefix Character

The default repeat prefix character is usually ˜. Generally, Kermit's repeat prefix encoding offers only a modest compression. On text files, it serves to offset the overhead of control-character encoding. On binary files, it tends to have no effect at all.

⟨ Dump initialization string 413 ⟩ +==
```
if (initLength > 8) {
  DebugBegin(pK -> debug, debugInit);
  DebugString(pK -> debug, "␣␣␣9:");
  DebugChar(pK -> debug, initString[8]);
  DebugString(pK -> debug, "␣Repeat␣prefix␣=");
  DebugInt(pK -> debug, initString[8]);
  DebugChar(pK -> debug, initString[8]);
  DebugEnd(pK -> debug);
}
```

A space character is used to indicate that no repeat prefixing will be done.

⟨ Build my initialization string 413 ⟩ +==
```
if (pK -> my . prefixRepeat) myInit[8] = pK -> my . prefixRepeat;
else myInit[8] = '␣';
```

⟨ Parse your initialization string 413 ⟩ +==
```
if (yourInitLength > 8) {      /* Repeat prefix */
  pK -> your . prefixRepeat = yourInit[8];
} else pK -> your . prefixRepeat = 0;
```

```
if (pK -> your . prefixRepeat == '␣') pK -> your . prefixRepeat = 0;
```

Repeat prefixing will only be done if both sides agree.

⟨ Adjust settings before responding 415 ⟩ +≡
```
pK -> my . prefixRepeat = pK -> your . prefixRepeat;
```

Extended Capabilities Bitmap

In addition to decoding the capabilities bitmap, this code also locates the extended capabilities that follow the bitmap. The capabilities bitmap is encoded by adding 32 to each byte. As mentioned earlier, the least significant bit is used to indicate if there is another byte in the field.

⟨ Dump initialization string 413 ⟩ +≡
```
if (initLength > 9) {
  int i = 0;
  BYTE thisCapability;

  DebugBegin(pK -> debug, debugInit);
  DebugString(pK -> debug, "␣␣Capabilities␣bitmap:␣");
  do {
    thisCapability = initString[i + 9] - 32;
    if (i < sizeof (capabilities))
      capabilities[i] = thisCapability;
    i++;
    DebugIntHex(pK -> debug, thisCapability);
    DebugChar(pK -> debug, thisCapability + 32);
    DebugString(pK -> debug, "␣");
  } while ((i < sizeof (capabilities)) && (thisCapability & 1));
  pExtended = initString + i + 9;
  extendedLength = initLength - 9 - i;
  DebugEnd(pK -> debug);
}
{
  DebugBegin(pK -> debug, debugInit);
  DebugString(pK -> debug, "␣␣Capabilities␣enabled:␣");
  if (capabilities[0] & 32)
    DebugString(pK -> debug, "␣(Locking␣Shift)");
  if (capabilities[0] & 16)
    DebugString(pK -> debug, "␣(Extra-Long␣Packets)");
  if (capabilities[0] & 8)
    DebugString(pK -> debug, "␣(Attributes)");
  if (capabilities[0] & 4)
    DebugString(pK -> debug, "␣(Windowing)");
```

```
     if (capabilities[0] & 2)
       DebugString(pK -> debug, "␣(Long␣Packets)");
     DebugEnd(pK -> debug);
  }
```

Most of these fields indicate my willingness to receive the corresponding item. For example, the "extended packets" capability means that I can receive extended packets. The "windowing" capability is the only exception; it indicates that I can both send and receive full-duplex.

```
⟨ Build my initialization string 413 ⟩ +==
   pK -> my . capabilities[0] = 0;
   pK -> my . capabilities[0] |= 2;        /* Extended packets */
   pK -> my . capabilities[0] |= 4;        /* Windowing */
   pK -> my . capabilities[0] |= 8;        /* Attribute packets? */
   if (pK -> your . maxPacketSize > 9024)
     pK -> my . capabilities[0] |= 16;      /* Extra-long packets */
   pK -> my . capabilities[0] |= 32;       /* Locking shifts */
   {     /* Build remaining fields */
     BYTE *source = pK -> my . capabilities;

     pMyExtended = myInit + 9;
     do {
       *pMyExtended ++ = *source + 32;
     } while (*source ++ & 1);
     ⟨ Build my initialization extended fields 422 ⟩
     myInitLength = pMyExtended − myInit;
   }


⟨ Parse your initialization string 413 ⟩ +==
   if (yourInitLength > 9) {
     int i = 0;
     BYTE thisCapability;

     do {
       thisCapability = yourInit[i + 9] − 32;
       if (i < sizeof (pK -> your . capabilities))
         pK -> your . capabilities[i] = thisCapability;
       i ++;
     } while ((yourInitLength > i + 9) && (thisCapability & 1));
     pYourExtended = yourInit + (i + 9);
     yourExtendedLength = yourInitLength − (i + 9);
   } else {
     pYourExtended = NULL;
     yourExtendedLength = 0;
   }
```

Before responding, I should disable any capabilities which you don't support.

⟨ Adjust settings before responding 415 ⟩ +==
```
{
  int  i = 0;
  for (i = 0;  i < sizeof (pK -> my . capabilities);  i ++)
    pK -> my . capabilities [i] & = pK -> your . capabilities [i];
}
```

Window Size

The window size value is only obeyed if the corresponding capability bit is set.

⟨ Dump initialization string 413 ⟩ +==
```
if (extendedLength > 0) {
  DebugBegin(pK -> debug, debugInit);
  DebugString(pK -> debug, "␣␣␣␣");
  DebugChar(pK -> debug, pExtended[0]);
  DebugString(pK -> debug, "␣Window␣size␣=");
  DebugInt(pK -> debug, pExtended[0] − 32);
  DebugEnd(pK -> debug);
}
```

Even if windowing was not negotiated, I still fill in this field so any later fields will be in the correct location.

⟨ Build my initialization extended fields 422 ⟩ ==
```
if (pK -> my . capabilities [0] & 4)
  *pMyExtended ++ = pK -> windowSize + 32;      /* Real window size */
else *pMyExtended ++ = 1 + 32;       /* window size of 1 */
```
See also page 423.

This code is used on page 421.

⟨ Parse your initialization string 413 ⟩ +==
```
if (yourExtendedLength > 0) {
  int windowSize = 1;

  if (pK -> your . capabilities [0] & 4)
    windowSize = pYourExtended[0] − 32;
  if (windowSize < pK -> windowSize) {
    pK -> windowSize = windowSize;
    if (pK -> debug) {
      DebugBegin(pK -> debug, debugInit);
      DebugString(pK -> debug, "Setting␣window␣size␣to␣");
      DebugInt(pK -> debug, windowSize);
      DebugEnd(pK -> debug);
```

```
        }
      }
    } else pK -> windowSize = 1;
```

Extended Packet Size

The extended packet size has two different interpretations. If long packets are enabled, but not extra-long packets, the extended packet size is taken as-is. If both are enabled (it's pointless to support extra-long packets but not long packets), then the extended packet size field is multiplied by 95 to obtain the actual limit.

```
⟨ Dump initialization string 413 ⟩ +==
  if (extendedLength > 2) {
    long packetSize = (pExtended[1] − 32) * 95 + (pExtended[2] − 32);

    if (capabilities[0] & 16) packetSize *= 95;
    DebugBegin(pK -> debug, debugInit);
    DebugString(pK -> debug, "␣␣␣␣");
    DebugChar(pK -> debug, pExtended[1]);
    DebugChar(pK -> debug, pExtended[2]);
    DebugString(pK -> debug, "␣Extended␣packet␣size␣=");
    DebugInt(pK -> debug, packetSize);
    DebugEnd(pK -> debug);
  }
```

```
⟨ Build my initialization extended fields 422 ⟩ +==
  {
    long extendedPacketSize = pK -> your . maxPacketSize;

    if (pK -> my . capabilities[0] & 16) extendedPacketSize /= 95;
    if (extendedPacketSize > 9024) extendedPacketSize = 9024;
    *pMyExtended ++ = (extendedPacketSize / 95) + 32;
    *pMyExtended ++ = (extendedPacketSize % 95) + 32;
  }
```

As with the normal packet size, I need to convert the negotiated value, which restricts the packet length field, into a limit on the size of the packet's data field. For long packets, the length field includes the data and the packet check. Reducing the negotiated value by three (the length of the longest packet check) ensures that the packet length field does not exceed the specified value.

```
⟨ Parse your initialization string 413 ⟩ +==
  if (pK -> your . capabilities[0] & 2) {
    if (yourExtendedLength > 2) {
      int packetSize = (pYourExtended[1] − 32) * 95 +
          (pYourExtended[2] − 32);
```

```
        if (pK -> your . capabilities [0] & 16) packetSize *= 95;
        packetSize -= 3;
        if (packetSize > maxPacketSize) maxPacketSize = packetSize;
    } else     /* Default extended packet size */
        maxPacketSize = 497;
}
```

Cleanup

One final piece of cleanup remains. The `maxPacketSize` was set to the largest of the various packet limits specified by the other side. This value is used to reduce the packet size limit in the `my` structure if necessary.

It's not a good idea to increase the packet size limit when the other end can accept packets larger than the local default. Kermit's general philosophy is that either side may know about channel limits of which the other side is unaware. The actual parameters used should satisfy restrictions placed by both sides. For example, if this code is used on a microcomputer transferring files to a copy of C-Kermit, the user may know that a smaller packet size is more efficient with their particular modem, even though the remote C-Kermit may be configured to accept much larger packets.

⟨ Parse your initialization string 413 ⟩ +≡
```
    if (maxPacketSize < pK -> my . maxPacketSize) {
      pK -> my . maxPacketSize = maxPacketSize;
      if (pK -> debug) {
        DebugBegin(pK -> debug, debugInit);
        DebugString(pK -> debug, "Setting␣maximum␣packet␣size␣to␣");
        DebugInt(pK -> debug, pK -> my . maxPacketSize);
        DebugEnd(pK -> debug);
      }
    }
```

Server Operation

Most Kermit sessions consist of a single transaction. The one exception is Kermit server operation. I've used the same approach that I used in XYModem to distinguish between a multiple-transaction session and a single-transaction session. The `serverMode` variable becomes set either by the `KermitServer` function, or by receipt of a non-file transaction. This same session layer is used for normal file receiving (with `serverMode` disabled) or for server operations (with `serverMode` enabled).

⟨ General Kermit variables 353 ⟩ +≡

```
int serverMode;
```

⟨Initialize Kermit variables 353⟩ +==
```
    pK -> serverMode = FALSE;
```

The server itself just sits and waits for a new transaction to begin. The special value of −1 for the timeout indicates that no timeout should be used.

I've not filled in the details of the various types of transactions, but it shouldn't be difficult for you to do so.

```
STATIC int KServer(KERMIT_PRIVATE *pK)
{
  int defaultTimeout = pK -> my . timeout;       /* Save this value */
  KProgress(pK, stsNegotiating);
  while (TRUE) {
    KResetSequence(pK);     /* Each transaction starts with packet 0 */
    if (pK -> serverMode) {     /* Suppress timeout waiting for packet 0 */
      defaultTimeout = pK -> my . timeout;
      pK -> my . timeout = −1;
    }
    StsRet(KReceivePacketReliable(pK));
    pK -> my . timeout = defaultTimeout;     /* Restore it */
    switch (pK -> rxPacketType) {
    case 'S':     /* Send-Init packet: receive file */
      KReceiveNegotiate(pK, pK -> rxPacket, pK -> rxPacketLength);
      StsRet(KReceiveFiles(pK));
      if (!pK -> serverMode) return kOK;
      break;
    case 'G':     /* Generic (G) server command */
      ⟨Handle Generic server command 426⟩
      pK -> serverMode = TRUE;
      break;
    case 'R':     /* Receive initiate */
    case 'I':     /* Initialize */
    case 'X':     /* Display text */
    case 'C':     /* Host command */
    case 'K':     /* Kermit/Application command */
      pK -> serverMode = TRUE;
    default: StsRet(KSendResponse(pK, 'E', (const BYTE *)
          "Command␣not␣implemented", 23));
      break;
    }
  }
}
```

A Kermit program that supports host mode *must* support three transactions:

- It must recognize the Send-Init (S) packet to begin receiving a file.

- It must recognize the Generic Command (G) packet with the Finish F sub-command, which terminates the server.

- It must recognize the Generic Command (G) packet with the Logout L sub-command, which terminates the server, and logs the user out, if appropriate.

```
⟨ Handle Generic server command 426 ⟩ ==
  switch (pK -> rxPacket[0]) {
  case 'F': StsRet(KSendResponse(pK, 'Y', NULL, 0));
    return kOK;      /* End of server */
  case 'L': StsRet(KSendResponse(pK, 'Y', NULL, 0));
    return kOK;      /* End of server */
  default: StsRet(KSendResponse(pK, 'E', (const BYTE *)
       "Command␣not␣implemented", 23));
  }
```
This code is used on page 425.

Public Interface

Typical usage involves the following steps:

1. call `KermitInit` to create a Kermit object,
2. call the various `KermitSet...` functions to establish the parameters for the transfer,
3. call `KermitSend`, `KermitReceive`, or `KermitServer` to perform a Kermit session,
4. call `KermitDestroy` to destroy the object.

The `KermitAbort` function can be called at any time during the transfer. The session function will return a few seconds later. Clearly, `KermitAbort` is only really useful in a multi-threaded system.

```
int KermitInit(KERMIT *pKPublic, SERIAL_PORT port)
{
  KERMIT_PRIVATE *pK;

  pK = malloc(sizeof (*pK));
  if (pK == NULL) return 1;     /* non-zero to indicate error */
  memset(pK, 0, sizeof (*pK));    /* Initialize structure */
  ⟨ Initialize Kermit variables 353 ⟩
  KInitWindow(pK);
```

```
    pK -> port = port;
    *pKPublic = pK;
    return 0;
}


int KermitDestroy(KERMIT kPublic)
{
    KERMIT_PRIVATE *pK = (KERMIT_PRIVATE *) kPublic;
    ⟨ Destroy Kermit variables 365 ⟩
    return 0;
}
```

The KermitSetFast function provides a way to quickly set some related variables that should allow faster connections. This could be used to provide a simple 'speed' setting that users can set to enable faster transfers. Notice that these particular settings tend to stress window size over packet size. Over typical settings, having more packets in the window is usually more important than having a large packet size.

```
    int KermitSetFast(KERMIT kPublic, int speed)
    {
      KERMIT_PRIVATE *pK = (KERMIT_PRIVATE *) kPublic;
      int packetSize = 90, windowSize = 1;

      if (speed <= 0) return 1;
      switch (speed) {
      default:    /* too-large value */
      case 7:     /* 270k window */
        packetSize = 9024; windowSize = 32; break;
      case 6:     /* 128k window */
        packetSize = 4096; windowSize = 31; break;
      case 5:     /* 64k window */
        packetSize = 2048; windowSize = 31; break;
      case 4:     /* 16k window */
        packetSize = 1024; windowSize = 16; break;
      case 3:     /* 4k window */
        packetSize = 512; windowSize = 8; break;
      case 2:     /* 1k window */
        packetSize = 256; windowSize = 4; break;
      case 1:     /* 1k window, half-duplex */
        packetSize = 1024; windowSize = 1; break;
      }
      pK -> your . maxPacketSize = packetSize;
      pK -> my . maxPacketSize = packetSize;
      pK -> windowSize = windowSize;
```

```
    if (packetSize > 500) pK -> my . preferredPacketCheck = '3' ;
    else if (packetSize > 90) pK -> my . preferredPacketCheck = '2' ;
    return 0;
}


int KermitSetDebug(KERMIT kPublic, DEBUG debug)
{
  KERMIT_PRIVATE *pK = (KERMIT_PRIVATE *) kPublic;
  pK -> debug = debug;
  return 0;
}


int KermitSetProgress(KERMIT kPublic, PROGRESS progress)
{
  KERMIT_PRIVATE *pK = (KERMIT_PRIVATE *) kPublic;
  pK -> progress = progress;
  return 0;
}


int KermitSetFileType(KERMIT kPublic, int fileType)
{
  KERMIT_PRIVATE *pK = (KERMIT_PRIVATE *) kPublic;
  pK -> fileType = fileType;
  return 0;
}
```

The three types of sessions currently supported are:

- Sending a group of files.

- Receiving files.

- Server mode.

Additional sessions could be added to send commands or request the server send a file.

```
    int KermitSend(KERMIT kPublic, const char *filenames[], int
           numFiles)
{
  KERMIT_PRIVATE *pK = (KERMIT_PRIVATE *) kPublic;
  int returnVal = 0;     /* No error */
  pK -> filenames = filenames;
  pK -> numFileNames = numFiles;
```

```
  pK -> currentFileName = 0;
  pK -> sending = TRUE;
  ProgressSending(pK -> progress);
  if (KSendFiles(pK) != kOK) returnVal = 1;
  return returnVal;
}


int KermitReceive(KERMIT kPublic)
{
  KERMIT_PRIVATE *pK = (KERMIT_PRIVATE *) kPublic;
  int returnVal = 0;     /* No error */
  pK -> sending = FALSE;
  ProgressReceiving(pK -> progress);
  if (KServer(pK) != kOK) returnVal = 1;
  return returnVal;
}


int KermitServer(KERMIT kPublic)
{
  KERMIT_PRIVATE *pK = (KERMIT_PRIVATE *) kPublic;
  int returnVal = 0;     /* No error */
  pK -> serverMode = TRUE;
  pK -> sending = FALSE;
  ProgressReceiving(pK -> progress);
  if (KServer(pK) != kOK) returnVal = 1;
  return returnVal;
}


int KermitCancel(KERMIT kPublic)
{
  KERMIT_PRIVATE *pK = (KERMIT_PRIVATE *) kPublic;
  pK -> userCancel = TRUE;
  return 0;
}
```

Bibliography

[1] American National Standards Institute. *ANSI x3.64, Additional Controls for use with American National Standard Code for Information Interchange.*

[2] Ward Christensen. my protocol. Forum message on CompuServe, reproduced in [15], April 1985.

[3] Frank da Cruz. *Kermit Protocol Manual.* Columbia University Center for Computing Activities, New York, New York 10027, sixth edition, June 1986. Available via anonymous ftp from `kermit.columbia.edu`.

[4] Frank da Cruz. *Kermit: A File Transfer Protocol.* Digital Press, 1987.

[5] Frank da Cruz and Christine M. Gianone. *Using C-Kermit: Communication Software for Unix, VMS, OS/2, AOS/VS, OS-9, Amiga, Atari ST.* Digital Press, 1993.

[6] Chuck Forsberg. Source code for `rz` and `sz`. Versions prior to 3.0 are public domain, later versions are owned by Omen Technology Inc.

[7] Chuck Forsberg. *The ZMODEM Inter Application File Transfer Protocol.* Omen Technology Incorporated, 17505-V Northwest Sauvie Island Road, Portland, Oregon, 97231, October 1988. Available on many BBS's and online services, including ftp://oak.oakland.edu/pub/misc/protocols as `zmodem8.doc`.

[8] Christine M. Gianone. *Using MSDOS Kermit.* Digital Press, second edition, 1991.

[9] Christine M. Gianone and Frank da Cruz. *A Kermit Protocol Extension for International Character Sets*. Columbia University Center for Computing Activities, 612 West 115th Street, New York, New York 10025, December 1993. Available via anonymous ftp from `kermit.columbia.edu`.

[10] Jerry Horanoff. *C-Modem File Transfer Protocol: Preliminary Documentation*. Carina Software Systems, September 1988. A half-duplex protocol which allows for a large negotiated window size. Available on ftp://oak.oakland.edu/pub/misc/protocols as `cmodem.doc`.

[11] International Organization for Standardization. *ISO/IEC 6429, Information technology — Control functions for coded character sets.*

[12] Tim Kientzle. Intelligent xymodem. *Dr. Dobb's*, December 1994. An earlier version of the XYModem implementation included in this book.

[13] Donald Knuth. *The Art of Computer Programming, Volume 1: Fundamental Algorithms*. Addison-Wesley, second edition, 1973.

[14] Ken Lunde. *Understanding Japanese Information Processing*. O'Reilly & Associates, Inc., 1993.

[15] Omen Technology Incorporated, 17505-V Northwest Sauvie Island Road, Portland, Oregon, 97231. *XMODEM/YMODEM Protocol Reference: A compendium of documents describing the XMODEM and YMODEM File Transfer Protocols*, October 1988. Available on many BBS's and online services, including ftp://oak.oakland.edu/pub/misc/protocols as `ymodem8.doc`.

[16] Keith Petersen. Modem/xmodem robustness improvement on eot tests succesful. Available from ftp://oak.oakland.edu/pub/misc/protocols as file `robust.eot`, December 14 1985. Describes early experiments with a NAK challenge to detect spurious EOT characters.

Index

A

aborting, *see* cancelling
ACK (Acknowledge), 71, 77, 79, 84–87, 91,
      93, 217, 236, 237, 241, 242, 249
    spurious, 85, 87, 248
      recovery, 93, 241
acknowledgment
    requesting, 327
alphabet, 16
    defined, 39
APC (Application Program Command), 77
application command, 32, 102, 104, 109
Application Program Command, 34
archiving, 7, 30, 134
ASCII, 70
    table, 71
attention string, 102, 106
automatic transfers, 34, 106

B

BELL (Bell), 71, 77, 79
blank compression, 121
block, *see* packet, *see* window, blocked
blocking I/O, 102, 158, 173, 266, 285, 358
Boy Scout, 4
BPH (Break Permitted Here), 77
Break signal, 106
BS (Backspace), 71, 77, 79, 235
burst length, 11, 102, 319
    adjusting, 326

C

Byrns, John, 94
byte
    different sizes, 131

C0, 71
C1, 71
CAN (Cancel), 34, 36, 71, 77, 79, 86, 96–99,
      106, 107, 235, 237–240, 243, 308
can't beat them
    join them, 256
cancelling, 36
    automatically, 36, 120
    Kermit, 36
    manually, 36, 107, 121
    session, 36, 107
    transaction, 36, 118
    XModem, 36, 86
capability
    longPacket, 234
carriage return, *see* end-of-line
Carriage Return character, 68
Catchings, Bill, 113
CCH (Cancel Character), 77
channel, 8–13
    defined, 8
    error-free, 9
    examples, 11
character
    control, 67

defined, 67
graphic, 67
character code, 69
character encoding, 69
conversion, 75
eight-bit, 125
character-set conversion, 187
checksum, 54, 86, 88, 92, 93, 116
Kermit, 65
weaknesses, 54
Christensen, Ward, 84, 94
Code Page 437, 78
Code Page 850, 78
code point, 69
coding conventions, 152
Columbia University, 113, 135, 143
compression, 50, 96
Kermit, 115
ZModem, 103
CompuServe B protocol, 34, 36, 64
constant names, 152
control character, 67
control escape, 22
control information, 5, 16
control prefix, 115
cooperative multitasking, 157
CP/M, 68, 83, 84, 113, 131, 434
CP/M, 83
files, 84
CR (Carriage Return), 68, 69, 71, 77, 79, 93,
    97, 99, 103, 106, 120, 121, 124,
    131, 132, 177, 182, 186–188, 212,
    213
overprinting lines, 212
CRC
basics, 55
calculation, 223, 276, 356
defined, 63
mathematics, 60
self-checking, 64
weaknesses, 65
CRC escapes, *see* ZModem, CRC escapes
da Cruz, Frank, 113, 143
CSI (Control Sequence Introducer), 77
CWEB, 151

D

data loss, 9, 10

DC1 (Device Control 1), 71, 77, 79
DC2 (Device Control 2), 71, 77, 79
DC3 (Device Control 3), 71, 77, 79
DC4 (Device Control 4), 71, 77, 79
DCS (Device Control String), 77
DEBUG, 160
debug, 217
debug module, 154
filtering, 163
handles, 162
using, 160
DEBUG_PRIVATE, 161
DebugBegin, 160
DebugBeginInternal, 160, 163
DebugChar, 160, 166
DebugDestroy, 160, 162
DebugEnd, 160, 164
DebugFile, 160, 163
debugging, 159–166, 222
DebugInit, 160, 162
DebugInt, 160, 165
DebugIntHex, 160, 165
DebugPacket, 271
DebugPrint, 162
DebugPrintF, 161
DebugPtr, 160, 165
DebugSetFilter, 160, 163
DebugString, 160, 164
DebugStringCount, 160, 164
DebugUInt, 160, 165
DEC Multinational Character Set, 75
DEL (Delete), 71, 77, 79, 97, 98, 114, 115,
    120
delay
channel, 11
disk, 217
disk module, 154
DiskAppendOpen, 180, 192
DiskConvertName, 184
DiskCopyText, 194
DiskDebugWarn, 183
DISKFILE, 178
DISKFILE_PRIVATE, 183
DiskFileDate, 181, 198
DiskFileMode, 181, 198
DiskFileName, 181, 199
DiskFileSize, 181, 199
DiskFileType, 181, 198

DiskGuessType, 187
DiskMakeNameUnique, 185
DiskRead, 180, 197
DiskReadClose, 180, 198
DiskReadFillBuffer, 195
DiskReadOpen, 180, 196
DiskReplaceOpen, 180, 192
DiskWrite, 180, 193
DiskWriteClose, 180, 193
DiskWriteDate, 180, 191
DiskWriteEOL, 184
DiskWriteFlush, 188
DiskWriteInit, 180, 189
DiskWriteMode, 180, 191
DiskWriteName, 180, 190
DiskWriteOpen, 180, 192
DiskWriteSize, 180, 190
DiskWriteText, 188
DiskWriteType, 180, 191
dividend, 61
DLE, *see* Kermit, locking shift
DLE (Data Link Escape), 71, 77, 79, 97, 126, 371, 435
duplex
    defined, 10
    full, 25, *see* full duplex
    half, *see* half duplex

E

ease of use, 7
efficiency, 5
eighth-bit prefix, 115
EM (End of Medium), 71, 77, 79
encoding, 10, 16
    control characters, 97, 114
    excess-32, 114
    five-for-four, 41
    four-for-three, 41
    Kermit, 114
        examples, 115
    none, 84, 91
    prefix, 40
    radix, 41
    ZModem, 96
encryption, 51
end-of-line, 68
ENQ (Enquiry), 71, 77, 79

EOT (End of Transmission), 71, 77, 79, 84, 86, 87, 93, 94, 217, 238, 239, 242, 243
    reliability, 242
    spurious, 86, 242
EPA (End Protected Area), 77
error correcting codes, 53
error rate, 9
    non-zero, 9
error recovery
    XModem, 85
error-correcting modems, *see* modems, error-correcting
ESA (End Selected Area), 77
ESC (Escape), 71, 77, 79
ETB (End of Transmission Block), 71, 77, 79
ETX (End of Text), 71, 77, 79
EUC character code, 73
extensibility, 5

F

failure, *see* cancelling
FF (Form Feed), 71, 77, 79
file
    collisions, 132
    creation date, 6
    modification date, 6
    permissions, 6
    record type, 6
    resources, 6
    size, 6
file errors, 179
file layer, 86
    XYModem, 244
file transfer
    reasons for, 31
file types, 179
FileExists, 182
filename, 6
flow control, 9
    hardware, 10
    software, 9
    transparent, 10
Forsberg, Chuck, 91, 94, 95, 112, 113
frame, *see* packet
FS (Field Separator/Information Separator 4), 71, 77, 79
full screen mode, 121

function names, 152

G

generating polynomial, 56
GL, 71
glyph, 67
GR, 72
graphic character, 67
gremlins, 8
GS (Group Separator/Information Separator
    3), 71, 77, 79
GTE Telenet, 95

H

half-duplex, 85
    defined, 10
    efficiency, 88
    importance of delay, 88
    Kermit, 117
    segmented, 25, 101
handle
    XYModem, 215
hard break, 69
header check, 239
header file gaurd, 160
hexadecimal, 41
Hiragana, 73
host commands, 33
HT (Horizontal Tab), 71, 77, 79, 182, 186
HTJ (Horizontal Tab with Justification), 77
HTS (Horizontal Tab Set), 77

I

international, 218
Internet, 12
invertibility, 75
ISO 10646, 74, 76
ISO 2022, 76
ISO 646, 70, 76
    table, 72
ISO 8859, 71, 76
ISO Latin 1, 71
    table, 77
ISO Latin 2, 71
    table, 77

J

Japanese, 73

K

Kanji, 73
Katakana, 73
KBuildMyInit, 411
KCrc16, 357
KDebugWarn, 355
KDumpCache, 387
KDumpInitString, 410
Kermit, 113–143
    attributes, 130–135
    caching packets, 129
    checksum, 65, 127
    compression, 115–116
    CRC, 128
    encoding
        caveat, 116
    error check
        type 1, 116
        type 2, 128
        type 3, 128
        type B, 121, 128
    file attribute codes, 130
    file attributes
        most important, 131
    file transaction, 118, 130–135
    full-duplex, 129
    half-duplex, 117
    host mode, 124
    initialization string, 119–120
    locking-shift encoding, 125–126
    module, 154
    overhead, 122
    packet, 116–117
        extra-long, 127
        long, 127
    packet format
        short, 117
    packet types, 117
    reducing prefixing overhead, 125
    reliability, 117
    repeat coding, 124
Kermit packet
    A (Attribute), 128, 130, 402, 406
    B (Break), 116–118, 120
    C (Command), 128, 137
    D (Data), 116–118, 402
    E (Error), 117, 120, 137, 398
    F (File), 116–118, 128, 137, 402

G (Generic Command), 128, 138, 425
I (Init), 128, 137
K (Kermit Command), 128, 137
N (Negative Acknowledge), 116, 117,
    129, 137, 140, 398–400
Q (Reserved), 128
R (Receive File), 128, 137
S (Send-Init), 116–119, 135, 137, 138
T (Reserved), 128
X (Text), 128, 137, 138
Y (Acknowledge), 116–119, 137, 138,
    398, 399
Z (End-of-File), 116–118, 402
Kermit the Frog, 113
KermitCancel, 352, 429
KermitDestroy, 351, 427
KermitInit, 351, 426
KermitReceive, 352, 429
KermitSend, 352, 428
KermitServer, 352, 429
KermitSetDebug, 351, 428
KermitSetFast, 351, 427
KermitSetFileType, 352, 428
KermitSetProgress, 352, 428
KFileRead, 362
KFileReadClose, 362
KFileReadEncode, 369
KFileReadOpenNext, 361
KFileWrite, 363
KFileWriteClose, 363
KFileWriteDecode, 371
KFileWriteOpen, 362
KFindCheckValue, 379
KInitCrc, 356
KInitEncoding, 373
KInitWindow, 391
KParseYourInit, 411
KProgress, 364
KReadBytesWithTimeout, 358
KReadByteWithTimeout, 360
KReceiveFileData, 404
KReceiveFiles, 409
KReceiveNegotiate, 412
KReceivePacket, 380
KReceivePacketCache, 393
KReceivePacketReliable, 400
KResetSequence, 390
KSendByte, 360

KSendBytes, 359
KSendFile, 402
KSendFiles, 404
KSendInitiate, 404, 411
KSendPacket, 376
KSendPacketFromCache, 395
KSendPacketReliable, 396
KSendResponse, 402
KServer, 425
KWaitForSentBytes, 360

L
last laugh, 35
Latin Alphabet 1, *see* ISO Latin 1
Latin Alphabet 2, *see* ISO Latin 2
layer
    reliability, 23
layers
    summary, 15
legibility, 75
LF (Line Feed), 68, 69, 71, 77, 79, 93, 99,
    103, 121, 124, 131, 132, 177,
    182, 186–188
Line Feed character, 68
linefeed, *see* end-of-line
locking shift, 40, 125–126
locking shifts, 124
long division, 61

M
MacBinary, 7, 30
Macintosh, 6, 7, 30, 68, 69, 79, 133, 136,
    157, 178, 194
Macintosh Character Encoding, 79
mainframe, 114, 121
mainframe terminal ports, 10
master, 36
master/slave, 36
MODEM, 83
modem, 8
    as backup tool, 32
    error-correcting, 13, 96, 101
MODEM2, 83
MODEM7, 83
modems, 12, 27
    error-correcting, 10, 12
    flow control, 10
module, 153

module interfaces, 153
MS-DOS, 30, 33, 68, 131, 133, 185, 188,
    194, 290
multi-byte characters, 73
multitasking, 9, 155–158
    applications, 156
    cooperative, 157
    polling, 156
    preemptive, 157
Muppet Show, 113
MW (Message Waiting), 77

N

NAK
    duplicate, 110
NAK (Negative Acknowledge), 71, 77, 79,
    84–88, 92, 93, 110, 218, 237,
    243, 438
NAK packet
    as request, 27
    duplicate, 26
NBH (No Break Here), 77
negotiation, 34
NEL (Next Line), 77
network, 11
networks, 12
    channel properties, 96
New Line character, 68
newline, *see* end-of-line
NeXT Character Encoding, 79
no news is good news, 26
noise, 85
    inter-packet, 239
NULL (Null character), 39, 44–46, 48, 71, 77,
    79, 92, 98, 104, 106, 115, 120,
    182, 186, 187, 230, 231, 266,
    290, 291, 300, 341, 344, 409, 415

O

Omen Technology, 112
OSC (Operating System Command), 77
overhead, 5

P

packet
    format, 18, 117
    header, 17
    header check, 21, 85
    sequence, 21

    sequence number, 239
    start, 17, 239
    type, 117
    types, 19
        ZModem, 100
    XModem, 84
packets
    average retries, 89
    changing size, 4
    multiple outstanding, 26
    ZModem, 98
PLD (Partial Line Down), 77
PLU (Partial Line Up), 77
PM (Privacy Message), 77
polling, 156
polynomials modulo 2, 62
PORT_PARAMS, 170
POSIX, 182
prog, 217
PROGRESS, 202
progress module, 154
progress reporting
    XYModem, 232
PROGRESS_PRIVATE, 204
ProgressDestroy, 202, 205
ProgressEndOfFile, 209
ProgressFileName, 202, 207
ProgressFilePosition, 202, 208
ProgressFileSize, 202, 207
ProgressFileType, 202, 207
ProgressInit, 202, 205
ProgressProtocol, 202, 206
ProgressReceiving, 202, 206
ProgressReport, 202, 210
ProgressSending, 202, 206
ProgressSetDebug, 202, 205
protocol
    defined, 3
    implementation, 4
protocol cheating, 91, 93, 236
protocol converters, 113, 114, 121
protocols
    half-duplex, 10
PU1 (Private Use 1), 77
PU2 (Private Use 2), 77

R

radio, 12

real-time, 156, 158
reliability
    defined, 4
    full-duplex, 23
    half-duplex, 23
    implementing, 29
    Kermit, 117
    scripted dialog, 24
    segmented half-duplex, 25
    XModem, 85
    XYModem, 241
    YModem, 92
requesting file, 105
retransmission, 11, 53
RI (Reverse Line Feed), 77
robustness
    defined, 5
RS (Record Separator/Information Separator 2), 71, 77, 79

S

satellite, 11
satellites, 12
SCI (Single Character Introducer), 77
scrap, 151
security, 106
serial, 217
serial error
    framing, 226
    overflow, 226
Serial errors, 167
serial I/O
    overlapping, 243
serial module, 154
serial port, 12
    errors, 226, 227
SERIAL_PORT, 167
SERIAL_PORT_PRIVATE, 171
SerialClose, 168, 171
SerialMakeTransparent, 168, 173
SerialOpen, 168, 171
SerialPause, 169, 176
SerialReadWithTimeout, 168, 169, 173, 174, 226
SerialRestoreState, 168, 172
SerialSaveState, 168, 172
SerialSend, 169, 174, 227
SerialSendBreak, 169, 175

SerialSetParity, 168, 173
SerialSetWord, 168, 172
SerialWaitForSentBytes, 169, 175, 227
session, 33
    initiation, 34
    XModem, 86
    XYModem, 256
SI, *see* Kermit, locking shift
SI/texttttLS0 (Shift In/Locking Shift 0), 71, 77, 79, 125, 126, 439
signal, 158
signature, 53
simplicity, 8
single shift, 40
slave, 36
SO, *see* Kermit, locking shift
SO/texttttLS1 (Shift Out/Locking Shift 1), 71, 77, 79, 125, 126, 439
soft break, 69
SOH (Start of Header), 71, 77, 79, 85, 92, 98, 239
SOP, *see* start-of-packet
SOS (Start Of String), 77
SPA (Start Protected Area), 77
space, 70
SprintNet, 95, 97
SS2 (Single Shift 2), 77
SS3 (Single Shift 3), 77
SSA (Start Selected Area), 77
ST (String Terminator), 77
start-of-packet sequence, 17
streaming, 22, 27, 101
    segmented, 25
STS (Set Transmit State), 77
StsRet, 155, 183, 221
StsWarn, 155, 183, 222
STX (Start of Text), 71, 77, 79, 89, 92, 98, 239
SUB (Substitute), 71, 77, 79, 177, 182, 186
SYN (Synchronous Idle), 71, 77, 79
system dependencies, 170–176, 197

T

terminating, *see* cancelling
termination
    not reliable, 35
text
    common format, 67

time
> conversion, 224

timeout, 168, 174

transactions, 29
> files, 30

transfers
> non-file, 32

transparency, 10

`typedef` names, 152

U

UCT (Universal Coordinated Time), 92, 232, 278, 292

Unicode, *see* ISO 10646

Unix, 7, 33, 34, 41, 45, 68, 73, 92, 95, 103, 131, 134, 136, 170, 180, 194, 231, 272, 291, 338

US (User Separator/Information Separator 1), 71, 77, 79

UUCP, 37

uuencode, 41, 42, 45, 46, 116, 132

V

variable names, 152

VT (Vertical Tab), 71, 77, 79

VTS (Vertical Tab Set), 77

W

walkie-talkies, 10

wide character sets, 74

window, 26
> blocked, 26, 319, 320, 324, 326, 391, 396
> optimal size, 28
> reducing, 29

windowing, 90

windows
> problems with large, 28

wire, 12

words, 39

WXModem, 90

X

XModem, 83–90, 215
> control packets, 84
> data packets, 85
> efficiency, 87
> error recovery, 85
> file layer, 86, 244

long packets, 89
> origin of name, 83
> packet layer, 234
> popularity, 83, 86
> problems, 86
> references, 94
> reliability, 85, 241
> session, 86, 256

XMODEM program, 83

XModem-CRC, 88, 246, 247

XModem-K, 89, 91, 246
> efficiency, 89

`XOFF`, 9

`XOFF/DC3` (Device Control 3), 9, 43, 95, 97, 99, 269, 440

`XON/DC1` (Device Control 1), 43, 95, 97, 99, 269

xxencode, 41, 42, 45, 46

`XYCrc16`, 223

`XYCrc16Constant`, 224

`XYDebugWarn`, 222

`XYFileRead`, 229

`XYFileReadClose`, 230

`XYFileReadOpenNext`, 229

`XYFileWrite`, 232

`XYFileWriteClose`, 232

`XYFileWriteOpen`, 230

`XYGobble`, 228

`XYInitCrc16`, 223

`XYMODEM`, 216

XYModem
> batch, 220
> crc, 220
> default, 216
> file layer, 244
> G, 220
> handshake, 252
> longPacket, 220
> module, 154
> negotiation, 219
> packet layer, 234
> progress reporting, 232
> public interface, 259
> receiving files, 251
> reliability, 241
> sending files, 244
> session, 256

XYMODEM structure, 218

XYMODEM_PRIVATE, 218
XYModemCancel, 261
XYModemDestroy, 259
XYModemInit, 259
XYModemReceive, 261
XYModemSend, 261
XYModemSetDebug, 260
XYModemSetFileType, 260
XYModemSetProgress, 260
XYModemSetProtocol, 259
XYNewFile, 219
XYReceive, 258
XYReceiveFallback, 252
XYReceiveFile, 252
XYReceivePacket, 238
XYReceivePacketReliable, 243
XYReceiveSendHandshake, 252
XYSend, 258
XYSendByte, 228
XYSendCAN, 235
XYSendEOTReliable, 242
XYSendFile, 251
XYSendFirstPacket, 248
XYSendPacket, 235
XYSendPacketReliable, 241
XYSendPacketZero, 244
XYSendReadAckNak, 237
XYSendReadHandshake, 245
XYSendSessionEnd, 256
XYSerialReadByte, 228
XYSerialReadWithTimeout, 226
XYSerialSend, 227
XYSerialWaitForSentBytes, 227
XYTime, 225
XYTimeToTm, 224

Y

YAM, 91
YModem, 91–94, 215, 246, 247
    checksum variant, 247
    fall back to XModem, 92
    file information, 92
    file layer, 244
    packet layer, 234
    references, 94
    reliability, 241
    session, 93, 256
    text files, 93

YModem-G, 9, 94, 241, 243, 246, 247

Z

ZCrc16, 277
ZCrc32, 277
ZDebugWarn, 275
ZFileCRC, 294
ZFileRead, 289
ZFileReadClose, 290
ZFileReadOpenNext, 289
ZFileReadSkip, 289
ZFileSize, 294
ZFileSystemFree, 294
ZFileWrite, 293
ZFileWriteClose, 293
ZFileWriteOpen, 290
ZGobble, 286
ZInitCrc, 276
ZInitWindow, 316
ZModem, 95–112, 263–349
    attention string, 102, 106
    crash recovery, 102
    CRC escapes, 101
    data subpacket, 101
    encoding, 96
    error recovery, 110
    file conversion options, 103
    file extended options, 104
    file management options, 104
    file transport options, 104
    free space, 105
    half-duplex, 96
    module, 154
    negotiation, 97
    packet header
        binary, 98
        hexadecimal, 99
        prefix-encoded, 98
    packet types, 100
    packets with data, 99
    popularity, 96
    prefix encoding, 98
    public domain status, 95
    references, 112
    restrictions on command transactions,
        105
    security challenge, 106, 109
    session, 107

streaming, 101
ZRInit flags, 107
ZModem packet
  ZAbort, 100, 107
  ZAck, 99–102, 105, 106, 108, 109
  ZCan, 100, 107
  ZChallenge, 100, 106, 108, 109
  ZCommand, 99, 100, 104, 105, 109
  ZCompl, 100, 105, 109
  ZCRC, 100, 101, 103, 108, 109
  ZData, 99–101, 103, 104, 108, 109, 301
  ZEOF, 100, 103, 108, 109
  ZFErr, 100, 107
  ZFile, 99–102, 108, 109
  ZFin, 99, 100, 107–109, 342
  ZFreeCnt, 100, 105
  ZNak, 100
  ZRInit, 100, 103, 105–109
  ZRPos, 100–103, 106, 108, 109
  ZRQInit, 99, 100, 105, 106, 108, 109
  ZSInit, 99, 100, 106, 108
  ZSkip, 100, 101, 103, 105, 108
ZModem-90, 112, 123
ZModemCancel, 264, 348
ZModemDestroy, 264, 348
ZModemInit, 264, 347
ZModemReceive, 264, 349
ZModemSend, 264, 349
ZModemSendCommand, 264, 349
ZModemSetDebug, 264, 348
ZModemSetFileType, 264, 348
ZModemSetProgress, 264, 348
ZNewFile, 276
ZParseZRINIT, 280
ZParseZSINIT, 280
ZPause, 287
ZReadBytesWithTimeout, 283
ZReadByteWithTimeout, 286
ZReadByteWithTimeoutFcn, 286
ZReadDecodeBytes, 299
ZReadDecodeHexBytes, 300
ZReadHeader, 304
ZReceive, 339
ZReceiveFile, 335
ZReceivePacketData, 309
ZReceiveStream, 311
ZSendAttention, 300
ZSendBreak, 287

ZSendByte, 286
ZSendBytes, 285
ZSendCAN, 301
ZSendCommand, 347
ZSendCrcEscape, 308
ZSendEncodeBytes, 296
ZSendEndSession, 330
ZSendFile, 333
ZSendFileData, 320
ZSendFileDataPacket, 318
ZSendFiles, 338
ZSendFillWindow, 317
ZSendGetZRINIT, 328
ZSendHeader, 303
ZSendHexBytes, 297
ZSendHexHeader, 302
ZSendZCommand, 345
ZSendZFile, 331
ZSendZSINIT, 329
ZTime, 279
ZTimeToTm, 278
ZWaitForSentBytes, 285

About the Attached Disk

Before you try to use the files on the disk, please read the following information carefully.

The disk facing this page contains all of the source code from the book.[1] Every directory on the disk contains a READ.ME file that explains what is in that directory. Please read these files for additional information. There are three main directories:

GENERIC This directory contains the C source code for the file transfer protocols and auxiliary modules. These files do *not* form a complete program. See page 154 for an overview of the files in this directory.

MISC This directory contains miscellaneous source code for radix encoding and CRC calculation from the earlier parts of the book.

SYSTEM This directory contains small stand-alone file transfer utilities for specific systems. These programs are *not* polished end-user applications; you should think of them as outlines demonstrating what changes need to be made to use the source on a particular system. Please read the READ.ME files carefully *before* compiling or using them.

Legal Matters

If you own this book, you are entitled to royalty-free use of the source code. There are certain restrictions, however. Please read the conditions at the top of each source file (reproduced on the other side of this page), and the discussion on pages xvi and xvii for details.

---

[1]The disk contents will also be available on the World-Wide Web at http://www.coriolis.com/coriolis, or via ftp from ftp.coriolis.com/users/o/orders.